White Man's Dreaming

To Jason and Charles

White Man's Dreaming

Killalpaninna Mission 1866–1915

Christine Stevens

Melbourne
Oxford University Press
Oxford Auckland New York

OXFORD UNIVERSITY PRESS AUSTRALIA

Oxford New York Toronto
Delhi Bombay Calcutta Madras Karachi
Kuala Lumpur Singapore Hong Kong Tokyo
Nairobi Dar es Salaam Cape Town
Melbourne Auckland Madrid
and associated companies in
Berlin Ibadan

OXFORD is a trade mark of Oxford University Press

© Christine Stevens, 1994
First published 1994

This book is copyright. Apart from any fair
dealing for the purposes of private study, research,
criticism or review as permitted under the Copyright Act,
no part may be reproduced, stored in a retrieval system,
or transmitted, in any form or by any means, electronic,
mechanical, photocopying, recording, or otherwise without
prior written permission. Enquiries to be made to
Oxford University Press.

Copying for educational purposes
Where copies of part or the whole of the book are made
under section 53B or section 53D of the Act, the law requires
that records of such copying be kept. In such cases the
copyright owner is entitled to claim payment.

National Library of Australia
Cataloguing-in-Publication data:

Stevens, Christine, 1946-
  White Man's Dreaming: Killalpaninna Mission 1866–1915.
  Bibliography.
  Includes index.
  ISBN 0 19 553574 X.
  1. Lutheran Church – Missions – South Australia –
  Killalpaninna, Lake, Region – History. [2] Aborigines,
  Australian – Missions – South Australia – Killalpaninna, Lake,
  Region – History. 3. Killalpaninna, Lake, Region (S. Aust.) –
  History. I. Title.
266.4194237

Edited by Angela Gundert
Designed by Derrick I. Stone Design
Typeset by Syarikat Seng Teik Sdn. Bhd.
Printed in Hong Kong
Published by Oxford University Press,
253 Normanby Road, South Melbourne, Australia

On his last visit to the ruins of Killalpaninna Mission Station, in 1964, Pastor Proeve was told that 'old Sandy' the Rain-maker, who for many years had camped near the ruins, had recently died. On an earlier visit Sandy had said to Proeve, 'You know me, I am Sandy, me make rain.' And when Proeve had responded with 'God makes rain', Sandy replied, 'Me believe in God, too. God and me make rain.' Many years earlier Sandy had run away from the mission school; 'Too much stick at school', he had said. Another old Aborigine, who was camped with Sandy, when referring to one of the Killalpaninna missionaries, had declared to Proeve, 'That feller must have been all wrong that Jesus has been here. I have looked everywhere and not found His tracks.'

Contents

Sources of Illustrations	viii
Introduction	ix

1	German Altlutherans	1
2	The Diyari	19
3	First Contact	45
4	Bucaltaninna and the Kolonisten	68
5	Flierl the First	87
6	Reuther and the Glorious 1890s	116
7	Old Rites, New Order and Mission Decline	164
8	Linguists and Ethnographers	202
9	'A Scattered Homeless Flock'	231

Notes	267
Bibliography	286
Index	293

Introduction

I first heard of Killalpaninna Mission in 1984, during my second visit to Marree and while researching the history of Afghan cameleers in Australia. It was a hot December afternoon, and an archaeologist friend and I had finally abandoned our sweltering tent, singularly pitched on the bare brown earth at the edge of this tiny outback settlement. It was a moment of submission, after constantly draping our small canvas shelter in wet towels and huddling within in brief reprieve. The December heat from mid-morning was humanly unbearable. We had managed a day and a half of this inferno before escaping to the cool confines of the only refuge for visitors foolish enough to venture here during the summer months, the century-old Marree Hotel. With temperatures of 40 degrees Celsius and more, its 30-centimetre-thick stone walls gave unimaginable relief. In fact, the entire town hibernated for many of the daylight hours during summer months. And there, in the cool shadows and patchy, spartan rooms, I was to hear, from the hotel's laconic manager, of the German missionaries of last century who came to the area, and of the crumbling ruins of their mission station on the western run of Etadunna Station (then owned by the hotel manager's brother), just 130 kilometres northwards, along the Birdsville Track.

I was later to learn that these newly arrived Germans, resplendent in top hats and coat-tails and moving heavy German wagons, had travelled to this remote desert place during the summer months of 1866–67. They had been near Marree in December 1866, and had travelled even further northwards as the summer months intensified. It seemed ironic that they had camped in this same heat on these same bare plains nearly 120 years earlier.

The story of these German Lutheran missionaries, and of the indigenous people of the area into which they ventured, was found primarily in the letters and reports that were sent back to the mission headquarters in Germany and to their headquarters in South Australia. Many were printed in the newspapers and journals published by the mission institutes that provided the mission personnel and by local Lutheran publications. Hermannsburg Mission Institute, Germany, which supplied the first missionaries for the South Australian project (from 1866 to 1874), printed reports in the *Hermannsburger Missionsblatt*. And after 1874, when the mission station was under the control of the South Australian Immanuel Synod and supplied with missionaries from Neuendettelsau Mission

Institute, Germany, reports were printed in the Tanunda-published *Deutsche Kirchen und Missions Zeitung*. Some reports were printed in the Melbourne-published Lutheran journal *Der Australische Christenbote*.

Other letters and reports to the Mission Committee in South Australia can be found in letterbooks now deposited in the archives of the Lutheran Church in South Australia, and in the South Australian Museum. This material, which is in handwritten nineteenth-century Gothic German, has not been easy to read and translate. I was fortunate to have several German-born translators, and am reliant on the accuracy of their difficult task.

The letters published in the Lutheran journals were, of course, designed to be read by a supportive Lutheran public, and it is unknown whether any omissions from or editing to the printed form were made. Letters in letterbooks were, however, unedited and thus an accurate record. The letters themselves are often vital and emotional testimonies, rich and revealing, and written 'on the spot', giving unique accounts of early culture contact between these diverse groups of people, although always from a German Lutheran perspective.

To view life for the Diyari Aboriginal people, I could, unfortunately, only turn to the above accounts, and to those of other Europeans living in or visiting the area, and to later European anthropologists and ethnographers. Without a tradition of a written language or written records, the Aborigines themselves had only oral accounts of an earlier life and of the events that changed the course of their lives and culture. Much of this oral knowledge has now tragically passed to the grave. A few old Aborigines hold remnants of facts, woven into songs and stories, about events that occurred after European contact. And a few retain elements of their traditional history and religion as it was transmitted in song, dance and story form.

Professor Ronald Berndt and his wife, Catherine, have spent a lifetime working among the Aborigines, particularly those in South Australia, and have published prolifically. Their knowledge, understanding and sympathy with these people has provided a basis for the chapter on the Diyari. I have also drawn on material from the anthropologist A. P. Elkin, who studied Aboriginal culture during the second and third decades of the twentieth century, and remains a classic authority, albeit European also. And I have drawn widely on material published by the linguist Dr Luise Hercus, a speaker of Wangkangurru, Arabana and some Diyari, who has spent several decades with old Aboriginal people from the north-east of South Australia documenting traditional histories and stories from their original owners.

There has been extensive use of the terms 'Aboriginal' and 'Aborigine' to describe the indigenous people of Australia, although the term 'European' has also been used when referring, predominantly, to the British and Germans in this account. However, it should be noted that to call these groups of diverse indigenous people by a single appellation (its connotation often denigrating) seems to be a perversion of their specific tribal identities. They had no collective name for themselves, as they did not interact with humans beyond their own island. Consequently, local tribal identity was all that was required. I too, therefore, have been forced to use the term 'Aborigines' when referring collectively to these original Australians.

The culture of Australian Aborigines has been permanently fractured and fragmented. There has been a general uninterest in Aborigines and disregard for their traditions since the beginnings of European colonisation of the continent. They were not counted in census surveys until 1967, nor were they granted the vote before that time. Even today Aboriginal health is appallingly infirm. Furthermore, their standard of living is equivalent to that of a Third World country, when the rest of Australia's population enjoys First World status and comforts. The life expectancy for Aboriginal men today is twenty-two years less than for other Australian men; for Aboriginal women it is fifteen years less than for other Australian women. Aborigines are seventeen times more likely to die from diabetes than their other Australian counterparts, indicating serious problems with the change to their diet.[1]

Unemployment for Aborigines today is at least three to five times greater than the national average. Alcohol has become ingrained as a social disease, in the words of one scholar, 'caused by the lack of a workable reality',[2] a state of hopelessness, depression and alienation. Aborigines are fifteen times more likely to be imprisoned than other Australians, and die significantly more often while in prison.[3] It has recently been revealed that Aborigines are twenty times more likely to be murdered than other Australians.[4] Aborigines have always used a degree of violence (corporal or capital, depending on the crime) in their society as a social control (as there were no accumulated possessions or capital to be taken away as punishment), for the necessarily rigid rules of small hunter-gatherer groups living in marginal country. But the violence of today is not that of social control. It is born of frustration, illness, poverty, injustice and social isolation. And it is not just the urban Aboriginal populations that endure these social consequences. Aborigines in remote areas also suffer poor sanitation, poor employment opportunities, poor diet and poor health, poverty, low self-esteem, alcohol dependence and domestic violence. With sexual promiscuity and poor education endemic among Aboriginal people, it has been mooted that the AIDS epidemic currently sweeping the world could be the 'last nail in the coffin of Aboriginal society'.[5]

The book is divided into chapters of unfolding 'enlightenment'—from the world of the Germans of nineteenth-century Europe, to their fear, cultural xenophobia and abhorrence at encountering the Aborigines of Australia, and to their attempts at recognising and documenting a dying culture. It should be read in chapter order. I have tried to let the missionaries speak with their own words, and to provide a window through their own eyes. Where it has been possible, I have tried to do likewise from an Aboriginal perspective, although this was more difficult since most documents were written by Europeans.

Killalpaninna Mission was the first Hermannsburg mission in Australia. The name was later changed to 'Bethesda', but was often referred to unofficially as Killalpaninna, a more enduring geographical reference name.

This particular contact history demonstrates the strength of the human spirit embodied in two very different cultures, meeting for the first time in history, and the changes each wrought on the other as a result. As such, the history of Killalpaninna Mission is a microcosm of the metamorphosis of Aboriginal

Australia. Apart from its social history context, to look back at this rich indigenous society, and to understand the emphasis of the imposing new culture are covert themes of the book.

I would particularly like to thank the Lutheran Archives in Adelaide and the South Australian Museum for their generous assistance with material for this project. And my sincere gratitude to the Institute of Aboriginal and Torres Strait Islander Studies (Canberra) for awarding me a grant for the project in 1991. I would also thank the following: the Mortlock Library, South Australia; the Mitchell Library, New South Wales; the Public Record Office, South Australia; the Hindmarsh Police Archives, South Australia; the Archives of the AIATSIS (Canberra); the descendants of the Vogelsang family (South Australia); and the translators, Dr Jurgen Tampke, Eleonore Reigert and Anna Huppauf. I am most grateful to the McGonigal family who so generously provided me with quiet space to write this book. I wish to thank Dr Luise Hercus for her time, advice and unerring support throughout this project. And lastly, and most importantly, I thank my husband, Andrew, for again supporting me in every possible way. My love and appreciation go beyond words.

Christine Stevens

1
German Altlutherans

It was not until the seventeenth century that the enormous island of Australia was first discovered by the human inhabitants of the then 'civilised' world. Seafaring explorers from Holland, Portugal, France and Britain traced portions of its coastline onto incomplete maps. Some rowed ashore in search of fresh water or food, but strangely, for more than two hundred years none of these 'visitors' ventured to explore on land. The amorphous landmass was considered empty and alien, occupied only by bizarre animals, unfamiliar plants and 'primitive' blacks. It was not until 1770 that the British navigator James Cook returned to his homeland with reports of the eastern coastline, and another eighteen years passed before the British claimed sovereignty in the form of a penal colony.

For many millennia the indigenous people of Australia had lived in virtual isolation from other cultures and were unique in that no other humans, beyond their own rich groupings, were included in their histories and mythologies (with perhaps a few isolated exceptions along the northern coastline). These people became known as 'the Australian Aborigines'. Over their own long history they had developed a complex and enduring culture and religion. But just as their land had generated no initial inquisitiveness in the 'visitors' to their shores, so these people received no initial interest from the newly arrived Europeans. Their land was considered unoccupied, for the Europeans saw the Aborigines as a kind of extension of the native animals. Indeed they were referred to as 'natives' even as late as the 1940s and 1950s. They did not farm the land in any way comprehensible to the Europeans, nor build permanent structures. They appeared to have no material culture beyond a few crude weapons and utilitarian devices. They wore animal skins or went naked. And their attempts at defending their land were deemed unnecessary aggression by the Europeans who, from the beginning of settlement, had to farm sufficient to feed an often near-starving European population. The indigenous people were considered an obstacle to European progress and various attempts were made by the occupying foreigners at virtual Aboriginal genocide, both physically, in parts of Australia, and culturally, all over the country.

Europeans came to this remote, barren, uncivilised, God-forsaken land for many reasons: forced (as convicted prisoners); to administer and police; to break free from seemingly inescapable poverty in a European homeland; as people persecuted for their religion; as wealthy entrepreneurs willing to chance and exploit a new opportunity; and as Christian missionaries with a predilection for the salvation of the souls of the 'primitive heathens' of this strange, untouched country. The Europeans brought with them an attitude of cultural and material superiority, as well as the nineteenth-century European notion of exploitation of resources for national and individual wealth. They brought superior weaponry, and proceeded to control and coerce the indigenous people, progressively manoeuvring them from desired areas of occupation. Within a very short time Aboriginal populations dropped drastically in places of European habitation—some the victims of the gun, others victims of European disease, still others pushed onto land traditionally belonging to different tribal groups, creating competition for local food, and conflict.

In the early decades of colonial rule European Christian missionaries became aware of the physical, intentional or unintentional, genocide that was rapidly occurring among the indigenous people. They saw their vocation as instrumental in the spiritual salvation of the souls of these condemned people, who were perceived as pitiable heathens, destined to die out as a race in just a few short years. They had never previously had the opportunity to hear the great message of the European Saviour, Christ, a message which could ensure entry into eternal life even for these 'primitives'. The Christian faith was considered the great linchpin around which civilised life revolved in nineteenth-century Europe. And Europeans were firmly entrenched in a sense of their own physical and cultural superiority, vindicated 'scientifically' by current Social Darwinism and its network of European theories. The Christian missionaries considered it their duty to give the Australian Aborigines hope in death, if not in life.

The story of Killalpaninna is of a particular encounter between two such differing groups of people—German Lutheran missionaries and the Diyari Aborigines of the north-east of South Australia. Both groups were from strong, well-defined cultural backgrounds; both tenacious, resolute, self-reliant and daring. These two disparate societies, diametrically opposed, met in the Australian desert, interacted for a period of some fifty years, and produced changes in one another, one group inexorably becoming more profoundly changed than the other. Such changes as have resulted from the Killalpaninna experience have contributed to the shaping of Australia's national attitudes and character.

Ironically, the German Lutheran missionaries of Killalpaninna Mission Station were themselves born of the zealous enthusiasm of a displaced and persecuted religious group. The mission was instigated by a convergence of 'Altlutherans' (old Lutherans) who refused to unite into the Church of Prussia. Instead they had chosen to emigrate to a far-flung, virtually unknown island between the Pacific and Indian oceans in the Southern Hemisphere. Their missionising intentions, which developed some twenty-five years after arrival, were meritorious in that they wanted no harm for the Australian Aborigines, only benevolence according to their understanding of it. Killalpaninna Mission did serve as a refuge of physical safety for the Aborigines in the north-eastern corner of South Australia. But at the same time it greatly facilitated the cultural disintegration of the indigenous people in this part of Australia, a people who had developed, over many millennia, a strong and unique desert culture with a deep spiritual dimension. Killalpaninna Mission expedited the loss of these spiritual foundations, the destruction of this unique culture, the loss of identity for the Diyari people and others in that part of the desert north. While performing its function of physical sanctuary, as well as Christian spiritual 'salvation', Killalpaninna Mission simply hastened the Aborigines' dependence on the invaders of their land: for food, for recreation, for European medication and drugs, for institutional support, and finally for European jobs and welfare. It was a tragic demise that befell the indigenous people right across their island continent, one that was irreversible, and has had enduring dire consequences. These original Australians became 'second-class citizens', dominated by another culture and people, victims of near genocide and virtual prisoners in their own country.

German Lutherans
By the nineteenth century Germany had resolutely established Protestantism (in the form of Lutheranism) as the primary religion of the German people. Its origins are traced to the Reformation as it occurred in that country under the leadership of Martin Luther. Luther (1483–1546) had been an Augustinian (Catholic) monk who became professor of Bible studies at the University of Wittenberg. Born into a poor and deeply religious farming family of Saxony, the young priest was awakened to the corruption within the Catholic priesthood while visiting Rome in 1510. Disturbed by his discovery, young Luther made a serious study of the Bible, struggled with his own spirituality and search for God, and concluded that the truth lay in the simple message contained within the New Testament. God had come to him in Christ. He did not have to struggle to find God. Hence Christ came to occupy an unqualified, central position in Luther's new evangelical theology. With the proclamation of this gospel message and the restoration of biblical evangelical thinking, Luther felt driven to reform within the Catholic Church what had been deformed, in his eyes, over many years.

Luther challenged philosophy in favour of theology. He expounded the distinction between laws and gospels, and debated God's righteousness, sin, grace, free will and faith, justification by works and justification in Christ, and he debated the theology of the Cross. The Pope summoned him for correction and discipline. But in Leipzig, in 1515, Luther denied the primacy of the papacy and the infallibility of general councils, spearheading the Reformation movement in Europe.

A year later came Luther's decisive break with medieval Catholicism, with the nailing of his theses to the church door at Wittenberg. These were threefold:
1 an appeal to the laity and an invitation to German princes to take the reform of the church into their own hands by abolishing tributes to Rome, and to abolish celibacy of the clergy, masses for the dead, pilgrimages, religious orders, and other Catholic practices and institutions;
2 an appeal to the clergy to establish a New Testament sacramental theology and communion, and to reject transubstantiation (the doctrine that the bread and the wine in the Eucharist are converted by consecration into the body and blood of Christ) and the sacrifice of the mass and its related abuses;
3 an exposition of justification by grace as distinct from justification by works (making faith a substitute for good deeds).

The theses were censured as heretical. Luther was ordered to burn his books and recant. But even before the emperor he refused. Luther was placed under ban by the emperor, and for a time was guarded by supporters. During this period he translated the New Testament, previously in Latin, into German, making it accessible to all Germans.

Luther was returned to his post at Wittenberg University a year later, there to face Catholic opposition. His Reformation theology divided German society, resulting in the Peasants' War of 1524–25, a predicament that saddened the abashed Luther. That same year he married a former nun. They had six children of their own, and raised a further eleven orphaned nephews and nieces. Confined to Saxony, Luther compiled a mass (which later developed into his 'German mass') and began the massive corpus of liturgical works that were to become Lutheran orthodoxy, and a translation of the entire Bible into German. At the age of sixty-three, in 1546, he died. Luther was buried, a poor and humble man, in the church in Wittenberg, but his radically new religious persuasion was to change the course of spiritual life in Germany.

In 1530 the Augsburg Confession, centre-piece of Lutheran theology, had been prepared by the scholarly reformer Philip Melanchthon under Luther's persuasion. Designed to settle a theological question of prime importance to Luther and his followers and one that conflicted with Catholicism (being the manner of Christ's presence in the Lord's Supper) the document was, not unexpectedly, rejected by the emperor. It took a further twenty-five years to receive legitimate theological status in Germany. However in 1530 five provincial German rulers did sign the Augsburg Confession, thus rejecting the instructions of Emperor Charles V to return to the Catholic faith. Furthermore, less than a decade after Martin Luther's death, such was the conversion to Lutheranism that it was decided by both Protestant and Catholic princes in Germany that their subjects should adopt the religion of their provincial ruler. One exception, however, was the Electorate of Brandenburg, later the Prussian state, whose ruler held to a liberal philosophy of religious tolerance, even though it might mean a division between the religion of the ruler and that of some of his subjects. The Prussian ruling family became Calvinist, and gradually divisions occurred between the ruling Calvinists and their many Lutheran subjects. Only Frederick the Great, who ruled Prussia from 1740 until his death in 1786, seemed undisturbed by this discrepancy.

The two centuries following Luther's death had been characterised by bitter European wars, partly religion based, between European Catholics and European Protestants. By the early 1800s religion had ceased to be a dominant political issue. However, Frederick the Great's successor, King Frederick Wilhelm III, a deeply religious man himself, saw his mission as unifying the Protestants of Prussia into one state church. Spurred on by the eighteenth-century emigration of French and Dutch Calvinists, and by the influence of pietism and rationalism creeping into Protestant thinking and weakening its religious doctrinairism, he planned a two-stage unification programme. It was to begin in 1817, the tricentenary of Luther's nailings to the church door at Wittenberg, and it would end with the tricentenary of the Confession in 1830.

But Wilhelm III met opposition from some Lutheran sectors, especially the recently annexed, orthodox-Lutheran eastern provinces. Among these farmers and villagers resistance to unification was unyielding. By the 1830s such opposition had reached its height, with the Lutherans declaring that unification upheld the Calvinist interpretation of the Holy Communion—that of Christ being spiritually present when believers took the bread and wine rather than the bread and wine actually becoming the body and blood of Christ, their unerring Lutheran interpretation. Unification was wholly unacceptable to them.

Less orthodox Lutherans accepted the unification proposals, but the resistance groups proved problematic to Prussian authority and rule. The king had compiled and issued a new liturgy, and given orders for its introduction and use in all churches in Prussia. The defiant Lutherans, known as 'Altlutherans' (meaning 'old Lutherans', for their resistance to change), declined to introduce and use this new 'royal' liturgy for two main reasons: it contained doctrines and statements at variance with their faith and confessions (like the Holy Communion interpretation), and, as a matter of principle, they declined to recognise the king as having any authority to dictate to them in matters of religion. They adhered to the belief that God had instituted two powers on earth, a political power (the state) and an ecclesiastical power (the church), and that both must be obeyed.[1] The political power should not interfere in ecclesiastical matters, nor alter the rights of the church, but was bound, as a Christian government, to watch over the privileges of the church. Conversely, the Altlutherans believed the church had no authority to interfere with the rights or privileges of the state. Its role was to preach the gospel to all men, even kings and authorities, but not to exact obedience, because the kingdom of God is not of this world.[2]

These rebellious Lutherans were coerced by the Prussian authorities in an effort to force them to conform. Stubborn pastors were deposed from office, churches forcibly taken, fines levied, goods and homes confiscated, imprisonment imposed, and the Prussian military employed to crush resistance. The Altlutherans were deprived of public, even private, places of worship, and resorted to clandestine meetings in the surrounding forests (ironically, not unlike their Aboriginal counterparts later, who were deprived by these very Lutherans of religious freedom and who, under threat and imposition, performed their religious rituals clandestinely in the Australian desert). Prussian spies were engaged to report on the activities of the Altlutherans (just as the missionaries later planted spies among the Aborigines), particularly in Silesia, and the spies were paid to find and arrest recalcitrant Lutherans, like those found administering the holy sacrament at night. Such persecutions made the Altlutherans steadfast and faithful to their principles. Many Lutherans, who had earlier conformed to unification, now left the state church and joined those who held fast to orthodoxy. New Lutheran communities arose in Silesia, Pomerania, Posen, Magdeburg, Halle and Berlin, and dissenters considered themselves purified by the fire of persecution.

The oppression of these Lutherans, however, was quickly increased. Every child of school-leaving age (fourteen years) who had been confirmed by a Lutheran pastor was officially classed by the state as not confirmed and was forced to remain at school—an effort to strike at rural labour. Non-attendance resulted in fines. Marriages solemnised by Lutheran pastors were deemed null and void. The children of Lutherans were to attend religious instruction from a state church minister under police enforcement. Children previously confirmed in the Lutheran church were re-confirmed into the state church, and guardians were appointed for them (a treatment akin to the pattern imposed on Aboriginal children and their families some thirty or forty years later).

After many years of suffering at the hands of officialdom some of these steadfast Lutherans called on a traditional Prussian right, that of emigration. A decade of negotiations later a substantial number eventually left their homeland to begin a new life in parts of the world where they could freely practise their religion. Most emigrated to the United States of America, but some 600 to 800 emigrated to the new British colony of South Australia.

The first Australian group emigrated through the benefaction of a Scotsman, George Fife Angas, London banker and shipowner and founder of the company that delivered the infant colony of South Australia, the South Australia Company. Angas had intended the new colony to be a 'place of refuge for pious Dissenters from Great Britain',[3] but the largest group of such dissenters were the German Lutherans. In 1838 Angas offered £8000 as passage money to Pastor August Ludwig Kavel, dissident pastor from the German town of Klemzig, in the Brandenburg administration district of Zuellichav. Kavel led the first group of 400 Lutherans to Australia, the majority from the 'Mark' and Silesia districts.[4]

In the late German summer of 1838 trunks of possessions were loaded onto barges at Tschicherzig on the Oder River, near Zuellichav, and families began their long trip by canal-system to the German port of Hamburg. As they travelled along the Oder through rural settlements and towns the Altlutherans were ridiculed and jeered. Passing under the bridge at Frankfort some were molested. But lusty singing of Lutheran hymns maintained morale while the huge convoy of barges moved slowly into the Spree and Elbe rivers, finally reaching the port city.[5] Families sheltered in farm buildings at the edge of the city before boarding the two British ships, *Prince George* and *Bengalee*, waiting in Hamburg harbour. A third ship, the *Catharina*, left two months later.

The emigrants travelled in the steerage, the lowest part of the ship's stern, below the water line. The air was stale, the space overcrowded, there were no beds—only chaff-bags and boxes—access to luggage was permitted just once a month, and most of the passengers were seasick. The small wooden ships tossed impetuously when the seas swelled, and were entirely dependent on wind to cover distance. It took four wretched months for the perilous journey to Australia. As well as human cargo, the little ships carried baggage, tools, sheep, bricks, 'staves', and boxes of merchandise. The *Catharina* alone carried 350 tons of such extra lading. They sailed through the Bay of Biscay and around the Cape of Good Hope. Four deaths occurred on the *Catharina*, and the figures for the other ships are not known.[6]

On 20 November the *Prince George* reached the port of Adelaide. Nothing but mangrove swamps and mudflats could be sighted from the ship, with a brown, flat, seemingly empty land stretching beyond. The Lutherans had embarked on their journey from the familiar cool, long, lush grasses and rushes of the Oder River. They disembarked four months later into scorched, sharp, dead grasses and the protruding tangle of mangrove roots at an 'unknown' place aptly called Port Misery on the Great Southern Ocean, and into the full force of an Australian summer. Disembarkation was lengthy, and passengers and crew had to wait for low tide, when ground surfaced among the mangrove swamps. Row-boats carried them from the moored ship, then the men waded ashore with women and

Port Misery, near Port Adelaide, South Australia, in the 1840s

children on their backs before laboriously carrying baggage, livestock and survival equipment in the same manner. The first arrivals prepared rough shelters in the swampy marshes, where they camped while awaiting the arrival of the *Bengalee*.

Plagued by mosquitoes and foreign insects, with only brackish water and subsistence food, it was a raw introduction to the prospect of a new life. The Lutherans spent a month in rough huts before making their way to the embryonic settlement of Adelaide and settling on the banks of the Torrens River, on land owned by Angas. They named their settlement 'Klemzig' after the home town of their leader, Pastor Kavel.

A month after the arrival of the *Prince George* and *Bengalee*, another shipload of German emigrants, again financed by Angas, sailed into Port Misery in a Danish ship, the *Zebra*, captained by Dutchman, Dirk Meinert Hahn, of Osterende. This group of 197 passengers had suffered stormy conditions, an outbreak of typhoid and another of scurvy, and ten deaths on the voyage.[7] They rested briefly among the mangrove swamps, camping in huts vacated by the earlier Germans. It was a month further into the Australian summer and conditions were extremely uncomfortable.

Lastly, in January 1839, the *Catharina* and its passengers arrived at the lonely port, to later establish their settlement at Glen Osmond in the Adelaide foothills.

Captain Hahn felt bound to see his charges, those 'plain and honest people' from the *Zebra*, settled before he embarked on the return trip to Europe, and used his influence to find them a suitable locale. Some 150 acres of land, set in the high hills above Adelaide near the Onkaparinga River, were leased from a syndicate of Englishmen against repayment from the profits of agriculture and livestock.

The *Zebra* Lutherans began the long and difficult task of transporting their belongings across the Mount Lofty Ranges to the Onkaparinga land, returning again and again to collect the remainder. The round trip was some 17 miles (28 kilometres) across uneven country, through virgin scrub, and over high, steep slopes. The first European exploratory trips had barely been made across the ranges, and there was as yet no trodden path. Many weeks were spent in pushing and pulling carts piled high with the necessities to rebuild lives and sustain existence in such an isolated place. The women and children walked the distance, while the men also carried goods on their backs and shoulders. But the struggles and conquests turned to relief and excitement as the beautiful spot selected lay spread before them. Plains thickly covered with 'kangaroo grass' were surrounded by well-timbered hills, and nearby the river offered precious water. Heavy rains had fallen in December and January, and waterholes and creeks were swollen. Freedom at last was theirs. In the shade of imposing gum trees, under the filtered summer sun, the Lutherans held their first service. They named the settlement 'Hahndorf' in honour of their considerate captain.

Liberty of conscience and religious freedom was now entirely theirs, and 'with their hearts of oak and arms of steel' they began the massive task of clearing and building a settlement.[8] Seeds and cuttings carefully carried from German soil were planted in the baked brown earth, and watered from the nearby river. While houses were being constructed the Lutherans camped under spreading gums and slept under the stars. The local Aborigines were peaceable, and, with few food resources, the Germans learnt to eat native foods. They cooked and ate pig-face in place of cabbage, and drank infused wild chicory roots in place of coffee. Strange lizards and snakes crawled about, and harmless stumpy-tailed reptiles frightened the women. Only the croaking of frogs in the creekbeds provided a familiar sound.

One of the first projects was, of course, the construction of a Lutheran church to service the community and act as a religious focal point; after which a school took priority. Finally land was divided and cleared for cultivation and pasturage, for these people were from a background of rural peasantry, accustomed to frugality, hard work and self-reliance. Cattle, oxen, sheep, horses were purchased and brought to individual landholdings. Fences, farm implements and handmade carts were fashioned from local wood and forged by local blacksmiths. The community had a close co-operation and unity among its members, and the German Lutherans began to feel a sense of ownership in the glorious heritage of their adopted country and in its free and noble institutions. Had they not taken possession of what was a wilderness; untamed virgin land, unoccupied? Had they not endured all the hardships and privations of pioneering in a new place, and contributed their fair share towards the opening up and development of 'their country'? They began to feel that, by moral and civil right, the prosperity and blessings which they were beginning to enjoy were their due, and that the full privileges of British citizenship should be granted them, which

German Altlutherans

Among the first immigrants to South Australia, J.E. Auricht and her daughter, Anna (later Vogelsang)

of course they were. Barely two years after the founding of the city of Adelaide, more than 10 per cent of the population of the colony of South Australia (then 5700 people) was German Lutheran.[9]

But nowhere in the records of these early German communities is there mention of the plight of those so-called 'peaceable' Aborigines. Nor is there mention of any sense of dispossessing another who may have occupied that land, regardless of the early assistance the community received in local food knowledge. The Germans, it could be said, were simply following the standard British practice of the colony.

In May 1839, just months after arriving in the new colony, the *Catharina* group initiated the first Lutheran synod, which was held under a gum tree at Glen Osmond. Kavel determined to establish a unified, single community of German Lutherans, in preference to the three scattered settlements, and representatives were elected to explore available land some 40 miles to the north of Adelaide. A month later a contract with Dutton, Metcalfe and Finnis was signed for the lease of 2080 acres in the Barossa district at £10 per acre.[10]

After signing the contract the Lutherans of the Hahndorf settlement, the most isolated group and those who had perhaps laboured hardest to establish their community, had a change of heart. The Hahndorf women complained that, after barely settling into new homes, they were now expected to abandon them, undertake another burdensome trek through yet more wild country and begin again.[11] As vindication the Hahndorf settlers cited the conditions under which they had leased the Hahndorf land (two of the English landholders being the same men who also owned the Barossa land), and asserted that they would not be released from their own contracted obligation. A petition dated 1 August 1839 and signed by fifty-one Hahndorf householders, the first signature being that of Kavel's own brother, F. Kavel (a teacher), was presented to Kavel and the representatives. It stated:

> The congregation at Hahndorf feels in conscience bound to declare that it cannot and will not leave Hahndorf until the gentlemen, Dutton, Captain Finnis and McFarlane, through their behaviour and withdrawal of that which they had declared themselves willing to give until the harvest, and, in general, by non-compliance with all their promises, which for the greater part has already occurred,—compel it also to be unable to keep it's [sic] word, and thus against it's [sic] will be induced to leave Hahndorf.[12]

'Land fever' had now gripped the colony, and the men who owned the Hahndorf and Barossa land held considerable power. Francis Stacker Dutton had been one of the discoverers of the Kapunda Copper Mine, and with his wealth and prerogative became a member of the first South Australian Parliament, and later was to be premier twice. Colonel Boyle Travers Finnis was assistant surveyor to Colonel Light before his appointment as surveyor-general, followed by commissioner of police, then four other public offices in South Australia. The German immigrants, however, were poor, rural peasants with little education, though proud, hardworking and virtuous. They were described as of a 'sedate aspect', fastidiously clean and with steadfast perseverance. They had arrived in the colony with little or no capital, grateful for an opportunity to live and worship freely. As such they were open to exploitation and were charged exorbitant rents for land in these early years, ensuring their poverty for a generation or more.[13] And with few economic resources, their preoccupation was with earning a living and modest establishment.

However, after receiving the recusant document from Hahndorf, Kavel, in an extreme act of persuasion and punishment, banned the Hahndorf settlers from the holy sacrament, claiming their withdrawal to be a breach of faith which would bring dishonour upon the Lutheran Church. The Hahndorf people, who had been administered by visits from Kavel, were left without an offertory pastor.

Pastor August Kavel, at forty-one years of age, was now at the peak of maturity, but declared himself to be 'a shepherd almost without a flock'.[14] Born in Berlin as the eldest son of a poor family, he was nevertheless given the opportunity to attend university. Kavel passed theological examinations to become a member of the Prussian state church and pastor in the village of Klemzig. But the young Kavel was one 'awakened' by Wilhelm III's persecution campaigns, and in 1835 he severed from the state church, taking with him a large number of his parishioners. It was Kavel who travelled to Hamburg, then to London, after merchants at Hamburg had told him of Angas' vision of the new colony of South Australia. For two years he remained in England before permission was given for his followers to leave Germany. Consequently Kavel escaped much of the persecution suffered by other Altlutherans. From London he issued a 'confession' of his faith, but joined his followers only when the *Prince George*, chartered by Angas, called at Plymouth harbour to collect their leader. Kavel saw himself as originator and organiser of the exodus, and the spiritual leader of the Altlutherans emigrating to Australia.

With the move to the new Lutheran settlement at Langmeil (meaning 'Long Mile'), in South Australia's Barossa Valley—named after a home town in Prussia—Kavel exercised great influence over his people. The Barossa community grew into the largest early German settlement in Australia. Kavel persuaded another dissident pastor and his group to join the South Australia community instead of emigrating to the United States.[15] And on 28 October 1841 Pastor Fritzsche's shipload of 274 Altlutherans docked at Port Adelaide after a horrific journey on the vessel *Skiold*. An outbreak of a highly contagious, unidentifiable disease had claimed the lives of one-fifth of the emigrants.[16] In Germany, too, Fritzsche's people had endured even greater hardships and suffering for their faith than had the earlier emigrants. They had defied Prussian authorities for a further three years, and yet, ironically, just before the *Skiold* departed Hamburg harbour, Wilhelm III died, and religious freedom was granted the remaining dissident Lutherans. Having already disposed of property and belongings, the *Skiold* Lutherans were compelled to proceed with their resolve to emigrate. Vexed by problems even before leaving Hamburg harbour, the ship eventually sailed on 6 July 1841. As it moved away from the dock, Fritzsche was heard to pray, 'O Lord Jesus, be thou our Compass, Rudder and Mast; and Thy breath speed us on our way'.[17]

The *Skiold* Lutherans were led by a man firmly committed to Altlutheran principles, who had studied for his theological degree at the University of Breslau in Silesia, bastion of Lutheran ideology at that time. Gotthard Daniel Fritzsche was born in Saxony in 1797. As a young man he was declared physically unfit for conscripted military duty and subsequently studied divinity under the dissident Professor Schiebel, who lectured openly on Lutheranism.[18] On graduation Fritzsche joined a secretly formed Lutheran synod with other dissidents, and performed Lutheran duties clandestinely. But Fritzsche's health again suffered, and in March 1840 he left the provinces to recuperate in Hamburg. While there he began preparations for the emigration of more Lutherans.

Fritzsche was an admirer of Kavel and his achievements, and although Angas was not now in a position to help, the pastor, accompanied by a Dr Hubbe (who later also emigrated to South Australia), travelled to England where they succeeded in gaining financial assistance. Together with money collected from emigré hopefuls, some of whom were possessed of means, the sum now collected was sufficient to fund the exodus. Meanwhile Fritzsche had become engaged to a young woman in Hamburg. But the couple postponed the marriage ceremony until it could be conducted by Fritzsche's hero, Kavel, in South Australia.

The *Skiold* Lutherans stayed briefly at the settlements of Klemzig and Hahndorf, the latter being the place where Kavel married Fritzsche and his fiancée. Eighteen families pooled resources to form a settlement at Lobethal, in the hills close to Hahndorf, while other families moved to the Barossa district to settle at Bethany.

When Fritzsche arrived in South Australia he was requested, by both the Hahndorf settlers and Kavel, to act as mediator between the fractured communities. And virtually from the day of his arrival the pastor was urged to serve the starved spiritual needs of the congregation at Hahndorf. He suggested Missionary Schuermann of Port Lincoln be called, but the Hahndorf settlers implored him, arguing that it would not be right to call a missionary from his field. Finally Fritzsche consented, but not before determining to make a thorough investigation into the Lutheran troubles in the new colony.[19]

Kavel meanwhile had created further schisms by issuing his own 'Protestations' against certain statements in the Lutheran Confessions, declaring that there were a number of doctrinal errors, and contending that the Confessions should be accepted by the church only insofar as they were in accord with the Scriptures.[20] This had further alienated the Hahndorf settlers, and, just before the arrival of Fritzsche, forty-one Hahndorf householders had sent Kavel a protestation of severance.

At the Bethany Lutheran Synod Convention of 1846 the final split occurred between the two groups of Lutherans. Kavel, now influenced by German Piety, had adopted premillennianism, or chiliasm, the doctrine of the 1000-year reign of Christ and the saints on earth after the Judgement (mentioned in Rev. 20: 2–7). Fritzsche's followers opposed this view, arguing that it was based on a wrong interpretation of the Scriptures, and Fritzsche himself rejected the doctrine. Furthermore, the two pastors disagreed over the authority of the Lutheran Confessions and church polity. Nerves were on edge, minds were agitated, and an atmosphere existed where the slightest provocation could result in serious consequences—and it did. In the heat of debate the chiliasts stormed out of the meeting. The result was a split in the Lutheran Church in South Australia into two distinct synods, Kavel's group forming the Evangelical Lutheran Church of Australia (ELCA), or the Immanuel Synod, as they were later called, and Fritzsche's group forming the United Evangelical Lutheran Church of Australia (UELCA), or the South Australia Synod, as it was commonly referred to. These groups were to remain as separate Lutheran entities for 120 years, only coming together in partial union in 1864 for the purpose of missionising to the Australian Aborigines in the north of the colony under a so-called Confessional

Union. However, this was not the first German Lutheran missionary attempt in Australia.

Early German Missionaries in Australia
The eighteenth and nineteenth centuries were the great age of discovery of new lands and peoples by expansionist, industrialised, European powers seeking trade and resources. The indigenous people of these 'new' lands were subjected to colonialism, with the imposition of European cultural and religious precepts. It was an age of enthusiastic missionary activity, with mission training institutions proliferating in Europe, preparing active personnel for the task ahead. Mission societies formed in rural provinces and cities, raising money for missionary activities, and donations of gifts were encouraged. Ebullient mission rallies and festivals were held to assist fundraising, as enthusiasm often exceeded available funds.

As a result of early negotiations between Kavel, Angas and the South Australia Company, the first missionaries in South Australia were German Lutherans, members of the Lutheran Mission Society of Dresden. C. G. Teichelmann and C. W. Schuermann worked among the Kaurna people of the Adelaide Plains and taught, in the German language, at the Adelaide School from 1839. The men had sailed from England in May aboard the *Pestonjee Bomanjee*, the same ship that conveyed the new governor, Colonel Gawler (who succeeded Captain Hindmarsh). It arrived at the colony in the second week of October, just five weeks before the arrival of Kavel and his Lutherans. Encouraged by Governor Gawler, the missionaries lost no time in establishing a school for Aboriginal children and proselytising among the indigenous adults.

Less than a year later, and also as the result of the same negotiators, two more German missionaries arrived in South Australia. Pastors Meyer and Klose expanded the existing missionary enterprises, with Meyer establishing a mission station at Encounter Bay. Schuermann, meanwhile, had left Adelaide for the new settlement of Port Lincoln, some 500 isolated miles distant. There he was to establish a Lutheran mission on 'reserves' recently set aside by the South Australian government for placating and pacifying local indigenous groups who had demonstrated a determined resistance to the European occupation of their country. Schuermann was to try to win their confidence, as Aborigines far outnumbered Europeans in this dangerously isolated part of the colony. And Gawler instructed the resident magistrate at Port Lincoln 'to distribute three pounds of flour every two months to all the natives who chose to assemble. Only those who had misbehaved and those who were wilfully shielding a criminal were to be excluded'.[21]

Schuermann had been sent to Port Lincoln at the specific request of Gawler a month or so before a murder that horrified the infant colony: the spearing by Port Lincoln Aborigines of a young white boy, son of a British settler, a few miles from the straggling township. Local Aborigines were subsequently harshly punished for any further crimes, whether among themselves or directed at the Europeans. A few months later a station owner and his hutkeeper were murdered by Aborigines, followed by an attack on another station and the murder of three more European men. Settlers fled to the township for refuge.

Schuermann accompanied a search party for the offenders, led by the government resident. Along the coast, about 12 miles from the township, they encountered a group of Aborigines known to be friendly towards local Europeans. One man was standing in water poised to spear a fish when one of the Europeans opened fire and shot him dead. 'About a dozen natives ran up, unarmed, shy and apparently friendly, but wanting the white men to go away.'[22] In disgust, Schuermann left the party.

Soon afterwards the governor despatched a detachment of soldiers to Port Lincoln under the command of Lieutenant Hugonin, with orders to apprehend the guilty Aborigines and, if necessary, answer force with force.[23] But according to Schuermann, Hugonin claimed he had been instructed to take all Port Lincoln Aborigines prisoner, whether alive or dead.[24] Later, however, and after blood had been shed, Hugonin was to learn (perhaps from Schuermann) that responsibility for the murders of the Europeans allegedly rested with one tribe only. He requested that Schuermann accompany him to help prevent further loss of life. For over a month the search continued. But soldiers were continually attacked at their posts by a silent, unseen enemy that would always disappear into the bush.

Eventually European officialdom surrendered the cause, the lieutenant agreeing with the government resident that the Port Lincoln Aborigines were far more numerous than was previously supposed, and that the whole Aboriginal population was inimical and intent on driving the settlers away. The hostilities continued, and in some cases settlers took their own violent, sometimes undiscriminating revenge. This was the experience of one of the first German Lutheran missionaries to work beyond the safer limits of Adelaide. Others, like the Killalpaninna missionaries, were also to encounter hostile resistance to the European presence and subsequent European revenge.

The Aborigines of Encounter Bay, however, seemed to offer more promise of European 'pacification'. Encounter Bay had been an early whaling station, where, according to one visiting British surgeon, W. H. Leigh (surgeon on the ship *South Australia* with the South Australia Company), whalers were 'living among savages almost as wild and reckless as they'.[25] When whales were dragged onto the beach to be butchered, there appeared 'scores of natives, marching in high glee to the scene of the action' to feast on the carcass, returning to their camps 'carrying large square pieces (of whalemeat) to their "lubras" upon their heads'.[26] With food as pacification, settlers in the area declared the Encounter Bay Aborigines 'far superior' to their counterparts in areas surrounding Adelaide.[27] Missionary Meyer began work there in September 1840, and in time the mission station attained a degree of prosperity, with the Dresden Mission Society sending further assistance. However, like the Adelaide mission, it eventually succumbed from lack of funds, and in 1848 Meyer accepted a post as assistant to Pastor Fritzsche in the Lobethal–Bethany parish.

Meanwhile, at Port Lincoln, Schuermann was encountering great difficulty with missionising in the area. Aboriginal opposition was intense, considerable time was needed to gain local confidence, and he continually faced financial problems. Schuermann stoically maintained the Port Lincoln Mission by supplementing his meagre resources with farming, labouring for six hours each day, and then devoting four hours daily to mission work.[28] But with the fracturing of the Lutheran Church in Australia, and the Dresden Mission Society in Germany openly siding with Fritzsche's faction, sponsorship was withdrawn, and

Schuermann was left to struggle on alone.

The Lutheran missionaries in South Australia had laboured long and hard during those early years, and by 1846 had published four pamphlets on Aboriginal dialects and customs. But one by one, due to lack of financial support, they were forced to abandon their enterprises, and by the mid-1850s all had joined Fritzsche's synod.

Lutheran Missionaries in the Far North

With few economic resources and a preoccupation with earning a basic living, the establishment process alone was sufficient to deter South Australia's Lutherans from engaging in independent mission activity for some time. Moreover, they already suffered a shortage of pastors. Besides the rift between Kavel and Fritzsche, doctrinal differences between the two synods, and the failure of the Dresden missionaries to achieve much success, did little to inspire others for almost a decade.

During this time both synods supported the Leipzig (previously Dresden) Mission Society in Germany, with Fritzsche's group taking a particular interest in their work in India. In 1854 the Evangelical Lutheran Mission Society of South Australia was founded on the suggestion of an ex-Leipzig missionary, J. Meischel, who was then living among South Australia's Lutherans. Meischel and another ex-Leipzig missionary, E. Appelt, had been serving in India when Leipzig missionaries there divided over the caste system, one group advocating abolition, the other insisting on a policy of compromise. Meischel and Appelt belonged to the former, but when the latter prevailed both men resigned and sailed for South Australia, joining the sympathetic South Australian Synod in 1860 and 1861 respectively.

In February 1860 Pastor Kavel, head of the Immanuel Synod, died of a stroke at Tanunda (formerly Langmeil), at the age of sixty-one. He was buried in the cemetery of the Langmeil church where he had been pastor, leaving the Immanuel Synod with two remaining pastors, Auricht and Reichner (also spelt Rechner).

During 1862 Meischel began to urge the South Australian Synod to take up its moral and spiritual duty and preach the gospel among the 'heathens' of its adopted country. The church council grew enthusiastic, and in September 1862 Auricht and Reichner approached the South Australian Synod with a proposal to unite the synods for the purpose of such mission work in Australia. They were keen to approach the highly successful director of the Hermannsburg Mission Institute in Hanover, Pastor Ludwig Harms, for assistance and personnel.[29]

Just four months later South Australia celebrated the successful crossing of the Australian continent by their illustrious explorer, John McDouall Stuart. The jubilant colony was filled with optimism and hope. Victoria's Burke and Wills had tragically perished during a crossing further eastwards, but Stuart had traversed the very centre, creating speculation about the possibility of European settlements further inland. His reports indicated huge tracts of land perhaps suitable for pastoral grazing, and an expectation of wealth from resources held by that land. Therein also lay an expectation of vast missionary potential. Auricht and Reichner travelled to Adelaide from the Barossa district for the return of Stuart, and while there paid a visit to Meischel. Together they revived a stirring appeal for mission work in Australia, written by Meischel thirteen months earlier, and now published in the church paper.[30] Both synods were enthusiastic and a combined mission rally was held to initiate the project. Ex-missionary Schuermann, now more comfortably ensconsed in a parish in Victoria, was asked to take charge of the mission project, but refused.

Months passed before Harms was approached and before doctrinal and constitutional differences were brought to the attention of the South Australian synods by Meischel. Harms, furthermore, declined to send missionaries to undertake work that involved congregations supportive of chiliastic doctrines, like those of the Immanuel Synod. A year after the mission rally the two synods again met in an attempt to resolve their differences. Both Kavel and Fritzsche were now dead, removing the major obstacles to reconciliation. A somewhat ambiguous compromise was reached, whereby the South Australian Synod agreed to the teaching of chiliasm 'provided it does not degenerate into enthusiasm [Schwärmerei]', and the Immanuel Synod revoked Kavel's 'Protestations', but held to the right to protest any passages of the Augsburg Confessions which in the future could allow the state to interfere with the church.[31]

Ludwig Harms, whose health had been deteriorating, lived long enough to agree to supporting the South Australian enterprise, considering it his spiritual duty to send missionaries to the 'heathens' of this new part of the world, and writing: 'In New Holland [Australia] numerous native tribes have been discovered in the inland salt-lake districts'.[32] Harms had been assisted by his younger brother, Theodore (also a pastor), who attained the directorship on Ludwig's death. The mission centre (which was still operating in Germany in 1993), in Harms' day, had trained and despatched missionaries to Africa, India, the United States and Greece, and now they were to extend their operations to Australia.

By the 1860s South Australia's frontier had advanced into the north-east of the colony (an area that became known as the Far North), as pastoralists in search of stock runs followed in the wake of explorers. While searching for the lost members of the Burke and Wills expedition, Alfred Howitt and John McKinlay had explored and described parts of the country. The unexpected discovery of rivers and a lake system (for 1861 was a time when floodwaters still lay on the low-lying plains), and of John King, sustained for three months by the Cooper Aborigines, were positive signs in this remote area.

A wealthy Scotsman and philanthropic entrepreneur, Thomas Elder, had already acquired a large land lease in this part of the colony in 1860, and had established a sheep station at Lake Hope. Other settlers also moved into the area, taking control of what had been Aboriginal country and grazing their stock protectively. It was an invasion of land that did not belong to these white settlers, and the pockets of Aboriginal resistance were harshly met with superior European weaponry. The Europeans refused to be deterred by hostility at their presence and continued to occupy large tracts of land, organising for police troopers to be stationed near Lake Hope to protect them from Aboriginal attack. Elder's manager, Henry Dean, wielded severe measures against local Diyari Aborigines who tried to resist stock encroachment on precious natural water supplies during a bad drought period.[33] In regard to this affair, and writing to his superiors on Christmas Day 1865, police trooper Poynter (stationed at Lake Hope) described the 'affray' between Dean and his supporters and the local

Aborigines, one that saw the deaths of four Aborigines and the wounding of several others, and concluded with the request: 'I have only 20 rounds of cartridges with me. I wish you would instruct Sergeant Wauhope to forward me 100 rounds as I have no doubt I shall want them'.[34]

The area stretching from the township of Marree at the beginning of the Birdsville Track, north-eastwards to Lake Perigundi, was traditionally the country of the Diyari people, and it was to this part of South Australia that the German missionaries were attracted during the 1860s. Perhaps the humane story of King's rescue by the Cooper Aborigines gave the Lutherans confidence that the people of these parts had potential Christian principles and may respond to missionising. Perhaps the great salt-lake system of the north-east, and reports of corroboree grounds hosting numerous Aborigines for ceremonial rituals (documented in Howitt's reports), suggested a concentration of population in that area or, at the least, a concentration of spiritual activity that was 'pagan', 'heathen', and must be superseded with the true religious principles of the Christian gospels. Perhaps stories of violence by European settlers towards Aborigines in the area, even early rumours of massacres, were the impetus for missionary interest in a specific part of the lake system in the north-east. The area around the generally dry depressions of Lake Killalpaninna and Lake Kopperamanna, a desolate, difficult place, curiously attracted not only the Lutherans of South Australia, but also German Moravian missionaries from the colony of Victoria at virtually the same time.

Thus, by the mid-1860s the stage was set for Lutheran missionary activity among the indigenous people in the north-east of the twenty-five-year-old colony of South Australia. Already facing potential physical genocide as a hindrance and unwanted element in the world of the new colonists, the Diyari were soon to face an expeditious cultural genocide with the arrival of the Lutheran missionaries into their country. The dislocated Lutheran community of South Australia had by now established themselves comfortably in German settlements which afforded religious freedom and economic opportunity. Perhaps they considered their good fortune and blessings to be a moral right as well as a civil right for being faithful to their religious principles. Perhaps their sense of achievement created a justification for having been sent to this New World by God to transplant Luther's divine message among the Australian Aborigines.

It is ironic that a people born of religious persecutions and repressions should themselves be the perpetrators of religious repression and persecution, albeit well-intentioned, among another minority group, as the Australian Aborigines soon came to be. It is ironic too that the success of these German missionaries pertained more to physical salvation among the Aborigines than to any spiritual salvation in a form comprehensible to them.

18 White Man's Dreaming: Killalpaninna Mission 1866–1915

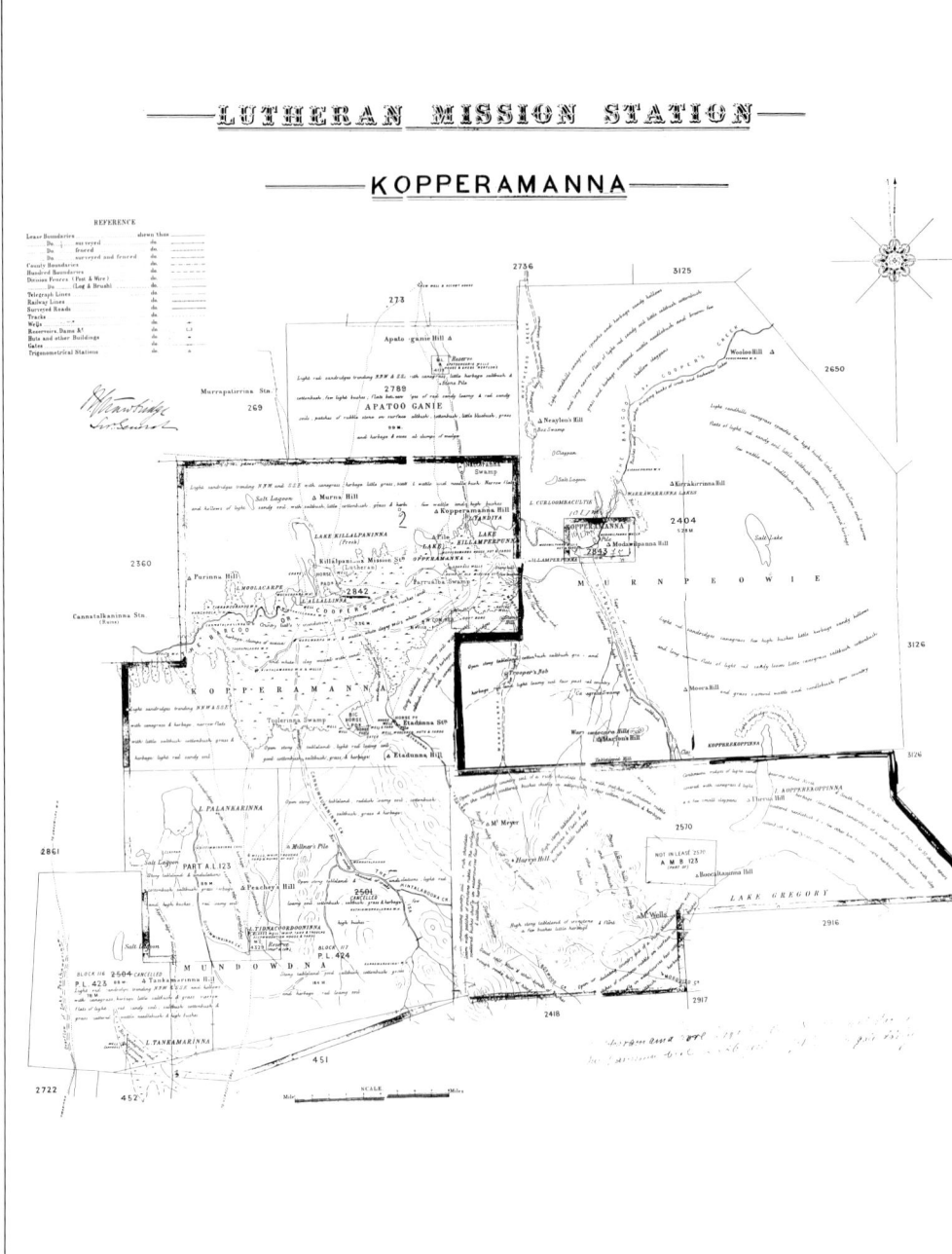

Map of Lutheran mission stations

2
The Diyari

The area into which the Hermannsburg missionaries ventured was the harsh desert country around the Lake Eyre Basin. The climate was extreme, with excessive heat in summer, and bitter cold on winter nights. Temperatures could reach 50 degrees Celsius in the shade, and could drop to below freezing. Summers were long, hot and dry, and the parched land had no assured rainy season. Between January and March rain sometimes fell, but there were years of none at all. The average rainfall was about 4 inches (100 mm) annually. Extended stony gibber plains, banks of sandhills, dry saltpans and waterless lakes formed the austere landscape. Floodplains held the most vegetation, with coolibah eucalypts, acacias, lignum (*Muehlenbeckia cunninghamii*) and samphire and glasswort swamps.[1] A few stunted trees lined creekbeds that were generally empty, for they and the empty lakes were fed at irregular, often lengthy intervals from monsoonal rains in the tropical north-east of the continent. The rains flooded massive low-lying plains, which in turn filled Coopers Creek to spill down through the gigantic ancient lake system until eventually, after especially prolonged northern rains, lakes Kopperamanna and Killalpaninna were filled. During such floodings and after local rain the surrounding desert would burst into an abundance of birdlife and wildlife, and small plants would carpet the ground. This was, however, a rare occurrence. For decades these lakes and creeks could lie barren and desiccated.

The Diyari and Their Country
The indigenous people of this area probably arrived on the Lower Cooper River system some 12 000 years ago.[2] They survived on limited food variety and limited resources, keeping their numbers at a sustainable level. Howitt estimated that about 1200 people were in the area in 1878.[3] As hunters and gatherers they used simple implements and weapons made from local materials (or traded from other parts), like stone, bone and wood. Their diet consisted of edible plants and roots, gathered by the women and older children, and small game such as lizards, snakes, birds and birds' eggs, frogs, rats, mice and small marsupials hunted by the men and women. The staple diet was a mixture of ground grass seeds and water, eaten either raw or cooked in the hot ashes of a fire to produce

a kind of bread. In pre-European times, and after good rains, there were 'miles of clay flats thickly sprinkled with the dry seeds'. They would be collected in large quantities and kept for future use in grass containers daubed with mud.[4] Several varieties of fish were caught in the creeks and lakes, by means of nets or grass weir-traps. Emu was an occasional delicacy, but kangaroo was rare. As the traditional diet was low in saturated fats, every opportunity was taken to incorporate animal fat, such as was observed by Howitt when the fat from a dead pelican was melted and shared among a group.[5] Game was cooked in the ashes of campfires, never boiled in water, which, of course, was scarce.

Pitjiri (also spelt 'pitchere'), a substance chewed and placed under the tongue, was a favoured narcotic. It acted both as a stimulant and a painkiller, and was described as 'very strong stuff', later likened to opium.[6] Bundles of dry leaves from the *Duboisia hopwoodii* were smoked and mixed with ash from the *Acacia salicina* bush (both harvested near the Mulligan River by the tribes in south-west Queensland). The ash and dried leaves were then gathered and further dried in earth ovens before being packed into net bags for trading purposes. 'When a stranger chews it for the first time it puts him out for so many hours, might be for a day', one old Aborigine recalled.[7] Pitjiri was used socially, a plug of the substance being chewed and passed from person to person at meetings or gatherings. It also increased resistance to pain, and on long expeditions was chewed to suppress hunger and prevent fatigue.

In summer the desert Aborigines lived in open bough huts, but in winter these windbreak shelters were covered with grass and sticks and smeared with earth or sand to make them windproof and rainproof. The huts, holding whole families, were often built in clusters near permanent water sources.[8]

The people of this area wore neither clothing nor foot protection. The women were quite naked and the men wore only a boomerang-carrying belt, a long cord (made from human hair) wound around the waist, with a large tassel hanging in front. The men wore their hair either long and wound into a flat hairnet (often decorated with a few bird feathers) or cut short. The resource of hair was primarily for the making of boomerang-belts, presented to males at their circumcision ceremony, but was also used for making fishing nets and utility bags. Many of the men wore beards, some tied with a cord in concentric circles to a point at the bottom. Initiated men had their front teeth extracted and a hole bored through the cartilage of the nose, with either a long, pointed bone inserted (taken out and used to extract thorns from the feet) or a pair of feathers, one through each side.

The men carried softwood hand-shields, both for protection and utility, each having a small cavity at one end in which fire-sticks were twirled with the hands until the soft dust ignited. They were renowned for their hunting skills with the boomerang ('kirra'), and all men carried boomerangs with individual markings and decoration, bestowed during Mindari ceremonies. These were not returning boomerangs but were of two types: a larger version for fighting and a smaller version for hunting, where the club, or waddy ('kaudri'), was used for killing larger game.[9] The very large, boomerang-shaped weapon ('marawiri'), kept at the camps except when in specific use, was used only for killing at close range (such as in pinya-execution clubbing). Made from heavy box-wood rounded on both sides, the weapon was too heavy and cumbersome to be carried about. As

Traditional winter sleeping hut of desert Aborigines

well as boomerangs the men carried hardwood spears (made from *Acacia aneura* or mulga), scraped to a point at one end, or jagged and pointed. Stones were also used for hunting or as weapons, formidable when hurled with great force and accuracy, with the dexterity of either hand. Adzes, for cutting branches to make huts or carving wood into weapons or utensils, were made by fixing a piece of broken stone (with a flat conchoidal fracture) to the end of a piece of wood. Flakes from this stone were used as scrapers and knives, tools for skinning, and cutting cooked game. Fishing nets were made from lake or flood-ground rushes, woven to a fibre.

The women carried hardwood digging-sticks ('wona'), for food-gathering. Six feet in length, they were the women's only weapon and could be quite redoubtable if employed for attack. Oblong wooden vessels ('pirra') made from the box-gum tree were used for water-carrying, seed-gathering and winnowing, and as tools for digging sand from around huts.

These desert people kept domesticated dogs that provided valuable assistance with hunting snakes and small marsupials, and warmth during the cold desert nights. The Aborigines took 'as much care of them as if they were human'.[10] However, in times of drought-stricken starvation, dogs were sometimes killed and eaten.[11]

The semi-nomadic tribes of the region kept to their own well-defined geographical areas. They knew the locations of every permanent water-hole in their territory, often far beyond, and water could always be found even during the most severe drought. They could bring underground water to the surface by digging 'soaks', and in desperate times would dig out hibernating frogs and drink from their underground water storage supply.[12] But when the lakes were full and the countryside transformed, food was abundant. Black swans, pelicans, ducks, fish, flocks of birds would all appear with the flooding.

This country belonged to the Diyari (also spelt Dieri) tribe, of which there were five divisions: 1 Ngadi-ngani (or Bukatyiyi), who lived around Lake Perigundi; 2 Pando-etya (or Pandola), who lived around Lake Hope; 3 Kunari-kana (or Kunari men), who lived around lakes Kopperamanna and Killalpaninna (Kunara being the local dialect for this specific area); 4 Paritiltaya-kana, who lived between Salt Creek, Lake Howitt and the Warburton River; and 5 Mardala (meaning stone hill), who lived to the south between Coopers Creek and the foothills of the Flinders Ranges.[13]

The Diyari's neighbouring tribes were the Arabana, the Thirrari, the Yandruwantha, the Pirlatapa, the Ngamani and the Wangkangurru. Not surprisingly, considering the severity of climate and paucity of food and other resources, the Aboriginal population of the Lake Eyre Basin at the time of early European settlement in that area was only around 3000 or so.[14] Given that this might have been reduced slightly by European disease from the east or further south, it can still be surmised that the area was probably never very densely populated. However, within the constraints of geography and tradition there was a profusion of tribal and cultural diversity, evidenced by the unique languages of each tribe, with some mutually comprehensible, and some people multi-lingual.[15] Languages were believed to have originated and developed during the Dreaming, the Great Creative Period (the 'Mura' to the Diyari). The Diyari language was described as 'poetical and rich in grammatical inflections' and with a complex sign language.[16]

The Diyari lived in local groups, enlarged family units of a man and his living descendants in the male line, with each group (each patrilocal clan) being part of the overall tribe of Diyari. The local groups were exogamous, the women leaving their own countries to live in the local countries of the men they married (although still within their own tribal territory). A local group 'owned' the hunting and food-gathering rights to its country, and members of other groups could only enter that country and hunt over it after permission had been granted. Each local group had a head man, usually the oldest male, and the headmen of the various groups constituted a council. This council met over matters of common interest and made important decisions regarding tribal management, like the maintenance of the moral code, the despatching of avenging expeditions, and the determination of the time for ceremonies. Young initiated men could be present at such meetings, but were not permitted to speak.

Great respect was held for elders (older men and women). By the time Europeans began to study the customs and culture of these people, male elders were exercising the greatest authority. Called 'pinaru', these powerful old men served as headmen, settled quarrels, made decisions, acted as spiritual leaders and, with their authority, monopolised the marriage stakes for young women.

The Diyari 23

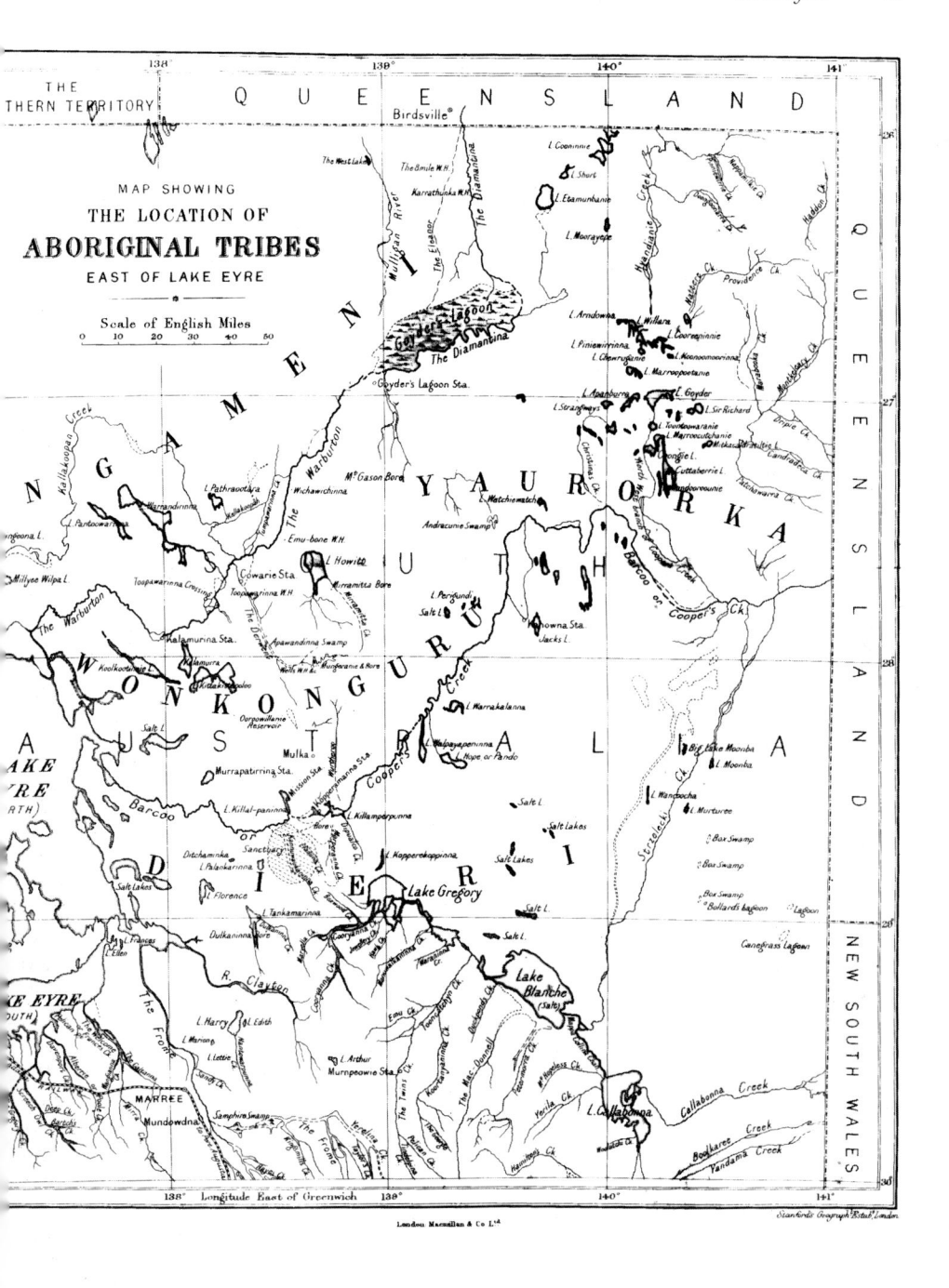

Map of Aboriginal tribes

Ginwillie, a Wangkangurru man, flaking stone knives from rock at Mungerannie Gap

To gain their positions of status and authority they must have 'knowledge' of tribal law and custom and of the mythological sanctions at the root of the social system. Old men and women had more time to contemplate spiritual matters, and more experience of the world at large. The young were busy with food-searching, resource-gathering and, throughout their life, gradually increasing their knowledge of the traditions, both secret and non-secret, until they too became old and powerful. Certain old men (called 'Walkabout Old Men' by the Lutherans) travelled among neighbouring tribes carrying news. They were given sanctuary, and expected to make long and elaborate speeches at council gatherings or at grand corroborees.[17]

Local Diyari groups were bound to their land by a bond between them and their spiritual ancestors, and were named for some natural feature in their country or some totemic, historical association. Furthermore, the Diyari (and others of the Lake Eyre Basin) were divided into two social sections, two matrilineal moieties (tracing descent through the female line), called 'Materi' and 'Kararru'.[18] Each social division was further classified into thirteen subdivisions called 'mardu'. These were specific totems, matrilineally traced, that denoted a person's own 'flavour' ('mardu'), and were named for a local animal or plant. It

Aboriginal men making weapons for hunting

was forbidden to kill or eat one's own mardu, or to marry within one's moiety. Consequently these social totemic clans were exogamous. Increase rituals were performed for the continuance of totemic species, and the owners of each specific totem held the rights and responsibility for their particular myth and its special ritual.[19]

These totemic ancestors were believed to have emerged from the ground, one by one, in the centre of Lake Perigundi during the Creation Period.

> Still quite stunted, and without developed limbs or sense-organs, they lay there around the Lake on the numerous sandhills that still exist in the region to this day. Here, exposed to the rays of the sun, they were gradually warmed, dilated, shaped, animated, strengthened and developed, until finally they [could] stand up as human beings and disperse to all points of the compass. The many sandhills that terminate at Lake Perigundi denote the representatives of the mardu that originated there, respectively the mardu themselves. At the place where these mardus emerged there is today an island located in Lake Perigundi.[20]

In addition, patrilineal ceremonial totems were inherited by the Diyari men. Known as 'pintara', they were acquired from a man's father, and named for a piece of country associated with a Mythic Being (a 'muramura'). The ownership of this totem related to the myth of that muramura and its associated ceremony. There was also a matrilineal ceremonial totem, one's 'marduka', which was the inherited pintara of a man's mother's brother, his uncle or 'kaka'.[21]

The Diyari terms for 'brother' and 'sister' denoted totemic relationship, persons belonging to the same social totemic clan. Alternate generations were categorised as forming one 'line', with marriage permitted between members of the same line. Hence, grandchildren could marry within their generation and could also marry within their grandparents' generation, but not within the parents' generation. Such categorising gave legitimacy to older, more powerful men claiming young wives.

Diyari Religion

Aboriginal religion revolved around a system of orally transmitted stories (called myths and legends by the Europeans) that explained Creation, history and law. It was believed that these stories originated from real events of long ago, before humans walked the earth, during the formation of the earth's landscape and the evolution of life forms. This period was called the Dreaming, or Dreamtime, and was perceived to be an era of timeless spirituality that determined all aspects and phases of existence. Mythic beings, the muramuras to the Diyari, shaped the environment, established the 'law', and were viewed as progenitors of the human species. Religious life focused on the paths (or Dreaming tracks) that were taken by these muramuras in their primordial travels across the landscape. A person's pintara and marduka (through birth and kinship) gave custodianship of a piece of country that was associated with the travels of one or more of these muramuras. It was the responsibility of that person not only to watch over this section of land, but to keep alive its myth, songs and ritual expression.

Aborigines believed that, either at birth or conception (the belief varied among tribes), a particular manifestation of a muramura entered a foetus or new-born baby as a 'spirit-child' to animate it. Spirit-children were of the Dreaming itself and carried with them some of its essence, thus endowing all humans with special qualities and sacredness. The Diyari believed that spirit-children entered newborns at the place of birth, and because they were a patrilocal society, this birthplace would ideally be in the local group territory of the father so that the child could inherit its father's mythic associations. As the child matured, it would learn that part of its totemic cult myth, with the associated ritual and knowledge of sacred sites, which constituted its secret cult life and that of its pintara group. Through initiation a child would be fully admitted to its particular cult. Because many Dreaming tracks were quite long, their myths and rituals were often shared between several local descent groups.[22] Persons belonging to the same mythological path belonged to branches of the one totemic cult and, as 'spiritual relatives', were normally friendly towards each other. A headman, who had to belong to the predominant moiety of that totem, presided over each local totemic cult.[23] Consequently the ritual–religious life of the Diyari consisted of various interdependent totemic cult societies.

The Diyari believed the entire countryside to be composed of memorials to the travels and deeds of the muramuras, who were responsible for everything: hills, trees, stones, plains, animals, plants, clouds, rain, wind, and sun. The muramura cults gave a sense of continuity and well-being, with moral, economic and social sanctions intertwined into the historical settings of the myths. The world of nature was personified and given an origin, and the necessary ritual enabled humans to make their own adjustment to natural phenomena. Such intimate knowledge and associations induced a passionate attachment to one's own special country. And so deep were its muramura associations that at times a person would be overcome with emotion.

Fundamental to Diyari belief was a form of reincarnation—that humans were ever-changing, immortal, returning at death to the Dreaming, and having the expectation of being reborn in human form, always with an essence of sacredness. There was no specific Land of the Dead; rather, 'a belief that humans were caught in an inescapable cycle marked by periodic transition'.[24] For the Diyari there was no final death, and no such concept as Hell. (Small wonder there was no word for 'sin' or for 'salvation' in their language, to the horror of the German missionaries.) Morality and ethics had no bearing on the fate of the spirit or soul, for it was continuous in a sacred life even after death. Each person, male and female, was a reincarnation of an ancestral spirit-being, hence everybody had an essential immortal, sacred essence.

There were both male and female muramuras, and their actions explained the prevailing environment, were lessons in ethical or unethical behaviour, or seemingly had no social or geographical significance at all. The myth of the wind muramura, Paltira, however, is an example of an environmental explanation.

During the Creation Period, Paltira stole a pounding stone and a large stone dish. But as he could not move the stone dish alone, he sang a song that caused the wind to blow and lift it onto his head, and he carried it south to Parachilna. This action explained, by personification, the presence of sandstone in the Parachilna area. The stone consisted of solidified sand, that same sand that constantly blew further northwards in Diyari country. Annual expeditions were made to obtain this resource for grinding-stones, and members of the tribe who had the wind for their pintara were responsible for its continuance through ritual re-enactments of the Paltira myth.[25]

The most important muramura to the Diyari was Darana, controller of the phenomenon of drought. Darana was believed to have been the first to come to earth, emerging from the ground at Kandrimoku Lake, some 16 miles east of Lake Killalpaninna.[26] He was controller of the sky and winds, and could cause droughts or make rain fall, especially around Lake Hope (called Pandu Pirna by the Diyari). At the time of his emergence a severe drought constricted the land. Humans (who were then in existence) could find nothing to eat, and had grown emaciated. Darana and his 'mili' (his retinue, who were still only partly formed) moved from the drought-stricken Lake Kadrimoka to a slope of Lake Killalpaninna specifically named Parakana. Before returning to settle at Lake Hope (at a place also called Parakana), Darana and his people sang and danced a rain song, wearing head-dresses made from bundles of bush collected from a sandhill called Pirilani (that same hill on which the mission station was later built) and tied together with human hair string, until the drought broke. On the slope of Parakana two very tall trees (named Karrawara, meaning 'the big eagles') later grew. It was believed that wherever Darana's feet trod during this period in history trees would grow. The Diyari's veneration of trees originated from this myth and its belief system.[27]

Samuel Gason, a policeman stationed at Lake Hope during the 1860s and 1870s, wrote:

> There are places covered by trees held very sacred, the larger ones being supposed to be the remains of their fathers metamorphosed. The natives never hew them and should the settlers require to cut them down, they earnestly protest against it, asserting they would have no luck, and themselves might be punished for not protecting their ancestors.[28]

In rain-making ceremonies, 'rain stones' (smooth pieces of glistening gypsum rock) were rubbed with fat, before the Dara-song called upon Darana to make rain. At the end of this ceremony an exchange of sexual partners would take place, in the manner of the exchange of Darana's time.[29]

Crucial to the success of rain-making were two oval-shaped stone balls ('hearts') known as Dara-ulu and believed to be the metamorphosed sons of Darana. The hearts were in the custody of the Darana totem's elders, who held the secrets of this important and potent totem. Death was the penalty for betrayal of such secrets, handed down to successive generations of those with Darana pintara, for secrecy was considered vital to the effectiveness of rain-making rites. Anyone attempting to disclose such information was seized and a sharp pointing stick, previously soaked in fluids from a human corpse, was forced into the anal sphincter to produce blood-poisoning without an external wound.[30] Should Dara-ulu be mutilated, it was believed that the entire population would starve as a result of drought. Should Dara-ulu be smashed, the sky would become red, dust would descend from the west and spread across the earth, and humans would die of fear.[31]

Diyari religion was centred around two critical factors, physical survival and spiritual survival. Spiritual qualities pervaded everything, from mundane activities like hunting and gathering, to lovemaking, sexual attractiveness, dancing and art, and to the most sacred of ritual activity. Without the power released by muramuras, it was believed humans could not physically survive. The world was a spiritual world only, and there was no division between sacred and profane. Everything in the physical world arose from the spirit-world, and everything re-entered that spiritual world again. There was a continuum of life and death, and every man and woman and every part of nature existed in a state of sacredness and spiritual harmony. Without this recognised harmony, endurance within this harsh, semi-nomadic lifestyle was weighty indeed. Such harmony gave hope and assurance that, with patience, renewal was a basic factor of life.

Religion thus acted as a buffer between humankind and nature, providing an assurance that humans were not entirely at the whim of the natural elements. Myth and ritual re-enactments assured them at least some influence over the forces that controlled them. For example, those Diyari whose pintara was the wind (Paltira) had the duty and privilege of singing the songs of Paltira, thus bringing about the wind, or at least having some control and understanding ('knowledge') of the wind phenomenon. Wind was an important element, for the Diyari were subjected to the oppressive, still heat of the inland summer (gaining relief from cool breezes), the hot, blowing summer winds, and hazardously wild windstorms that regularly whipped the desert sands, clouding the skies to darkness and blowing for days on end.

'Increase rites' were performed for the maintenance of natural species (hence food). For example, as Minkawonpala was the particular Kardimarkara muramura (ancestral snake) regarded as the dispenser of carpetsnake ('womas'), the men with woma for their pintara or madurka would ritually dig for the large, fat, non-venomous and edible variety at the site where Minkawonpala, after wandering the Cooper Creek country, burrowed into a sandhill at a cave at Kadipirie (Cattapirie) near Kunauana. The men would shed arm blood and sing sacred songs for the increase and maintenance of this species.[32] Kardimarkaras, who lived in waterholes, were greatly feared, for they were thought to devour humans who ventured near.[33] Female Kardimarkaras were said to regurgitate live human beings several days after they had been swallowed, whereas the males simply killed and ate. The fossil remains of large, extinct marsupials, like the diprotodont found near Lake Callabona, were referred to as Kardimarkara. These remains were believed to have dated from the Creation Period, and as such to be endowed with 'life potency'.[34]

Initiation

Initiation rites were performed on young boys and girls at puberty, the first rite being circumcision and hymen-cutting. They were highly formalised rituals, traditionally held at the same time, often with the same stone flakes used in the operation.[35] Hymen-cutting was followed by a seclusion period, before the girls were symbolically returned to life, 'reborn' as young adults. Rites were also performed on girls to promote the growth of breasts, as the focus for girls was on physical maturity and childbearing. But, as men were the greater custodians of religious life (at least after European contact, when the first accounts of the customs of these people were documented), boys received a series of rites and instructions as socialisation into religious affairs. (Although the details of the ceremonies seemed the focus for the European documenters, there is no doubt that the focus for the Diyari was on acquiring 'knowledge' of stories and their rituals.)

Initiation for boys began at about nine years of age, when a married woman, not of the same moiety nor related to him in any way, approached him one evening to quietly slip a string, made of human hair with a mussel shell attached (a 'kuri'), over his head. The action would cause a disturbance, for everybody at the camp would then know that the boy was soon to be circumcised. The boy would run from the camp, his mother would wail and a symbolic fight would ensue, with the father attacking the elders and insisting his son was too young to undergo the painful operation.[36]

The circumcision ceremony, performed at a later date, began with initiants throwing sand around a specially designated area beyond the camp (to which the males only had retreated) to symbolically drive out 'kutchie' (evil spirits) and keep in the muramuras. Then, with group wailing, as the novice youths passed into a ritual state of death, blood was collected in a wooden bowl from the arm veins of initiated men and passed around for all, including the initiants, to sip. Blood was also smeared on the bodies of the boys, symbolic of both death and revival, before the nasal septum was pierced and tooth evulsion took place. A piece of damp clay was pushed into the gums to stop bleeding, while the drawn teeth were placed inside a bunch of emu feathers, smeared with grease and kept for about a year before being buried. It was believed that if the teeth were thrown away on extraction the Eaglehawk might cause larger ones to grow in their place, resulting in death.[37]

The boys were partially segregated for a period before the circumcision operation.[38] It was preceded by several ritual re-enactments involving men of the novices' own patrilocal descent group, before the novices were 'smoked' with branches of lighted green boughs (to counteract dangerous influences) and a 'human circumcision table' arranged. The boys were carried, one by one, along a pathway made by smoke dancers and arranged on the men's backs for cutting. A boy's foreskin was sometimes handed to the parents of his betrothed, who would pass it on to the man who cut the daughter's hymen, to be briefly placed in her vulva to establish 'a sympathetic union between them'.[39] The women then performed the ritualised dance of the mythical Minmara (a group of women who originally performed circumcision), at a fire-throwing ceremony near the circumcision ground, before again retreating. Each initiant's father stooped over his son and, inspired by a muramura, gave the boy a new name.[40] Before circumcision his name ended with 'ana', but afterwards the new name ended with 'ina', denoting the transformed status.[41]

After circumcision the boys were taken to a male-only camp until their wounds healed, given two bullroarers, and their hair was bound in a 'bun', symbolic of their new status. Headbiting rites, to promote the growth of hair, followed, the scalps opened by a sharp stick and bitten by the old men until blood flowed profusely. Blood was again spurted over the youths before they were taken back to the main camp and 'sung-in' by the men and the women. Soon afterwards they would be taken on a pilgrimage to sacred sites within their own local descent group territory.

A year or so later the youths underwent the second stage of initiation, called the 'wilyaru'. The initiant's arm vein was cut so that blood could spurt across his body and infuse him with strength, and cuts (cicatrisation) were made with sharp flints on the nape of his neck to produce the public scars of a wilyaru. He was then presented with a bullroarer, marked with individual totemic identification and attached to a string of human hair, as a symbol of power. According to the anthropologist Ronald Berndt, at this second important ceremony all youths underwent subincision (an incision made to the urethra from underneath the penis which was allowed to heal but whose scab was regularly knocked off for blood-letting in prescribed rituals and ceremonies).[42] But according to Howitt only selected youths, chosen by elders and taken by surprise while hunting with the men, became 'kulpi' (subincised).[43] A kulpi, according to Howitt, was the highest stage of initiation, bestowing the status of a 'thorough-man' and a position of envy for others. A kulpi controlled important tribal matters, took the principal role at grand corroborees and ceremonies, and only he could appear before the women completely naked.

A period of segregation followed the wilyaru (of Howitt's version), or subincision (of Berndt's account), during which (according to Berndt) full initiants spurted blood from their penis incisures over the youths to the accompaniment of ritual singing and dancing. Now the youths could become active in the sacred life of the men, with its regular ritual incisure piercing that formed part of the religious re-enactments.[44] Furthermore, it was only after wilyaru (according to Howitt), or subincision (Berndt), that a male could marry.

The youths were taken to the 'tjurunga storehouse' of their particular totems—often a cave—where bundles of sacred wooden boards were untied, ritually handled to the accompaniment of songs, and whose incisions were explained. The markings symbolised the mythic actions of an initiant's own mythic ancestor, and it was believed that at his death his spirit would seek the place where its tjurunga rested.[45]

When the wilyaru returned to the camp, with healed wounds, the sisters and mothers made a great fuss. However, he was forbidden to speak to them until he had given each a gift.

The stages of male initiation necessarily stretched over a number of years, as youths developed into manhood. It was a progressive preparation of males for custodianship of the traditional religious knowledge and as primary intermediaries between the various local descent groups and the spirit world with which they interacted.

Red Ochre Expeditions

Ochre paint, made from claylike earth mixed with water, played a significant role in ceremonial life. The smooth, soft clay paint was finger- or hand-patterned onto bodies and faces, and onto sacred objects. It was used, and traded, in several colours across the continent, each ochre colour having a geographical and a spiritual significance. White ochre, found near the Lachlan River, was believed to have been kept by the giant kangaroos of the Creation period and were smeared over the body and face of the mythological Wirroowaa. Yellow ochre was the sacred ochre colour of the Yirritja moiety of north-eastern Arnhem Land, while black ochre was produced by many groups from the charcoal believed to be the remains of campfires made by the mythic ancestors during the Creation time.[46]

The sacred red ochre ('karku'), found in South Australia's Flinders Ranges and collected by the Diyari and other tribes of the general area, was believed to be the blood of the ancestral Emu, Kuringii. Kuringii was chased by two ancestral Dogs, Kilowilinna and Perilingunina, from the Innaminka area, down the Cooper to Mt Alick (which was believed to be Kuringii petrified), where the Emu turned, dodged the Dogs, and made for the Flinders Ranges, travelling due east. The first hill of the ranges was where Kuringii had met a Man with a pack of Dogs, one particularly savage brute being named Thorijurra. Here the Emu was killed by the Dogs, with the Man's assistance, the Man being instantly turned into a hill. The blood from the Emu, it was believed, formed the red ochre deposit at the sacred cave, Jerkinna. The Dogs entered another cave to rest, and died. There they metamorphosed into huge dolomite limestone boulders with the original pair, Kilowilinna and Perilingunina, represented by two high peaks—St Mary's Peak and a peak unnamed by later Europeans.[47]

Every July or August a party of seventy or eighty Diyari men, some handpicked for their fighting prowess (for the journey had its dangers), made the annual red-ochre-gathering expedition ('pukartu') to Parachilna Creek near Jerkinna Cave. The expeditions followed the path of Kuringii, members were selected by the elders, and the round trip of some 300 miles took eight to twelve weeks. Most accounts indicate that women were never in an ochre party. However, one describes the role of women as mediators for entry permission from the local tribal custodians, using the tradition of sexual favours as payment.[48]

The pukartu was not only an expedition for resources for Diyari use and trade, but was also both a religious pilgrimage and one to test fortitude. Sometimes youths were initiated just before the mine was reached; and when the party did arrive at Parachilna Creek, near the sacred cave of Kuringii, the men and youths had to build a sacred fire and perform an all-night dance based on different phases of Kuringii's chase. Next day, in single file, their bodies greased with goanna fat, the men and youths would walk solemnly to the cave. As they passed the limestone rocks of the metamorphosed Dogs, the men hurled stones in vengeance. They climbed the hill to a flat area, where the younger uninitiated males were left, while the initiated proceeded, chanting the Emu song in anticipation of gathering his 'blood' (the Murragurta). Only ochre dust could be collected (not the larger pieces), in a coolamon vessel. The men then moved on to the rocks symbolising the Dogs to paint their bodies with the ochre before running to Jerkinna Cave, where the leader would initiate them into the Murragurta rite. All body hair was burnt off with a glowing firestick and scattered about to represent emu feathers.

The men would then descend the hill and return with their ochre to the sacred fire. Only now could they eat and drink, and only that which they had carried with them in wallaby pouches. They were prohibited from drinking at the sacred spring nearby. Sacred springs served as conservation game reserves, and no game could be killed in the area between the sacred fire and the sacred ochre cave on penalty of death. Women were excluded from this sacred place, also on penalty of death.[49] The red ochre powder was mixed with water from the creek (or with urine, if water was short), patted into loaves, and each man carried some 77 pounds of solid substance, supported on his head by a headring, back to Diyari country.

The pukartu's successful return was always made at night, by surprise and design, announced by the humming of a bullroarer swung at high speed. Yelling, clapping and dancing arose at the camps. The women were not permitted to speak to their men until sunrise, when the 'return ceremony' was over. But for weeks afterwards the talk was of the adventures of the journey.

Red ochre, that sacred substance representative of the blood of mythic ancestors, contained iron oxide, as does haemoglobin in human blood.[50] Its function was renewal and cleansing, both spiritual and physical. Apart from its ceremonial usage, red ochre was employed as an ointment for wounds, bruises and swellings, as a magic charm to abate the heat of the sun or the force of the wind, as decoration on ritual objects, in rain-making ceremonies, in the rituals of transition from boyhood to manhood, and as a medium of transcendence from sickness to health, from death to renewal or from uncleanliness to cleanliness. It was that special substance that changed the secular to the sacred, and present reality to the state of Dreaming.[51] Karku was traded by the Diyari (whose economy was partly based on its annual harvest) during the large ceremonial gatherings in the north-east of South Australia.

Mindari Rituals

Red ochre was the theme of a long series of myths and rites to ensure its preservation and continuance within Diyari culture, the most important being the Mindari ceremony. Indeed the Mindari was the most significant ceremony for the people of the Lake Eyre Basin. The return of the pukartu would herald this annual event of increase rites to celebrate the Emu ancestor. It was an occasion of large gatherings of tribes from distant parts, a platitude of peace between them to amicably settle disputes, and an opportunity to trade in resources. Red ochre, as well as string tassels and netted bags, were exchanged by the Diyari for such commodities as pitjiri (from south-west Queensland), softwood shields and hardwood spears and boomerangs (from the tribes of the east), slabs of stone (from the west), and feathers (from the north).[52] The Mindari also served as the next ceremony for the initiants after wilyaru.[53]

The leader of the Mindari was a man whose marduka was Mindari (Emu totem), and the marduka men (sister's sons) made the necessary preparations for the ceremony. Two special objects were fashioned, the 'itikaru', made from lignum and painted with charcoal, and the 'kopi', a representation of the Emu's heart, made from burnt gypsum stone wound with string.[54]

The night-time ceremony spanned five consecutive nights. On the given day, appointed for its full moon, the host tribes would welcome arriving parties with singing. At sunset the men, in two distinct groups, shaved all hair from their faces and bodies, tying head hair high with emu and cockatoo feathers. The kopi men painted themselves with white ochre and charcoal, and carried the itikaru; the 'wimabala' men with red ochre, and carried the 'Emu's heart'. The wilyaru remained unpainted and unadorned.[55] The women retreated to a distance from the camp to dance, and the men left for a piece of hard, prepared ground where a small boy, elaborately decorated with down and feathers, stuck by blood, danced into the large ring of men. The wilyaru then followed and the young boy ran out of the ring. Throughout the night the itikaru was worked backwards and forwards by novices in turn, assisted by an experienced pintara or marduka, while the men danced with a boomerang in each hand. Every now and then a man would drop out and, taking a woman of his own moiety away from the ground, would have sexual intercourse with her. The woman would then return to the women's ground, and the man would resume his place in the dance. The ceremony ended at daylight with men and women of opposite moieties having sexual intercourse.[56] The groups would retire to sleep for the day, before the ceremony recommenced at sunset.

On the last evening the young wilyaru were carefully dressed, their hair tied high with cord, the tails of marsupial rats ('thilpa') fastened to the top, feathers of the owl and emu fixed to the forehead and at the ears, and a girdle of hair wound around the waist. Their faces were painted with red and black ochres and they were each given two boomerangs by members of their own moiety, for they had become the new Mindari men. After handing food to the old Mindari men, the new members were given a signal from the ceremony's head-man to cook and eat emu.[57]

34   *White Man's Dreaming: Killalpaninna Mission 1866–1915*

Aboriginal men dressed and decorated for ceremony

Sexual excitement was a feature of certain ceremonies and was probably believed to add effectiveness to the increase rites. It possibly also served to link the tribes in peace and friendship, and to be an occasion for expressing the common unity of the participants.[58]

Nevertheless, Samuel Gason found such ritual behaviour too indigestible for his Victorian palate. He described the increase rituals as 'altogether so obscene and disgusting, I must, even at the risk of leaving my subject incomplete, pass them over by only thus briefly referring to them'. He noted the Mindari rituals as 'Indescribable Customs'.[59] Howitt, in his description of the Mindari ceremony, simply referred to the young men going through 'many extraordinary evolutions'.[60]

The Kopperamanna plains were often chosen as the site for Mindari ceremonies, consequently the area became important as ceremonial and trading grounds. Other sites were Lake Etamunbanie (near Pandi Pandi), Wadrawadrinna Waterhole (near Innaminka), Cooncherie Waterhole, and Lake Howitt.[61] Ngarlangarlani, near Lake Killpaninna, became a Mindari ground, certainly after the 1870s.[62] Ironically, considering the missionaries' preoccupation with Aborigines transgressing the 'sacred' Christian sixth commandment (adultery), the Diyari origin of the name 'Killalpaninna' (correctly 'Kirla wiljpaninna') pertains to 'kirla' meaning 'vagina', and here referring to the mouth of a cave.[63]

'Doctors' and Magicians

If a man or a woman had a mystical or metaphysical experience which was related to the tribe and deemed significant, such as an important dream, muramura sightings, or having been swallowed and regurgitated by a female Kardimarkara, he or she might be thought to be possessed by sorcery.[64] If special powers were believed bestowed, that man or woman became a 'kunkie' (called a 'sorcerer', 'native doctor' or 'magician' by the German missionaries). Kunkies were healers of the sick, exorcising malevolent spirits by removing poisons from the body, and curing by using local, natural materials.

Gason refers to several local diseases, like a skin infection known as 'witch', and a childhood disease called 'mirra'.[65] He also reported a disease known as 'mooramoora' (indicating that it was especially mysterious and particularly virulent), unquestionably smallpox, and existing among the Diyari before direct contact with Europeans.[66] Many old men and women bore pockmarks on their faces and bodies, and from the graves indicated to him, a great number had already died from this European disease that came from the colonised east.

The kunkie would also perform rain-making rites. According to Berndt, this was accomplished by 'undoing a rain bundle secreted in his beard'.[67] But it seems there were several methods of rain-making practised among the Diyari. The kunkie (as Rain-maker) had custody of the rain-making bullroarer, keeping it from public view to retain its spiritual potency. Gason described this ritual as one of the Diyari's 'grandest ceremonies', a bloodletting rite, with the old men taking the leading role.[68] Another method of rain-making was to rub goanna fat into the body of a boy (in the same manner as it was rubbed into the Dara-ulu of the gypsum rain-making stones), the grease causing steam to rise from his body, and the steam in turn forming a cloud from which, it was believed, rain would fall.[69]

Some forms of sorcery or magic, however, could be practised by any adult. 'Pointing the bone' was probably the most widely distributed such form and was generally used to avenge a death. This practice (according to Reuther) was traced to the Kujimukana muramura story of a Boy (Kujimukana) assisting a Man to find water. The Boy then drank from the waterbag, forgot to close it and the precious liquid ran out. Kujimukana was subsequently killed by Others for his negligence. But his friend and protector, the Man, carefully trimmed the flesh from the dead Boy's bones and proceeded, in revenge, and by means of the bones, to inflict death upon 'the entire multitude of people'.[70]

In Diyari culture, the 'bone', traditionally a human tibia or fibula, would be pointed in the appropriate rite and 'sung'. The Diyari believed that the bone 'moved' invisibly from the pointer to the victim causing the victim's soul to be drawn into the bone.

According to Missionary Otto Siebert the bone was first moistened with drops of blood from a penis incisure, before being soaked with blood from a man's arm vein. A second man bound the bone by a cord (made from human hair and attached to the lower end of the bone) to two fingers of the first man. The second man then drew steadily and strongly on the cord so that the arm of the first was shaken about. Suddenly the second man grabbed the point of the bone and smeared it with clay, to prevent the imprisoned soul from escaping, and the bone was wrapped in emu feathers and buried in the ground. It was left for several months to become soft, which became the period of the victim's illness. After removal, it was slowly burned, signifying that the 'bewitched' person was now dead. If, however, that person did not die, it was believed that in some way a counter 'bewitching' had taken place.[71] The power of the bone could be ameliorated, but only by locating the sorcerer and persuading him or her to draw all power from it by steeping it in water.[72]

Death Rites

The disposal of a corpse was by burial only.[73] The two large toes were tied together, and the body sewn into a net before being taken to soft ground where a grave was dug with a conical mound at one end.[74] A digging-stick was placed in the mound for a woman and a spear for a man. The body was carried to the gravesite on the heads of three men and, to ensure that the person was indeed dead, it would be dropped onto the ground in such a way that the neck was broken. At the burial site the corpse was placed on the heads of the kneeling carriers and a kunkie, holding a thin rod in each hand, would stand opposite and address it, enquiring as to the cause of death. Any of the three below could act as interpreter, and could give the corpse's answer. Sometimes death was attributed to 'innocuous magic', but on other occasions the name of an enemy from another tribe would be given. In such cases the bearers would throw the body onto the ground and begin wailing, their minds intent on the necessary revenge killing. The body would then be placed in the grave and covered with bushes and pieces of wood to prevent the ravages of wild dogs.

Before burial, however, and at the graveside, a non-relative would cut away the fat adhering to the muscles of the face, thighs, arms and stomach, to be passed in a prescribed order to relatives of the deceased's matrilineal moiety,

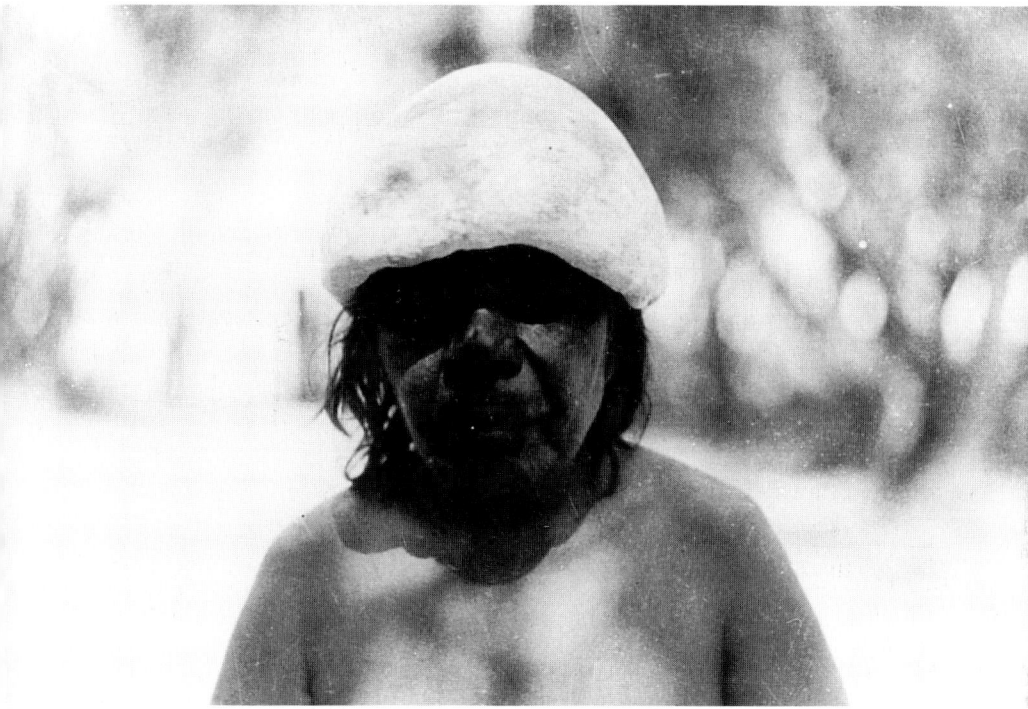

A widow wearing the heavy mourning cap made from layers of gypsum paste

and ritually eaten.[75] The members of the burial party, ritually painted with ochre, then began a day and night of loud mourning.

A dead man's camp would be deserted immediately after his funeral, and his few possessions abandoned. His relatives would continue the lamenting with great wailing, the women cutting themselves, and both sexes smearing their bodies with white ochre to signify mourning and to render the body of the mourner more visible to the spirit of the deceased, allowing the spirit to 'see' that it was being properly mourned. The 'totem soul' of the deceased was believed to be present at the grave during burial, and would follow the mourners back to camp, keeping hidden for most of the time within the shade of a bush but occasionally exhibiting itself in the form of an eagle that would cry out directly at the mourners, or a crow that would sit unusually still in the presence of humans. During evening mealtimes the mourners would place food aside for the spirit.[76]

On the death of a man, his wife and tribal sisters would shave their heads and, using a hair-net as a covering, would add gypsum paste (ground gypsum stone) to their heads until a hard cap formed. This heavy mourning cap was worn for a period before being placed on the grave, or smashed when the widow remarried.[77]

Mourning for the very old, however, was short. And stillborn babies and very young children were buried with no mourning at all. The bodies of stillborn children were frequently ritually eaten,[78] perhaps in an effort to embrace the embryonic spirit within the matrilineal moiety and its special mardu, thus giving it more substantial spirit-life.

It was believed that the deceased's spirit, which entered a person's body at birth, left it at death, but did not immediately return to the spirit-child centre. Part of it remained in a special 'mourning ring' constructed near the graveside, and part remained near the corpse. During this time the spirit was prone to wandering, often far afield, and associating with muramuras and 'kutchie' (spirits).

Some months later the mortuary party, accompanied by a kunkie, would return to the grave to conduct further rituals. The deceased's spirit was then summoned by the kunkie, lured to the grave by a smoking fire made by the widow or widower, and 'caught' by the kunkie. He would place it in his stomach, using it as a special spirit agent in divination, and then release it to its spirit waterhole (muramuras associated with waterholes being 'revivifiers'). A piece of ground beside the grave, facing the direction of the deceased's Dreaming spirit, was cleared so that the spirit could rejoin its spirit double as a manifestation of that Mythic Being. At a later time the special mourning ring was thrown into a waterhole.[79] After these final rites, living relatives (pintara and marduka) took responsibility for the deceased's country and its relics and rites.

Revenge Parties (Pinya)

Few deaths were attributed to natural causes, mainly those of the very old. If a seemingly unexplained death occurred at a relatively young age, or a normally healthy person fell ill and died, it was believed that somebody, as sorcerer, was responsible. A revenge death was arranged to redress the account, and this could be carried out by a number of means, using either weapons or sorcery.

The most direct revenge action and one that produced terror among the Diyari, was the armed pinya (execution) party. A pinya would travel great distances if necessary to avenge a death. But before setting out the men (only), selected by a council of pinaru and decorated with the characteristic plaited band and white ochre, would engage in a temporary exchange of wives to express unity and fellowship.[80] At a day's distance from their destination the pinya would travel only at night, to avoid detection, and spies were sent to check that the accused was in camp and where he slept.

On the designated night, at the deepest hour, the pinya, painted with white ochre, crept to the camp and surrounded it. The pinya leader called to the accused man, waking him in terror with the customary lies about coming out and not being hurt. Frightened people emerged from their huts, and tree-boughs were distributed among the women for shaking, to muffle the sounds of the execution. The accused was killed by clubbing.

At dawn the elders among the pinya party washed the pinya weapons with water in a receptacle, and one passed the 'cup' between the young men so that they may receive some of the strength of the victim by drinking his blood (a ritual that had later parallels for the Christianised Aborigines during the rites of the Lord's Supper).[81] Fat tissue from the victim's kidneys was used to anoint the weapons of the elders, and was ritually eaten by the fully initiated men to enhance their strength.[82] Such revenge killings would frequently spark feuds between the various groups (both internal and inter-tribal), to which there seemed no end.

The leader of a pinya (the 'mudla-kutya') was usually the elder brother of the dead person, or, as a substitute in his absence, a near relative. The elder brother ('neyi'), the most honoured, was guardian to the younger brothers ('ngadada'). He was duty bound to stand by, help and protect, even to the death. If the younger brother was to be a pinya victim, the neyi must offer himself in his ngadada's place.[83]

Pinya party members were decorated with the tails of small marsupials tied to beards and hips, while on the head of the leader was a large cap, balloon-shaped and fashioned from the fibres of plants, with the inside filled with emu feathers. The outside of the cap was decorated with bird feather-down and two strings of animal tails. When a pinya approached a camp, the old people of that camp, and especially the old women, could, in fact, turn the course of events. Without saying a word they could take away the pinya decoration, thus expressing their disapproval and causing the pinya to turn away. If this occurred, a woman from the camp would be given to the leader of the pinya to appease the family of the deceased for whom revenge should have been taken.[84]

Women, Marriage and Children

Kinship, moiety, mardu and totemic clan exogamy were essential aspects determining prospective marriage alliances, and such alliances, forbidden within moieties and within mardu, and permitted only between the same or alternate generations, were generally by arrangement. Cross-cousins lived in a 'kami' relationship to one another, and were not allowed to marry. For marriage to be permissible between young people there must exist a 'ngadada' relationship between them as well as a 'noa' relationship to each other. Furthermore, the balancing of marriages was of great interest and importance to local peace and harmony among the patrilocal groups.

There were several methods of marriage arrangement, the most common being betrothal, which was arranged through the mother of the girl sought and the mother's male brethren, the older 'neyi' of that girl. Consent of the elders of both local groups was also necessary. Infant betrothal was the normal form, and often a potential daughter, before birth, was promised to either a man of an alternate generation, or to a man's son or nephew of her own generation. Often, too, an infant sister was exchanged on promise for one of the sisters of the man making the request. But if the mother of a girl refused her daughter, her word was considered final.[85]

Another form of betrothal was the concomitant birth of a boy of one moiety and a girl of the other who were in the correct relationship to one another. In such a case, a few days after the births, the two mothers would discuss a betrothal and declare their children 'tipamalku noa mara', that they should be man and wife. As a mark of the marriage promise, the naval strings of the babies were bound together with emu feathers and the members of each family discussed acceptance. The two babies then became noa to each other.[86]

The Diyari and surrounding tribes were polygamous, and a man who married the eldest daughter had the right to also marry her sisters. He may, however, transfer that right to one of his brothers. However, male elders, with their power

Aboriginal woman winnowing munyeroo seed to be crushed on a grinding slab

and status, monopolised the marriage market at the expense of younger men (possibly traditionally to some degree, but certainly after European occupation, when they began fighting for status and authority among their young). Allegedly their motives were not only sexual but also economic and social, to ensure there would be an efficient provider of food in an elder's camp when the old man and his old wife were no longer capable. Young Diyari girls of fourteen years old were expected to be sexually mature and physically capable of food-gathering. Elkin claimed to have been told that young girls were being married to old men to protect them from the 'loose living' otherwise resulting from liaisons with only partially initiated youths.[87] Boys were not permitted to marry until all stages of initiation had been completed, and consequently were considerably older than girls of marriageable age. However gifts, which may be adequate provision for old age, could be made to an elder, the promised husband, to buy marriage rights to a particular young girl.[88] Wives could also be gained from capture during conflict, or given as mollification in potentially violent situations (such as pinya).

Gift-giving had an important role in Diyari culture. At a marriage betrothal the man was obliged to make gifts to his prospective wife's parents, or to the prospective wife's mother's brother. And from the time of betrothal a strict taboo of not seeing or speaking existed between a man and his prospective wife's mother. The new husband had also to avoid his father-in-law, as well as the relatives who arranged the marriage. He stood in a position of inferiority before those to whom he was indebted, and this was expressed in an attitude of reserve and avoidance, and in making gifts to the father-in-law.[89]

In addition to having a wife, or a number of wives (regular marriages), a man had one or more 'secondary wives'. Conversely, most women had more than one 'husband', or at least more than one man as a lover, as married women were permitted to take a paramour (or even several paramours) providing the affair(s) were kept discreet and did not publicly embarrass the woman's husband. Such lovers were often drawn from those younger men who had not yet found wives. If the couple were brazen and the older man felt he was made a public fool, a serious fight might result, or worse, a revenge murder.[90]

Secondary wives were in fact the primary wives of a man's tribal brother (or brothers). If that man visited his tribal brother, his secondary wife would be given to him for the duration of his visit.[91] Known as 'pirauru' (or 'piranguru'), these extra sexual encounters probably served the function of binding groups not immediately living together. Moreover, such extramarital sexual relationships occurred during large temporary gatherings of diverse people, as was the case during the Mindari rituals.

Later, when Diyari wives were offered as peace overtures and in hospitality to European men who moved into their area, and were blindly accepted, the 'loan' put the Europeans into debt and into a pirauru-type relationship, with its privileges and obligations.[92] If the European man failed to make gifts in return, or fulfil obligations, trouble would follow. Clashes that began with this fundamental misunderstanding often ended in murder, with Aborigines demanding gifts (most likely food) as their right, and Europeans denying and showing resentment. When the German missionaries sent back women offered to them on their arrival in Diyari country, the rejection was interpreted as a hostile act with perhaps a violent intention. Furthermore, the advent of visitors was heralded by the Diyari custom of riotous noise and beating of the ground, giving an appearance of hostility and adding to the fear and suspicion of the newly arrived Germans.[93]

Women thus performed the function of mediators or conciliators during situations of potential conflict. They could be a powerful force in stopping the incessant fighting, from individual scuffles to group or inter-tribal warfare. If one party began threatening another, in desperation the latter may send some of its women to placate and signal their desire not to fight. If the attacking party was willing to withdraw, its men would have sexual intercourse with the women, before peaceably sending them back. But if intent on attack, they would return the women untouched, and combat ensued.[94] Furthermore, a regular method of settling a quarrel between two opposing parties was the temporary exchange of wives.

Women and children were never intentionally harmed during warfare. If the women wished to stop an advancing enemy, they would dance in front of them, cutting themselves as they pushed against sharp weapons, until the enemy (comprised of men only) felt shame and sorrow and ceased the attack. After peace was established the women were sexually lent to the enemy in gratitude.[95] Individual fights between two Diyari men could be stopped by the wailing and beseeching of a woman or a group of women. Such fights often started with one man referring to the sexual parts of a male or female relative of the other, an arousing and provocative action, or he might mention the name of a dead relative, knowing a fight would result.

Regardless of their power in saving lives and forging marriage alliances Diyari women were perceived by Europeans as having little real power in their society and as playing a minor role in religious matters. Bound by their physiological functions, they were thought to perform only a secondary or supplementary role at the ceremonies to which they were permitted, while the men became extremely powerful through their monopoly of the spiritual sphere. Aboriginal men did perform secret, sacred ceremonies which women were forbidden to attend. But, significantly, there were just as many female characters in the Dreaming mythology as male characters.[96] Women's supportive role may well have been held in high regard in the past, and perhaps changed over time. But, more critically, it may have changed rapidly after European conquest, when such customs were first documented.

According to various studies, women traditionally did play a prominent (if not equal) part in important religious ceremonies. Archaeology has confirmed old grinding dishes (used only by women) at significant ceremonial sites. And interviews with older Aborigines have indicated that the role of women in spiritual matters did change after European contact, when the traditional way of life became threatened and the old men felt their authority waning.[97] Women were allegedly present for all major religious ceremonies in the Lake Eyre Basin region, with only two exceptions—the Kangaroo History and rain-making ceremonies—although women performed their own rain-making ceremonies.[98]

'History' songs, 'Creation' songs and songs about the 'law' would be sung around the campfires, listened to and learnt by both sexes from their earliest days. Learning the great corpus of oral traditions was time-consuming, and it was not until both men and women were old and had more leisure time that they could acquire a large repertoire from which to draw and teach. Both sexes had their own particular secret ceremonies, and both sexes had an intimate knowledge of their country.

In Aboriginal society childhood was considered a preparation period for adulthood and marriage.[99] Children grew up in an open milieu, with little but certain rites and sacred objects hidden from them until full initiation into adulthood. Consequently they were prepared for independence and marriage at an early age.

Infanticide was practised by the desert tribes, although not indiscriminately.[100] In times of drought or starvation, young babies and children might be killed, and miscarriages (known as 'maudra-dungana' or 'belly knead') might be induced. All sickly and deformed children were destroyed, generally by being smothered in sand, having sand poured down their nostrils, or being hit hard on the head, so that they would not be a burden to the tribe. The offspring of very young girls were also sometimes destroyed as they were considered 'immature and not worth preserving'.[101] And newborns were sometimes killed during droughts or severe summers, when food and water were already scarce. Despite (in the eyes of Europeans) this seemingly callous attitude towards infants when deemed necessary, the Diyari were described as having a great love for children.[102]

Samuel Gason, one of the first Europeans to encounter the Diyari, described them as possessing 'in an eminent degree the three great virtues of hospitality, reverence to old age, and love for their children and parents. Should any stranger arrive at their camp food was immediately set before him'. And yet Gason also described the Diyari as a 'treacherous' race, with no sense of wrong, living in constant dread of each other:

> while their enmity to the white man is only kept in abeyance by fear. Kindness they construe into fear; and, had it not been for the determination and firmness of the early settlers, they would never have been allowed to occupy the country. The tribe is numerous, and if they knew (and it is feared they will eventually learn) their own power, the present white inhabitants could not keep them down, or for one day retain their possessions.[103]

Colonisation and Land Loss

South Australia was formally colonised by the British in 1836, and a letter from the Colonial Office in London to James Hurtle, colonial commissioner for the new colony at its very inception, loosely outlined a passive means by which land might be ceded from Aboriginal control into European hands. An officer was to be appointed to protect the interests of the Aborigines (the first protector of Aborigines), all ceded Aboriginal land must first be offered to the colonial government, and the protector must be furnished:

> with evidence of the faithful fullfillment [sic] of the Bargains or Treaties which you may effect with the Aborigines for the cession of lands, and you will take care that the Aborigines are not disturbed in the enjoyment of the lands over which they may possess proprietory rights and of which they are not disposed [sic] to make a voluntary transfer.[104]

Clearly the significance of land, and more particularly specific land, to the Aborigines was not understood by the Europeans. Nor was the cession always passive or peaceful. The colonists obviously considered that a sharing of land space—where, to these people from a more densely populated part of the world, there certainly seemed an abundance—was fair and realistic. Australia was deemed *terra nullius*, a land without owners, by the newcomers. And it seems they considered their initial method of 'take-over' democratic and humanitarian: 'On the cessation of lands you will make arrangements for supplying the Aboriginal proprietors of such lands not only with food but with shelter and with moral and religious instruction'.[105]

Weather-proof sheds were to be erected for the dispossessed Aborigines, and they were to be supplied with food and clothing and even 'gratuitous medical assistance and relief', 'at a small cost', in exchange for an equivalent in labour. But not for long was their labour sought. In the early days of the colony, as the struggle for black emancipation from slavery in America gained sympathy in Britain and Europe, the Colonial Office issued an order forbidding settlers in the British colony the employ of Aborigines, lest they be accused of practising slavery.[106]

With the loss of land came the loss of a cultural and spiritual base for the Aborigines; a loss of their spiritual essence, their Dreaming double. And with the arrival of the settlers to occupy their land, and the coming of the missionaries to impose a new spiritual and cultural order during the mid-nineteenth century, the world of the Diyari tribes changed rapidly and irrevocably.

3

First Contact

On the cool spring morning of 9 October 1866 the Barossa Valley German community gathered at the Langmeil church to witness a historic event. From the early hours, wagons, buggies and riders poured into the township, the church filled, and people spilled into the streets. German hearts were stirred as the pastors of both synods stood solemnly while the newly arrived missionaries were formally dedicated. They were Johann F. Goessling and Ernst Homann, recent graduates from Hermannsburg, and their 'Kolonist' (layhelper) assistant, Hermann H. Vogelsang. The trio were joined by Johann Ernst Jacob of Mount Torrens, a local member of the German community who had volunteered as an extra layhelper. Each man solemnly stood to receive the pious blessing of benediction. Goessling preached the farewell sermon and Pastor Auricht led a prayer of thanksgiving.

After a farewell meal the German community escorted the mission party in festive procession to Angas Park (now Nuriootpa). The missionaries were formally dressed in black top hats and heavy coats with tails and, as their strong German wagons laboured under the weight of survival essentials, the Langmeil and Bethany brass bands struck up a stirring march. Hundreds of wagons and horsemen lined the streets, and German families strained for a glimpse of the brave missionaries. A thousand pounds had been collected to fund this expedition.[1]

Rain began to fall, and few eyes were dry. The children of the Langmeil school sang 'O most blessed are ye heralds / Who the saving message spread, / Whom the Lord had sent far distant / To the blind and to the dead.'[2] As the rain intensified crowds gathered in the Nuriootpa Hotel and a few enthusiasts accompanied the missionaries to Dimchurch, where the party spent the first night.[3]

The German Lutherans of this less than thirty-year-old 'British claimed colony' were possessed of that nineteenth-century cultural and religious xenophobia that characterised all of Europe at the time. Their missionaries were obsessed with an overriding passion to spread the religious faith of their culture to the perceived 'underprivileged heathens', those 'primitives' of the New World. It was considered imperative by the European Christians, regardless of personal sectarianism, that these heathens emerge from their state of ignorance and darkness, and 'develop' along the cultural lines of Europe. These German Lutherans believed such metamorphoses could be accomplished among the 'primitives' of Australia by the message of Luther's central theme, the Christian gospel, being carried to these people. The missionaries themselves were newly arrived in the colony, imbued with enthusiasm and zealousness and impelled by a dispossessed body of German immigrants now attempting to take possession of the future of another culture. German Lutherans and Diyari Aborigines met in the inhospitable Australian desert, their alienation from each other creating fears, misunderstandings and hostility.

The Journey Northwards
The missionaries travelled northwards with a local German settler as guide. Through the gently rolling hills of the beautiful Barossa Valley they slowly made their way, past the settlements of Kapunda, Bethel, Rhynie, Auburn and Leasingham, where the missionaries met with a shipmate, Wilhelm Koch, who, less than a year later, was to join the enterprise as the mission's schoolteacher. They were welcomed along the route at various German homes to 'overnight' in comfort.

As the party of five men, with seven horses, two wagons and two dogs, progressed northwards from the Clare Valley, past the tiny settlement of Melrose and down Horrocks Pass, 'civilisation', as such, was gradually left behind. Through the folding hills and giant river redgums of the spectacular pass (named after John Horrocks, who had been the first European to explore this far northwards just twenty years earlier, using the first camel employed in the colony) the missionary party gained their first taste of the Australian bush. And, emerging from the high ground of the pass, the scene before them changed dramatically. A great, flat, empty plain spread as far as the eye could see, and a turquoise sea shimmered beyond as the men glimpsed the tip of Spencer Gulf in the far distance. While crossing the plain the two dogs disappeared after chasing an emu. One was found near Port Augusta a few days later, the other walked to Mount Torrens, its former home some 200 miles away.[4]

Near Port Augusta the guide left the party to return south. Further provisions had arrived by boat, and the missionaries spent an uneasy night at a local seafront hotel frequented by bawdy sailors.[5] Relieved to be leaving this wild frontier town, the Lutherans embarked on the most difficult part of their journey. The landscape became ever harsher, the air ever drier, the temperatures ever higher. Through endless plains of saltbush and bluebush their heavy wagons, loaded to capacity, lurched and rolled. Water was difficult to find, and feed for the horses dwindled. The men spent hours each day in search of a campsite where the horses could pasture. 'But the Lord was with us', wrote Goessling, 'and although we were absolutely inexperienced in such matters, we always fared well.'[6]

The wagons, however, were cumbersome and difficult to manoeuvre in the soft, sandy soil, their wheel distance too narrow to track with the wider (English) transport-wagon markings. The horses struggled to pull unevenly balanced vehicles whose wheels were partly in wagon tracks and partly on irregular ridges. The party progressed at an awkwardly slow pace, slowed further by breakages of wagon wheels. Furthermore, between Edowie and Parachilna one of their best horses was lost. In Port Augusta the Lutherans had met an English team-

Homann, Goessling, Jacob and Vogelsang set out from Tanunda (Langmeil) for the inaugural journey into the north, 9 October 1866

ster, a Mr Edgar, who had agreed to take a few things on for them. Fortunately Edgar came to their assistance over a broken wagon. He yoked his horses to the Germans' heavy wagons and pulled them to Beltana. Here the missionaries purchased horses from Edgar before travelling on, through Leigh Creek, Patsey's Spring and Owieandana, to Umberatana Station, one of Thomas Elder's pastoral leases. The last part of the track was extremely rough, passing through dry creekbeds and over steep banks. Small stones played havoc with the wagons and horses. The wheels began to dry out from the intensity of the heat, with rims coming loose and requiring periodic wedging into place. One horse lost a shoe and the party was detained while Vogelsang, a blacksmith by trade, plied his art.

Throughout the journey water shortage was dangerously acute, and the energy and time of each man was constantly occupied with physical survival and physical mobility. It was a new role for the scholarly theologians, and when they finally reached Umberatana Station to rest for a few days Goessling was to write of the journey thus far:

> But I will state that, as far as these difficulties are concerned, which are so prominent, they really recede when compared with the difficulties one has in spiritual things, namely so little time and quietness in order to edify oneself. And when the soul does not receive proper care the body suffers with it; and if the right joy in faith is lacking then the external things do not go well either. Still, in spite of everything

we are in good spirits, and hope to remain so. Our hymns have not been silenced and, God willing, they shall not be silent any day.[7]

Nevertheless, the Germans had arrived at Umberatana Station exhausted, sunburnt and dishevelled, their initiation into the Australian desert truly under way. They were made welcome by Samuel Stuckey, Elder's manager, and there they also met John Buttfield, a former Methodist minister and now sub-protector of Aborigines.

There was plenty of water and feed for the horses at Umberatana Station, and the animals recovered quickly. Here the missionaries had their first encounter with the new form of Australian outback transport, Afghans and their camels. Imported and employed by Thomas Elder to service his large pastoral leases in the dry, arid north, these exotics and their dromedaries were to play a vital role in the opening up and development of the interior of the continent. The first shipment of commercial camels, with their Afghan attendants, had been unloaded onto the Port Augusta docks on New Year's Day 1866, less than a year previously. Strings of pack camels were being used as a highly successful alternative to horses and wagons for cartage purposes in the north. As the Germans were leaving Umberatana a camel string and a few Afghan handlers were arriving at the station with a load of wool from Lake Hope Station, another of Elder's pastoral leases further northwards, close to the missionaries' destination.

The Lutherans had passed through rich grazing land near the Flinders Ranges, but in stark contrast the country further north became increasingly poor. The hapless wagons continued to give trouble. Vogelsang's broke its axle while crossing a small shallow creek, and he and Goessling worked for hours to repair it before the party could proceed. Delays continually tested patience and perseverance. Shortly after leaving Mt Freeling Station the back wheel of Vogelsang's wagon broke, shattering the spokes. An enforced stay of eight days at Mt Freeling resulted, while Goessling and Vogelsang repaired the wheel. It was 6 December before the journey resumed, and summer was fast descending. While the men were camped in the dry creek bed of Ducks Ponds they were to experience another of the mysteries of the north. A sudden, heavy, overnight thunderstorm turned the creek into a flowing river, and the Lutherans scrambled to prevent their wagons and possessions from being washed away. Now the washed-out wagon tracks caused even slower progress and the men arrived at Blanchewater Station on 15 December, just before the arrival of the sub-protector of Aborigines, who was returning from a patrol of his territory of responsibility.

Buttfield advised the Lutherans not to go to Lake Hope, which had by now become their destination. There a small police outpost existed for the protection of the new settlers in the area. According to Buttfield Lake Hope was only infrequently visited by Aborigines. Instead he advised the Lutherans to proceed to Lake Kopperamanna, which was close to Manuwakaninna Station homestead (also owned by Thomas Elder), for Kopperamanna was thought to be a popular meeting place for local tribes. The sub-protector also advised the men to investigate the place by horseback as it would be impossible to pull the heavy wagons over the 50 miles of sandhills.

But Buttfield had further unexpected news. He informed the astonished Lutherans that another party of German missionaries, three Moravian brethren, had already arrived at Lake Hope and were contemplating leaving for Kopperamanna in an attempt to establish a mission station there.

On 22 December the Lutherans reached Manuwakaninna, and were Christmas guests of the manager. 'We had come increasingly concerned about the Christmas celebration', wrote Goessling from the remote homestead to Pastor Harms in Germany, 'because it was the spiritual privation which caused the most suffering, and the longing for a shelter to properly conduct divine service.'[8] But now:

> The four of us have our own small house here, with a chamber and two bedrooms. It is a cool place and at last we can escape the ever present Australian 'bandits' [flies]. We need not worry about food and drink as everything is provided here in plenty. Our horses enjoy a lush meadow and our dogs at last can rest in the shadow of our wagons.[9]

A first opportunity to pause and recuperate; to reflect on the enormous changes in lifestyle and countryside, and to contemplate spiritual matters, and each man's service, as the men remembered Pastor Harms' words: 'Be faithful and diligent in the reading of your Bible; live in your Bible, let it be your daily manna'.[10] They saw again, above the main entrance to the Hermannsburg Mission Institute, the epithet now emblazoned on their hearts:

> With this (symbol) you will be victorious: with this cross on the banner the first Christian emperor, Constantine, conquered Heathenism in the Roman Empire. With this cross on which the Lamb of God has bled to death, our missionaries shall overcome the heathens, as well as their king, the devil, and under this cross our mission house shall stand, against the portals of Hell.[11]

Just eight months earlier the three Germans, who now sheltered at Manuwakaninna homestead, had stood before an altar in the near 1000-year-old church of Peter and Paul at Hermannsburg in Germany. It was a Whitsunday morning when twenty-six missionaries were dedicated for service in various mission fields across the New World—India, Africa, America and the first group for Australia. The words of the speaker on that day perhaps haunted the men as they lay on their bunks in the Australian desert:

> This day is a day of painful parting. We are about to bid farewell to these our dear brethren, whom we have learnt to love and esteem. They are about to leave us to go to foreign countries, and we most likely will never see them again on earth. This is also a day of joy as we witness here the answer to our prayers that the Lord may send labourers into His harvest. My brethren, take heed therefore unto yourselves and unto the doctrine; work out your own salvation with fear and trembling.[12]

Pastor Harms had addressed the congregation:

> Go now my brethren in God's name; keep your eyes fixed on Him Who hath loved you with an everlasting love and shed His lifeblood for you, and has called you into His service. Everything for Christ, the last breath, the last bit of strength, the last drop of blood. May His love permeate you, and guide you in all your ways, and prepare for you a last resting place, be it in the African soil, in India, America or Australia . . . We have not the hope that we shall meet again on earth, for the motto of every true missionary is: 'In this world we shall not meet again'. Let us all strive

that we shall meet again in Heaven. O what joy will that be![13]

Less than a month after the dedication service, on 5 May 1866, Homann, Goessling and Vogelsang had sailed for Australia on the ship *Sophia* with Pastors Heidenreich and Hellmuth and their families, who were to take up positions at Lobethal and Bethany. Homann was in charge of the mission group, and he and Goessling were to receive a modest salary of £6 a year, with £4 10s for Vogelsang and £4 2s 6d for Jacob. The mission committee in South Australia were to pay all mission accounts.[14] Since leaving Germany the formidable task ahead was daily contemplated.

But for now a brief respite—spiritual tranquillity and physical sanction at Manuwakaninna homestead, the cool rooms sheltering the Lutherans from the blazing heat of their first summer Christmas. Shimmering heat hazes danced above the ground as the parched earth smouldered. No snow bells tinkled, no white-laden fir trees glistened outside; just the shimmer and rustle of a cool breeze passing gum leaves, and the endless stillness and heat. Goessling was to write: 'It is sad that even here on the station the natives run around naked'.[15]

Moravians and Aborigines

After Christmas celebrations the Germans immediately set about the task of determining the best place for their mission station. Following instructions from the mission committee at Tanunda they tenaciously made their way to Lake Hope, only to discover that Buttfield's advice had indeed been sound. There were just a small number of Aborigines in the area and the place offered little prospect for the sheep and cattle station considered necessary to the mission enterprise. At Lake Hope they met the three Moravian missionaries, who had temporarily taken shelter at the tiny Lake Hope police station. Stationed there were three troopers, Samuel Gason, John Morton and P. T. Skenner.

The Moravians, of the Mission Society of the Brethren in Europe, were also attracted to the Coopers Creek area from reports connected with the ill-fated Burke and Wills expedition. Intimation of hundreds of Aborigines in the area made the location attractive. By June 1862, nine months after King was found alive with the Cooper Aborigines and the bodies of Burke and Wills were recovered, the Brethren decided to extend their own activities of a mission station at Ebenezer on the Wimmera River. They established Victoria's Aid Society of the Brethren among the Blacks in Australia and determined to send missionaries to the Aborigines of the Cooper, 'to bring the blessings of the Gospel to the still numerous tribes of newly discovered Burke-Land and Albert-Land, before the white settlers arrive with their diseases and brandy'.[16]

Four missionary graduates were sent from Germany to Australia for this purpose: C. W. Kramer, W. Kuhn, G. Meissel and H. Walder. But a severe drought prevented attempts by the Moravians until July 1866 and by then the four had been sent to various intermediary postings. Finally, in July 1866, Kramer, Meissel and Walder met in Adelaide, in a prelude to the journey to the interior. As preparations were under way, Kramer wrote: 'May the Lord graciously continue to help and Himself prepare the way, so that many of the poor blacks at Coopers Creek may still be saved before they become acquainted with the vices of the white settlers'.[17]

Homann conducting an open-air sermon to Diyari tribespeople at the Killalpaninna site

The Moravians arrived at Lake Hope on 3 December, just a few weeks before the Lutherans, and after an equally difficult journey. Their original destination was further north, at Howitt's Depot (probably today's Innaminka), near the spot where Burke and Wills died. But after a gruelling journey, and the realisation that from Howitt's Depot they could not maintain a connection with the supply town of Port Augusta, the Moravians settled for a time at Lake Hope to assess the countryside. Probably at the instigation of the sub-protector, but also due to the lack of water at Lake Hope, they travelled the 40 miles to Lake Kopperamanna. From Kopperamanna Walder wrote:

> The Natives (I believe chiefly through the good influence of the police) were right glad to see us; in fact a number have come down from Perigundi to meet us. After our horses will be fit again for an arduous journey, we shall proceed Coopers Creek-ward, on a reconnoitery [sic] tour, to see whether there is any possibility of conveying stores to there, that is to live there. At Blanchewater Mr Buttfield overtook us, and few days we spent together here, among Blacks and Whites. Yesterday Mr Buttfield left again. The German Lutheran Missionaries are expected to be here in a day or two.[18]

But before the Lutherans arrived at Lake Hope the Moravians had fled from Lake Kopperamanna to the sanctity of the tiny police outpost. The Aborigines were indeed gathering, but in anger.

With the arrival of the Lutherans, the groups amiably joined forces for exploratory trips to Lake Kopperamanna and Lake Killalpaninna, which was suggested by Gason as a favoured site. Kopperamanna, however, seemed favoured by the Moravians as, 'Natives from over a hundred miles in radius meet here'.[19] They settled by the shores of Lake Kopperamanna, 45 miles north-west of Lake Hope, in early February 1867, and during that same month Kramer claimed to have eight Aboriginal boys in his 'school'. Suspicious and curious elders quietly watched as the Moravians attempted to communicate with the schoolboys and tried to learn the Diyari vocabulary. Before the Moravians had left Adelaide arrangements had been made for government ration stores to be distributed among the Aborigines. A ration depot was consequently established very early at Kopperamanna, drawing Aborigines to the area in large numbers. A year later the Moravians were to write:

> The natives sometimes number 700 to 800. Our neighbourhood is an asylum for tottering blacks with white heads, native women covered with wrinkles, hanging skin, young and old blind native skeleton cripples who must be carried from place to place. These invalids have flocked here to enjoy government benevolence in the shape of rations. Daily our one room school is filled.[20]

The Lutherans had travelled via Lake Kopperamanna to Lake Killalpaninna, another 10 miles distant, 'this lake being much frequented by the Aborigines on account of the wood, which yields for their Support'.[21] On 31 January 1867 'The first mission station has been founded near the shores of this lake, and the brethren have given it the name "Hermannsburg"—and rightly so', announced Theodore Harms to German readers of the *Hermannsburger Missionsblatt*.[22]

Goessling described the area near Lake Killalpaninna, where there had been no 'decent' rain for three years, as 'just like Elija's times in Israel'. The four Lutherans perhaps saw themselves akin to the patriarchs of Old Testament days, in the desert wilderness taking God's message to the nomadic tribes. Conditions were certainly considered primitive. The men were now suntanned, bearded, and cloaked against the fierce sun. The lake was still filled with water from the previous flooding, but the land around was parched and empty, and in the throes of drought. Dead animals lay putrefying at empty waterholes. Goessling drew references to God's punishing the Aboriginal people for being heathens just as He had punished the people of Israel when the fiery figure of Ezekiel was unable to bring them to their senses.[23] The Lutherans had already seen some of the 'barbaric customs' of these Aboriginal heathens and they were certain that these people were in urgent need of spiritual help.

When the Germans arrived at Lake Killalpaninna they found a 'fairly good number' of Aborigines, 'physically well built, but spiritually in a pitiful condition', camped around the lake. No sooner had the pious delegation begun to unload their wagons than Diyari men sent women to them for sexual purposes. Outraged, the Lutherans sent them back, unaware of the custom of appeasing a suspected enemy attack. This rejection, of course, was understood by the Diyari to be a sign of hostile intention, and aroused suspicion and fear, especially as the

Lutherans used exaggerated gestures of disdain and disgust no doubt interpreted as hostility) to force the women away. When the women attempted to stay (to stave off warfare) the Lutherans employed their horsewhips to rid themselves of the abomination.[24]

But these pale strangers did not attack, and instead began to set up camp nearby, confusing the local Diyari. However, suspicion and distrust, and in particular, fear, remained. Shortly after this encounter the Lutherans were appalled when they witnessed the eating of a dead child. They reported that the Aborigines 'eat them like nasty pigs', and almost returned to the south after the repulsion of the experience. Goessling wrote that this heathen practice and other 'animal-like behaviour' was the reason that these people were close to extinction.[25] The Lutherans, too, were repelled by the practice of polygymy and polyandry.

Aboriginal Resistance to German Presence

Relationships between the two groups soured, the Germans abhorring the Diyari practices, the Diyari fearing hostility and possibly resenting the presence of such strangers in their midst. They and their neighbouring tribes had already experienced violence at the hands of white men in the area. Henry Dean, manager of Elder's station at Lake Hope, had forced a group of Diyari from their traditional waterhole at a time of severe drought, leaving four dead in the encounter. Lake Hope and Manuwakaninna stations were running increasingly more stock on the sparse resources of the country, and now more white men were moving onto land at Lake Kopperamanna and Lake Killalpaninna. Over the next few weeks the Diyari of that area united in an attempt to oust the potentially destructive strangers. As warriors prepared for battle, the missionaries sensed an atmosphere of inexorable tension. The 'bush telegraph' (communication between Aboriginal groups) was fast and efficient. Very early the Lutherans were to experience this effectiveness as:

> Scarcely had the good brethren the missionaries of the Moravian Brethren, arrived at Kopperamanni [sic], than we already saw a short time later a black, with a wurra in his girdle, appear over the sand dunes; it was the telegraph; for like wildfire the news went around the lake: Over there white people have arrived, Kullu wilparro (one wagon), nanto (horses), barro Ellno (three people), they live in a valle (hut), where the others (we) lived.

Hours later the Lutherans, through an Aborigine with a letter tied to a stick, received a message from the Moravians informing them of their arrival at Kopperamanna.[26]

Less than two months after the arrival of the two missionary parties, a large inter-tribal corroboree was held at Perigundi. There, agitated by the Perigundans, it was determined that all 'white fellows' in the area be killed. It was now the hottest month in the north and the Germans were living in small rough huts 'the size of a baking oven', with temperatures of 93 degrees Fahrenheit in the shade. Homann was suffering from eye irritation and Goessling from heat exhaustion. The men were beginning to grasp a few words of Diyari and to 'study' the customs of the local people, most of which were considered 'barbaric'. An old Diyari man, 'whom we have working for clothing, food and tobacco (they do not know any other pay), and who adheres to us really faithfully' (probably Pickally) informed the Germans of the plot for a massacre. The Lutherans quickly passed this information on to the Moravians.[27]

The Moravians, however, did not give the rumours much credence as all seemed harmonious about them. But over the following week the atmosphere began to change. One day, while preparing the mail, Kramer was taking down the letter balance (scales) from the roof rafters of his hut when old 'King John' (as he was known to the Germans), the local, powerful tribal elder, came to the doorway. When Kramer turned with the metal balance in his hands, the old man thought it was a gun and screamed 'Murder! Murder!' as he ran away. A few minutes later he sent a fish to Kramer to placate him, and next morning brought a second fish himself. He was given the usual tobacco in return, and for some days King John disappeared. In the meantime many Aborigines began to pour into the area.

Suddenly a Diyari man at the Kopperamanna Station began to yell and wave his arms. Kramer was told, 'Blackfellow big one growl longa you', as he looked towards the camps through his telescope. A large crowd of wild figures, highly decorated, were preparing for a corroboree. Kramer immediately rode to Killalpaninna to warn the Lutherans, and on his return was told the attack was planned for the following day. Three horses were kept tethered and saddled for a quick get-away and the Moravians took turns at keeping watch with loaded revolvers.

During the following two days unusual quiet presided. When the Aborigines learned of the preparedness of the Germans they decided to wait for a moment of surprise. On 14 March a crowd of tribespeople gathered at Killalpaninna. Tension was high at both stations. On that same day the Moravians were making plans to depart when, 'Suddenly we saw smoke rising all around the lake as a sign that something was coming. The boys soon came and told us that the police from Lake Hope were approaching. Meanwhile they rode past our place and on to Killalpaninna, in order to stay there for the night.'[28] The troopers, by coincidence, were simply out on a normal patrol, unaware of the terrifying situation. But their arrival was certainly timely, 'as if sent by the Lord', and probably saved the lives of the two German groups. Police presence nearby, and guns, was enough to frighten the Aborigines at Kopperamanna, and they, too, withdrew from menacingly encircling the Moravians.

When the troopers arrived at Kopperamanna they found some three hundred to four hundred Aborigines gathered, and it was rumoured that more were journeying there. Despite their presence, an attempt was made on Vogelsang's life as he was returning from Kopperamanna to Killalpaninna. The Kolonist was accompanied in the wagon by a 'trusted' Aborigine called Jammilli, who insisted on returning to Killalpaninna, allegedly to collect his clothes (but who secretly had informed others of Vogelsang's lone trip). While still in view of the Kopperamanna settlement, Jammilli jumped from the wagon.

> He runs into the bushes, takes an instrument, which makes a deep, whirring noise, and makes a din. Then he jumps on to the wagon again, and laughs. Brother Vogelsang looks around about and sees over 40 blacks get up in front of him at these signs and sneak along the track through the bushes with their weapons. At the same

time he notices that his axe, which he had in front of the wagon, was lying at the back, and it didn't slide there, he knows that. The air isn't clear, he notices, comes to a halt, waves back to the station and fires [his revolver]. In a flash the police are on horseback and came to his rescue.[29]

The Aborigines at Kopperamanna were subsequently interrogated, with Gason (who spoke Diyari) acting as interpreter. 'A chief named "Old Man Tonney" spoke in his Native Tongue that the Wild natives were going to attack the missionaries but he prevented it, and told them if they interfered the Police would come down on them from Lake Hope, and he also stated the Blacks did not like the Missionaries.'[30] No further action was taken.

After the troopers returned to Lake Hope the Germans naturally felt insecure and threatened, especially as black informers told them that tribes from even further away were approaching to join the campaign to oust the whites. A large group of mixed tribespeople had gathered at Perigundi that month to devise a plan for exterminating all settlers in the north, as far south as Blanchewater, beginning with the missionaries.[31] The Lutherans, however, unequivocally felt they could not defend themselves with firearms; it was against their principles and their Christian purpose. Moreover, such use would jeopardise their chances of successful missionising. This attitude frustrated the small local police force, whose territory was vast, but, on the other hand, a massacre of German missionaries would be highly damaging to police repute. In a report to his superior John Morton warned of the danger for the missionaries. To their headquarters 10 000 miles away in Germany, the frightened Lutherans made a plea: 'What shall we do? If we defend ourselves and shoot heathens it would kill the mission prospects forever and we would never be forgiven by them. If they kill us and eat us "our lives end under their teeth" and this is not a desirable end. The Lord must assist.'[32]

On 6 April the Moravians and Lutherans held a memorial together, praying for protection. And for a time they sought refuge at Bucaltaninna Station (28 miles to the south-east) with the owner's wife, Mrs Milner, alone there as her husband was driving stock. The Lutherans left stores, blankets and other goods at their base at Killalpaninna, in the charge of the faithful Pickally (or 'Mackey') and his 'lubra'.[33]

A deputation from the mission committee sought an audience with George Hamilton, South Australia's commissioner of police. It was suggested that Homann be made a Justice of the Peace, to swear in emergency 'special constables' in the absence of troopers.[34] This would legitimise local stationers to use firearms or force against attacking Aborigines, again absolving the missionaries. Meanwhile the Moravians made a plea to Hamilton for police protection at Kopperamanna, for themselves and 'some more Black-fellow-masters [the Lutherans]'. The petition was penned by Walder, arguing that Kopperamanna was about equidistant between Lake Hope and Manuwakaninna stations and thus an ideal location for a police station in the far north. Walder concluded: 'It is therefore evident that for a time, or till Gospel power brings dark forces into subjection, we cannot hold ourselves without Police Protection and are consequently compelled to pray to Governments for the Same.'[35] Both groups also made application for land for an Aboriginal reserve and mission station.

Meanwhile, six troopers from the Blinman Station, accompanied by Buttfield, rode to Lake Hope to investigate the situation. Together with the three from Lake Hope, they rode onto the mission stations, only to find that the Germans had left and that all was quiet and peaceful. When they reached Killalpaninna, four days after the missionaries had left for Bucaltaninna, the troopers found that local Aborigines 'had not taken or destroyed a single article' left by the Lutherans.[36] They were told, by innocent-faced people who feared reprisals, 'Blackfellows no growl, only Monkey-yabber', and asked, 'What for Whitefellow go away, Blackfellows No Hurt them'.[37]

During subsequent talks with the sub-protector, Diyari tribesmen demanded that they have their own country and their own indigenous food supply, claiming that there would then be peace between them and the whites. In his report Buttfield wrote:

> These children of the desert fear further encroachments upon their territory. They are jealous for their heritage, and cannot distinguish between the motives of the Missionaries and those of ordinary settlers. Their love of their country is an encouraging feature in their character. They travel south some 200 miles for ochre and they find that the ranks of once flourishing tribes have been greatly reduced and white men occupying the country, and doubtless view with alarm the gradual occupation by strangers of the country northward.[38]

Meanwhile letters had arrived at Hermannsburg in Germany from Goessling and Homann, relating the seriousness of events unfolding in the Australian desert. Harms reported in the mission periodical, 'If it [the mission] still exists, it needs our prayers'.[39] Fear was now held in Germany for the safety of the missionaries, that they might already have been killed and eaten by the 'Papua' (the Aborigines).

Retreat and Reorganisation

In early May 1867 both missionary parties were sheltering at Bucaltaninna Station. But as Goessling was suffering sunstroke and needed medical treatment, the Lutherans retreated further southwards, to Lights Pass, taking with them, as evidence of some success, the 'faithful' Pickally. The Moravians, whose headquarters were some 1000 miles away in the colony of Victoria, were forced to persevere at Bucaltaninna, and gather courage and resources before another attempt among the Aborigines.

Police protection was swiftly granted the missionaries, with formal agreement to move the outpost from Lake Hope to Kopperamanna procured before the end of May. Hamilton, however, supported a larger force for the area, as troopers were constantly required to watch over these intractable missionaries known by the Aborigines not to use firearms to defend themselves. The commissioner suggested that the cost of establishing a second outpost at Kopperamanna be met by funds previously set aside for the Aborigines themselves. Three troopers were to be permanently stationed there and the three from the Lake Hope Station would patrol the area. These extra police numbers suited the local pastoralists, and support was added by pastoral entrepreneur Thomas Elder.[40]

But regarding the application for land, official notification was not given for a full six months. The Moravians had requested an Aboriginal reserve of 100 square miles, and the Lutherans government rations for their Aborigines in addition to reserve land, namely: 'The extent of the country requested is at least 50 square miles including both the lakes of Killapaninna and Allo Allanenni'.[41]

Eventually both mission enterprises were assigned a lease of 100 square miles of 'waste land', as Aboriginal Reserve land, 'until such a time as a change may be necessary'. In the case of the Lutherans, this was twice as much land as requested. It was country that was not yet surveyed and each mission body was asked to supply a rough sketch of its respective areas. The conditional clause, however, disturbed the Lutherans, as the expense involved in constructing a mission station required an assurance of permanence. But they received a letter from the acting protector of Aborigines stating that they 'need not apprehend being removed by the Govt. as long as their Missionary work is being carried on'.[42]

In June 1867 the Moravians requested an extra 150 acres for their mission buildings, but it appears the grant was denied.[43] Goyder, the colony's surveyor-general, considered the missionising attempt 'a very expensive one' and raised doubts about the duration of the enterprise: 'There can be no harm in guaranteeing the Missionaries an undisturbed occupation so long as the land is devoted to missionary purposes—but I think it would be undesirable to alienate land upon a mere experiment such as this is'.[44] Land had now become a precious resource for a potentially wealthy colony, and it was not in the interests of local pastoralism for land to be constrained by mission stations (albeit mission stock stations). And in the case of the Moravians, Goyder's doubts were soon vindicated.

A third request, by the Lutherans, was the matter of rations for the Aborigines at their station. Government officials were concerned about charges for freight and cartage, and the Lutheran Mission Committee refused to bear this cost. In 1868 a deputation headed by Reichner, president of the mission committee, pleaded the same privileges accorded the Moravians. Supported by the protector of Aborigines, it eventually succeeded. The 'civilising' of Aborigines, and their conversion to Christianity, were deemed both honourable and necessary, as outlined by the Colonial Office at London in 1836. It would be a malingering colonial government that was not seen to support such a programme.

German Brides

By September 1867 the prospect of a second Lutheran missionising attempt seemed foreseeable and propitious. Police protection was assured, the lease of Aboriginal reserve land granted and regular ration supplies for Aborigines affirmed. The missionaries were now awaiting the arrival of their German fiancées, already on the high seas aboard the ship *Sophia* (that same ship that had carried the missionaries themselves to Australia). It was the policy of Harms that his graduates be accompanied by wives in the field, for homemaking and companionship in strange, isolated, often dangerous places, and no doubt to prevent any unfortunate 'shortcomings' on the part of his orthodox emissaries. Harms taught that a missionary must be aware that the 'devil' was always present!

Margarethe Veit, the fiancée of Goessling; Luise Wendland (accompanied by her housemaid, Magdalene Duvel, and four boys from a previous marriage), fiancée of Homann; and Wilhelmina (called Dorothea) Heistermann, fiancée of

Left: Missionary Johann Goessling and his wife, Margarethe Veit
Right: Hermann Vogelsang and his first wife, Dorothea Heistermann on their wedding day, 1867

the Kolonist Vogelsang, stepped onto the dock at Port Adelaide in early October. Luise Wendland had previously lived with her Hermannsburg-trained missionary husband in southern India and Africa, where he had died. She had grown to love southern India, 'but I had no desire to go to Australia'.[45] Ernst Homann was initially appointed to India, but the appointment was changed at the request of the Barossa Lutherans. 'Before Homann departed he begged that I should follow him with the children to Australia. How difficult it was to give an answer.'[46] Luise Wendland, two years Homann's senior, had been 'housemother' at Hermannsburg after her husband's death. Her health had suffered from her many years in mission fields and she was not now a strong woman physically. When Homann told Harms of his marriage proposal to Luise Wendland, the director exclaimed, 'You should not have proposed to the House Mother. She is weak and cannot stand further strain'.[47]

The wedding at Lights Pass was to have been a spectacular triple affair. Grand preparations were made, with the baking of cakes and biscuits and German delicacies. The German community busied itself for the happy day, and the missionaries and their fiancées undertook the massive task of taking a customary cake and making a personal visit to everybody they knew in the community. A week after the arrival of the fiancées, the wedding ceremony took place at the Lights Pass church. The triple wedding, however, became a double, as Goessling was still very ill. He and his fiancée married quietly at Rosenthal. He was advised not to return to the north, and left the enterprise to accept a position as pastor in Victoria. Later he was again to take up missionising, but this time in the cooler climate of New Zealand, among the Maoris.

A Second Attempt
Eight weeks after the Lights Pass wedding, in mid-December, the missionaries and their wives began their journey northwards to Killalpaninna. The women climbed into waiting wagons in their long-sleeved, ankle-length black dresses, arranged over their many petticoats. The men wore long frock-coats and top hats—at least to begin in respectability and style. Luise Homann's two eldest boys remained at Tanunda, for schooling, with the faithful 'Lene' (Magdalene Duvel). Goessling was replaced by Wilhelm Koch, who, although not a trained missionary, was described as 'a talented young man, who was planning to join the ministry'.[48] The 19-year-old Koch, born in Bremen (Germany) and grammar-school educated, had lost both parents and was forced to discontinue his studies for lack of finance. He had a brother in Australia and had decided to join him a year or so earlier.[49]

Of the journey back to Lake Killalpaninna, Homann optimistically wrote: 'We hope in four to five weeks to be at the old station'. But in reality, a gruelling eight long weeks later his new wife wrote, 'If we had not trusted in God we would have perished in misery. We left at the beginning of December and we nearly died of thirst and hunger in the Australian heat'.[50] Cured meats and German cakes and biscuits were soon consumed and the party was forced to live on birds and any wildlife they could catch. A constant thirst gripped them, the wagons repeatedly broke down and horses refused to pull. Exhausted and thirsty, some of the animals ran away. 'So we arrived after unspeakable fatigue at the Lake Kopperamanna.'

There the German women met their first Australian Aborigines, 'who looked with astonishment at the first white women'.[51] The Aborigines were amazed at the amount of clothing worn by the white women, and how they suffered in the heat in their long dresses and long sleeves. Conversely, 'How our hearts sank when we saw those poor neglected folk amongst whom we would have to live. Director Harms had warned us at the farewell. "We are sending you to the most difficult mission field to work, amongst the poorest people of Papua and you will need much heaven-sent strength, and our prayers." It was sandy desert where we were sent!'[52]

When the Lutherans arrived at Kopperamanna they found the Moravians back at their old station. But they were not to stay for long. Although a police outpost was now established at Kopperamanna, they increasingly felt the isolation from their headquarters in Victoria, and soon afterwards abandoned their northern mission station, never to return.

The Lutherans travelled on to Lake Killalpaninna. Luise Homann's first impression was bleak: 'the barren sand hills of Killalpaninna at last. Before us was the great lake and some miserable huts of the natives, hardly any trees, no bush, only barren sandhills. None of us imagined that our mission field would be so barren and deserted.'[53] The Germans were suffering from sand-irritated and fly-infected eyes (trachoma, known as 'sandy blight') as they groped to construct crude shelters to protect themselves from the fierce sun. Several earth huts were dug as living rooms and kitchens, while the wagons served as bedrooms. The Diyari, pacified by fear of police nearby, and by the availability of food to supplement a dwindling traditional supply, assisted with constructing the primitive shelters, and the German women cooked meat and baked bread 'for many hungry souls every day, trying at the same time to learn their difficult language'.[54]

Food rations were intended only for the sick, the old and infirm, orphaned children, and women with infants under twelve months. But in reality, through lack of native food, they were often also distributed to able-bodied people. The daily allowance for each Aborigine, it was deemed, must not exceed one pound of flour (or one pound of rice, as a substitute), 2 ounces of sugar, and half an ounce of tea. Daily allowances were to be entered into a ration return book, causing laborious entry work and copious correspondence. Cartage costs were high to this isolated and inaccessible outpost, borne by the South Australian government for two years, until, at the end of 1869, the mission enterprise itself offered to convey the stores at 20 per cent less than the usual rates. Ration supplies could now be controlled and guaranteed, and by mid-1868 Homann was reporting that 'More Aborigines are gathering around the station to get food. They feel obliged to stay and the more they receive the more they have to ask for. If the drought continues, they will become dependent, for food suits our purpose.'[55] This cartage charge became an added source of income for the station. The mission teamster for many years was the Kolonist Ernst Jacob.

Homann and Koch worked hard to master the Diyari language so that they could begin teaching and preaching. After a few months they were joined by Frederick Watske, an extra Kolonist, and his young wife.[56] More permanent buildings were constructed from wood and mud gathered from the lake-bed. The first substantial building was the Homanns' house, built on the highest sandhill. Koch was to write: 'If you stand on the sandhill and glance in every direction, one must admit, that in spite of many things lacking, the Far North of South Australia has its beauty, and the more often one has a look at the country, the more one will begin to love it'.[57] Small trees growing beside the lake were cut for building material. But the Diyari soon became agitated and distressed with this activity, and the missionaries were to learn that 'some of the trees were those under which Aborigines were born and now had to die, because they were born under those trees'.[58] Homann wrote: 'One tried to make up for the damage done by immediately taking some grass from the ground and putting it into the tree hole'.[59] The Diyari pleaded with the Germans not to cut further trees. Presumably this was not heeded, for the missionaries continued to build their settlement, using this example to insist that the 'heathen' belief system was untrue.

During 1868 the commissioner for Crown lands transferred the Moravians' Aboriginal Reserve land at Kopperamanna to the Lutherans at Killalpaninna.[60] The Lutheran enterprise was consolidating to a firmer footing. But 1868 became a year of severe drought that forced local English settlers to move their stock to other parts. As Bedford Hack and his station workers (from nearby

Manuwakaninna Station, some 60 miles away) passed near the mission station they offered to sell cows and sheep to the Lutherans as domestic livestock. Bedford Hack presented Luise Homann with a pair of chickens, and the Germans could now have dairy food and eggs added to their austere diet. The local water, from a bore sunk into the underground Great Artesian Basin, tasted unpleasant, with its high content of salt, saltpetre and magnesium, and there were no fresh fruit or vegetables. The women suffered from the summer heat and the dry desert air, and longed for the cold, crisp smell of Germany. The Milners, from Bucaltaninna Station, were also moving stock when Mrs Milner was brought to the mission station suffering heat exhaustion. For weeks she was nursed by the German women, but she finally died, the first European buried at the station.[61]

Young Willie and Bernhard, Luise's youngest sons, were the first to master the Diyari language, as they spent much of their time playing with the Diyari children.

> After the first necessary buildings were erected my dear husband and Mr Koch started to give lessons to the native children, who at first had no desire to learn. We were surprised, however, to later find that there were some very docile pupils in these poor neglected folk. Until then they had lived only on snakes, lizards and plants and anything else at the time to be found. Now they receive well baked bread, sheep meat, and also tea and rice. They lived in an earth hut, which was also a school room for some time. The following year a good, spacious school house was erected. On Sunday mornings we had our German divine service in our house, and in the afternoon the natives came with their wives and dogs and a few young children for service in our house in their own language. Their odour was terrible. My beloved Ernst fainted quite often. They had to be asked to come, these poor people who had never heard of Christianity.[62]

Two Cultures Meet
In these early years there were ten Germans living at the station, including Luise Homann's two sons. The teamster, Ernst Jacob, was generally absent, on the road between Killalpaninna and Port Augusta, collecting and delivering goods and stores for both the mission station and for other stock stations in the area. It was a drought period and the numbers of Aborigines camped near the mission station continued to increase as word spread about available rations, and as the tribes were pushed from their traditional hunting and foraging grounds by European pastoralists. Aborigines faced severe penalties, even death, if caught killing white men's stock for food. Pickally attached himself to the mission station, with Homann writing: 'He lives an unexpected lifestyle for a heathen and is not particular in all the heathen rites. His faith to the missionaries has brought him into mortal danger.' Certainly Pickally's allegiance to the unknown and untrustworthy strangers in the first months, when there was considerable fear and resistance, was unusual, and no doubt perceived as a betrayal by the local tribesmen. It is not known whether he had had some association with Europeans previously. However by 1868 Homann considered Pickally 'a fully fledged Christian' and the first convert, even though he was not yet officially baptised. Homann enclosed his photograph in a letter to Hermannsburg, writing that it was

written on the old fellow's face that 'out of the cannibal has become a lamb'.[63]

By 1868 Pickally was acting as an intermediary between the Lutherans and the Diyari at the camps, useful to both cultures for transferring information between them. He was able to inform his own people of some of the beliefs of the Germans and some of what happened in that mysterious place, the makeshift 'church'.

The Germans moved their settlement several times before finally settling at the edge of the lake, on top of high sandhills but close to the water. During the summer of 1868 they suffered the desert scourge 'sandy blight', with winds endlessly blowing the dry sandy soil, the hard grit irritating the eyes, and swarms of flies spreading infection. The women wandered blindly, groping about their crude huts, eyes bandaged in pain and as protection. One Sunday a well-known (to the Aborigines) kunkie (doctor) visited the Homanns' hut in an effort to relieve the missionary's wife, to exorcise her painful affliction. He was elaborately decorated with feathers on his head. He blew into Luise's eyes, claiming that a bad spirit was in there causing the sickness.[64] 'This kind of magic thinking was very popular among the people', reported Luise's husband.

In July 1868 the Homann's daughter, Elizabeth, was born at the station. 'When the natives heard the news they came from as far as 100 miles. They had to see the white child which they claimed as theirs because she was born on their soil', wrote Luise Homann. 'They were very astonished because she was a "Mittalali" ['Mangthanda pala'], which means a bald head. Elizabeth did not have a curly head like their few children who were born. She was a blonde.'[65]

Before long there were twenty-two pupils in the school. The young scholars enjoyed hymn-singing, providing Homann and Koch with an opportunity to call together the older Aborigines to hear their children performing. It was hoped that these gatherings would attract older people to the station for instruction in Christianity. Those who were attracted, however, especially in the early days, were the young and the very old or sick. The elders, who held power and dominance in their society, not surprisingly clung to traditional ways, and were suspicious and sceptical of the new culture. Of such traditional power and influence, Homann was to write: 'Meaningless secrets, which have to be kept by the young men and the old under threat of a death sentence if divulged are told to them. In this way these Old Men keep their authority, and the more devilish one of them is the more he is feared by the others.'[66] And of the young Aboriginal pupils, Homann wrote: 'When we try to teach them the Bible and the Bible's history there are a lot of misunderstandings because the children still sing in the way of the heathens'. Of the attitude of Aborigines in general: 'Belief in salvation is nothing that they can see, or grab with their hands, or put into their mouths, and all that counts for them is physical things'.[67]

Homann and Koch struggled to teach Christian principles, having difficulty with a language where words had many meanings and where there were no equivalents for 'hell' and 'sin', essentials to the teaching. Such concepts were not present in Diyari culture. When listening to a lesson where the concept of hell was being explained, a group of Diyari laughed, saying, 'But we like fire. It would be nice in hell.' Furthermore, it was reported to Germany by the frustrated Lutherans that when the schoolchildren were asked whether they loved God, they would always answer, 'Yes'. And when asked why they loved Him, would

Sketch of the early settlement at Killalpaninna, c. 1870

answer, 'Because He has saved us'. But when asked what the Saviour had saved them from, they did not know. This thwarted Homann, and rendered the teaching of Christianity, so based on man's guilt and estrangement from God, virtually impossible. 'Heaven does not attract them all that much, nor do they worry about Hell. Hell is just a warm-fire place, and Heaven a nice fertile country where there are plenty of things to be enjoyed.'[68] Neither were there understood to be words for 'mercy', 'justice' and 'sanctity' in the Diyari language. A baffled Homann reported that 'If we had some of the words now I could immediately, with some of the boys and with old Pickally, commence baptism classes'.[69]

Homann and Koch would wander across to the Aborigines' camp, on the opposite side of the lake. They would stand in front of huts and sing hymns, which, to the Aborigines, sounded like a mystical chant, a type of 'enchantment'. The elders were frightened by this practice of perceived 'magic' and its unknown effects, and many pleaded, 'Why don't you go home?' But Homann wrote: 'The more time I spend among these heathens the clearer I see just how black Satan is and how much power Satan has over these heathens; how much stupidity and silliness he has caused among them.'[70] 'Our people [the Aborigines] live here in a way just giving in to the demands of the flesh ... but looking at these Aborigines we can see the whole abnormality of giving in to that, and how unsatisfying and unclean life is without the proper guidance of the Lord.'[71]

At one time Homann was invited to the night funeral of an esteemed Aboriginal man (probably a kunkie). He watched by moonlight as the corpse was wrapped in a net bag, and carried to the grave pit. When asked who had killed the man, one of the bearers replied that it was kutchie (the Devil) in the form of a bird. Questions were then asked of the corpse, and it 'answered' with a strange whistling and other bizarre noises. Two of the young Aboriginal boys who now attended the mission school were frightened and buried themselves in the sand, praying to the Christian God, according to Homann. The mourners then proceeded to eat from the corpse: 'The women behaved as though they were mad. They jumped into the grave and demanded with great longing to eat from the dead body. But when I asked them not to do so, because it would not be good, they refrained from their plans.'[72] At least, perhaps, until the missionary was out of sight.

Droughts, Sandstorms, Disease

By November 1868 the country was unrecognisable from the time of the Lutherans' first arrival two years earlier. Temperatures were 100 degrees and more, and the hottest months were not yet upon them. The lake had almost dried out and waterholes in the area were turning ever saltier. All greenness had completely gone and the waterbirds were fast disappearing. For miles around there was only grey desolation and sand. Several stations nearby were abandoned, as there was simply no feed or water for stock. The health of the missionaries had deteriorated, with only fetid drinking water, and very little of it, no fresh vegetables and the insufferable heat. At this low point they were hit by a violent sandstorm. Sand blew fiercely all day and on into the night. The night temperature was measured at 90 degrees and the air was thick with swirling grit. Homann managed to nail the window frames of his house, while his family pushed against the front door to counter the tremendous force of the wind. But the door blew in, pushing the Germans to the far end of the house. The kitchen roof and one entire room blew completely away. Suddenly the storm stopped and quiet reigned. The missionaries sank to their knees in relief: 'A moment ago it seemed our houses were not strongly built and would completely collapse. Indeed how much would the terror have blown us off the face of the Earth if the Angels of the Lord were not protecting us.'[73]

The drought continued throughout 1869, delaying progress on the construction of mission buildings. It was difficult enough to locate suitable materials, but this was exacerbated by the deep sand through which heavy materials had to be dragged, and the long distances to be covered back to the station. By November 1869 Sunday sermons were well attended by Aborigines (probably to ensure their position in the ration line). When the mission bell rang on Sabbath mornings the Aborigines noisily strode across the sandhills from their camps to remain unusually quiet for the sermon in Diyari, during which Homann used the words 'extremely dirty' for 'sin', and 'clean and obedient' for 'sacred'.

Mission Aborigines and schoolchildren were given ration clothing as an incentive (for it was special, different, and gave them status) and for European modesty, and told not to give this clothing away to other Aborigines. But, being a community society, ration garments also began to be worn by people at the camps, often in a manner that never failed to amuse the Germans, regardless of their annoyance at ignored directives: 'Often one wears a waist-coat on his body, on top of this a coat and over this a shirt. Another one can walk around for days with nothing else but a waist-coat on—which they prefer to put back to front', wrote Koch.[74]

The drought broke in mid-1870, and for this brief period the Aborigines began moving away from the mission station. Native food had become plentiful again. Younger Aborigines, however, were easier to keep at the station than older people. But by early 1871, with the summer heat, came what the Germans perceived to be 'drought' (the dry season) once more. A few Aborigines were now being employed on the station as stock hands, and the Kolonisten and station hands were kept busy moving stock from one waterhole to another; 'Like the fathers in the Old Testament we wander from place to place with our herds'.[75] The Kolonisten had to be mobile and self-sufficient, carrying essentials for human existence and food, erecting temporary, rough shelters at each watering hole, and fencing in the stock and diligently shepherding each time they made a move. Young Watske and his hardy wife lived almost constantly in this way.

Work at the mission was divided into the theological and educational in the hands of Homann and Koch, and physical station work undertaken by the Kolonists Vogelsang, Jacob and Watske. There were now some 1500 sheep, 40 horses and 6 dairy cows to be attended, for the mission station was reliant on the success of the stock station.[76] Tensions over work and authority between the two factions mounted. The Kolonists worked hard to establish their difficult undertaking, as well as to provide the labour and supervisory skills for the mission buildings. Homann and Koch largely concentrated on learning the Diyari language, and teaching and preaching, although Homann was in charge of the overall enterprise. Resentments flared between the two groups. To make matters worse, Koch was living with the Homanns and the two were perceived as in collusion. 'The colonists made a lot of trouble for the missionary and his assistant, Mr Koch. They wanted to run their section of the duties and the missionaries also. It was also the case in Africa', reported Homann's wife.[77]

As the drought persisted more Aborigines gathered near the mission station for the available rations, and twenty-eight pupils now attended the school. Fifty or sixty had gathered near the station and many were suffering from diarrhoea and other illnesses (caused in part by pollution of natural waterholes by European stock). They were given European medicines and placed on 'invalid diets'. The Germans too suffered a series of illnesses, thought to be caused by the foul-tasting, smelly water, until they were able to dig a well and obtain better drinking water. Homann and Koch were informed of the poor condition of one old Aborigine, but he died just as the Germans arrived at his hut. The missionary was perturbed by the wailing and crying of the other Aborigines who rushed into the hut, covering their heads and bodies with sand and throwing themselves onto the hot ground. Due to the prevailing heat, the corpse was to be buried that same day, and Homann attended the burial ceremony. When the kunkie asked the corpse to name his killer, the answer came as, 'Killed by bad earth' (foul water). The bearers carrying the corpse threw it onto the ground to ensure death, and it was duly buried. (Homann does not mention the ritual eating of the corpse in this case, perhaps due to the causes of its death.)

In April 1871 the Germans were to experience a grievous setback. Young Koch developed a virulent fever—'we claim through the perspiration of the natives, which seemed like poison'.[78] There was no medical care for hundreds of miles. A few days later, towards evening, the once strong young man became weaker and weaker, and the mission staff gathered helplessly in the Homanns' living room. Koch's trembling body finally stilled at about 4 a.m., a deadly sweat ran down his face and, just before he died, he screamed, 'Good Lord have Mercy on me!' Wilhelm Koch was buried 'on a sandhill' at Killalpaninna, not yet twenty-one years of age. His loss was greatly mourned, especially by Homann.[79] (To the east of the settlement, on a hill, is the cemetery with the graves of Mrs Milner, Koch and Vogelsang's first child.[80])

With Koch gone there was no teacher for young Willie Wendland, and the boy was sent south on Jacob's next trip, to join his brothers at Tanunda. The Homanns, furthermore, considered the influence of Aboriginal children potentially detrimental to his Christian development as 'he was adopting some of their tribal habits'.[81]

Magdalene Duvel travelled north to join Luise Homann as companion, and together they shared the burden of domestic work and psychological austerity in this intimidating place. 'It was very hard and hot work, in the sands of the north of Australia and we unburdened our hearts to each other frequently. If we had known all this before, we would not have gone amongst the poor Papuaes in Australia.'[82] Luise was heavily pregnant and soon after the departure of her son, gave birth to a second daughter, Louise. Dorothea Vogelsang also delivered a baby, a second son but, like her first, it too died. On 22 May 1871 Hermann Vogelsang wrote a short but poignant note to the chairman of the Mission Board: 'The Lord, according to His unfathomable wisdom, took our only beloved child last night, between 6 and 7 o'clock into His Kingdom, after a sickness of 8 days, having Thyphoid [sic]. Please be so kind and register this.'[83] 'Our small graveyard on the sandhill had an increasing number of graves', wrote Luise Homann.[84]

Revenge, Refuge and Retreat
As the 1871 drought continued and worsened the Kopperamanna and Killalpaninna lakes progressively dried out. Aborigines fished the concentrated numbers trapped in the drying salt waters, and gorged in anticipation of an imminent food shortage. According to the Lutherans, increased fighting followed such gorgings and during the Easter festivities of 1871 one young Aboriginal man was bashed to death. A revenge party gathered a few miles from the watering hole where Watske and his wife were shepherding mission sheep. The father of the dead man visited Watske, seeking the murderers, and Watske rushed to the Aborigines' camp to persuade them not to avenge with blood. But the father confronted the German, spear raised, and Watske returned to his hut. He watched from the doorway as about 100 Aborigines made preparations around campfires. Among them were 'a number of notorious people already known to the authorities', and a number of Aborigines from further south.

Next day the dead man's father informed Watske that the murderers lived at a camp near the mission station and that a party was leaving for blood revenge. Watske quickly sent a message to Homann, 'passed by the same person who had once tried to club me to death', wrote the missionary.[85] Homann immediately summoned the leader of the pinya (probably the father or the older brother and his party), 'admonished them and asked them to come to the evening sermon and prayer'. But as soon as darkness fell the avengers attacked Aboriginal campsites opposite the mission settlement. The murderers being sought, however, managed to escape and take refuge at the mission station. Next morning the dead man's father visited Homann, saying he would be content with wounding one of the accused, but was refused as, according to Homann, 'All this was deception and prevention'.

Three days later the pinya returned to the mission station during the night and crept into the Homanns' house, where the murderers were sheltering. One screamed, awakening the Germans, who drove off the avengers. 'The urgent demand to shoot at the fleeing persecutors, of course, we rejected', reported Homann.[86] 'They looked like devils, painted with blood, feathers and chalk', wrote his wife.[87] An angry group stood a menacing vigil outside the Homanns' house throughout the night, and two Aborigines stood guard at the schoolhouse door, 'to catch Brother Vogelsang and myself should we dare go out there'. Vogelsang defied them and walked to the schoolhouse, with Homann eventually following. 'The Aborigines who surrounded us were so close that they could hear what I said—"We don't intend to shed blood but the Lord will protect those who believe. And I will oppose the enemies with the Word".' The pinya did not touch the Germans, but left for the Aboriginal camps nearby.

The avengers then returned to the area near Watske's hut. Homann sent for the Kopperamanna troopers, and barely hours later they galloped up, heavily armed. The avengers, meanwhile, were demanding sheep from Watske, and when he refused they became raucous and angry and began thumping the ground. At that moment the troopers arrived on the scene, revolvers at the ready, and the Aborigines fled.

Rumours subsequently resurfaced regarding large groups of mixed tribal people intent on driving the Europeans from their land. Homann claimed some of these collaborators were known to him. They were mission-station Diyari, who had even attended church services.[88]

After the sadness of Koch's death Homann continued the schooling alone, as well as his preaching duties. He was still awkwardly battling with alternatives to the critical words and concepts missing in the Diyari language: 'This is the most difficult and painful task for us all. All other problems are small in comparison. The desert, the heat, the distance and alienation, are of minor consequence, in comparison to the fact that we are still not able to teach the True Word.'[89]

But the drought continued to worsen throughout 1871, and the lack of water became grave. The Lutherans tried to dig wells, but with little success. Their bore water barely sufficed, as so many now depended on it. The livestock were eventually driven to a neighbouring station. There had been no rain at all for eighteen long months. 'The poor natives practised black magic and held terrible corroborees, their heathen dances, but the rain didn't come.'[90] Homann sent repeated letters to the mission committee describing the critical condition currently at Killalpaninna, but he always received the reply, 'You have become faint hearted and lost your faith—the rain will come'.[91]

Just before the birth of their third child, August, the Homanns endured a terrifying experience. Luise was constantly anxious for the safety of their children, especially as the Germans had witnessed local infanticide and cannibalism. One afternoon young Elizabeth, their eldest daughter, disappeared. In a frantic state, the mission team searched for hours among the sandhills. Finally Haemmerling, a German worker now employed at the station, found the little girl among a flock of sheep, clutching two lambs in her arms and crying, so afraid that she had squeezed one to death. She was taken home to the relieved Homanns.

Soon after this event Luise Homann, with her small children, left Killalpaninna in Jacob's wagon. She was to make preparations for her two eldest sons to leave for Germany to complete their education. It was a difficult five-week journey southwards, through drought-stricken desert country. The small children suffered the effects of stale water and exposure and had to be attended by a doctor at Hookina.

Luise Homann was never to see her eldest sons again. Both died, within a few years of each other, in Germany. She was never to see the mission station or the Aborigines of the north again either. A few weeks after her departure lack of water forced the missionaries to retreat to Mundowdna Station. It was eight days before Christmas, 1871.

4
Bucaltaninna and the Kolonisten

The station at Killalpaninna was abandoned at the end of 1871. The drought had worsened, water became desperately short and two of the women were heavily pregnant. Through searing heat and a parched, desolate landscape the despondent group made their way to Mundowdna Station a hundred miles to the south. They found refuge with the station manager and camped in makeshift shelters under the canegrass thatch that protected station vehicles. Nearby was a 'sweet' freshwater spring.

This second retreat produced despondency and pessimism; the enterprise appeared doomed to failure. Plagued by a critical shortage of drinkable water, harassed by persistent drought, stressed by the unpredictability of rain, the isolation and the harsh conditions, the Lutherans almost gave up at this point. Had it not been for the tenacity and idealism of the mission labourers, those unordained Kolonisten, the enterprise could well have ended within two years of this retreat.

Missionary Schoknecht
Coincidentally the mission party was joined at Mundowdna Station by the missionary sent to replace Goessling. Carl Schoknecht was a new graduate from Hermannsburg. He was travelling from Port Augusta in Jacob's wagon when he found the desperate group of Germans struggling to survive in appalling conditions. Homann had left the party and was travelling south to consult with the committee, and the two men had missed each other by travelling alternative routes.[1] The journey had already introduced the newcomer to the northern country, for he became desperately ill himself. And water shortage was such that on several occasions the horses were forced to continue for two whole days in the intense summer heat without drinking. And when the men did find water it was little more than a thick, yellow, clay-like fluid, as waterholes along the route were almost dry. It was surprising, to the new missionary, that the beasts survived.

Carl Heinrich Martin Schoknecht was born to farming parents at Dargun in the Duchy of Mecklenburg-Schwerin in 1841. At the age of twelve he was orphaned on the death of his father (his mother having died when the boy was only six). At fourteen he began work as an apprenticed coach builder, but by the age of twenty-two resolved to enter the mission seminary at Hermannsburg for training. Schoknecht was given a friendly reception by Ludwig Harms and was admitted as a student. In 1866 he entered the seminary, graduating two years later with the desire to be posted to India. Instead he was to be sent to Australia. But his journey was delayed when war broke out between Germany and France that same year, and it was not until peace was declared a year later (in 1871) that the young missionary sailed for that new continent.[2]

Circumstances, however, dictated a series of contravening events that determined his time as missionary in the Killalpaninna experience to be the shortest of all.

Carl Schoknecht arrived at Mundowdna Station three days before the Christmas of 1871. As he later wrote: 'Because of the privations, the fierce heat and the bad drinking water I arrived in our vehicle at Mundawadana [sic] dangerously ill and in an unconscious condition'.[3] He had expected to arrive at the mission station further northwards by New Year, but to his surprise he found a leaderless group of countrymen languishing in temperatures of 104 degrees and more. Watske's wife and Dorothea Vogelsang were close to delivering their babies, and the primitive huts and sheds offered the barest protection against the sun's burning rays. They were open to wind, weather and insects, and it was exhausting for everybody simply to survive the days. It was in these shelters that the mission workers cooked, slept, held their religious services, and the two women gave birth. A day after its delivery, the Watskes' baby died. Two hours before the child's death the newly ordained Schoknecht performed his first baptism. He then performed his first funeral. The exhausted and distraught mother languished for five weeks before recovering. Dorothea Vogelsang's baby was close to death too, but miraculously survived.

The group stayed on at Mundowdna as the long drought months dragged on. In the south, a disillusioned Homann was negotiating the mission's future. Together with his wife and children again, and aware of his wife's sufferings of the past, Homann perhaps felt that he could not further subject them to the north, and stressed the futility of persevering with this impossible project. But the joint synodal committee was adamant that their avocation not fail, that Homann not give up at this point, and a decision was made to dig deeper wells in the hope of striking drinkable water.

Meanwhile, in late January, after an unexpected downpour of rain, Schoknecht and Vogelsang rode to the mission station to check the water supply. Rain had reached the lake at Killalpaninna, but there was such a crust of salt on its bed that the precious liquid was quite unpalatable. The surrounding claypans also proved too salty. Grass was beginning to sprout on the brown plains, but it would soon die as the country quickly dried again. It took the pair a full month to ride to Lake Killalpaninna, survey the area and return to Mundowdna. Schoknecht described the place as 'miserable': 'everywhere only sand; playing with us, building a new hill here and there. Australia is a very poor country . . . the poor Aborigines are at such a low level of development of human civilisation because Nature can only offer them so little.'[4]

By February Homann was reluctantly returning northwards accompanied by two well-diggers. At the request of the mission committee he had been made a

Justice of the Peace, which enabled him to recruit protection assistance.[5] Hope for water soon faded, however, as even when an underground supply was tapped, it, too, proved salty and undrinkable. Vogelsang and Watske accompanied Homann and the well-sinker south to debate the issue.

A meeting of all delegates who were in charge of the mission enterprise was to be held at Tanunda to decide its future. The National Bank was pressing Reichner with a mission account overdrawn by nearly £140, and a decision was made to sell some of the mission stock to George Debney (owner of Mundowdna). Homann argued a case against continuing the work, citing the lack of suitable water to be the main obstacle. The last worthwhile rain had fallen in April 1869, nearly three years ago. And it seemed futile, he argued, to sink more wells for it appeared all underground water was undrinkable due to its high salt content. Besides, Homann continued, a water source must be sufficient to sustain the mission stock, as the station relied on income from this source and depended on animal husbandry as a food resource. Furthermore, there seemed little chance of successfully growing fruit and vegetables. And Homann relayed how he had to turn Aborigines away from the station because the Lutherans could no longer give them any of their dwindling water resources.

Homann was reportedly 'seriously maligned' at this meeting, perhaps by the Kolonisten present, and accused of 'certain charges' (not specifically documented) which he denied, but whereupon he stated: 'Since you can't use a missionary whom you have robbed of trust, I resign my position'.[6] Homann was immediately offered a pastorship (by a member after the meeting), at the Bethlehem Lutheran Church in Flinders Street, Adelaide, which he accepted (although the Homanns had hoped to move to America).

The committee at Tanunda was now pledged to the project and did not intend to surrender the station without a more concerted effort to find a suitable water source. A request was made to the commissioner of Crown lands for financial assistance for the sinking of wells, 'for the benefit of the Blacks (and to prevent our Missionaries in the future from driving away the poor Natives for want of water)'.[7] There are no records of a reply, but by this time (1871) the Lutheran congregation in South Australia had raised £3500 towards the mission's support and, encouragingly, the first return from the sheep had been £470.[8] Vogelsang and Watske returned to Mundowdna, to Schoknecht and their wives.

But further well-sinking attempts also failed. The committee was advised, by several pastoralists in the Far North, to move the station 130 miles to the east, to better soil, where local building materials were more abundant and where it was rumoured there was drinkable water from springs. The new area would have to be properly investigated, the government again approached for land leasing, a ration supply re-established and a new Aboriginal language learned. The committee determined to persist with the Lake Killalpaninna area, even though the difficulties seemed insurmountable at times, and their chances of success were in no way assured.

For five long months the bedraggled mission workers remained in their crude shelters and awaited the end of the drought in the north and the end of the debate in the south. Confined to their beggarly conditions they were unable to travel far as they had no wagons. For most of this time the mission wagons were either in the south or were engaged in ferrying well-diggers back and forth.

Furthermore the party was immobilised by the extremity of the drought conditions. In February Schoknecht wrote to headquarters at Hermannsburg: 'Work here demands an enormous amount of money and strength which could have been better diverted elsewhere. But this is the Lord's good intention, because His ways are beautiful, here we can only watch His miracles.'[9]

Bucaltaninna Mission Station

As the weather cooled, towards May, Schoknecht, the Watskes and the Vogelsangs decided to return north to their station. They could no longer rely on continued hospitality from the owner of Mundowdna Station. And although apprehensive, with Schoknecht writing, 'We know not what the Good Lord intends to do with our mission; or where He wants us to go . . .', they were nevertheless anxious to continue their work.

During this drought period the mission livestock (some 2000 sheep and 50 horses) had been cared for by an English shepherd at the furthermost settlement with a functioning waterhole, Cooraninna, about 40 miles from Lake Killalpaninna and 70 miles from Mundowdna Station. The police outstation for the north and the northernmost mail station had also been relocated to this waterhole.[10] Ernst Jacob had occasionally checked mission stock during his journeys back and forth with well-diggers. But now the livestock had to be driven back to the Killalpaninna area, for the late autumn and early winter was providing more favourable conditions. There was even the occasional night frost and some rain. The animals began doing well, but mission work was slow and quiet. Schoknecht studied the Diyari language, but few Aborigines now seemed to be in the area. The missionary complained that:

> They cannot refrain from wandering to look for food. They come naked looking for snakes, birds, rats, springs, small beetles and small berries. Occasionally they murder each other, and they sing and dance in an animal-like state of depravity. Their singing and dancing is like a terrible misery and frightful complaining howling, and of God they have only the darkest imagination.[11]

In August–September 1872 the sheep were driven to Port Augusta by a stationhand hired from Beltana to be shorn and sold, and eleven bales of wool stamped 'LM'/FN (Lutheran Mission) were shipped to Britain. (During the unsettled 1870s the mission sheep were shorn at various stations in the district.) In October 1873 thirty-five bales of mission wool fetched almost £430, and 195 wethers sold for £132.[12] Food rations for the Aborigines were again re-established at the mission station, and Jacob was kept busy carrying supplies from Port Augusta. In October another attempt was made at well-sinking in preparation for the coming summer, but it too was unsuccessful. And in November a new flock of rams was collected by Jacob to increase the stock by breeding.

But once again the shortage of water during the summer months threatened the mission's future. All attempts to dig for drinkable water failed and discussions in the south turned to surrendering the enterprise. However, Germany refused defeat, stating: 'The question is whether to give up Australia, and we say no. Everything points to it and we have been advised to do so, but we still have not fully recognised God's will. So we plan on a new station.'[13] By this time Homann had retired from the enterprise, but Schoknecht was considered still 'fresh'. It was believed, both at headquarters at Tanunda, and in Germany, that this important mission was the possible salvation—not only spiritual but even physical—from potential genocide, of the Australian Aborigines in the north of the colony. Their numbers had so rapidly declined in the few decades of colonisation that it was feared they would die out as a race.

The new station was to be at Lake Tankamarinna (now on Dulkaninna Station), a small salt-water lake about 50 miles south-east of Lake Killalpaninna, where drinkable water was rumoured to be found. In the summer of 1873 the mission brethren prepared to move to Tankamarinna, dismantling their homes and laboriously loading the precious material onto wagons to be carried southwards to the small lake. The committee at Tanunda enquired about purchasing the lease, only to discover, after the mission party had already begun to settle there, that it was held by the owner of Mundowdna Station. He declined making it over to the missionaries, but offered to allow them to build a mission-house beside the lake providing they did not disturb his sheep and cattle.[14] This, however, was quite unsuitable, for income from the mission's livestock primarily maintained the economic viability of the enterprise. Sufficient land was needed to continue and develop the sheep station.

Once again the disillusioned Lutherans had to move on. Having barely arrived at Lake Tankamarinna, burdened with building materials, personal possessions, families and livestock, they were forced to return to the Killalpaninna region. Intestinal infections, from the lack of fresh drinking water, plagued them and Schoknecht purchased bottles of the opium-based bush medicine, chlorodyne, from the Blinman store. With every small purchase, or transaction involving money, pedantic lists had to be carefully compiled and sent to Reichner. One such list of goods from the Blinman store for this period was tabled as 'pills, yards of brown calico, oil cloth, clay pipes, meerschaum pipes, postage stamps, a pair of Blucher boots, seal-skin slippers, cotton handkerchiefs and more chlorodyne'.[15] Exhausted and overstrained, Dorothea Vogelsang and her small son went south to rest and recuperate.

With this move the Lutherans decided to settle at Bucaltaninna, the cattle station closest to Killalpaninna that had recently been abandoned by the Milner brothers. There was still a little water in nearby Lake Bucaltaninna, and although it was quickly drying out, the sorry band 'didn't have the courage and didn't see any reason to try again at Killalpaninna'.[16] They decided to rebuild their mission station near the lake, and for the next few months were kept busy erecting buildings and settling families. But soon after arriving, Carl Schoknecht, with crushed resilience, was recalled to the south over the future of the enterprise and his future as its missionary. He never returned to the north.

Synodal Split and the Kolonisten
In late 1873 the Evangelical Lutheran Synod of South Australia met at Hahndorf to discuss the worrisome mission and determine a plan for its flagging future. It was decided that the entire enterprise be handed over to Harms in Germany, with the proviso that mission work continue among the Aborigines there. Should missionising discontinue, the mission stock station should revert to the South Australian Mission Committee.

Harms did not reply to the proposal for some time. A rift was occurring within the Lutheran Church in South Australia, primarily over the Immanuel Synod's connection with the unionist General Synod. This caused disparity within South Australia and between South Australia and Hermannsburg in Germany. During this time Schoknecht was recalled by Harms and transferred, leaving the future of the mission again tenuous. Schoknecht, however, felt committed to the enterprise and was recalled twice before relenting, reluctantly, in November 1873.[17] He was later to describe this period of his career: 'There followed two years of disappointment and hardship, with an occasional glimmer of hope, followed by further disappointments and failure—in short, two years of misery and want, which I can't and shan't describe'.[18]

Schoknecht accepted a posting to a parish in the Wimmera district (Victoria), among a colony of German immigrants.

Meanwhile Vogelsang and Watske were left to run the station, now located at Bucaltaninna (after the new site had been inspected by the committee for approval). Ernst Jacob, the teamster, was almost continually on the road as the supply and service arm. And Hermann Vogelsang did not see his wife and small son for nine months, until they again joined him in May 1874, when his son was approaching his second birthday. During this period the mission station was without an ordained missionary, and the Lutherans were unable to celebrate the Eucharist. Nor could there yet be any baptisms among the Aborigines that were being proselytised.

The stock station, however, began to prosper. In September 1874 forty-four bales of mission wool were sold at auction and shipped to England on the *Royal Shepherd*. And in November Reichner received a credit with the National Bank for the sum of £631 3s 8d for proceeds from the wool sales.[19] In anticipation of stock station success an application was made to the commissioner of Crown lands for more land to enable expansion beyond the 200 square miles initially allocated (around lakes Killalpaninna and Kopperamanna). The lease sought was that which had been granted to the Milner brothers to 1867, a run situated about 30 miles west of Lake Hope.[20] Stirring support was again penned by Meischal, and published in the church paper. It gripped the hearts of Lutherans in South Australia, providing sufficient incentive for the government to assent. A government lease of 1000 square miles of land was granted the enterprise, and a 'reserve' of 100 square miles the local Aborigines, the latter a request from Harms in Germany. The 1874 public gazette of land leases listed 2294 and 2295 as now leased by Reichner at a fee of £2 10s per half year.[21]

When Harms' official reply to the request for German control of the mission station eventually arrived in the colony, in May 1874, the South Australian committee was dissatisfied with its vague, non-committal tone. The synods of the joint committee were at variance themselves, and Reichner and Carl Schmidt were appointed to investigate a more promising station site. The two Germans consulted government members in Adelaide and were introduced to William Gosse and Ernest Giles, who had both recently explored extensively in Central Australia. The explorers offered advice on the nature of the country further northwards, the character of the Aborigines there and the means of communication to and from, and gave the men reports and maps to study.

At this time, around 1874, there was intense interest in the newly explored Centre. South Australia's McDouall Stuart had crossed the continent more than a decade earlier (which resulted in the northern country being annexed to the colony of South Australia), and the expeditions of Gosse, Giles and Warburton revealed that the centre of this huge island was not just a desolate wasteland. Reichner and Schmidt gave a promising picture to the committee at Tanunda. William Gosse had reported favourably on the region around the Finke River, of fertile land and Aboriginal communities which aroused considerable interest among the Lutheran community. By all accounts a mission in the Centre could prove a less arduous task, with an easier climate and the possibility of a large pool of potential Christian converts. Killalpaninna had been plagued with setbacks from its inception, and was still facing potential failure.

Goyder (the surveyor-general) supported the proposal of a Lutheran mission station in Central Australia, and Boucaut (the commissioner for Crown lands) agreed to allocate 200 square miles of country as a mission reserve. The land comprised two strips that bordered the northern foot of the James Range and enclosed a section of the Finke River. Full details, with explorers' reports and maps, were sent to Harms in Germany, and in January 1875 the director's enthusiastic reply and ready consent reached the Barossa Lutherans. In Harms' view the new proposal held a promise of potential that the old station obviously did not (no doubt formed from the correspondence that he had received over almost a decade). The reply, however, advised that the station at Bucaltaninna not be abandoned, as it might prove useful in the future as an intermediate station.[22] Hermannsburg would now take full control and responsibility for the new station, and would train and supply missionaries. Harms declared that South Australia must accept full financial responsibility for the mission's material affairs, and both parties were to have a claim to its property.

Harms' letter was published in the local church newspapers of both Lutheran factions, ELCA and UELCA. It was again a time for Lutherans to declare common ground and a common course of action. But in March 1875 the Immanuel Synod met at Carlsruhe, and for two full days debated the value of continuing with missionising among the Australian Aborigines:

> President Oster expressed the opinion that, after serving 12 years on the Mission Committee, he had little confidence in continuing Mission Work among the aborigines of Australia's dry Interior. He favoured an assessing of all Mission property, dissolving partnership with the Immanuel Synod, and supporting a new Mission undertaking which Director Harms was planning for New Zealand.[23]

At length a resolution was passed that the Immanuel Synod would cede its share of the property to Harms for use at the new proposed mission in Central Australia, on condition that Harms took responsibility for its direction and support. It was added that, 'In the event of Mission work among the aborigines of this land becoming impossible, Synod's share of the Mission's property shall revert to the Hermannsburg Mission'.[24]

In mid-May, at a meeting of the joint mission committee at Lights Pass, Reichner (president of the Immanuel Synod) announced that his synod had authorised him to press for an immediate dissolution of the mission partnership, 'in order that it might escape from the long and miserable, enforced inability to get anything done'.[25]

But when reports of the new proposal for Central Australia reached the Kolonisten at Bucaltaninna, they (Vogelsang and Jacob) threatened to withdraw their labour if the enterprise was transferred. Watske and his wife, whose health was suffering, had already withdrawn their services.[26] Having invested nine struggling years to establishing a mission station and stock station in the north of South Australia, Vogelsang and Jacob were unwilling to begin again. The Kolonisten declared they could not answer before God and their own conscience for deserting these Aborigines in order to care for another group. Besides, land had been granted the enterprise, rations were being supplied to the Aborigines in that area, and the local language had been learnt. Why give up all that had been achieved over nearly a decade of struggle?

The conviction and idealism of these stalwart Kolonisten (and no doubt the groundwork already prepared) stirred the conscience of the Immanuel Synod members and they determined to persevere in the north of South Australia. Further attention was given the project and the belief was declaimed that as the layworkers could hold out with the livestock in this part of Australia, surely missionaries, too, could continue working the old mission field. The Immanuel Synod now no longer had to contend with factional problems of a joint mission committee, and could maintain an independent station dedicated to perpetuating the Lutheran faith among an otherwise abandoned group of 'heathens'.

The two synods were now distinctly separate bodies again, with the larger body (at that time), the South Australian Synod, intent on establishing a new mission station in Central Australia, and the smaller body, the Immanuel Synod, in control and supporting the old mission (now located at Bucaltaninna). The joint mission committee, formed in 1863, was dissolved in 1875. All jointly owned property at Bucaltaninna was to be assessed and distributed between the two Lutheran synods in the order of weighted support. The South Australian Synod was also to be compensated in cash for buildings.

A deputation was sent to Bucaltaninna to divide the assets and livestock. The stock share to the Immanuel Synod was to be some 1600 sheep, 50 goats, 20 horses and 10 cattle.[27] The Kolonisten, who had toiled so hard for so long to develop and sustain their station stock, were to lose almost two-thirds to the new enterprise. The Hermannsburg Mission Institute now supported the South Australian Synod, withdrawing from the old mission station, and naming the new station on the Finke River 'New Hermannsburg', the name originally given to the mission station in the north of South Australia.

New Hermannsburg came under the supreme direction of Theodore Harms, with support from the South Australian Synod, while the Immanuel Synod elected its own committee and turned to the theological seminary at Neuendettelsau in Bavaria (Germany) for pastors and missionaries. Their petition met with apparent enthusiasm and willingness to help, but the young male student considered suitable for the enterprise had not yet finished his studies. Accordingly the Kolonisten at Bucaltaninna operated their station alone for three long years without an ordained missionary, and with the smaller share of the livestock. And the Immanuel Synod's mission committee was now burdened with a bank overdraft of £270 against the enterprise.[28] The mission station somehow had to become self-supporting again, for it was a continual source of expense to the struggling committee. In June 1874 alone the following list of stores was ordered from Bignell and Youngs Drapery and Fancy Warehouses of Port Augusta for the staff and Aborigines living at the station: '2000 lb flour, 250 lb sugar, 43 lb tea, 10 lb tobacco, 25 single blankets, 12 blue shirts, 6 tomahawks, 100 needles, 2 lb thread, 2 axes, 12 quart pots, 12 pannickins, sewing machines, iron bedsteads, mattresses and chairs'.[29]

Kolonist Hermann Vogelsang
While polemical debates were waged and restructuring of factions occupied the Lutheran bodies in the south, the struggle to survive and succeed continued for the isolated mission party. Hermann Vogelsang was now thirty-seven years of age, a physically strong man, an idealist and a staunch Lutheran. A short, thick-set, stocky figure, stiff-backed and with a square jutting jaw, the downward curve of his tight mouth was testimony to his strength of conviction and physical fortitude. He had sight in one eye only, having been blinded in the other at the age of two years.[30] Whether supervising black shepherds and the mission sheep, leading the daily, open-air prayers, or hammering and forging with hot metal in the 'smithy' shelter, a fierce sun beating through canegrass roofing, this wilful German exuded a profound zealousness and compelling passion; in the words of George Farwell, 'the rock upon which all storms burst and dissipate their force'.[31]

Two years after joining her husband at Bucaltaninna, after a protracted respite of nine months, Dorothea Vogelsang had fallen gravely ill. There were few medicines at the isolated station, and no medical advice to be sought for hundreds of miles. She must be taken south, and soon. Her worried husband loaded the mission wagon, by now a locally made one and not the heavy, narrow-based German type. He made her as comfortable as was possible inside the wagon and, scooping up young Heinrich, their 3-year-old son, set out on the long journey to Adelaide. The track was rough, with ruts and stones and wash-outs, and the long, lonely trip dangerous for a sick woman. Dorothea bore the journey stoically for weeks, but when approaching Hookina, north of Hawker in the Flinders Ranges, she suddenly worsened and died. Devastated, Hermann Vogelsang left his small son tied in the wagon and walked the three miles to the settlement for help. When he returned with assistance, the unhitched horses had wandered into the bush and were lost. The grieving husband and son buried Dorothea in the cemetery at Hookina. There was no time for lamenting for, before they could continue their journey south, they had to search for the missing horses.[32]

After his wife's death, in April 1875, Hermann Vogelsang and his young son stayed at Tanunda for three months, mourning his great loss. This squarely built man was tough in spirit as well as in body. He was a relentless man of God, stern, intolerant of frailties. But God had dealt him his greatest test. His beloved Dorothea, about whom he wrote with such feeling and tenderness in his letters to Germany, had gone. In the last such letter, after her death, he wrote that he was in 'the deepest despair', and in 'very great pain', and, quoting from Psalm 42, 'My tears have been my meat, day and night'.[33]

Hermann Heinrich Vogelsang was born at Schwenningdorf, on 17 March 1838. At three years of age he was sent to live with an uncle and aunt who had no family of their own. The childless couple took a keen interest in mission work

Hermann Vogelsang on horseback, probably near Lake Bucaltaninna, c. 1870s

and, while living with them, young Hermann would read reports of the mission fields. At the age of fifteen, at his real father's request, he was sent home to learn the blacksmith trade, although he had wanted to be a coppersmith. At Hevel, in the Province of Osnabrueck, he heard Pastor Ludwig Harms preaching at the Neuenkirchen Mission Festival. Later he was to hear him again, and in 1854 young Hermann approached Harms offering his services as a laypreacher. He was subsequently employed by a member of the Hermannsburg Mission Board and a close friend of Theodore Harms, Pastor Borcher, on his glebe. In one letter of 1854 to his parents young Hermann asked for clothing and boots, as 'everything here has to be just right' and he was only receiving 'pocket-money'. And in the manner of a typical teenager today, the 16-year-old requested his shoes or boots be 'in a real fashionable style, otherwise I won't take them'. Furthermore, he reported that 'Pastor Harms is to go to prison because he has hit a boy who had not attended church and school'. Harms' sentence, however, was annulled after his large congregation protested. The young Vogelsang also related the persecution of the Hermannsburg Institute; and 'they say this man [?Harms] is mad; this chap makes all people poor. Oh there is so much to tell you, all the

Dorothea Vogelsang, first wife of Hermann, with the couple's son, Heinrich, c. 1873

money, wrong doings, you know how it always is . . .'[34]

For five years Hermann worked Borcher's land, attended services and festivals at nearby Hermannsburg, and eventually approached its director, Ludwig Harms, to offer his services to the mission institute itself. In 1862 Hermann received a call from Harms requesting that he take charge of the horse team on the institute's farm. He was also given the task of carting stones, timber and other material for the erection of the new mission house and additions to the old. Four years later young Vogelsang was sent home to his parents for a brief visit and farewell before his ultimate dream was to be realised—the call to a mission field as Kolonist. His field was to be South Africa. But two weeks before he was due to sail Hermann received a letter from Harms asking him to prepare to go to Australia instead.[35]

Hermann was twenty-eight when he sailed for Australia. Before he left Germany an uncle (possibly the uncle with whom he had lived for so long, his 'adopted' father) presented him with a German sword, perhaps a family heirloom, perhaps for protection. It became a souvenir of the Old World he was soon to renounce and a talisman, a 'magical' object that terrified the Aborigines who believed it held supernatural powers. Whenever it was drawn as a threat in potential situations of conflict, its inherent power brought immediate pacification and peace.[36] Once, during early conflict encounters, when the missionaries were surrounded by painted tribesmen brandishing spears, the small man dismounted from his horse, strode between the tribesmen and drew his German sword. As he gripped the shining weapon and raised it slowly above his head the tribesmen silently and passively retreated. It was reputedly the magic of this weapon that they feared, its bewitching power, and perhaps the power of this stocky man.[37]

Hermann Vogelsang's intense convictions and faith found expression through physical strength as well as through the word of God. It was due to his strength and perseverance, and to that of that other laypreacher, Ernst Jacob, that the Killalpaninna Mission endured beyond its first decade.

After three months of mourning at Tanunda, Vogelsang again set out for the north, this time accompanied by the mission's newly appointed schoolteacher, Carl Meyer. Vogelsang's young son was left in the care of Reichner and his wife. As the party passed through the Lower Flinders Ranges near Hookina, Hermann fell into a deep gloom, and when they arrived at the mission station Hermann's house had been burned to the ground in his absence. Even small mementoes and little treasures that had belonged to his dead wife were now also destroyed. But his convictions and strength once again emerged and, with Meyer, he was soon energetically rebuilding.

Carl Meyer, Schoolteacher

As it would still be several years before the chosen Neuendettelsau student was ready for the field, a suitable person to at least open a school at Bucaltaninna was sought. The mission committee commissioned a consecrated elder of the Langmeil congregation, Carl Meyer. He was formally inducted into the position of schoolteacher and spiritual head at the mission station. Together with his wife, Meyer travelled to the station with Hermann Vogelsang in the mission wagon. At about this time a trio of committee members, representing both synods, was sent to inspect the mission run and its stock so that it could be divided between the two enterprises. Reichner, Graetz and Droegemueller travelled by train, coach and hired buggy, and a month after taking Meyer north, Vogelsang collected the three men and drove them to Bucaltaninna. They arrived at the station in early September and spent a week inspecting Killalpaninna,

Kopperamanna and Bucaltaninna. Pessimistically, Droegemueller, of the South Australian Synod, reported to his president that: 'conditions at the Mission generally were very depressing. The missionaries who had left had certainly not exaggerated their difficult lot. The Church and the committee made many mistakes in the past which must now be admitted, as they had not felt inclined at the time to believe their missionaries.'[38] The livestock was subsequently divided into the allocated shares, but the buildings were deemed worthless, as they were little more than crude huts.

Missionaries H. H. Kempe and W. F. Schwarz were sent from Hermannsburg (Germany) to the new station in Central Australia. The South Australian government generously increased the size of the proposed mission reserve to 900 square miles, and promised a supply of rations for the Aborigines. In late October 1875 (nine years to the month after the first mission party had set out from the town) the Central Australian mission party left Tanunda. They camped at Mundowdna Station while some of their men travelled to Bucaltaninna to collect the allocated stock. Kempe described Mundowdna as 'a very barren place with bad water, which, at least to human taste, was unpalatable'.[39] Yet it had been this 'sweet' spring water that had sustained a hardened Killalpaninna group as they sweltered in makeshift quarters in the summer of 1871–72.

The men who travelled to Bucaltaninna inspected Meyer's school, visited the Aborigines' camps (where about 100 were now living) and when Pastor Heidenreich, now superintendent of the proposed station in the Centre, inspected the freshwater wells alongside the dry lake, he reported, shallowly, and somewhat unsympathetically, that he 'felt disappointed that the earlier missionaries had declared this place hopeless—for missionaries working in this locality could consider themselves fortunate when they compared their lot with that of Mission stations in Africa'.[40]

The livestock was selected by Heidenreich before the men rejoined Kempe and Schwarz at Mundowdna. Meanwhile Haemmerling and George Mirus started out with a flock of about 3100 sheep for the Finke River. The rest of the Central Australian party had not yet left Mundowdna when news arrived that, due to excessive heat and lack of water, the drovers had already lost 700 sheep along just one 40-mile stretch of country![41] The cold realities of the north were just beginning to touch this new group of Lutheran missionaries.

Although Meyer was still unfamiliar with the Diyari language, he started gathering pupils for his school and, using the English language (more commonly known among Aborigines than the German language), began to teach in an open-air 'classroom' (any convenient spot where shade could be found), for there was as yet no school building. In fact, near Bucaltaninna local building materials were so scarce that the German families lived in crude (possibly bough and mud-type) dwellings. Hermann Vogelsang, who already had a working knowledge of the Diyari language, had been instructed by the committee to assist Meyer in the school. Within a short time there were twenty-one pupils learning to read and to repeat tracts of Luther's small catechism by heart, explanations given in a simplistic form by Meyer. To keep the pupils and mission Aborigines busily occupied, and to prevent attempts at straying back to the camps, the schoolteacher introduced mat-making, and possibly other mission activities, because 'there is [sic] not many other things for them to do because this part of the country is unfit for agriculture [*sic*] purposes'. Meyer sent twelve mats to the Aborigines' Office at Adelaide in 1878.[42]

Johann Ernst Jacob

The mission's hardy teamster, in 1875 forty years of age, had spent most of the past nine years on the dangerous desert track between each mission station location and the nearest service town of Port Augusta. His task was to collect rations for the Aborigines, food supplies for the mission staff, and machinery and other necessities for the enterprise to function in its isolation. He also carried baled wool to the port after shearing seasons. For some time Jacob carried for the forwarding agents Tassie and Co. (of Port Augusta) to other stations along the route, for a rate payment of £7 per ton as far as Mundowdna Station, and to stations further north at a rate of £25 to £30 per ton.[43] This brought extra income for the mission enterprise but put Jacob on the road for even greater lengths of time. The port town was some 400 miles to the south, and the round trip took two to three months. Consequently, by the time one trip was over it was time to begin the next, as food and supplies would again be running short, or a repair or certain piece of machinery was required. Jacob bore this hard life for many years, with long, virtually continuous journeys through the desert, in intense heat and bitter cold.

During these lonely odysseys Jacob grew close to the northern landscape, its nuances, changes and subtle beauty. The sunsets were spectacular, the nights wide, black and dazzling, the clarity of the morning air invigorating and sharpening the landscape focus, and the dry heat intense. When he passed the beauty and majesty of the Flinders Ranges, ruched and folded, misty blue and purple at a distance, followed by a sea of saltbush and bluebush, he knew he was drawing close to the port town. A few days at a local hotel, while delivering and loading, and he was again approaching those elegant ranges.

Tall, slim and softly spoken, Ernst Jacob was physically a direct contrast to Hermann Vogelsang. Both, however, shared a passion for the 'salvation' of the Aborigines, and for their Lutheran beliefs. Jacob was respected and well liked by the people of the north, both black and white. He had the demeanour of a child it was said, that elemental happiness and simplicity. Yet he could be found deep in philosophic thought, and was a lover of 'good books'. He was a gentle man of wisdom, yet his task was perhaps the toughest of all, and certainly onerous. Ernst Jacob could speak English and Diyari fluently, and of course his native German. He has been described as emerging from deep serious thought very suddenly, like the weather breaking, and erupting into humour and liveliness.[44] He had a quick wit and keen sense of humour, 'always quick off the mark with his witty remarks', 'always ready to crack a joke', although on several occasions Jacob's sense of humour caused him trouble. On the first difficult journey in 1866 Jacob provided the wit and humour that enabled the Germans to bear the awesome conditions. But one night he put a lizard in the sleeping bag of one of the missionaries and the joke was not received with the expected reaction![45]

Jacob was a Silesian, the son of pious Altlutheran parents who had defied the Prussian authorities during Frederick Wilhelm's reforms. While working in Germany he had read about the Hermannsburg mission fields, and was 'inspired'. Many of his close Silesian neighbours were emigrating to Australia as persecuted Altlutherans, and stories were returning to the Silesian villages of the wretched condition of the black 'heathens' there. Young Jacob was not a trained missionary, just a simple miller by trade, modest and industrious, but he determined to travel to Australia himself, and to find a way to serve God there, among these black heathens. At the age of twenty-five he purchased the ticket for a passage to Australia, and at the beginning of 1860 he arrived in the colony of South Australia. Jacob found a job with Pastor Fritzsche at Lobethal, familiarised himself with the surrounding countryside, and allegedly awaited an opportunity to work among the Australian Aborigines.

Six years passed before he was engaged as a member of the mission party bound for the north-east of the colony. He was the only member who had any knowledge and experience of Australian conditions and countryside. Those previous six years gave Jacob the background for the unenviable task of teamster, and the fate of being almost constantly on the road in some of the harshest country on the continent. Yet even though this mild man endured the excessive hardships of his job, he is said to have always remained tranquil in spirit and gentle at heart.

Goods, food, and machinery ordered by the missionaries or by Reichner would be shipped from Port Adelaide via the shipping agents Elders, Smith and Co. of Port Adelaide (a company part owned by Thomas Elder) to the forwarding agents, Tassie and Co. at Port Augusta, and from there to be carried by Jacob in the mission wagon to the station. A steamship, aptly yet indecorously named the *Lubra*, generally carried supplies for the mission. One such order included: '13 Kegs, 10 bags of flour, 1 plough, 5 cases of sundries, 1 bag of potatoes, 1 Cross, and bottle mark, 1 bag of saddlery, 3 casks of wine, and 3 packages'.[46] That same consignment included rations for the Aborigines (forwarded by the Adelaide-based sub-protector of Aborigines, J. H. Biggs), being '1/2 ton seconds flour, 100 lbs sugar, 4 lbs tea, and 5 lbs tobacco', already a diet and addiction foreign to these desert dwellers.[47]

The Kolonisten and schoolteacher, and their wives, managed to keep their small enterprise alive for nearly five years without an ordained missionary. Aboriginal youths and men were trained to assist with the sheep and cattle, and Aboriginal women were engaged in domestic chores. Bucaltaninna became predominantly a sheep station, worked by black labour. Donations towards its operation and maintenance still came from the Lutheran community in the south, at about £1200–£1500 a year, but income was now derived from sheep.[48]

By the mid-1870s the narrow German mission wagon had been abandoned for the standard British version, not only for its trackability, but also for its capacity for the standard two-bale width, the floor of the tray holding the customary eight bales of wool. The Kolonisten at Bucaltaninna had persisted for many years with their special German wagon, shipped to Australia specifically to carry the precious product of the early stock-station ventures. And it took a rather bizarre incident to force the change to the British version. During one busy shearing season the special wool wagon had sat for several days loaded in its awkward fashion and ready for the journey to the port. But Jacob was occupied with other pressing matters at the station. Although it was barely springtime, the traditional shearing season, the sun beat its relentless heat into the hessian-bound wool. On returning from the paddocks one evening the Kolonisten noticed smoke rising from the wagon. Suddenly the entire loaded vehicle burst into flames and in no time had burned to the ground. There was nothing but ashes and hot metal, the result of spontaneous combustion. The shocked Germans no longer had their special wool wagon. They had lost that season's wool clip and the mission income from it.

After recovering from that fateful season, however, Bucaltaninna Station began to prosper. The German Kolonisten, with their methodical procedures and disciplined work, profited by Aboriginal labour and by the Aborigines' intimate knowledge of the countryside. And once during a dry spell, when stations in the neighbouring areas lost some 57 000 head of sheep, all 500 mission sheep survived.[49]

But more often it was a struggle. Drought continually threatened the station's future, the lives of the stock, the numbers of Aborigines that the mission could accommodate, even the lives of the Lutherans themselves. During one lengthy dry period, when the surrounding water soaks had all evaporated, Vogelsang himself came close to perishing. Alone he had driven the station horses to a distant waterhole but the horse he was riding became debilitated from thirst, slowing the journey precariously. Hermann's water-bag quickly emptied. The German became so weak from heat and thirst that he could barely stay in the saddle. Miraculously, both horse and man reached the waterhole. By then, however, Hermann had become so enfeebled that he collapsed as he tried to dismount. When he regained consciousness he found a local Aboriginal woman bending over him, giving him water in her cupped hands.[50]

So severe was the drought of 1876 that it became impossible for Jacob to make the round trip to Port Augusta for food supplies. What had been waterholes along a penetrable track were now simply dry, dusty hollows, rendering the Bucaltaninna group dangerously stranded in a drought-stricken desert. The school was closed and the mission's Aborigines were asked to leave, to seek their own sustenance in the bush. Food resources at the station were perilously low. With their last bit of flour baked into bread, the dismayed group were sitting around an empty table when the sound of grinding and creaking caused a rush to the door. A strange wagon, enveloped in dust, drew to a halt, the wagoner on the verge of collapse from heat and fatigue. He was carrying flour to an isolated station 100 miles further north, and declared he could go no further. He asked whether he could leave the flour there, and would carry it on when conditions improved. When the mission party explained their predicament the wagoner permitted them use of the flour, provided it would later be replaced. To the Lutherans this incident was no less than a miracle, a sign from God that He was indeed protecting them and that they were indeed engaged in His divine work. 'This obvious help of the Lord mightily comforted and strengthened the mission people.'[51]

On New Year's Day 1877 the drought broke. The joyous sound of rain enlivened the desert, at once bringing forth hibernating fauna and causing the mission party to sink to their knees in gratitude. Rain filled waterholes, the wagon was once again despatched for provisions, and the school re-opened. Divine Service resumed on Sundays in makeshift school quarters. During 1877 the flood gushed down from Queensland, filling the great lake system, transforming the surrounding landscape and creating green pastures around Lake Bucaltaninna.

As optimism soared, Bucaltaninna was judged not to be the most suited place for a permanent mission station. There was no firewood and little native food in the area. Lake Killalpaninna was considered a better location. The move back to the original lake, however, had to be postponed for a time. Hermann Vogelsang was going south again, this time to end his widowerhood. The irrepressible Hanovarian was to marry Anna Maria Auricht, a 22-year-old step-sister to the Langmeil church pastor, and daughter of Christian Auricht, who had emigrated to Australia from Posen in the *Prince George* with the first group of Lutheran dissenters.[52] Young Anna Maria had been introduced to Hermann, the 45-year-old widowed laypreacher, on one of his visits to Tanunda. She had agreed to become his wife, for it was her pious duty, and they were married at the Langmeil church. In early September 1877, the second Mrs Vogelsang embarked on the journey to Bucaltaninna to begin her thirty-seven-year crusade in the north.

When Hermann Vogelsang returned to the station as a married man, Meyer, whose health had suffered, went south to seek medical advice. Before he left Bucaltaninna, the first seven Aboriginal pupils allegedly 'applied' for instructions in preparation for baptism (or were deemed ready). Meyer left the school in the care and guidance of Vogelsang. Fortuitously, while Meyer was convalescing in the south, the candidate from Neuendettelsau, Johannes Flierl, arrived in South Australia.

With the arrival of the new missionary came a restructuring and a new beginning for the mission station. Ernst Jacob was exhausted from the physical and mental strain of his nomadic occupation. His spirit was almost broken and he was described as being 'moved to tears of near despondency'.[53] At this point the mission committee relieved him of his position as teamster, appointed Jack Hester (who was later to become mailman along the Birdsville Track), and placed Jacob in charge of the mission's sheep. But just before he began his new job, Jacob travelled to Tanunda to marry the widow Elizabeth Irrgang, an elder sister to Hermann Vogelsang's new wife. Elizabeth had two small sons and three daughters from her first marriage, and she had been widowed for two years.

The couple's 'honeymoon' was spent on the old track to Bucaltaninna, for Jacob one journey that differed vastly from the rest. Elizabeth took her youngest child, Johannes Gustav (later known as 'Jack'), with her, leaving the other children in the care of family members at Tanunda. One morning, when the Jacobs were only two days' journey from the station, and when Ernst was busy hitching horses to the wagon, a party of surveyors with camels passed nearby. Their leader knew Jacob, and when he saw the German and his familiar wagon at a distance he rode across to greet and congratulate him. As the surveyor approached on camel-back, the wagon horses reared and bucked in terror and raced into the distance, for horses have a profound fear of camels. Elizabeth was already seated in the wagon and she (and presumably her small son) disappeared with the terrified horses. She managed to gain her balance and find the reins but by the time the horses could be controlled she was many miles from her husband and completely lost. The countryside was quite unknown to her and the frightened and dismayed woman laid the reins aside to let the horses take the lead, in the hope that they would travel along their familiar route to the mission station. Two days later she did reach Bucaltaninna, her husband not arriving

Left: Hermann Vogelsang and his second wife, Anna Auricht, on their wedding day
Right: Ernst Jacob, with Elizabeth Irrgang and her son, Johannes ('Jack'), probably on their wedding day, 1879

until a full day later. Anxious for the fate of his new bride, Jacob had little choice but to walk the distance to the station, hoping that she would be there safely when he arrived. Jacob said of the incident that 'Even if the Devil himself had congratulated us on the wedding, the outcome could not have been any worse'.[54]

Ernst Jacob and his wife lived in a tent for the first decade of their marriage. Again the quiet German's life was nomadic, moving the sheep from place to place following feed and water. Young Johannes became free-spirited and close to nature and animals. He developed strong bonds with the Diyari children, his only playmates, speaking their language fluently from a very young age. Jacob employed Aboriginal shepherds to assist him and the men camped in family units nearby.

Jacob's family would sleep under the stars on hot, still nights, and the Silesian loved to chart the southern skies, pondering at the wonderment of God's magnificent creation. He developed a considerable knowledge of astronomy after hours of studying the clear, black, celestial spaces hung with bright stars and glistening galaxies. Always sunburnt, tall, and with a short, full beard, Jacob resembled an image of his biblical namesake. Like a Patriarch in the desert he gently tended his flocks, spoke quietly to his Aboriginal shepherds, and led a humble and simple existence while keeping his faith with God. Jacob conducted prayers before evening meals for the Aboriginal shepherds, and followed with Bible stories. He was kind and considerate to his black brethren and they respected and loved him. It is alleged that an English station hand, when he discovered he would not live for long, wanted to be comforted by being close to this warm and gentle, spiritual German. The Englishman moved from further northwards and set up camp near the Jacobs' tent.[55]

When the Jacob family was back at the mission station they would occupy a room in the home of the Vogelsangs. The two sisters had been brought even closer by their isolation and the harsh realities of their irregular life of servitude. It was not until the late 1880s that the Jacobs had a permanent home of their own, the house constructed by Ernst Jacob of rubble masonry at Etadunna waterhole. Its massive 22-inch-thick walls stand to this day as a memorial to permanency at last, and to the workmanship of this dedicated man.

5
Flierl the First

Missionary Johann Conrad Flierl and the schoolteacher Carl Meyer were delayed at the Beltana Hotel on their trip northwards. They had reached this point by post coach and railroad, but their luggage and the mission wagon that was to carry them to the station were delayed in Port Augusta. There were wild bushmen about, and offensive drunks at the hotel, and the new graduate from Neuendettelsau was unimpressed with the inefficiency and prosaic life in the Australian bush. The pace of bush movement, the desolate countryside and the lack of communication and control in these remote parts were awesome new experiences.

Meyer had sufficiently recovered in health and, by resolution of the synod, was solemnly ordained with Flierl. As they travelled northwards, the young graduate observed the dramatic change in landscape, from the 'nice German town' of Tanunda to the brown emptiness around Beltana, 'no longer the beautiful green of the Fatherland'.[1] Flierl became excited at the sight of 'a beautiful lake with clear water', but Meyer simply laughed, for it was a mirage.

Flierl passed the time at Beltana studying the Diyari language. When at last the mission wagon arrived, loaded with provisions from the port, the last section of Flierl's journey to Bucaltaninna began. It was nearing the end of September, springtime and reasonably green for the north. At night the party camped beside small creeks beneath majestic gums. The men slept under the stars, held conversations in three languages (German, English and Diyari), and cooked over a campfire. The young missionary revelled in the outdoor experiences, writing that these Australian meals were 'thoroughly enjoyable, even though all the luxuries of our civilised world are missing'.[2] Flierl preferred to walk beside the wagon rather than endure its discomfort, the better to familiarise himself with waterholes along the way. Dead cattle and sheep lay strewn beside these few water sources, a grim reminder that the countryside was not always so hospitable. The precious liquid was transient, and the carcasses offered cruel warnings that this sole source may not now be fit for human consumption. Nevertheless, to survive, the men and horses were compelled to ignore such threats.

Flierl the First, as he became known, spent seven crucial years at the mission station. With the move back to the shores of Lake Killalpaninna, they were years of solid establishment; of building, both in the physical and the spiritual sense, of instituting mission routine and rules, and a permanent (though fluctuating) Aboriginal community based around the station. Aborigines from a wide area gathered, primarily for rations and protection. Many were landless, homeless, driven (often violently) from their tribal country by uncompromising settlers and foreign, prohibited animals. These 'mission Europeans' never took up guns, although their rigid enforcement of rules and regular work was, for most Aborigines, an unhappy accompaniment to the positive fundamentals of food and protection—a cultural genocide in preference to a potentially physical genocide.

Flierl himself was to experience emotional tensions between compassion, genuine concern and sympathy for the Aborigines, and an abhorrence and despisal of their perceived depraved condition. Flierl admired the Aborigines' survival skills in the desert and their ability to track and to move about, but he understood virtually nothing of their religion and culture during his time in South Australia, nor did he show any interest in or recognition of the existence of such attributes.

Flierl's First Encounter with the Diyari
During Flierl's journey with Jacob and Meyer he met a party of about thirty Diyari camped near the northernmost township of Government Gums (later called Farina). The Germans made an exchange of flour for firewood and clear drinking water. Flierl was fascinated by the Aborigines' 'primitive' lifestyle, and he wrote back to Germany describing their 'leaf' and 'grass' huts, their nightfires to keep away bad spirits, their method of digging their bodies into the sand at night to keep warm, their hospitality and their great passion for smoking tobacco (which was rapidly replacing the chewing of pitjiri, as it was being made so readily available). Flierl described the Diyari's smoking habits as 'charming': the way the mother of the hut would reach for the pipe, light it with a lump of wood carried by the child, inhale with powerful puffs, and then pass the pipe to her husband—a touching family affair! Smoking, according to Flierl, was not as detestable as the popular chewing of pitjiri, customarily carried in a moist chewed lump, rolled in burnt wattle-leaf ashes and stuck behind the ear for safekeeping. From there it was passed from one mouth to another, until it again ended behind the ear of the original passer. The smell of chewed pitjiri was exceedingly unpleasant to the Europeans.[3]

The Diyari were travelling north to their own territory, and the two groups joined for the journey. A 'colourful procession', according to Flierl, trailed around the mission wagon. Some of the Aborigines had acquired pieces of European clothing, but, to the amusement of the Germans, they were not worn in the usual European manner. Women wore men's trousers, 'old greybeards' (male elders) were in women's skirts, and others were traditionally naked. The women carried heavy bundles and provided the daily food by digging for root vegetables. The men went hunting with wooden spears and brought back 'miserable offerings' (according to the missionary), in the form of mice, rats and lizards. As was their community-based custom, the Diyari offered to share their meagre meals with their travelling companions, but the offers (considered too unsavoury by the Germans) were refused. The Germans, however, did exchange flour for swan eggs, which 'tasted quite well'.[4]

On this journey the missionaries were privy to news reports from 'Aboriginal big-speakers' (or 'Walkabout Old Men' as they were called by the Lutherans), information that, according to Flierl, covered 'every little unimportant detail, with an expression in the eyes and a seriousness which would have demanded a more worthwhile cause'.[5] The big-speakers would emphasise each point, moving their whole body with such enthusiasm and conviction that everybody was persuaded to agree with everything said, even, as Flierl put it, 'if one doesn't understand all that much of what he is saying'. Most of the discourse related to seemingly mundane matters (to the Lutherans), such as food. But one 'lecture' concerned a pinya. A tribe in the north was rumoured to be forming a pinya against a member of this band. Great fear struck the members. But as the mission party broke away from the group when they neared Bucaltaninna, the outcome of this drama is unknown.

The Germans reached Bucaltaninna on 17 October 1878 (after a thirty-day trip from Tanunda). Flierl wrote: 'Just as day was nearing an end, to the right I saw a beautiful group of trees. We walked towards them and finally stood on the shores of Lake Bucaltaninna that evening.'[6] Recent rain had filled the lake. The water gleamed darkly as the sun slipped behind sandhills. Between the sanddunes, and surrounded by a group of small trees, stood the mission house, 'somehow looking white on a canal which connected the upper and lower parts

A group of Aborigines dressed in government ration blankets and European clothing

of the lake'. Barking dogs signalled the arrival, and immediately thirty or so spotlessly dressed Aborigines rushed out in greeting. Behind them came the Vogelsang family. That evening the black pupils sang in English. 'So far I like it here very much', wrote Flierl, 'and I hope that the Master will give me strength enough to continue the task for which I have been selected.'[7]

'First Fruits': Aboriginal Baptisms
At Bucaltaninna about fifty Aborigines were attached to the station and several hundred 'camp blacks' lived in huts among the surrounding sand-dunes. Many were Diyari, but there were also many who belonged to neighbouring tribes: Ngamani, Kujani, Wangkangurru, Wonkarapana and others. Most spoke several dialects as, in their adversity, the tribes freely intermixed. The missionaries concentrated only on the Diyari language which, according to Flierl, was not difficult to learn; one could get by with the main words and declined nouns to convey the general message. A translation of the New Testament into simple Diyari began.

On 6 January 1879, less than three months after Flierl's arrival at Bucaltaninna, the first twelve Aborigines were baptised. They were the pupils of the school, whose ages ranged from twelve to twenty years, and who had been prepared in catechism by Vogelsang and Meyer but were awaiting the arrival of the ordained missionary. They were the 'first fruits' of the twelve-year enterprise, solemnised and celebrated on Epiphany Sunday in a makeshift schoolroom under grass thatching. The twelve were scrubbed and neatly clad in European clothing. They were given German, Biblical or English first names, and kept their tribal names as second names. After the ceremony each was given a new English Bible, donated to the Lutherans by the Australian Mission Friends Society. Among the newly converted was a 20-year-old lame man, named (at his baptism) Henry Tipilanna, and his young sister, named Susanna; also Johannes Pingilinna, Godfrey Mildimirana, Benjamin Dulkilla and his wife, Louise, Gustav Tilchiliana, August Mahuliliana, Bernhard Irana, and Bertha, Clara and Rosa. But within months many of the baptised were no longer at the station. Some had returned to their old lifestyle, others had been castigated, and one had been expelled entirely. 'Lame Henry' and a few others, according to German accounts, stayed faithful.

The Move Back to Lake Killalpaninna
In late 1879 the mission station was moved back to the original site on the banks of Lake Killalpaninna, a decision made two years earlier. This was a major meeting place for Aborigines in the north, it had a good supply of native food, and there were local building materials at hand. With the move a serious new beginning was made. The station was renamed Bethesda, for the biblical 'pool of healing'. It was now equipped with an ordained missionary, an ordained schoolteacher and his wife, a stock station manager and blacksmith (Vogelsang) and family, a sheep station manager (Jacob) and family, and a team of Aboriginal station hands and shepherds. It was intended that the station become a substantial and permanent mission station, established to service the Aboriginal communities in the north, and to engage in pastoral enterprise, considered a lucrative activity in the new colony.

Killalpaninna Aborigines making sun-dried bricks from the mud and rushes of the lake bed. Theodore ('Jack') Ruediger is at the windlass

The original structures were renovated and repaired, and much of the lay brethren's time was engaged in constructing new buildings. Financial resources were short, but every advantage was taken of local building materials. There was no stone in the area, but there was wood from the short, stunted trees in the nearby scrub, clay from the lake bed for handmade bricks, rushes and canegrass from the edges of the lake for thatching. With the aid of the Aboriginal men at the station the Germans made hundreds of bricks from clay and chopped reeds, which were dried in the sun. After school the Aboriginal boys, under the supervision of Vogelsang, helped with the building programme. Living quarters for the Germans were the first completed, then for the various categories of mission Aborigines (the married couples, the single female quarters, the single male quarters), followed by the schoolroom and store houses. It was a year before the church was constructed, with the schoolroom serving that function in the meantime.

Sunday, the Lord's Sabbath, was the highlight of the week. A typical Sunday began with the mission staff arising when the sun was still low over the sand-dunes. A hand-bell signalled all Aborigines, those from the mission quarters and those sufficiently interested from the camps, to breakfast. Everybody crowded into the schoolroom, which also served as a dining-room (and church). One Aborigine would be chosen to say a morning prayer, after which everyone would join together in a hymn. This pre-breakfast ceremony was held in Diyari. A few extracts from the New Testament were read and explained, all would kneel while Flierl or Meyer uttered the morning prayer, everyone joined in the Apostolic Faith, there was more praying and singing, and finally breakfast was served.

A morning service held in German for the mission staff followed, then a service in Diyari. The hand-bell was rung again, to call the mission Aborigines, scrubbed and dressed in their Sunday best, and any willing camp Aborigines. The service was conducted by Flierl or Meyer, and concluded with a special message for the day. It was one of three—a morning, an afternoon and an evening service—held each Sunday for the Aborigines. The Lutherans were certainly persistent in these early years, but the Aborigines showed little real interest in Christianity, apart from the material benefits at the mission station.

During the week school-teaching, with its emphasis on religious instruction, occupied Meyer and Flierl, together with translations into Diyari. Like their earlier counterparts, the men struggled with equivalents for European spiritual concepts and words. A school day would begin with a prayer and singing (the only part the Aborigines seemed to enjoy), followed by a religious hour, a little catechism and a Bible story, after which reading, writing and arithmetic seemed to take second place. The pupils varied widely in age, from very young to old, and most did not take their lessons seriously. Very few stayed at the school for long—a couple of months seemed to be the average period—before going 'walkabout'. The task of teaching was further exacerbated by the lack of teaching resources. Eventually the missionaries secured a limited number of teaching booklets (Diyari readers, written by Flierl, and printed in the south) that contained key parts of the Lutheran teaching, and a dozen individual blackboards. But there were too few to distribute to all pupils and only the sick and lame could have their own reader. Under such difficult teaching conditions it was hard for the Lutherans to maintain enthusiasm and dedication. Those pupils who stayed at the school for a time appeared to learn quite well, but eventually they would run away like the rest. When they returned, as many often did, they would have forgotten almost everything learnt and had to begin the lessons all over again.

Flierl described Aboriginal men as lazy, for they could not see the value in 'work' in the same way that the Europeans viewed it. The Aborigine, wrote the missionary, 'lies on his back and dreams most of the time'.[8] For a short time he could be persuaded to attend the school, work on the mission buildings or tend the sheep, but he would soon tire of this and return to his old leisure ways, Flierl complained. The women, he added, were worse, making the lives of the mission wives even more difficult with their unreliability with domestic help. If they were to turn up for domestic duties, they would have an air of restlessness and a miserable expression: 'All they want to do is run around the sand hills and play and have fun'.[9] The Aboriginal men could not be left to their building or station tasks, but had to be supervised constantly, even with shepherding. The Kolonists wasted 'precious time' (a concept of prime importance to the efficient Germans) supervising the pastoral enterprise, while the missionaries themselves,

Ernst Jacob, now manager of sheep enterprises, with his swag and accompanied by two Diyari shepherds, c. early 1880s

although they saw their concerns principally as spiritual, spent needless time supervising matters at the mission headquarters. Aborigines' 'laziness' was considered by the Germans to be the beginning of all evil with these 'heathens'. Training them out of laziness was deemed no small task, and not measurable by the same standards as would apply to Europeans. This laziness the Germans attributed to the Aborigines' poor native diet and to their 'dissolute' way of living. 'Therefore at the beginning we are satisfied with very little progress', wrote Flierl.[10]

The Kolonisten were engaged in continuously supervising working Aborigines. There were now 5000 sheep, 45 cattle, 9 horses and 350 goats to tend.[11] Dingoes constantly ravaged sheep stock and Aborigines helped with their eradication. In 1880 they brought in 233 dingo scalps. Flierl felt that with a limited German staff engaged in constant supervision, and limited ration food and clothing, expansion on either the stock station or with missionary work seemed impossible. Often the mission staff felt they were not making progress on any front.

Despondency enveloped the Lutherans. Flierl wrote: 'Oneself seems to fall into the same kind of common laziness which seems to surround this whole enterprise; a product of the difficulties one continually encounters ... Although one doesn't initially notice it, one seems to fall into the general trot of just doing one's daily work'.[12] And on another occasion: 'We missionaries don't put in a full strength, which is also necessary to overcome the situation'.[13]

It was a frustrating vocation. Aborigines themselves were reluctant, in the eyes of the Germans, to take their new opportunities seriously, using every advantage to slip back into old customs, just as a little progress appeared to have been achieved. Of the nine candidates who began baptism classes in 1879–80, only four were baptised in the late Sunday afternoon two-hour ceremony.

Many of the younger 'converts' returned periodically to camp life, or sneaked away from the station to engage in night-time ceremonies. Perhaps due to the power of persuasion of the pinaru, from fear of tribal punishment, and certainly a confused spiritual viewpoint, these young 'converts' also underwent initiation into their own spiritual culture after (or before) Christian baptism. Young men would have been taken with a pinya party (as traditionally practised), for initiation into the bravery of the expedition and the expected courage of the executed, or from duty if related to a 'victim' of the bone. Perhaps young, newly baptised men would remember the Eucharist, and the blood and body of Christ, as the wooden bowl and executed victim's blood was passed around in the dawning light of a pinya camp for all young initiants to sip. Perhaps young, newly baptised men would silently recollect their first pinya experience as they stood in the mud church at Killalpaninna and sipped from the silver Eucharist Cup solemnly passed along a row of black 'converts'.

Flierl had now mastered the Diyari language, hymns had been translated and sermons were conducted entirely in the indigenous language. The average attendance at Sunday services was about forty-five Aborigines, but numbers could swell to 100 or so, especially during dry periods when native food resources were low. Some came to ensure their ration supply, others for the diversion. On the occasions when many did arrive for the service they crowded into the schoolroom, spilling out of the open doorway and around the building. The room was cramped, hot and humid, and the need for a church became

Johannes Flierl the First with one of his protégés

urgent. In 1880 construction began, with the clay bricks handmade during the cool season.

The first Aboriginal weddings were held in the schoolroom in early 1880, before construction began on the church. Two baptised couples had a full European Christian wedding, with the brides in white, the grooms in tailored

Johannes Pingilinna and his wife, Rosina. Pingilinna, a Diyari man, left his home country to accompany Meyer to Elim Mission Station in Queensland, and to proselytise among the Aboriginal people there. In his absence his wife died

Mud-brick church at Killalpaninna, erected during Flierl the First's period

suits, a best man for each couple, and a congregation of scrubbed mission Aborigines. 'Camp blacks' attended the occasion, no doubt from curiosity, and looking somewhat at odds with their mission compatriots. One was swathed in a woollen blanket, others wore an assortment of clothing, while some were virtually naked. The father of the bride, an old 'greybeard', arrived in just a shirt, his hair and beard smeared hard with white ochre, a sign of mourning the recent death of his wife. The service was held in Diyari and German, with Flierl officiating. One of the German wives became alarmed when she noticed a green lump behind the ear of one of the bridegrooms. As she watched, a green fluid trickled down the man's neck and cheek, and she whispered to her husband, enquiring as to the nature of the 'growth'. He smiled as he quietly explained the habit of pitjiri chewing.[14]

At the solemn ceremony Flierl emphasised the monogamous duties of married Christian couples, of Christian morality (in the hope that the old permissive customs would be laid aside), and the couples signed registry papers (European legal custom quite foreign to these people), presumably in the script taught to them in the school. The legal papers were then sent with the next mailcoach to the appropriate government department in Adelaide. A celebration with cake and wine followed. Flierl, however, was to ungraciously describe the day, to his counterparts in Germany, as a 'miserable occasion', and in a wave of depression wrote: 'Their (the Aborigines') bottomless depravity, the Devil and the bad people who call themselves Christians (the local wild, white bushmen) seem to hope with all their might that we will fail in our task. Sometimes I am fearful as to whether the Good Lord is still with us.'[15]

As the mud-bricks for the church lay drying in the sun an appeal for financial assistance was sent to Germany by Reichner. The result was a donation of 4000 German marks, together with gifts of German altar-cloths and communion vessels.[16] As the site for the sacred building was being prepared at the top of a sand-dune, a human skeleton was unearthed while the foundations were being dug. 'So', wrote Flierl, 'the church will be above the grave of a heathen.'[17]

Mission Aborigines, under the supervision of Hermann Vogelsang, began laying bricks but, as they had no concept of building a European structure, everything again had to be supervised. It took months for even the basic structure to take shape, but on Sunday 11 April the church was consecrated for use. It stood 50 feet long, 15 feet wide and 12 feet in height from packed lime floor to wooden ceiling. Seven windows directed light into a mud-brick interior and lit a German altar, decorated with crucifix and lights, sent by mission friends in Bavaria. The roof was galvanised iron, covered with cane thatch for coolness. A bell tower 40 feet high was its distinguishing feature, and became, from a distance, the first visible sighting of the mission station. Inside, church seating was divided between that for converted Aborigines and for those who were still pupils of the catechism. Renewed enthusiasm followed the consecration of a proper house of worship at last. But still missionary progress was painfully slow and success in conversion abysmally small. Flierl and Meyer would regularly visit the camps nearby to preach and attempt to teach, but with little success.

Flierl's First Trip (1881); the Possibility of Outstations
Perhaps the establishment of outstations might be the answer, with the missionaries travelling out to the Aborigines to either preach to them on their home territory or to persuade them to come back to the station? Perhaps they would respond better to regular servicing at their tribal grounds? To test these theories and to make some assessment of the numbers in the surrounding district, Flierl, in July 1881, with an Aboriginal guide and two horses, embarked on a survey of the country and its occupants beyond lakes Kopperamanna and Hope, through the region of the Perigundi people. It was the cool season, floodwaters had recently come down from the Cooper, and the Aboriginal population was expected to be at its peak. There was no better time for such a survey, yet the journey was not successful.

Contrary to expectation, the pair saw very few Aborigines between the mission station and the country of the Wangkangurru. While journeying north-west they met an Aboriginal family with two small daughters, and Flierl managed to 'enrol' the girls for the mission school. Near Salt Creek they were led to a large camp of Wangkangurru celebrating initiation rites. At Salt Creek the river was swollen and the large gums gave shelter to two camps that faced each other across the water. As Flierl approached he could see the Aborigines setting nets to catch fish. He spoke to each group about the new religion and his desire to take a few of their young people back to the mission. Gravely the elders held council, and four young boys, between the ages of ten and twelve years, were chosen to accompany the German. Initiation was very much in the minds of these people, and perhaps the 'new religion' was a special kind of magic that might be unwise to ignore. Perhaps they sent the boys as a gesture of goodwill and friendship, to stave off violence from these foreigners. The boys were given jam (a luxury obtained from a nearby station) and firewood by their people, and sufficient clothing to cover their offending body parts by Flierl. At sunset the band set out for the mission station.

On the second day, however, just as the party was packing provisions obtained from a local station (five loaves of bread and half a sheep), one Wangkangurru boy announced he had to return to his tribe as his lubra would be crying too much. Flierl could not believe that such a young boy, 'with barely a hint of a beard' could possibly have a wife or lover.[18] He could do nothing to prevent the boy from leaving. Suddenly two others leapt to their feet and fled with him. Flierl was forced to journey back to the mission station with what was left of his meagre 'gathering', two little girls (one bitterly unhappy) and one youth.

Impressions of the Aborigines
Tired and disillusioned, Flierl took a rest in the south soon after his 1881 journey of unsuccessful proselytising. His sympathy for, and comprehension of, Australian Aborigines was perhaps at its lowest point. In his assessment they were the 'lowest of all primitive peoples'. 'Most "natural" people have at least some kind of ethical standard', he reported to the Germans of the Barossa Valley, and wrote back to Germany:

> but among these heathens there are no ethics or morality at all. They have shrunk to the levels of animals, to the lowest levels possible. Unlike other civilisations, like the Indians or the ancient Greeks or Romans, who actually philosophised about the purpose of mankind and the nature of being, and managed to produce something that would last, the people here don't know anything about a steady or orderly life ... Of the sanctity of marriage and women, the honour of virgins, which means something to the wandering Indians of North America, those depraved people (the Aborigines of Australia) have no idea at all. Like the animals of the fields they run around naked, build their huts where ever they find their miserable food, and then they continue their wanderings. To satisfy their animal-like love seems to be their only purpose in life, otherwise they do not know, or demand, anything else. Their whole life centres around eating, drinking, sleeping, dancing and associated things. These blacks are people who only live for the moment, and have no concept of the past and no concept or hope for the future. There is no trace of a deeper meaning to life, no folk lore, no sages, no remainders of the stories of the past, or ancestors.[19]

Flierl was now fluent in the Diyari language, had spent three years with these people and this was the impression he had formed. A product of nineteenth-century cultural and religious xenophobia, the German went on to report: 'They see life on this earth, and they regard their own lives as never-ending. Although they see death all around them all the time . . . they nevertheless continue to argue strictly that they never have to die.' He had heard of the 'Muramura'—'about whom or whatever I can't find much'—thought they resided in old gum trees, and that the Aborigines believed they made humans out of clay. He understood the equivalent of the Devil to be the kutchie, that spirit which was greatly feared. 'Of false idols our black people know nothing. They put themselves in the place of God . . . The black people claim that they are in charge of rain and wind, frost and heat, animals and plants and birds, and illness and death: in charge of those things themselves!'[20]

Flierl acknowledged that the Aborigines had a large number of 'secrets and reminiscences and rather strange habits, most of which are somehow connected with immortality', and that he knew little about this side of their lives. But he simply dismissed what he did not know with the qualification that 'The things that happen secretly are normally Immoral'. His reports to his fellow Germans (both in Europe and South Australia) served to reinforce the current European notions of Aborigines being so 'primitive' as to be without religion, and shed little new light on a people not encountered by Europeans before. Flierl was a religious fundamentalist, incurious about other cultures, a staunch evangelist by character. He spent the major part of his life among indigenous, tribal people while engaged in missionary work, yet throughout his writings from Australia he shows almost nothing learned from the Aboriginal people, nor any real understanding of their culture.

While Flierl was in the south in 1881 he received letters from a few of his 'converted' Aborigines at the mission, including one from Henry Tipilanna, 'Lame Henry' of the first baptismal group. The letters were a source of great excitement in the south, and were duly sent on to Germany. Perhaps the years of struggle had not been quite in vain; a new glimmer of hope tantalised. 'Lame Henry' had written, humbly and affectionately, that he regarded himself as the 'younger brother' of Johann Flierl. Now that he was a baptised Christian he regarded the esteemed missionary as his 'neyi' (older, hence more important, brother), with himself in the lesser role of 'ngadada' (younger brother who had a great respect for the older). As they both now belonged to the same religion, the same cult totem or Dreaming spirit in his understanding of Christianity, he consequently considered himself a 'spiritual brother' to the German. Lame Henry's affiliation with the missionary was perceived somewhat differently by the Germans in the south, where his desperate plight and Christian yearning were taken as a positive sign of both need and success.[21]

The following extract was published in the Neuendettelsau mission journal of 1882:

> I am now sitting in the school and haven't achieved much good. It seems to be difficult to do well in the school and although you always admonish us, we don't seem to succeed. I now ask you to tell the people far away to teach us about our sins. Only a few of us are really happy ... On the birthday of Master Jesus I was very sad. I was sitting in the opening in front of the church and looking up at the cross and was crying with desire. As the day progressed I didn't become any happier and didn't go to the Holy Sacrament. At night we were all at church. Teacher Meyer gave us this word of love and made us at last happy, and we felt a little better.

Henry's agonising letter, written in mission Diyari by a Christian Aborigine, together with another to the South Australian committee a year later by a young Aboriginal mission girl named Rosalee, and the visit to the Barossa community of Meyer accompanied by a baptised Aboriginal husband and wife, gave a new impetus to the flagging enterprise. The Aboriginal couple stayed in the Barossa for several weeks, a public display of the successes in the north. The German community was pleased with their quiet and humble behaviour. They were impressed with their heart-rending hymn-singing in church, and touched by the husband's solo hymns in his own language.

1882 Visit from the Mission Committee
As a result of these successes the mission committee sent an inspection party, in July 1882, to investigate the situation at Killalpaninna. The gentlemen, including the committee's president, travelled on the new railroad to Farina (previously Government Gums). The journey was now easier and swifter thus far. Apart from a deputation sent to divide assets in 1875, this was the first inspection of the station by the controlling committee. They were met at Farina by Flierl and embarked on a seven-day journey, on horseback and on foot, to the mission station.

This part of the journey was also vastly improved, as the South Australian government had recently completed a rough road between the northernmost township of Herrgott Springs (now Marree) and the settlement of Birdsville in Queensland, and had sunk some thirty artesian wells along its route. This embryonic Birdsville Track was constructed primarily to assist development in the north, allowing drovers from Queensland and from the north-eastern corner of South Australia to bring their cattle to the stock markets in Adelaide more reliably. The wells were sunk to 3000 feet, tapping the Great Artesian Basin that spread beneath the desert interior. And although water reached the surface at very high temperatures, it was drinkable, even for humans. The closest well to Bethesda was the Kopperamanna Bore, which now provided a regular and reliable water source to the mission station. With these artesian wells an unlimited amount of water became available. And with the new railhead at Farina the mission supply wagon now collected from that point and was no longer forced to make the long journeys to Port Augusta. Farina became a substantial service town of stone structures. But just two years later the railroad was extended to Herrgott Springs, giving that town greater importance, as the most northerly point able to be reached by rail. This further shortened the distance for the mission supply wagon. For thirty years the township of Herrgott Springs served as the closest point of civilisation and human contact for the mission personnel, apart from neighbouring cattle stations.

In July 1882 the tired, dusty inspection party at last sighted the bell-tower of the mission church. They were greeted by an enthusiastic hymn from the mission Aborigines, rested at their quarters, and then taken on a tour of inspection of the entire station lasting three weeks. Each of the mission buildings was assessed, the gentlemen watched thirty pupils at work in the schoolroom, examined their exercise books, listened to their singing (from 'those rough and uneducated mouths'), attended the Sunday services at the church, and explored the mission country. One committee member presented an Aboriginal pupil named Gottfried, who had distinguished himself by being both baptised and able to take the class for a spelling lesson, with a black overcoat. Gottfried was told he could wear it to church on Sundays.[22]

The party dined communally, with about thirty mission Aborigines, on bread, meat and tea in the mission dining-room, and were impressed to see those 'former heathens' kneeling and thanking the Lord for their supper. They noted a 'pronounced difference' between the mission Aborigines and 'those wild camp blacks who attended the Sunday services'. A head count showed seventy-seven 'camp blacks' at one service, a pleasing number for the controlling body. After another Sunday service, Reichner handed out gifts to the Aborigines present, on affirmation that their lives were now enriched by the Christian religion, 'that they had been lifted from the dust', and that they promise very truly to stay faithful to the mission station forever. According to Reichner, in his report to Germany, some blacks could not stop the tears.[23]

The inspectors were impressed with what they saw. Perhaps it would be necessary to send more missionary personnel, particularly urgent for those Aborigines at Salt Creek (too far away to be serviced from Killalpaninna) and at the Diamentina River in Queensland, where it was rumoured Aborigines were receiving inhuman treatment from European settlers. Reichner reported to Neuendettelsau: 'Mission friends, all the work has not been in vain, and many poor heathen souls will be eternally indebted for the love shown to them'. A month later another 3000 German marks arrived at the mission board in the Barossa to assist the Bethesda project.[24]

Only one incident marred the visit. A young black mission girl, on an errand to the 'camp blacks' for Meyer's wife, returned clasping her bloodied head. She had been 'molested', reported Reichner, by a young man from the camp because she had refused to become his wife, or even to have sexual relations with him (she had possibly been betrothed to him many years earlier, perhaps as a newborn). The molester was found, brought to the station, punished (the method being undocumented), and then released. Soon after the inspection party returned to the south they received a letter from a young Aboriginal girl called Rosalee (sometimes spelt 'Rosalie'), possibly the same girl.[25] The letter was probably initiated by the mission staff as a social convention of gratitude, and as a propaganda exercise.

Flierl's Marriage

From mid-1882 Missionary Flierl had urgently to complete the construction of his own partly built house at Bethesda. He was to be married in late 1882 and, as confidence and optimism had increased regarding mission work, he wanted his new wife to settle contentedly at the station. At Tanunda he married Luise Auricht, another daughter of Pastor Christian Auricht of Tanunda, and halfsister to Elizabeth Jacob and Anna Vogelsang. No doubt Luise Auricht was no stranger to mission work in the north of the colony.

The newlyweds spent their honeymoon travelling northwards towards Killalpaninna. An overnight rest at the hotel at Farina gave the new Mrs Flierl her first encounter with a 'dirty bush pub' and 'rough bush people'. So dirty and uncomfortable did the Germans find their room that they slept for only a few hours, lying fully dressed on the filthy beds.[26] They were met at Farina by the 'faithful' mission black, Joseph Enchilina, with horses and a light carriage. Joseph led the way to Killalpaninna on horseback and Flierl drove the carriage. By the second day Luise was suffering from the dry desert air and becoming excessively tired. It was late spring, dry, with a foretaste of summer heat. She slept for most of the time in the carriage, the endless, brown, flat miles seemingly stretching to infinity. Cameltrains, loaded with baled wool and led by turbanned Afghans, passed unobserved by the missionary's wife. On the second

Horse-drawn mission wagon in which the new wives of the mission staff travelled northwards to the station

day Flierl sent Joseph ahead to look for water, but he returned without any. There had been so little recent rain that the regularly used waterholes had dried out. The horses were quietening with thirst as the small party continued over a white, stony desert, the sun burning from a cloudless sky and the air searing with heat. There were no artesian wells this far south. Mirages danced teasingly, creating beautiful lakes on distant horizons that disappeared as soon as they were almost reached. The new Mrs Flierl sat passively under the carriage's cover, beside her husband, no doubt wondering at her life ahead. The north was already facing a potential summer crisis.

Suddenly Joseph appeared in front of the carriage, beaming broadly. 'He's found water', shouted Flierl. Jacob's sharp eyes had spotted a dismal puddle in a creekbed, left from a recent shower of rain. Small holes in dry, hard-baked creek depressions could sometimes carry water for several days, whereas large holes were quickly exhausted by animals. And beside such large holes the party had already seen and smelt the decomposing carcasses of the native animals that had come too late. What little water might be left in these larger holes was quite undrinkable by humans. Flierl carefully filled waterbottles with the brown liquid before allowing the horses to quench their thirst. It was two more full days' travel before the party would reach the first well, and Flierl doubted whether the horses would make the distance. He was well aware that not all travellers were this fortunate; that hardly a summer passed when somebody did not die of thirst out there.

Luise Flierl was being introduced to the harsh realities of life in the north of the colony. The brown water was boiled over a campfire and added to coffee beans to make it palatable and 'hygienic'. Flierl believed that coffee beans killed the germs in stagnant water, and not the boiling of the water.[27] Typhoid was a common infection in the Australian bush in the nineteenth century, but the mode of transmission of the germ was not understood at that time.

On arrival at the mission station the missionary's wife was welcomed by the women there, both black and white. Rebecca, whose husband Joseph had been Flierl's guide, took a special interest and pride in the new white woman. Luise walked through her new home of three modest mud-brick rooms. The walls were uneven due to the small crooked branches of the Cooper trees from which the framework was constructed, the roof was a rough thatch of rushes from the nearby lake. The house looked like a peasant house from deep rural Germany. She gazed out over the surrounding sandhills and stumpy growth to the lake beyond. It was late spring, almost early summer, and the lake was still full of water. These were considered the good times, for the flooding occurred only once in every five to ten years.

Indeed, when Lake Killalpaninna was filled with water, the area abounded with waterbirds and wildlife, and the mission was filled with an air of vibrancy. Black swans bred in the rushes at the lake's edges, hundreds of pelicans swarmed into the area scooping fish from the lake in their enormous bills. The cacophony of birdcries disturbed mission activity, and the abundance of wildlife distracted the mission Aborigines. Camp Aborigines spent their days fishing with nets made from rushes, selling the surplus of their catch to the mission station. The Germans took moonlight swims in the lake, and boating became a romantic pastime.

But as water began to evaporate, with the passing of long, hot summer days, the liquid became brackish and insalubrious. Fish died, birds migrated and animals departed. The lake became a smelly salt sump filled with the odour of decay. Hundreds of fish lay dead in the salt pools, and wild animals, hoping for a final thirst-quenching lap, became stuck in the deep muddy edges and slowly died. The centre of the lake was half a mile from the station, generally far enough for the stench not to offend. But when the desert winds blew from the west a sickly decaying smell hung in the air at Killalpaninna.

During the summer months hot winds would whip the air like the blast from a furnace, and sandstorms darkened the sky, sometimes for days, leaving an aftermath of sweeping and cleaning that occupied everybody. At such times life at the mission station could be miserable. But on clear, cool days the desert air was euphoric, and the brilliant orange-magenta sunsets exhilarating.

The new Mrs Flierl, having arrived at the station at the beginning of summer, 'had to pay the usual price to enter the desert'. With the sunlight at its strongest and the wind blowing sand, she suffered the pain of swollen, festering eyes, unable to be opened, and the sitting for days in a darkened room. Her fear of blindness was so strong that, with so much crying, the salt tears flushed away the debris and her condition improved. Luise soon acclimatised, familiarised herself with the Diyari language, and became an influence at the mission station. On the verandah of her house she taught the Aboriginal women to sew, with shirts for the black workers the first items to be produced. The black women were taught the arts of domestic science, but were unhappy and uncomfortable

The house of Flierl the First and his wife at Killalpaninna

in their bondage. They were dressed like 'decent' European domestics, in sleeved, long, floral dresses covered by a full apron, their hair neatly tucked beneath a scarf. Instructed in the correct demeanour for their new position within mission society, they were expected to assist the mission wives. But as the German women complained that their own domestic tasks took twice as long after explanation, instruction and supervision, they preferred to do their own housework and baking. Consequently the black mission women were often bored, filling their days at the schoolroom, spasmodically attempting lessons, or visiting the Aboriginal camps, which was strongly discouraged by the missionaries.

Flierl's Second Journey, 1883

In the early 1880s there were approximately fifty Aborigines living at Killalpaninna, with about fifty 'camp blacks' living nearby in traditional shelters. The male mission Aborigines were employed in manual labour at the station: shepherding, building, repairing, shearing. Unlike most 'employed' Aboriginal station hands in the area, at least some were paid wages (albeit meagre). However, during 1883–84 there was almost no rain in the north of the colony. It was a very trying year, with Flierl writing:

It is really surprising how the poor Aboriginals are able to exist; therefore the stores from the Government have been very beneficial to the old people among them. A great many old people have been on the station, and were glad to receive rations from the Government, which they were greatly in need of, and I am most certain that if they can be supplied with rations regularly, they will prefer staying here than roam about as they did in former years.[28]

By 1884 there were twenty ration depots in the Far North: fourteen at stock stations, four at police stations and two at mission stations (Hermannsburg, and Killalpaninna). But not all stock stations had ration depots, and in 1888 one hungry group of Aborigines passed through Coondambo Station, stopping briefly to kill some of the station sheep. 'But', as the sub-protector of Aborigines reported, 'they must kill sheep or starve as there is no living thing for them to hunt.'[29]

During this dry period the German botanist and patron of exploration in Australia, Baron Ferdinand von Mueller, who lived in Melbourne, sent Flierl experimental seeds for cereal-growing, but the missionary responded with: 'I am sorry I have to state that this last year we had not sufficient rain to make any experiments ... The rainfall has only been sufficient to make the necessary feed grow'.[30]

However, the notion that the establishment of mission outstations might be the solution to proselytising persisted, and after the inspection party's favourable report to Germany it was agreed that another missionary would be sent from Neuendettelsau. One of the missionaries at Killalpaninna would then be freed to establish 'interior branch missions'. Although Flierl's 1881 attempt failed, he made a second journey into the desert in 1883, this time with the intention of reconnoitring for the establishment of branch missions. 'There are also a good number of natives further north who live on friendly terms with those down here, but as they prefer to live in their own country I think it would be better for them if the mission work could be extended to them', he wrote in a report to the committee.[31]

On the first trip Flierl had travelled up the Cooper east of Lake Hope to Lake Perigundi, and from there had journeyed northwards to Salt Creek, before returning south to the mission station. Part of the purpose in going so far northwards was to observe the oncoming flood, as word had reached the mission station that the floodwaters were on their way southwards, and none of the mission personnel had yet experienced this phenomenon. At Lake Hope Flierl had watched in fascination as muddy, yellow floodwater streamed into the dry, salt-white lake bed, the level rising silently among naked sandhills. On this journey he observed endless miles of creeks and lake beds filling from a seemingly inexhaustible source. The realisation dawned as to the volume of water required before Lake Killalpaninna began to fill, the head of the great wall of water entering it through a straight canal between sandhills.

Unused to riding horses, and more accustomed to the German practice of walking alongside packhorses, Flierl had taken many weeks to make the first journey. His elderly Aboriginal guide, Benjamin Dulkilinna, knew the country to the east, and without him the German would have become hopelessly lost in the maze of bends and sandhills. Although Benjamin was unhappy about the tedium of walking instead of riding, he was bound to the German's reduced pace, for Flierl could barely ride. The missionary came to depend almost desperately on his Aboriginal guide, and once, after a nightmare in which Flierl dreamt that the horses had become stuck in a muddy sea, he awoke bathed in sweat and fear. Unable to find Benjamin in the dark silence he panicked and unhobbled the horses, fearing the premonition. They ran away, and in terror he lit bushes, in an attempt to see, and screamed for his black guide. Benjamin was asleep nearby, and awoke, unimpressed by the German's foolishness and panic. The Aborigine managed to retrieve the runaway horses next morning, and the pair continued their journey to Salt Creek.

After leaving the floodwaters the slow journey on foot created water shortage problems, and the men suffered dehydration. Flierl became so ill that Benjamin suggested he rest beneath a small shady bush while he rode off in search of water. But the missionary stubbornly refused, perhaps afraid that the Aborigine might abandon him. The pair were fortunate to reach a grazier's station alive. Flierl was badly dehydrated, but his guide recovered quickly. The missionary was to write: 'Especially valuable in the natives here is their fine sense of observance, through which they are the best trackers in the world and extremely valuable companions for the whites in the Dessert [sic] and wilderness'.[32]

Flierl attributed the failure of his first proselytising trip to an abundance of native food at the time. With recent flooding the Aborigines had been uninterested in moving to some other place when they considered themselves already in a veritable Garden of Eden. Wildlife was plentiful, and it was on this trip that Flierl experienced at first hand the killing of birds with the boomerang, 'a strangely shaped piece of wood which they throw in a very skilful way'.[33] The young girl that Flierl had brought to the mission station after his first journey attended the mission school for several years and was later baptised as 'Anna'. But her parents soon left the station to live with the camp blacks nearby. As a baptismal candidate, Anna may well have been psychologically compelled to stay on at the station. She was later married to a young Christian Aborigine, Timotheus Maltilinna, and they became a 'reliable couple' at the station.

Timotheus had already worked on cattle stations in the area before arriving at the mission station at the age of sixteen. A well-built, strong young man, he was well liked by the Germans for he was perceived as being ambitious in the European sense. His native Wangkangurru name was considered unpronounceable, so the Germans renamed him Maltilinna (a Diyari name meaning 'the gentle'), with the Christian name of Timotheus.[34] Timotheus was a good scholar, an eager workman and was described as 'docile'. He brought skills from his employment on cattle stations—repairing saddles, harnessing and breaking horses, and droving. He was also considered a good influence on other Aborigines at the station, for 'he was practically the only one who gave no reason for complaint'. He was multilingual, speaking Diyari and English as well as his native Wangkangurru, and was considered intelligent, with initiative, for he soon asked for baptismal instruction. Flierl took Timotheus with him on a reconnaisance trip westwards, using this opportunity to give him further Christian instruction. 'In the long evenings in the small calico tent, by candlelight, the candle stuck in a tin, we read the english [sic] Bible, and he absorbed all explanations thankfully and eargerly [sic]. One could be a friend and companion to him without any disadvantage.'[35] Timotheus Maltilinna soon became a shining example of success at the station, with Flierl sending back to Germany a glowing description and account of this Aboriginal youth.

But the wedding of Timotheus and Anna was fraught with drama. The Lutherans had begun using a traditional custom, arranging marriages between young mission Aborigines, to keep them from straying back to their old ways, and to strengthen the bond with the mission station. In this case, the initiation necessary before marriage was baptism. And in October 1884 the mission community prepared to celebrate a double, black, Christian wedding, between Elias and Sarah, and Timotheus and Anna, all baptised Aborigines. However, among the people at the camps intense opposition arose to the proposed mission marriage of Timotheus and Anna. The couple belonged to the same group (either moiety or mardu), hence marriage between them was forbidden by Aboriginal law. Furthermore, Anna had been promised to a much older Wangkangurru man (a pinaru) from Salt Creek. The young Aboriginal couple, however, were told by the Germans that there was no reason for their not marrying, as they were not blood related in the European sense, and wedding plans were urged to proceed. The camp blacks were outraged, and Anna's parents snatched their daughter from the mission station. But the young girl escaped and the double wedding ceremony took place peaceably in the mission church. 'With this happy wedding an old bad custom of the natives was undermined', wrote a satisfied Flierl.[36] The couple lived in a small verandah enclosure adjoining Flierl's house, and later moved into a two-roomed house beside that of the missionary.

Flierl's second journey northwards occurred a year before the marriage of Timotheus and Anna. The German had learnt to ride a horse by now, and he carefully selected his Aboriginal guides, Elias Palkilinna, a young Diyari man, and a Wangkangurru man named Nathanael Ninpilinna.[37] (These men were obviously baptised mission people, as evidenced by their biblical first names, and initiated traditionally, as evidenced by the ending of their second names.) Flierl planned to travel as far as the Herbert River, for a branch station was now proposed within Queensland following concern over the plight of the Queensland Aborigines. Some European pastoralists had determined their own solution to the spearing of their stock, or simply the 'Aboriginal problem', by massacres planned to coincide with known large gatherings of Aboriginal people, and several had occurred at the north-eastern corner of South Australia and into Queensland.[38] Flierl's own guides on this journey had related how their people had been run off their land, some taking revenge—probably killing stock—which resulted in the reprisal massacre. And one still night, as the trio were camped in a small hollow on the great stony plains of the Simpson Desert north of Birdsville, Ninpilinna sang Flierl a sad lament about the massacre of his people who had lived nearby, and of how he had narrowly escaped. Just before the trio reached the Diamentina and Herbert rivers, 'a Sub-Inspector L. of that area' had passed through a stretch of over 100 miles of that same country with his trackers: 'We hardly saw one Aborigine, only a few in the service of whites. Only in the west near the South Australian border a few thin boys were looking for yams in the sand. They introduced themselves in Wonkungurru [sic] . . . "Antas mulu julku!" (We both are sand hillers!).'[39]

It was evident that Killalpaninna had become a focus and a sanctuary for Aborigines in the north-eastern corner, their entire population now estimated at

Timotheus Maltilinna (Merrick) with his wife, Anna, and their children

no more than 1000 or so. But with so few encountered on the journey into Queensland, a second station in that area appeared excessive.

On the way to Salt Creek, Flierl and his Aboriginal guides were forced to rest one of the horses that was in pain with a pack-saddle irritation. Flierl then foolishly left his guides to travel alone for a few days. On the second day he became hopelessly lost in countryside that had, to an untrained eye, no distinguishing features. When the German finally confronted his perilous predicament it was midday, scorchingly hot, and his waterbag was empty. Flierl was well aware that a man could quickly die of dehydration and sunstroke in these conditions. But, like a miracle, there appeared in front of him 'a couple of black boys who were searching for "Jewa", a small edible bulb dug from the ground'. They took the German back to their group of about thirty Aborigines camped nearby. Flierl had only a vague recollection of where his own camp was situated, but the next day two men led him safely back to Ninpilinna and Palkilinna. He later wrote that:

> Our newly found friends proved themselves honest and noble. I promised myself never again to go into a strange district without a native leader, or at least travel

along a plain track. This of course applies to any white person in the wild north. Yes, unexelled [sic] path-finders and trackers are our Australian natives and already on this account worth to be looked after by the Government and the settler. Many a white person has been saved by them especially from dying of thirst and much more good could be done by them if people would thankfully procure their services in this large dessert [sic] country of Central Australia. They can identify footprints of small and large wild animals and also tell cattle, sheep and horses also humans and vehicles, as well as being able to tell if these are old or new, from today or yesterday, they also have endurance and patience to find cattle which have gone astray. They distinguish markings which we would not recognise.[40]

The second journey was expected to take six weeks. With five horses and good camping equipment the party had set out in the cool season of 1883. They travelled north-eastwards to Salt Creek, from there to a cattle station named Berlin, and then journeyed northwards to the junction of the Diamentina and Herbert rivers.

After purchasing flour from a local station (at the exorbitant price of one shilling a pound), the party turned east and crossed into the Great Stony Desert, described by Flierl as a 'particularly hapless desert with small red stones, and so lacks fodder and wood that for days one didn't find anything thicker than a finger'.[41] The men were forced to cook with dried cattle dung as fuel. They had, as yet, seen very few Aborigines, and between the Great Stony Desert and the Queensland border there was just one more cattle station, and no Aboriginal people at all. In Birdsville, described as consisting mainly of a hotel and store where prices were 'sky high', Flierl also saw very few Aborigines. The party travelled north-west from Birdsville to the Mulligan River (source of the famed pitjiri), but still very few Aborigines were encountered. Despondent, Flierl returned to Bethesda Station.

Arrival of Flierl the Second
Meanwhile the new missionary from Neuendettelsau, a cousin to the senior Johann Flierl, was on the high seas bound for Australia. 'Flierl the Second', as he became known, or simply John Flierl, arrived at Killalpaninna in October 1883, at the beginning of summer. Like most of his compatriots he was initiated into life at the desert mission station with the eye infection that tormented every summer season, with the summer of 1883–84 particularly hot and trying. A scorching wind blew sand for days, and the nights were stiflingly hot and still, so that the Germans were forced to sleep outdoors to gain relief from the slightest cool breeze. They would pull small iron beds onto the verandahs and fall exhausted upon a cotton mattress. There had been no effective rainfall for a year, and the sheep and cattle were suffering. Young Flierl wrote: 'The heart of the Aborigines here seems to be dry and hard just like the country they live in'.[42]

John Flierl became schoolteacher to eighteen black pupils, many of whom had already attended in the past but had run away to go walkabout. Undoubtedly many had a smattering of the German language by now, but certainly the new missionary had to learn the Diyari language as quickly as possible. School lessons were conducted each morning between 9 and 12, five days a week.

On first encounter Flierl the Second took an interest in Aboriginal customs, although this was more a fascination with sexual freedom and polygamous practices, particularly those of old men possessing several young wives while the young men were left with old women. But he soon followed convention, adopting the mission's stance and stereotyped interpretations, such as relating these sexual practices to the Aborigines' depraved state, of their having no 'higher God', of their superstitions and bedevilment. His early descriptions quickly duplicated, almost word for word, those of his older cousin. He wrote back to Neuendettelsau that the Aborigines: 'live in the depths of the sins of the flesh, without a God, without hope . . . almost like animals in their rawness, with no past and no future . . .'[43]

By 1884 Killalpaninna had matured into a community in its own right. The nearest service town was the railhead centre of Herrgott Springs about 105 miles to the south. Although Killalpaninna was primarily a centre for Aboriginal 'care', both spiritual and physical, the mission station personnel and settlers in the area interacted over joint stock problems, water shortages, the use of the Kopperamanna bore and the hiring of trained black mission workers, whether they be skilled Aboriginal shearers, black drovers and station hands, or black women trained as domestics at the mission and in demand to assist station wives. The mission Aborigines had their own black cook, a young woman baptised during the winter of 1883. There were now eighteen buildings at the station: a church, 3 houses for mission personnel, 2 stores, a school, 2 dormitories for the Aboriginal children (one for girls and one for boys), a baking house, a dining house, 3 individual houses for black couples, a separate large house of 6 rooms for Aboriginal couples (only recently completed), a smithy, a saddlery and a couple of sheds. All the structures were of clay and wood, with roofs of galvanised iron. Aborigines living at the mission had increased to approximately seventy, with another seventy camp blacks living nearby. During the cool season of 1884 more buildings were to be constructed. In need of permanent dwellings were married, baptised, Aboriginal couples who still lived in tents. The construction of a mortuary was also planned. Aborigines from wider parts came within radius of the mission station as the 1880s moved forward and European settlement in the interior progressed.

But with all this apparent success, by early 1884 only twenty-two Aborigines had been baptised. Many who had begun instruction never completed it: 'If only God would give the black people steadfastness', wrote the senior Flierl. Of the nineteen candidates beginning the 1883 classes (6 had already been previous candidates) only eleven endured.[44] And of the twenty-four now baptised (15 adults and 9 children), seven had died by 1884 (5 adults and 2 children), for those who submitted to baptism were predominantly the sick and the elderly. But the Lutherans clung to fervent hope. Lame Henry, veteran of the 1879 'first fruits', was considered an exemplar of the potential for Christianity that the Aborigines may have. He had embraced and remained faithful to the new religion, providing an abiding support to the black Christian community. Aborigines would gather around him to listen to his Bible stories. Together with other converted Aborigines he would visit the camp blacks with the missionaries and assist in the preaching among the heathens. The old 'greybeards', however, sitting placidly outside their wurlies, would listen calmly and incredulously before moving quietly away to engage in fishing or hunting, leaving the enthusiasts vexed and disappointed.

Towards the end of 1884 Lame Henry's health deteriorated and in early 1885 he died. It was a sorry loss for the Germans. He died just two weeks before the death of another successful black convert, Simeon, who was also sick, but, unlike Henry, was an old man. Lame Henry's death was not documented in any detail, but that of Simeon was. Ill when he came to the mission, Simeon quickly embraced Christianity, and was carried to his baptismal ceremony in a specially prepared chair. A month later he died 'triumphantly', having claimed to have seen a vision of the Holy Angels and the Lord Jesus, and with the departing words, 'Oh Lord, take me to Thyself'.[45]

With the severing of Aboriginal people from their land and resources, the mission station served as a source of spiritual nourishment for the few, and physical nourishment and sanctity for the majority. Aborigines were being described by the European stationers in the area as 'parasites', and were despised for 'hanging about' the stations looking for food handouts. 'The better ones', wrote Flierl senior, 'stayed around our mission station, where our missionaries and lay-helpers always carefully looked after their souls and bodies.'[46]

Soon after the young Flierl and his wife, Emilie, arrived at Killalpaninna in 1884 his older cousin made a third trip into the desert to determine a location for a second mission station. Flierl senior travelled westwards to Lake Eyre, then northwards to the Warburton Creek, but clearly the numbers of Aborigines left living in their tribal homelands were too few to warrant another mission station. Killalpaninna, with its quota of government food rations, had become so well known that the largest concentrations of Aborigines in the north-east of the colony were located around the mission station itself. The extra missionary sent to serve a branch mission spent his time teaching school pupils at Killalpaninna. Flierl senior concentrated on translating the New Testament and other Christian works into the Diyari language.

By the mid-1880s some Aboriginal Christian couples were presenting their babies for Christian baptisms, and naming them with solid German or biblical names. In 1885 one such couple had a young son baptised Gustav, and another had their young son baptised Daniel. The use of tribal second names began to be dropped, and mission Aborigines became known simply by one name. The first part-Aboriginal child was baptised in 1885, and during that same year an epidemic of influenza killed an unknown number of Aborigines in the area. Tiny Emma, the 1-year-old daughter of Johannes Pingilinna, died from influenza while her father was so ill with the infection that he could not attend her funeral. At the graveside Flierl senior proudly noted the calm reactions of his mission Aborigines, who stood quietly and sadly, while the camp blacks cried and screamed uninhibitedly, a certain sign, thought Flierl, that the Christian blacks knew the baby to be at peace with Jesus, for she had been baptised into the 'true faith'.[47]

But mission success remained elusive. At times when rains brought economic relief to the stock station, and much-needed physical relief to the Germans, many of the Aborigines, even those baptised, deserted the station and returned to their old ways. Bush foods were then plentiful, corroborees were held, and groups pursued traditional life patterns. Sometimes converts would suddenly and unexpectedly disappear from the mission to follow station work elsewhere, the sense of permanence and attachment to one small locale alien to the

Flierl the First **113**

Wedding of Flierl the Second and Emilie Gallasche at the German settlement of Hahndorf

Aborigines' cultural milieu. By evening the Germans would listen, with hope and encouragement in their hearts, to young Aborigines in their mission houses singing Christian songs in their native Diyari; by next morning several would have disappeared. It was a vicious circle for the Lutherans. During droughts, when resources and economics were stretched to the very limit, large numbers camped near the station hoping for food handouts, while others attached themselves to the mission station itself as potential converts. Disillusionment and disappointment sapped the missionaries' energies and fortitude. But the two Flierls were to react quite differently to their continual blighted hope, and to take divergent paths during the forthcoming years.

During 1884 just five adults and three children were baptised, the sheep station brought £700 in revenue, £300 was donated from Germany and £200 from the Lutheran community in South Australia. But salaries for mission workers totalled £115, wages paid to white labourers £408, and wages paid to 'blackfellows' amounted to £59. At the end of 1884 the mission station was £678 in debt.[48]

Flierl Senior Posted to New Guinea

In 1885 Johann Flierl senior was transferred from Bethesda (Killalpaninna) to a missionary post in New Guinea. Without the establishment of an outstation, there was neither the need nor were there funds for two trained missionaries at Killalpaninna. Flierl senior had estimated that, at best, there were about 1000 Aborigines in the north-east of the colony (an area as large as the whole of southern Germany), and that most of them could be serviced by Bethesda. On the other hand, New Guinea, recently annexed by the German Empire, had an estimated black population of 1 million, a substantial missionising potential awaiting Lutheran conversion. A few German missionaries were already there, on the coasts to the east, west and south, but there were none yet in the north. The Neuendettelsau mission headquarters were hoping to begin work in the north before the settlers, planters and merchants had a chance to corrupt the local blacks. The New Guinea Company, based in Berlin, held a monopoly in trade, and it was they who eventually granted Flierl access to the country when he was having difficulty procuring a passage. The company's representatives at Cooktown, in northern Queensland, where the missionary was awaiting a visa and a ship, received the advice and Flierl was given a free passage in a first-class cabin on one of their vessels. Flierl became the founder of the Evangelical Lutheran Mission of New Guinea, a missionary organisation still active in Papua New Guinea.[49]

Johann Flierl had been delayed at Cooktown for six months, and during that time had managed to establish that second mission station which had eluded him for so long. He had been concerned for the Queensland Aborigines for some years (since his journey across the border in 1883), after reports of massacres and brutality by the European settlers and police, writing: 'in that colony least of all was done for the poor blacks'.[50] In 1885 he successfully instituted a mission station, naming it Elim, among the Koko Yimidir tribe at Cape Bedford (15 miles north of Cooktown) for the 'countless natives which over-ran the district'.[51] The Queensland colonial government sanctioned the proposal and promised financial assistance provided Flierl stay at the station for a period of five years. An

Aboriginal reserve of about 60 square miles was established on the northern bank of the Bloomfield River, and the mission station later became known as Bloomfield Mission.

But when the opportunity came for the missionary to leave for New Guinea he arranged for Carl Meyer (who had served at Bucaltaninna and Killalpaninna) to be transferred to his position. Johannes Pingilinna, tiny Emma's father, travelled with Meyer to Cape Bedford, and for several years assisted him there.[52] Of Pingilinna's service in Queensland the Germans were to write that, 'In spite of the fear and distrust of this people to go into strange surroundings and among strange blacks and despite their love and affection for the brown land, he (Pingilinna) still declared himself willing to go with these words, "In the name of Jesus I go where he calls me".'[53] Johannes Pingilinna's wife died while he was serving in Queensland.

The committee at Tanunda appointed Bernhard Riegert (a Lithuanian Lutheran) as schoolteacher at Killalpaninna, and the younger Flierl took control as primary missionary. Just before Flierl senior's departure an attempt was made to strengthen the fragile black Christian community by organising it along the conventional lines of a Lutheran church community in Europe, but using a known Aboriginal social convention. Three male Aboriginal Christians were selected as neyi ('elder brothers') whose job was to advise and assist the missionaries. They were expected to mediate among the black Christian community (like the Elders of a church community), settling arguments and making sure that everything ran smoothly. Every Sunday a meeting would be held to discuss the affairs of the community.[54] All mission Aborigines' weapons were collected and burned, and they were made to promise never to make any more, or to use them again.

During his last days at Killalpaninna, Flierl senior wrote, 'Our desert here has many advantages, in particular the advantage of a relatively healthy climate'. He was apprehensive of the tropical forests of New Guinea, the constant heat and tropical fevers.

> And I have found here a comfortable home. But the naked fact remains that here in Australia all we have is now the country of the white man with his herds, and an ever dwindling number of Aborigines. In New Guinea, on the other hand, an enormous field of heathens, thousands of Papua, where we can go and missionise them. So I am happy to sacrifice the comfort I have built up here. I am happy to leave the orderly condition here, to have established everything here, and again start from the beginning and build up a new mission enterprise. My dear wife will follow me in my task.[55]

On first arrival in Australia, Johann Flierl had described the country as 'the most miserable of all fields for missionaries'.[56] Towards the end of his life, however, after forty-four years as an active missionary, Flierl was to write: 'I must admit and say clearly that in the seven years in the Australian desert I felt well. I would have liked to stay there had I not been transferred to New Guinea. They were in more than one sense the best times of my life.'[57]

6
Reuther and the Glorious 1890s

Missionary Reuther caught his first glimpse of Killalpaninna at the beginning of December 1888. The mud-brick tower loomed above a line of shrubby trees as the 27-year-old bumped over a rough sandy track. It was again early summer, and the younger Flierl had travelled south to collect his assistant and be present at Johann Georg Reuther's ordination. The countryside in the north had not received rain for six months. Animals were dying and water was difficult to find. 'I can understand the joy of the Children of Israel when they found fresh water during their walk through the desert', wrote the enthusiastic new graduate of the journey to the station. He described the mission as 'a nice pretty village', and reported, in innocence and simplicity, 'Certainly patience has already achieved a great deal'.[1]

Reuther was young and idealistic, and held great hope and enthusiasm for his own opportunity in the transformation and salvation of these people. His senior and mentor, the young Flierl, on the other hand, had become tired and disillusioned, and was aware of the true situation. Convert numbers were still small, and even those who had been baptised or confirmed repeatedly strayed, returning to their old religion, to the power of the pinaru, and to the pull of their wandering ways and tribal lifestyle. To add to the instability and corruptibility of these people (as seen by the Lutherans), European station hands—single men working the surrounding properties—were overtly engaging in sexual relationships with local Aboriginal women (whom they often found to be sexually liberal), including those from the mission station itself.

But young Reuther was still fresh and enthusiastic. And, encouraged as were all missionaries in the field, he married within a year of arriving in the colony. He had been introduced to the daughter of Pastor Reichner, chairman of the Immanuel Synod's mission committee, while staying with the family at Lights Pass. Pauline had been widowed for three years after her husband, a young pastor, was said to have died 'grieved by the disunity and squabble in the Church at that time'.[2] She was six years older than Reuther and had three boys from her first marriage, but as the missionary wrote:

> I thank God that now He has given me a help-meet, according to His will and we thank God that now her sad widowhood should be changed into joy ... Although I

Reuther and Pauline on their wedding day, Tanunda, February 1889

knew that, I had a hard task before me, I did rejoice that He has given me the duty to lead them to heaven. And why shouldn't I rejoice since Pastor Stolz [Pauline's deceased husband] was a martyr of the Church for he only did the will of God and sacrificed his life for it. Though I had the opportunity to marry quite often but God always led it so to do His will that I did not entertain the idea.[3]

Reuther was to be the longest-serving and perhaps best remembered of the ordained missionaries at Killalpaninna. For eighteen years he worked among the Diyari and other tribes, becoming a respected leader among the northern community, and being sworn in as a Justice of the Peace in the courtroom at Herrgott Springs in 1896.[4] He left a corpus of literature from his observations and study of the Diyari people amounting to thirteen volumes of work relating to their culture, geography, religion and language, with a four-volume dictionary of the Diyari language. Together with the missionary Carl Strehlow (who served at Killalpaninna as Reuther's assistant from 1892 to 1894, and at Hermannsburg in Central Australia from 1894 to 1922), Reuther made a complete translation of the New Testament into the Diyari language (just as Luther had translated the New Testament, the heart of his theology, into the German language from the Latin). He also translated Lutheran hymns and psalms into Diyari, as well as into the Wangkangurru and Yandruwantha dialects.[5] Reuther was not the first, nor perhaps the most skilled linguist or ethnographer at Killalpaninna, but he was certainly the most prolific and energetic. He gathered a vast collection of Aboriginal artefacts and native foods, a total of 1308 items in all, which he later sold to the South Australian Museum.[6]

During Reuther's eighteen-year period there were many staff changes. But for most of this time Reuther controlled the spiritual and educational aspects of the mission as well as the stock station management. Add to this his frenetic collecting, collating and translating, and the overwhelming burden of his job becomes obvious. It was a burden that was to cause him grave health problems and possibly a propensity for chronic depression. Reuther was an emotional and sensitive man. Perhaps he was aware of his place in history and his role among these unique people, particularly evident to him after visiting academics directed their interest to the Diyari and related tribes during the latter part of the 1890s and the early twentieth century. Perhaps, in collecting, collating and translating such a huge body of material, Reuther sought not only to make Christian literature accessible to the 'poor backward heathens', but also to preserve what was widely perceived as the fragments of a dying 'primitive' culture. He was on the spot and, being a man of intense idealism and religiosity, saw it as his personal duty to do as much as possible in this capacity. Perhaps there was even a hint of a recognised role for himself in the prestigious field of late nineteenth–early twentieth-century anthropology.

Reuther, it seems, saw himself as a kind of patriarch, a biblical leader in the desert of Australia. With an older wife, a new-born child every year for the duration of his wife's fertility, his Aboriginal flock of converts, his missionising zeal and fearlessness among them, his placing of the Word of God in the language of a 'pagan' tribe and his publishing of the Word for future pagans to read, his position could indeed be perceived as biblical in flavour, even lofty in missionary terms. And despite his disciplinary methods and his interferences in traditional ceremonies, Reuther was nevertheless popular among the Aborigines at Killalpaninna. His successor, Wolfgang Reidel, although no venerator of his predecessor, wrote: 'I must admit the blacks here [at Killalpaninna] are very fond of Reuther'.[7]

Reuther's contribution to the knowledge and ethnography of the Diyari cannot be overlooked. His dedication to his work at the mission, his years of toil in the difficult northern desert, and his compassion for and relationship with the Aborigines of the area, and with the mission workers, combine to make him the most outstanding of the missionaries at Killalpaninna. And yet he was to be driven from his field by ill-health exacerbated by accusation and malignant gossip, his years of dedication forever under a cloud of suspicion.

Johann Georg Reuther, son of a weaver, was born at Rosstall, near Nürnberg in Central Franconia, on 3 September 1861. It was the same month and year that John King, the only member of the Burke and Wills advance party to survive the crossing of the Australian continent, was found by Alfred Howitt. King was living with the Aborigines of the Coopers Creek area, whose progeny may well have been at Killalpaninna during Reuther's time there.

Reuther was the oldest of seven children. He received only a basic provincial education before completing military service in a supplementary reserve in Neuberg on the Danube. He then became a postman and railway worker. But on Christmas Eve, 1885, while awaiting the arrival of mailtrains on a chilly railway platform and listening to the joyous sound of church-bells ringing out the Christmas message, young Reuther claimed to have received a vocation. From thenceforth he would dedicate his life to propagating the word of Christ. He entered the Neuendettelsau Seminary the following April, at the age of twenty-five. Study at seminary level was difficult for a young man with such a rudimentary beginning, but he somehow managed to complete his examinations. On 12 August 1888 Reuther was commissioned for service in Australia and a month later he embarked from Genoa for a journey that would profoundly change his life.[8]

Killalpaninna Aborigines, 1890s

After a marriage ceremony at Lights Pass, on 28 February 1889, Reuther and his new wife were welcomed at Killalpaninna with a dinner by the German staff. And while they were sitting over this meal, mission Aborigines gathered outside the doorway and began to sing the hymn, 'Great God We Praise You'. Reuther wrote to Neuendettelsau: 'It was a moving sight to see those happy faces singing. I could not stop myself from crying. In moments like this I would like all you mission friends in Germany to see so closely the power of Christianity and what effect it has on humans, and to what changes it can lead.'[9]

Optimistic words from an idealistic newcomer. In reality, however, missionising was not progressing well. Killalpaninna had become a refuge and ration station to many dispossessed Aborigines. Groups of people wandered between portions of their tribal country still accessible (legitimately or illegitimately) and the safe precincts of the leased land around Killalpaninna, now designated 'Aboriginal Reserve land'. During the late 1890s about 200 Aborigines lived on mission-leased land.[10] As before, they were essentially sick or old, and just two years later the young missionary wrote that 'Children have become a rarity', with Strehlow, three years later again, writing: 'I don't think our blacks will survive for much longer. At the camps there are old, decayed men and old, ugly women. It is rare to see a child. The only welcoming sign is a bunch of barking dogs, which seems to take the place of children, for the blacks can ride for days without seeing a black', and 'Our people here are dying out, getting old before their time. Only few surpass forty.'[11]

Aboriginal camp near Killalpaninna, c. 1895. Note the combination of European clothing and traditional nakedness, of aluminium billycans and mugs and traditional tools and weaponry, and traditional huts now covered by old clothing and government-issue mission blankets to keep out wind and sun. These people were known as 'camp Aborigines' by the mission staff, for they lived on the other side of the Lake Killalpaninna, away from the strict control of mission authority

Converts came and went, as the situation dictated, for it was, of course, often not genuine interest in the new religion and culture, or conversion at all, as the missionaries had dearly hoped.

A year after the arrival of Reuther a baptised couple wandered back to the station from a walkabout of quite some time. After a severe dressing down from the missionaries the couple appeared repentant (to the Lutherans). But one morning, shortly afterwards, they were gone again. 'Although the blacks can see their sins they are not able to understand the temptations of the bad enemy, because a free and unrestrained life in sin and lust is so pleasurable to the flesh', wrote Reuther somewhat more cynically.[12] 'The situation wouldn't be as bad', wrote Flierl, in disgust over a 17-year-old mission girl returning to her white labourer lover,

> if the blacks themselves didn't enjoy the sin of the flesh so much and if they would refrain from staying clear of the devils in disguise of humans. But the opposite is the case. As soon as there is a white fellow around immediately a group of blacks surround him and often the black men are proud of their daughter or even their wife if they have the dubious honour to have given birth to a halfcaste. They call them, with great pride, a white lubra.[13]

The missionaries attempted to arrange marriages between baptised mission men and women in order to try and keep them virtuous and faithful. The young Aboriginal mission men were still engaging in relationships with older women from the camps, as generally they had not yet been promised young girls. The Lutherans became obsessed with such transgression of the sixth commandment (adultery), and perceived this to be the root evil of the Aborigines' heathen ways: 'above all it is the sinning against the sixth commandment that makes a human being most poisonous in his soul and hardened . . .', wrote Flierl.[14] And they were only too willing, and quick, to marry off young baptised mission Aborigines at the expense of contravening Aboriginal marriage codes. Some of the young mission men complied for the sake of a young bride, even though they took the risk of traditional retribution. Paranoia arose over European labourers in the area openly seducing the Aboriginal girls while introducing their male counterparts to the temptations of alcohol. By 1892 this paranoia was translated into controlled passage through mission country (after the flooding of the Cooper disrupted the normal droving route to and from Queensland) and into the placing of spies among the mission Aborigines to report on illicit sexual activities. The mission station provided ferries to carry passengers and goods across the flooded Birdsville Track near the Kopperamanna run, with Hermann Vogelsang in charge. As Reuther wrote, 'We agreed to do this service to make sure that no bad white people are able to get near our enterprise and become a danger to the black people'.[15] After an Englishman awaiting ferrying made sexual suggestions towards one of the baptised Aboriginal women (which, it seems, were accepted), Reuther was furious. He placed four so-called reliable informers (which he called 'spring people', or 'Kammakampara') among the mission Aborigines to report on any such incidents. Such spies, however, could meet with fatal consequences from their people if their deception was discovered.

> I had to take disciplinary methods at times. We preach to them on Sundays and they go back to their old ways on Mondays. Its either Christ or Satan. Disciplinary methods have caused a fearful impact. Three times I found it necessary to interfere. The first time a man wanted to avoid discipline and went to the camp of the heathens because he did not want to admit publicly what had happened. I said God would find him. He caused a public nuisance and should publically ask God's forgiveness.[16]

By enforcing public confession, Reuther hoped to shame mission Aborigines before their Christian counterparts. 'We try to keep the better ones at the station by paying them more wages', wrote Reuther in 1891, 'And also provide them with old age security in contrast to the other enterprises where black people are sent away when they cannot work anymore. But we still have problems over keeping them here and problems with other white settlers who would very much like to see us go.'[17] Some mission Aborigines were being paid wages of between 3 and 5 shillings a week. One man (probably Timotheus Maltilinna) earned up to 10 shillings a week.[18]

During the early 1890s there was a concerted effort not only to convert, but to forcibly eradicate the old culture. Two years before Reuther's arrival, Flierl the Second had burned all the 'kira' (boomerangs) that belonged to the mission

Aborigines, insisting the Aborigines would be better advised to rely on the Good Lord as their protector.[19] Many Aborigines appear to have given in to the dominant culture at the station, recognising the advantages of regular food, sanctuary and medical treatment. Perhaps some sought to learn the powerful ways of the new religion. But life at the settlement was rigid and confining. They were forbidden to mix with camp people or engage in ceremonies, and they lost contact with Aboriginal 'news'. In 1894 Strehlow wrote:

> Many could not put up with this 'healing barrier' against a decaying and decadent influence, so they returned to heathenism . . . After attending Christian classes for a while some became worse sinners than before and actually opposed us. We see the evidence in those Christians who were once at the station and have left. They are living more immoral lives than before.[20]

A year after Reuther's arrival, a 12-year-old girl who was attending the mission school was impounded at the station to ensure that she would not be taken back to the camps by her parents. The girl was then placed with a black Christian family at the station. But the parents secretly visited the Aboriginal family, appealing to their traditional beliefs by telling them that their daughter was 'bewitched', and that their own child would also be bewitched if their daughter was to remain with them. The girl was immediately released.

But some Aboriginal children who were born at the station knew nothing of camp life and were actually afraid of camp Aborigines. When the 15-year-old daughter of Johannes Pingilinna, young Maria—mission born, raised and educated—became seriously ill in 1895 she stoically lay on her death-bed in the Reuther home for two months.

> She was not interested in the heathen way and was frightened when a heathen entered her room. One day I was with her when one of our black shepherds, a heathen koonkie (magician) passed by, and when Maria heard him she called out angrily, 'Please take that man away. He is a miserable human being and a liar. My koonkie is Jesus' . . . Maria died, repeatedly asking us to pray for her. It was touching how much she loved and was devoted to Mrs Reuther, who had become a loving mother to her.[21]

During the 1890s the old pinaru system was still very much in operation. The old men had power and control over the 13- and 14-year-old girls as wives, and some daughters were still betrothed from birth. In 1891 Flierl and Reuther refused to release a young girl who was living at the station but had been promised to a particular old man.[22] Reuther gives no further details about this incident. But in his diary, in January of that year, he reported a general uprising at the mission station, led by one of the 'first fruits of Flierl's 1879 baptisms', and a month later 'a storm among the native women'.[23] Reuther wrote that 'A number of those blacks at the station are only with us halfheartedly and still hold old weaknesses'.[24] But there is no evidence at Killalpaninna that the mission Aborigines were locked in at night to prevent them wandering to the camps. At the Hermannsburg Mission Station in Central Australia, Aboriginal children were allegedly locked in the schoolrooms or in separate dormitories at night.[25]

The missionaries worked to gather young Aboriginal people to the station, give them work, baptise them, marry them to each other, and hope they would

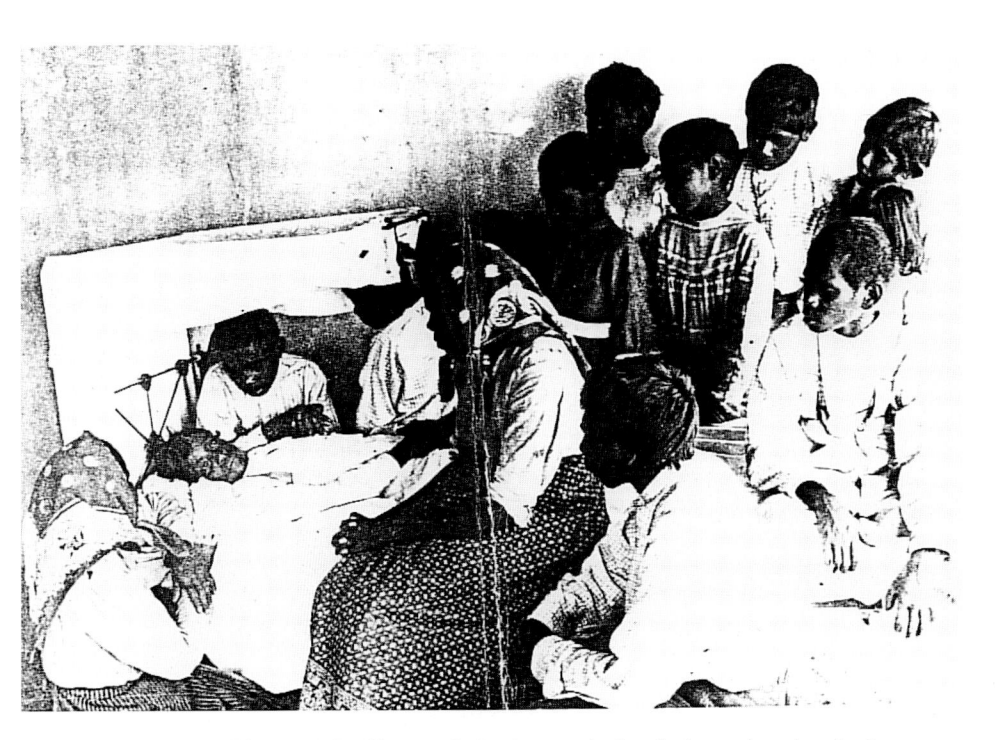

Possibly the 15-year-old Maria Pingilinna, mission born, raised and educated, on her deathbed in the Reuthers' home, c. 1895. She was afraid when a 'heathen Aboriginal healer' entered her room, saying 'My kunkie is Jesus'

not be tempted back into the circles of promiscuity. But the Lutherans failed to understand the power and strength of the traditional spiritual world of these people. In the 1890s the ritual re-enactments and dances to which mission Aborigines escaped in the heart of the night plagued Flierl and Reuther. At some 10 miles distance from the station the Diyari would gather for Mindari ceremonies. And just 2 miles from the station, across the sandhills but out of sight of the missionaries, was the traditional site of the Storm History, an important ceremonial ground known as 'Ngarlangarlani' to the Aborigines, and Lake Allallinna to the Europeans.[26]

When Flierl and Reuther heard in advance of one impending nocturnal ceremony, they rode to Ngarlangarlani to observe and interrupt the heathen activity. In the distance they saw the dozens of campfires flickering, and as they rode closer could hear the sound of perhaps hundreds of voices: 'Suddenly we were unexpectedly right among them. When they asked us what we wanted we said we want to give you the word of the Good Lord', wrote Reuther. They attempted to gather the Aborigines in a circle for a different kind of religious ceremony, but 'it wasn't easy to search at night because the night is black and the blacks are also black. We didn't see many. Some said they would come and pretended to be on their way, but suddenly they disappeared. Others said they had to worry about their dogs, or there was an old man or woman they couldn't leave alone.' About

'Camp Aborigines' and 'mission Aborigines' preparing for a ceremony out of sight of the mission station.

ninety Aborigines were pressed into listening to a Lutheran service, while about a hundred slipped away to another spot.

But the Germans followed, and again attempted to interrupt. Reuther wrote:

> This time my interrupting of their dancing and singing (Mindari) was not appreciated at all. For the whole day yesterday they called the emus and they were expecting them at any moment. I must admire their patience doing that. One of the men sitting there painted with white lines hit the ground at regular intervals with a piece of wood accompanied by murmuring and singing until the arrival of the emus. The blacks wanted to get rid of me as quickly as possible, but today I thought, 'No, I'll be staying!'

Even with threats of violence, the Germans dogmatically stood their ground:

> Seven men coloured in the most beautiful way were dressed as emus. A bunch of emu feathers was placed on each of their heads, and extended three feet above the head and covered the neck. The blacks thus dressed were then sent away, and attempted to hide behind bushes. Now they called the women, who had stayed behind a sandhill. The white-painted magician hit the wood against the ground as much as he could and another one hit two pieces of wood together. Everyone was now waiting anxiously for things to happen. Finally one of the seven emus arrived, and in the end all of them came closer and closer, to disappear in one of the huts.

Reuther, no doubt familiar with the sexual nature of the next stage of the ritual, chose that moment to attempt again to preach the Christian word. He does not indicate what followed, but wrote, 'I decided my closer visits to the camps of the blacks should occur more often', and in his report of the matter to Neuendettelsau requested a third missionary.[27]

Reuther and Flierl thenceforth interfered at all known Aboriginal ceremonies in this manner. Whenever they heard that a dance was to be performed they would appear at the spot and force a Lutheran service instead. This undoubtedly caused resentment, not least with the pinaru whose authority and power was being undermined. In 1896 an Aboriginal uprising was planned near the mission station. Word leaked to Reuther that the intention was to kill 'the missionary', and rumours reached the Germans of a large corroboree planned for the western sandhill. Reuther boldly announced he would go there to investigate. He took with him the newly arrived missionary, Nathaniel Wettengel (Carl Strehlow's replacement after Strehlow was posted to Hermannsburg in Central Australia).

The two Germans walked across the dry lake channel, climbed a large sandhill and saw before them a huge gathering of Aborigines. Reuther fearlessly strode into their midst, followed by a well-armed Wettengel. Reuther demanded the name of the person who had threatened to kill the missionaries, and was directed to a fierce-looking man who was gesticulating wildly. Reuther and the Aborigine argued in Diyari for some time, while the German kept one hand in his pocket, so that the Aborigine finally asked whether the missionary was armed. As the crowd silently gathered to witness the revenge of the German, Wettengel—certain his own hour to meet his maker had arrived—Reuther slowly withdrew his hand and produced, not a European firearm, but a pocket Bible! With the suspense of the situation he had the crowd 'in the palm of his hand'. Reuther motioned for them to sit in front of him. He selected a text from the Bible, and began to read.[28]

Most of the mission Aborigines lived in mission housing, either in small two-roomed married couples' houses, or in segregated dormitories for either males or females, 'like they would be in an institute'.[29] A few camped nearby as there were not enough houses for everybody. 'With lantern in hand I frequently walked through the station at night', wrote Reuther, 'to see if everything was in order.'[30]

Aboriginal women did the cooking for the Aboriginal mission community in a kitchen adjacent to the large communal dining-room. Pauline Reuther supervised the kitchen, and the Aboriginal women were expected to dress neatly in the mission style of peasant Germany—scarf, a long dress over petticoats, and a white working apron. Shoes, however, were forsaken. By 1891 there were forty-two Aborigines living at the settlement, but sixty-five regularly came to the station for meals. They ate at one long table, after prayers before the morning and evening meals. On Mondays the Aboriginal women were expected to do the weekly washing of clothes. Sewing, mending and knitting groups were supervised by Emilie Flierl. During the late 1890s there was a mission shop where Aborigines could buy handmade clothes (sewn by the black women) from their wage packets, 'and if they have a little money over they keep it', informed Reichner. 'It is better to let them have a little in hand, like children ... It teaches them to practise economy.'[31]

Housework at the Aboriginal quarters was supervised by the wives of the missionaries. All Aborigines at the station were given designated tasks, and even the children had daily duties. The Aborigines hated the monotony of this daily work, which was a concept quite alien to their culture. This 'working' day after day, to a different set of material values, seemed fruitless and pointless. One Aboriginal couple left the station in 1886, the man pointing out to Flierl that he had been sick for some time and that it was the 'work' that was making him sick.[32]

The fanatical attention to cleanliness and order imposed by the methodical Germans—their sweeping, washing and preoccupation with getting rid of dirt— was extraneous to the Aborigines. Soil and sand was part of the natural world of Aboriginal Australia, integral to desert life for these inland dwellers, and not a matter for revulsion and consternation, as they were now taught. Reuther, furthermore, instigated a pre-condition for all Aboriginal pupils before daily acceptance into the schoolroom—the cleansing of the body at the edges of the lake. Thorough washing was also expected on Sundays, before services in the church. 'The natives are washed and combed in a way they never experienced in their natural life', testified Reuther during the inquiry before the 1899 Select Committee into conditions for Aborigines in South Australia.[33]

Mission Aborigines grew to regard illness (feigned or otherwise) as a relief from the compulsion to attend the long, tedious services in the church.[34] And any distraction during these monotonous regularities was a deliverance. When a bird flew into the church and could not get out again, it caused laughter and enjoyment. Old Aboriginal women would languorously stretch across the pews and close their eyes, saying they were tired of sitting on the seats. However, hymn-singing was an enjoyment, although to German ears the resonance was 'like a thousand musicians with so many sounds and so many interpretations that we couldn't have had enough musicians in Europe to present the variety we have here during singing'.[35] One old fellow would close his eyes and emphasise every sound, accompanying it with pressure from under his armpit. One old woman had to wait until the end of every word before 'singing' that word. Reuther would play harmonium, and later Jack Irrgang would accompany him on an organ that had arrived at the station on the mission wagon in September 1899.[36] The sound of these exotic instruments had immense appeal for the mission Aborigines, and singing time (hymn periods) was popular. An Aboriginal choir was formed, causing no end of frustration for the Germans attempting to train members to sing together and in key.

In 1891 twenty-four of the sixty-five mission Aborigines worked as shepherds at the station, while twenty-eight of the sixty-five were baptised. Those baptised adults were all married couples, with the exception of two. A total of sixty Aborigines had been baptised since the mission began, but sixteen had since died. At least sixteen of the remaining forty-four, however, had reverted to their old ways. Occasionally one of the errants would be spotted by the missionaries, 'But we don't succeed in evoking any kind of guilt feeling in them', wrote Reuther.[37]

By the 1890s Aboriginal law was coming into confrontation with European law. In June 1889 Flierl reported to the police that a local pinya had killed one of the black shepherds working on the mission station. All nineteen of the pinya

Killalpaninna Mission settlement at its peak, c. 1901, seen from across Lake Killalpaninna

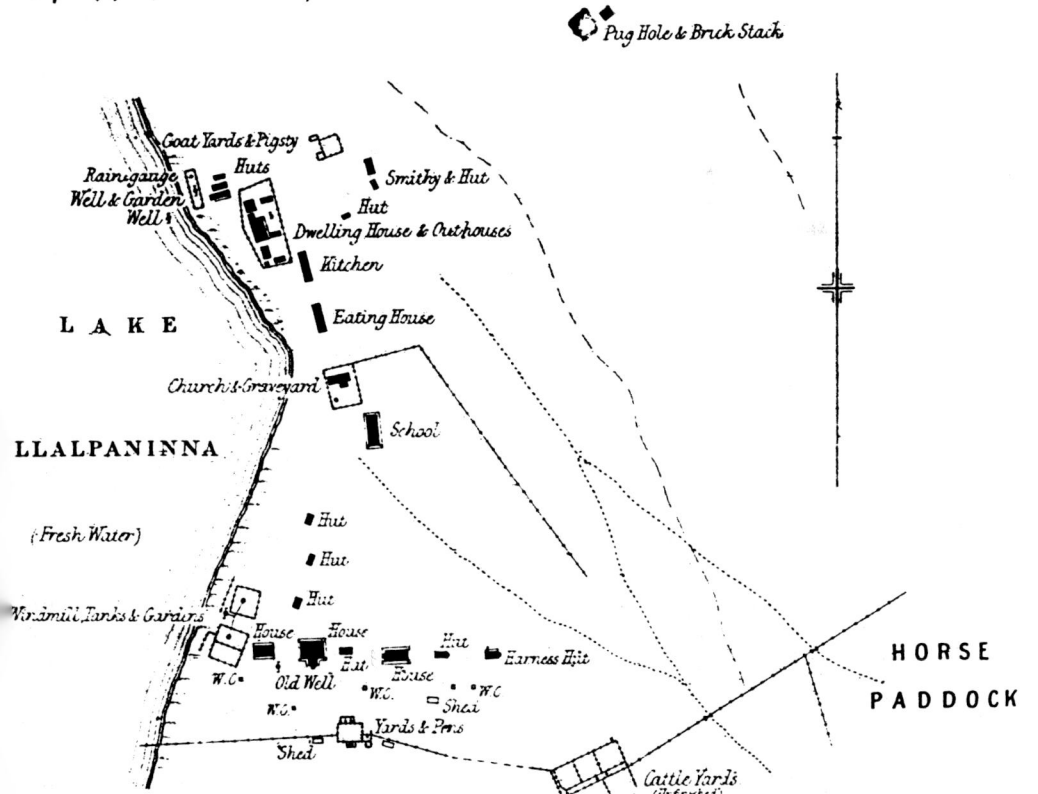

Plan of the Killalpaninna settlement Pastoral Lease 2842, dated 1899

party were captured and taken to Port Augusta for trial. The ringleader was singled out and sentenced to death as an example of European justice to these heathen people, and as an attempted deterrent to any more such traditional 'barbaric' customs. The other seventeen (one had died in the meanwhile) were placed on a good-behaviour bond.[38]

But Aborigines living at Killalpaninna were generally considered non-violent towards the missionaries and their families, and were deemed honest and trustworthy, at least within the mission station itself. During a visit to Killalpaninna in 1904 the Russian scholar Professor Yashchenko noted that 'Pastor Reuter [sic] locked neither his own door, nor the doors of storehouses and granaries'.[39]

By 1893 Reuther was complaining to Neuendettelsau of the increasing number of part-Aborigines who were without fathers, castigating the white so-called 'name-Christians' and envying his New Guinea counterparts their isolation. He claimed that European pastoralists were trying to lure strong working Aborigines from the mission station to their own stations, but that the Lutherans had managed to keep most of those baptised in earlier times.

Killalpaninna Aborigines suffered enforced isolation from their own communities and compliance with a new set of laws and rituals. In 1894 an old mission man was discovered visiting the camp Aborigines and exchanging news with them. He was immediately sent back to the station and forbidden to enter the camps again. But after nightfall he continued clandestinely to return. Other complaints were also made about him, and he was given the option of camp life or 'honest Christian life'. He chose the former and, according to Carl Strehlow, 'has become a good heathen again'.[40] Mission life and camp life were not compatible and many mission Aborigines could not cope with the separation from community and custom. For this reason many left the protection and provisions of the mission station, while others were reluctant to ever join the sanctuary proper, choosing instead to live close by in the hope of receiving the government rations of blankets, flour, sugar and tea, and to be near the protection provided by the Killalpaninna missionaries.

Dismissal of Flierl the Second
John Flierl had worked as sole missionary for over three years before the arrival of Johann Georg Reuther. He had only the assistance of Lithuanian schoolteachers Bernhard Riegert and his wife. All other employees were engaged on the stock station enterprise. Flierl's job included that of missionary and stock station manager during a difficult period when the mission station was over £600 in debt.[41] As it relied so heavily on the stock station for economic survival, Flierl could devote only a portion of his time to missionising activity. Reuther consequently was placed in charge of the school pupils and helped with much of the missionising work. Flierl, as general manager, took charge of the accounting and controlled the overall business venture, as well as performing baptisms and giving sermons on Sundays. The two Kolonisten, Vogelsang and Jacob, were in charge of the daily station tasks, and managing the Aboriginal labour with which they largely operated their enterprises.

But even after the arrival of Reuther, missionising success continued to be

Flierl the Second with baptismal candidates Rebecca and Joseph

Reuther and the Glorious 1890s **129**

elusive and painfully slow. There were constant set-backs, in particular, again, the breaking of the sixth commandment, the sin that so occupied the Aborigines and so preoccupied the Lutherans. The missionaries were obsessive about Aboriginal liaisons with white labourers, fearing the depravity of these whites and the promiscuity of the Aborigines. In 1889 Flierl was to write:

> 'What are we to do about it? Should it lead us to giving up our work which at times seems so futile? No! The answer is 'no, no, no!' How the Devil and his tools would triumph if they could so cheaply win the battle. We will fight here until our last breath; as long as our God admits us and as long as He does not command us to retreat. There are still people around us who are in the service of the flesh and sin, in conjunction with the Prince of Darkness, which threaten to ruin these poor black folk. It means the more for us to be faithful and industrious, to fight the sins committed on these poor people. More than ever we must proceed with work, love and dedication.[42]

But in reality Flierl himself was beginning to fall from grace. Frustrated by the lack of any real success at Killalpaninna, haunted by the sins of the surrounding European males (many of whom despised these German missionaries who occupied good grazing country and tried to control and moralise over the local Aborigines) and subjected to the physical and psychological 'thirsts' of the desert, Flierl the Second turned to the comforts of that common bush pacifier, alcohol, to dull his disappointment and dissatisfaction. He had found mission life at Killalpaninna intolerable. Each summer he was afflicted with the painful desert eye infection and endured blindness for days on end. And both he and Reuther suffered homesickness for the cool green comfort of the German countryside. Irritated, frustrated and probably depressed, Flierl argued and interfered with the labourers and stock station personnel.

In the summer of 1889–90 Flierl and his wife took a three-month holiday from the station.[43] Soon after Flierl's return to Killalpaninna, Reuther was reporting in his diary that, 'In the night from 2 to 3 [of February] I was in Kopperamanna because of Brother Flierl who was drunk. God have mercy that it may not occur again.'[44] Two weeks later Reuther recorded 'A small opposition between Brother Flierl and Vogelsang. How good it is when brethren live together in harmony and unity. Pray God that it would be like that here. As it is now it cannot continue. Lord give us means and help.' A month later the Ruedigers ('Jack' Ruediger was then engaged as teamster) and Flierl refused to attend Holy Communion as 'they were both estranged from each other', and Reuther wrote that 'It is very hard for the mission people to insert such matters into the diary'.[45]

In 1887 Flierl had clashed with Vogelsang and several of the station workers. In July of that year, Thomas McMahon, a well-sinker working at Kopperamanna under the supervision of Vogelsang, wrote to the protector of Aborigines in Adelaide complaining of Flierl's conduct towards the Aborigines at Killalpaninna. McMahon accused Flierl of tyrannising the Aborigines, with the result that about seventy had recently left the station and that many of the camp blacks had also moved away. McMahon claimed that Vogelsang had reported the problem to the mission committee, but at a meeting in Tanunda Flierl had accused Vogelsang and a part-Aborigine named Weaver of being the cause of the retreat. Vogelsang, he claimed, was subsequently called upon by the committee to withdraw the complaint. Vogelsang's reply was 'that he never would so long as he was in the right', and 'that what took them twenty-two years to accomplish, Flierl has upset in six months . . . in hunting the Blacks away'.[46] Flierl subsequently banished the troublesome Weaver, who found employment, and sympathy, with McMahon (and Vogelsang) at Kopperamanna.

In his letter of complaint McMahon wrote that 'There are incidents where the blacks lost confidence in the Missionary'. One mission Aborigine named Godfrey (probably the baptised 'Gottfried'), had made 3000 bricks and should have received £1 per thousand. Allegedly Flierl paid him nothing.[47] The wellsinker accused Flierl of turning his hand to the colonial experience of being more involved with the stock station management than with missionising. McMahon claimed that there had been only one visit to the mission station by a committee member in the past nineteen months, and that had been for the purpose of sending 800 fat sheep and 40 cattle to the Adelaide market. He accused Flierl of neglecting to teach English to the Aborigines, replying to one young Aboriginal boy that 'he wanted to learn cockatoo yabber'. And he accused Flierl of hiding a 'lubra who was implicated in the Cowarie murder' from a police sergeant, only to call to her when near the hiding place and have her appear. In that way the sergeant would witness the authority and control of the missionary over these people.

A police officer was sent from Herrgott Springs to report on the situation at Killalpaninna:

> I fail to detect any of the complaints and irregularities . . . neither have I seen or heard of harsh treatment being displayed towards the Blacks by the Manager Rev. Mr Flierl; on the contrary they appear to be well treated and cared for by the Missionaries . . . they [the Aborigines] are naturally of a lazy disposition, they leave the Station rather than work; another reason why they leave is to attend Corroborees which are held in different parts of the country several times every year, but Mr Flierl informs me that they almost invariably return to the Station and as a rule they never remain for any lengthened period in one place.[48]

Flierl and Ruediger continued to squabble and in early April 1891 Ruediger and his wife left the station for the south. Three weeks later the teamster returned, having taken his complaints to the mission committee, and with the news that an investigation was forthcoming. On 19 May, Reichner and his family arrived at Killalpaninna. Two weeks of inquiry followed, with even the shearers being interrogated. Ruediger and Vogelsang were interviewed at length in the presence of the two missionaries. Emotionally, Reuther wrote that: 'This day the brethren Ruediger and Flierl stood up against each other until at night in the presence of Brother Vogelsang and myself. I could barely take it for sorrow, because of all the accusations. O dear, sin is the ruination of men, blessed is he who is aware of it and takes it to heart.'[49]

Flierl was accused of arriving at the mission station 'totally drunk and soaked' on whisky, after visits to Herrgott Springs.[50] Ruediger was probably the teamster on these occasions. Flierl, however, did admit to drinking three glasses of schnapps on one occasion, and to once having purchased six bottles of cognac, but he was accused of being seen drunk at least four times, twice at Etadunna, once at Herrgott and once at Killalpaninna. On one occasion he was observed cradling a bottle of whisky in his arms like a little child, on another he was found in a drunken state with two Englishmen and, worst of all, he was in the presence of mission Aborigines, purportedly selling sheep to a local pastoralist. (Alcohol was, of course, banned for Aborigines at the mission station.) Reuther confirmed some of these allegations.

But they did not end with drunkenness. Flierl was further accused, by Ruediger, of stealing a horse that had belonged to a visitor to the station (Dr Heinrich), branding it with the mission iron, and selling the horse to pocket the money. Jacob confirmed this story. Ruediger added bitterly that Flierl was a fellow who did not get on well with anybody, attesting that he was subservient to Reuther, supposedly his assistant.

In forlorn defence John Flierl pleaded 'thirst' when he had met the Englishmen, claiming he fell asleep and did not wake until Reuther arrived on the scene. He pleaded that, other than that incident, he had never been drunk, and denied the story of selling Heinrich's horse. But on further interrogation of others at the station Flierl's position weakened.

Flierl was found guilty of misconduct and asked to resign. Vogelsang had refused to stay if Flierl were to remain, and Reuther agreed that Flierl had lost the trust of the Aborigines and would never get it back. 'It was a dreadful day for me to hear how a missionary was deprived of his office. O Lord be merciful and gracious to this Brother', wrote Reuther.[51] To save face with Lutheran supporters, Flierl was offered a position at Bloomfield Mission Station in Queensland, provided he would forgo alcohol. But the young missionary decided against staying in Australia; 'I will probably go to my father-in-law . . . I will go to America'.[52]

Ironically, three months after the resignation of Flierl the Second, rumours reached the Killalpaninna missionaries that Carl Meyer, serving at Bloomfield, was in trouble for being drunk. An immediate investigation was again made by Reichner.[53] Meyer, now reclusive and alcoholic, was dismissed after being accused of accepting bribes from a bêche-de-mer captain to recruit Aboriginal men from Bloomfield to work on luggers.[54]

John Flierl, with his wife and child, left Killalpaninna for the south, and soon afterwards for America. Reuther was made general manager and Hermann Vogelsang took control of the stock station, effectively reporting only to Reuther. It was at this time that the decision was also made to pay wages and not only rations to working male Aborigines.[55]

Stock Station Management

Farming European stock in the Australian desert was a precarious endeavour—an unpredictable climate, repeated droughts, and great expanses of uncertain, dry country across which animals had to be driven to markets. At times the Killalpaninna cattle would go mad with thirst, or were plagued by blinding dust storms.

In 1884 a water bore was sunk by the South Australian government into the edge of the Great Artesian Basin at Herrgott Springs. It was not particularly successful, but two years later a second attempt produced 81 000 gallons of water each day. Other government bores were progressively sunk along the track leading to Birdsville, the route down which cattle were driven, the famed Birdsville

Etadunna Station drafting yards. 'Jack' Irrgang (left) took over supervision of the sheep station on Jacob's retirement, c. late 1890s

Track. In 1890 one was sunk at Lake Harry that produced some 120 000 gallons a day. And in 1897 a bore sunk at Kopperamanna produced a massive 800 000 gallons of water a day. This, of course, was a great boon for the Lutherans, who had leased this stretch of country. The Kopperamanna bore itself was subsequently leased by the South Australian government to both Killalpaninna Mission Station and Thomas Elder (of the Beltana Pastoral Company), in equal proportions for stock use. The mission station, from about the mid-1890s, had developed an outstation at Kopperamanna, stocked mainly with cattle. Another outstation at Etadunna had earlier stocked sheep, for it had had a better water supply.

In December 1899 the 155-square-mile northern pastoral run adjoining Killalpaninna, Murrapatirrinna Station, was leased to the mission station for 'Aboriginal purposes'. Previously owned by Henry McConville, it consisted mainly of sandhills, but did have a stone house and good well. The station was added to an Aboriginal land lease of 595 square miles surrounding the Etadunna sheep enterprise. With the mission's own 321-square-mile lease, the extra land now gave the Lutherans 1071 square miles of country to run their stock.[56] In 1903 the new leases were designated an Aboriginal Reserve, the contentious AL 145.

Etadunna Station, 12 miles south-east of Killalpaninna, was chosen as a base for the sheep stock, before the sinking of the Kopperamanna bore, as it had three good wells, one used for drinking, one for gardening and one for watering sheep stock. In 1891 Ernst Jacob was permanently stationed there as overseer, and Jack Ruediger became mission teamster. Large shearing sheds were constructed by

German labour hired from the south, and from the south came German shearers for the annual season, held for one month, beginning late July or early August. Jacob and his wife cultivated an impressive (by desert standards) vegetable garden from one well, and managed to supply the mission staff. Kopperamanna, however, had just one well (in addition to the government bore), Killalpaninna likewise—a 40-foot-deep depression on the eastern side of the sand ridges. However, this vital water source was only productive for a short time after flooding, and would fail quickly. It was worked by a windlass, but sanded in at the top in drought years. Lack of water at Killalpaninna produced continual difficulties for the Germans, who were forced to rely on 'Aboriginal soaks' (water that seeped to the surface after digging into sand), or water carried from elsewhere. In 1890 the mission stock count was some 14 000 to 16 000 sheep, 300 cattle and 150 horses.[57] The stock was branded LM (for Lutheran Mission).

In late 1890–91 rain fell in the north of South Australia and the floods came down from Queensland, again filling the lake system. Reuther wrote: 'I have never seen a rain like that ever ... The blacks didn't thank the Good Lord for the rain, but thanked the blacks in Queensland for the rain, which they believe they have sent down for them.' The Aborigines near Killalpaninna sent gifts to the Queensland Aborigines in gratitude.[58] With these rains came an abundance of native food. Reuther watched 'one Aboriginal man and his woman preparing a meal from 60–80 eggs, 7–8 lizards and one rabbit [not native of course]'. When asked whether just the two of them intended to eat all of it, they replied, with a smile, 'Yes'. The abundance was duly celebrated with ritual dancing, and the Sunday services at the mission station were less than popular. Only elderly people remained in such times of plenty. The rest, according to Reuther, 'were having a good time'.[59]

Floodwater filled Lake Killalpaninna and flowed across the plain between Killalpaninna and Kopperamanna. The flooding was so severe that cellars filled with water, mission workers traversed the station by boat, and snakes swam about in an effort to find dry, high ground. The Lutheran settlement, built on top of high sandhills, was virtually an island surrounded by water.[60] Vogelsang was forced to bring goods from Kopperamanna to Killalpaninna in a flat-bottomed boat, and with this modest conveyance managed to make a little money for the mission purse by charging a small fee for ferrying teamsters who were stranded on the northern side of Coopers Creek. The income idea, and the control of traffic through mission country, was considered potentially beneficial to the enterprise, and Vogelsang was stationed at Kopperamanna (12 miles to the north of the mission station) for the duration of the flooding. The idea had a dual purpose: 'We have agreed to do this service to make sure that no bad white people are able to get near our enterprise and become a danger to the black people', wrote Reuther.[61]

Reuther would visit Etadunna during the shearing season, often for days at a time, perhaps for the company of fellow Germans. But more pointedly, his presence kept watch on relationships between the Germans and the Aboriginal women at Etadunna. On 2 August 1891 he thanked God that 'the shearing is finished without any mishap with the exception that the kitchen was burnt'.[62]

Large herds of goats, for meat, milk and dairy produce, were kept at both Killalpaninna and Kopperamanna, for they were hardier than dairy cows.

About 200 were shepherded by Aborigines at Killalpaninna, and yarded by night. But the animals were extremely destructive to the fragile desert environment, voraciously consuming the already sparse vegetation that grew on the tops of sandhills, particularly the sandhill canegrass so necessary for the prevention of soil erosion.[63]

Black Labour

Mistrustful of British-born labourers, whom they considered to be drifters, unreliable and undisciplined, the Killalpaninna missionaries avoided employing any on their stock stations. They were viewed as immoral, with a taste for too much alcohol and only too ready to exploit the perceived promiscuity of the Aboriginal women.[64] And only when absolutely necessary were German southerners employed as station hands. Consequently there was a concerted training of Aboriginal stock workers. A few trustworthy European labourers (mostly German), however, had to be hired to supervise and teach the blacks. But they were employed only after a written agreement clearly describing the job and emphasising moral duties was signed.[65]

Uniforms and neat work-clothes were provided for the black workers. Batches of dozens of moleskin trousers, cotton shirts and bush boots were purchased by the station. Dozens of collar studs were sent from the south for church on Sundays. Mission-trained Aboriginal stockmen became highly sought after in the area, often to the disapproval of the Lutherans, who tried to keep them

Although the Lutherans were paranoid about Europeans' moral standards and drinking habits, they were sometimes employed at the mission's stock stations to supervise Aboriginal workmen.

faithful to the mission station. At around the turn of the century some were earning up to 15 shillings a week (presumably at other stations).[66] They had proven efficient and steady workers.

In 1900 Reuther, as head missionary, received a salary of £50 per year, his missionary assistants, Siebert and Wettengel, received £25 each, the Kolonisten £20, Pastor Kaibel (then the president of the mission committee), £31 13s 4d, and employed Aborigines at the station received salaries ranging from over £15 per year to as low as 2 guineas. The average full-time salary for an Aboriginal male (as only males were paid) was around £10 per year.[67] There were at least forty Aboriginal men employed at the station in 1900. The cost of their employment was perhaps some £400 a year. Wages for white station hands were probably similar to the wages being received by the Kolonisten, about £20 a year, bringing the cost of employing a similar number of white labourers to £800. By 1900 many of the Aboriginal men were skilled stockmen, fencers and shearers, and needed little or no overseeing by white supervisors.

Kopperamanna and Vogelsang
In 1894 Hermann Vogelsang was sent to the outstation at Lake Kopperamanna on a permanent basis. His main task was to prevent trespassing by drovers, like those of 'Cattle King' Sidney Kidman, who were encouraging their stock to graze indiscriminately on the mission run's grassy floodplains instead of moving them on for several miles each day in accordance with droving regulations. Kidman's men were illicitly fattening their cattle on mission land after the long drive from Queensland, and the cattle were consuming vegetation across vast areas as the huge herds passed through mission country.

Whenever flooding occurred Vogelsang continued to ferry stranded people and stock across Coopers Creek. Propelling the punt with oars, Vogelsang even carried stranded camel-teams and their Afghan attendants, with the camels' legs tied together and the animals rolled onto the punt. And he continued to police this public area of mission land for trespassers and unwanted and 'unsavoury' characters. The task was often prodigious for the 56-year-old German. During the 1903–04 flooding one of Kidman's drovers was bringing 32 000 sheep from beyond Birdsville to the Farina railhead for freighting to the Adelaide markets. Vogelsang and the drover built a bridge above the waterline for the sheep to cross. Construction occupied the Kolonist, his Aboriginal assistants and the drover for a full week.[68] Sir Sidney Kidman, knighted for his pastoral successes, was well known to the Vogelsang family, Kidman and Vogelsang having first met on the train from Herrgott to Adelaide.[69]

In 1896 the Vogelsang family moved from their temporary quarters at Kopperamanna into a mud and thatch house built beside the Kopperamanna lake. The government bore was just a few miles from the house, on the main stock route from the north. Accordingly, the Lutherans were given the right to control access to water from the bore and drovers were required to send notice to the station when intending to enter mission country to water their stock. The mission levied a charge for travelling stock at a rate of 2 pence a head for camels, a penny for horses and cattle, and 9 pence per 100 sheep. Afghans, with strings of pack camels carrying supplies to isolated stations and returning south with the products of inland ventures, would water their thirsty animals at the bore.

Kopperamanna settlement, c. 1900

Hawkers, with their enticing wares for isolated communities, stopped to water horses or camels. Occasionally a donkey team was watered. When the land to the north was especially dry, and travelling cattle were deprived of water for long periods, the beasts would smell the bore water for several miles and great mobs of thirsty cattle would break into a run and stampede perilously close to the Vogelsang home in their desperate rush. From August to September 1901 the levy was collected on 14 000 cattle and 12 000 sheep. The passage of such enormous numbers of foreign, cloven-hoofed herds through the north-east of South Australia, especially through such areas as the Kopperamanna lease, has contributed immensely to the extensive ecological damage wrought on this fragile desert country.[70]

Mission cattle were grazed at Kopperamanna, with Aboriginal stockmen working the station under the supervision of Vogelsang. And the German, although not an ordained missionary, acted in that capacity at Kopperamanna. Each day he conducted morning and evening devotions in Diyari with his Aboriginal employees, as well as Sunday services at the outstation. But on Sundays of special religious significance, or Communion Sundays, the Vogelsang family, and possibly some of the Kopperamanna Aborigines, would ride in the buggy to Killalpaninna for services at the church.

The Herrgott to Birdsville mailcoach also passed through mission land near Kopperamanna and would call fortnightly at the Kopperamanna homestead. Consequently the homestead became the unofficial post office for the mission station, with Vogelsang emptying the mailbag, collecting mission mail and selling stamps. The homestead also operated as a refreshment staging post, with meals served to passengers at the family table, and the Vogelsang daughters acting as waitresses.

Vogelsang's management met with a mixed reaction from his Aboriginal employees. He controlled by a combination of strict discipline and Christian compassion, using superstition, fear and even corporal punishment. On one occasion there was a near strike when an Aboriginal refused to go to work until he was given his tobacco ration. A number of others joined him in support. After several attempts at persuading the renegade, then threatening him with the stockwhip, Vogelsang 'had the stockwhip slashing around his legs'.[71] The man's supporters hurried from the scene, and both they and the dissident stockman returned to work. Some Aboriginal employees longed to break loose from the rigid conformity and strict work ethic; like Gustav, who one evening 'opened his heart' to Anna Vogelsang. But she too had learnt to control through superstition and fear: 'She took him by the hand, led him into the house and showed him the picture depicting the human heart when governed by the Holy Spirit, and the human heart in which evil dwells'.[72] Soon afterwards Gustav had an opportunity to escape from Kopperamanna. He was sent by Vogelsang to procure tobacco from a maildriver camped near the bore and was tempted to flee from the station. But the fear of the 'new magic' inherent in the picture that Mrs Vogelsang had shown him came to his mind and he was afraid of the consequences for himself. Gustav reluctantly returned to Kopperamanna. However, after an argument with other Aborigines at the Kopperamanna camp, Gustav went to the Vogelsang house to bid the family farewell. This time he unequivocally intended to leave. Anna Vogelsang again took his hand and led him to the picture of the crucified Christ. But Gustav refused to look at it, withdrew his hand and fled. He never returned to the station.[73]

Etadunna Outstation
From 1878 to 1890 Ernst Jacob was manager of the Etadunna sheep station and supervisor of the Aboriginal shepherds. Each shepherd, accompanied by his wife, looked after approximately 600 sheep. During dry seasons the sheep were watered from one of the Etadunna wells, the task accomplished by each shepherd dividing his flock into two groups of 300 sheep, and taking each group to the well on alternate days. When feed was especially scarce the shepherds cut branches from the small boxgum trees on the floodplains and hand-fed their charges. During periods of flooding the sheep were driven to dry ground.

Aboriginal shearers were trained at Etadunna and many became well known in the area for their skills and speed. Elias Palkilinna and Johannes Pingilinna became champions, clip-shearing an average of eighty sheep a day. Two shearing sheds were constructed, one for white shearers and one for black shearers, and each season a team of between five and seven Germans arrived from further south to work the white shearers' shed. There was always keen competition between the two sheds. Hermann and Anna Vogelsang were often engaged as cooks for the shearers.

During a prosperous period, income from the sheep could average £1000 to £1600 a year, and in the flood year of 1892 three wagons made a total of five trips each to the railhead at Herrgott to carry baled wool shorn from more than 20 000

Etadunna Station homestead, built c. 1890 by Jacob with the help of Aboriginal labour

sheep. The mission teamster, Jack Ruediger, and his 18-horse team were on the road continually for many weeks. In April of that year the Jacobs' house at Etadunna was completed and for the first time the family had a permanent home.

Like Vogelsang at Kopperamanna, Jacob led the daily prayers at Etadunna Station, and held services on Sundays in the Diyari language. And for special Sundays the Jacob family would ride, with horse and buggy, across the sandy track and through the floodplain to the mission station church. On these occasions services would be held in German for the white staff, after those already conducted for the Aborigines in Diyari.

The 1890s were indeed boom years for the sheep enterprise. They were years of repeated floodings of the Cooper, producing abundant feed and water for the stock and allowing stock numbers to build to record figures. However, with conditions so bountiful in this normally dry region, a new introduced animal species was breeding in immense numbers in the colony. By the early 1890s the rabbit numbers reached plague proportions in the north of South Australia. When the rabbits first arrived, Reuther employed two white labourers and twenty Aboriginals to kill the animals with sticks. They worked under Jacob, who had retired from sheep management in 1890. The men laboured for a month at the gruesome backbreaking job, but in vain. Rabbits continued to increase in enormous numbers and began to threaten the existence of the sheep stock. They were consuming grass and other critical feed at an alarming rate, and within a short time the Lutherans were forced to reduce sheep numbers to about half those previously stocked. Rabbit became the staple meat diet at Killalpaninna. But in December 1894 a great heatwave and dust storm killed millions of the pests. A year later 388 bales of wool were produced, and two extra horse teams were hired for cartage to Herrgott. Income from the wool that year reached £3000, which was donated to the Immanuel Synod's other two enterprises, at Hermannsburg in Central Australia (taken over two years earlier) and at Bloomfield in Queensland, and the house was built for the Vogelsang family at Kopperamanna.

In 1897 the record number of sheep shorn at Etadunna reached 28 000, at a staggering rate of 1100 per day. But the rains had slowed, flooding had stopped, and the lakes and creeks were again drying out. In late 1897 drought once more gripped the north, and 22 000 sheep died in its wake. The floodplains were again bare. When Reichner was asked what he intended to do about the plight of the Killalpaninna enterprise, he replied: 'We bought 7000 sheep and we leave the feeding of them in our Lord's hands. Our duty is to fold our hands in prayer, and glorify our Lord by putting our firm confidence in Him.'[74] Reuther wrote: 'Just as Egypt is dependent on the annual floods of the River Nile, so Bethesda is dependent on the regular flooding of the Cooper River system, which fills the lake. Water then stays there for years making life possible in the Australian desert.'[75]

After the sudden failure of sheep and the constant shepherding and protecting, the mission station turned its attention, from around the turn of the century, to farming cattle. There had been a particularly bad drought in Central Australia and cattle stock were moved southwards to Killalpaninna. Jack Irrgang (the son of Elizabeth Jacob) was sent to Hermannsburg to drive 600 to Killalpaninna. The country across which the cattle had to travel was difficult and harsh, and desiccated by drought. The route ran through the junction area of the Macumba River from the west, and the Kallakoopah Creek (a branch of the Warburton River that runs for about 150 miles, with a dangerous bog at its lower region). In flood times this area became a maze of water channels. And in dry times the water courses took endless twists and turns with treacherous crossings of sandhills. The explorer Peter Egerton Warburton was the first European to venture there and he had become completely lost on a number of occasions.

Irrgang selected a skilled Aboriginal stockman from Killalpaninna to accompany him, and carefully surveyed the country for a suitable route along which to drive the beasts, as the pair rode around the northern end of Lake Killalpaninna and on towards the Finke River through this tortuous countryside. At Hermannsburg he engaged extra stockmen for the droving job. But on the return journey even waterholes that had been charted just weeks previously had already dried to nothing but sand. The party, and stock, were saved from perishing of thirst only by a heavy fall of rain during a critical part of the journey.[76] Fortuitously the rainfall was not so heavy as to plunge them into the opposite problem of being trapped by watercourses. Three cattle drives were made from Hermannsburg to Killalpaninna during this time. In 1901 Theodore Ruediger left Hermannsburg with 448 head of cattle for Killalpaninna. Twelve died *en route*.

The years 1901 and 1902 saw a severe drought across the inland of Australia. Only 3154 sheep remained at Etadunna in 1901, producing just 57 bales of wool.

The Vogelsang family with the Kopperamanna Aborigines beside the 'native' kitchen at Kopperamanna Station

No German shearers were hired that season. Dingoes preyed on the drought-weakened sheep, and the finances of the mission station became a source of endless worry. Wages were lowered for the staff in an effort to weather the economic crisis. Temperatures soared to 120 degrees Fahrenheit in the January of 1902. Mission horse teams could no longer be used for cartage as there was no feed or water along the track. For over a decade local pastoralists had been engaging Afghan drivers with camel transport for their cartage purposes. These exotic animals had proven better suited to the dry conditions of inland Australia, and it was at this time that the conservative Lutherans began to engage camels and Afghan handlers for mission cartage.

During this drought crisis, finances from the enterprises fell so low that only special collections enabled the station to continue. In Adelaide £700 was raised, and Neuendettelsau, in Bavaria, contributed a further £500.[77] Reuther, who was also frenetically working on his translations of the New Testament into Diyari, and on his ethnographic collecting and cataloguing, became ill from overwork and fatigue, and was forced to take a rest in the south. Wettengel was left in charge of the mission station, with its constant problems, like decisions about the moving of stock to ever-dwindling food sources in the drought-ravaged region.

While Reuther was travelling southwards his father-in-law, the president of the mission committee, died. Ludwig Kaibel succeeded Gustav Reichner, and in 1902 Kaibel visited Killalpaninna for the first time, before going on to Hermannsburg. In 1903, 8.5 inches of rain fell and another 7.55 fell in 1904.

Strehlow and the Purchase of Hermannsburg

After the dismissal of Flierl, Pastor Georg Friedrich Leidig took over his position, but stayed for only two months. At the same time, Johannes Bogner was appointed to Meyer's position at Bloomfield. He travelled north with Leidig, visiting Killalpaninna on his journey, and served at Bloomfield for four years until his transfer to Hermannsburg and then Killalpaninna in 1902. But his own period at Killalpaninna was shrouded in discord and controversy.

After Leidig's departure Reuther ran the station as sole missionary until Neuendettelsau sent a replacement some six months later. The newly graduated Carl Frederick Theodore Strehlow arrived at Killalpaninna in July 1892. Thus began the partnership—in April of the following year, after Strehlow had grasped the Diyari language—that saw the translation of the New Testament into the Diyari language. The task took Reuther and Strehlow four years to complete. When the project began Reuther requested a third missionary for the station, claiming the importance of the translation not only for church purposes, but also for private reading for the Aborigines.[78]

But in the year of Strehlow's arrival the UELCA faction of the Lutheran Church severed its connections with the Hermannsburg Mission Institute in Germany, citing a disagreement with 'unionistic' sympathies harboured by the current director, Theodore Harms' successor, Egmont Harms. When theological differences split Lutheran synods in America, Theodore had sided with the Ohio faction over the interpretation of Luther's 1530 Formula of Concord. But South Australia's UELCA synod was strongly 'confessional' and aligned with Missouri synods (accused of being 'Calvinistic'). Egmont Harms was to take an even stronger stand against the Missouri position and steps were taken at Hermannsburg to amalgamate with the Prussian State Church (achieved five years later). Relations quickly soured with the displaced Altlutherans of UELCA, and by 1893 UELCA had cut all ties with Hermannsburg in Germany.[79]

UELCA, consequently, was not prepared to continue with mission work at the Hermannsburg Mission Station in Central Australia, as it no longer had support from Germany. Pastor Heidenreich, president of the UELCA Mission Committee, tried to persuade the synod to purchase the mission station from the partnership, but the synod decided instead to put its small funds into 'home' mission work and its recently established college and seminary. Heidenreich himself attended the auction of assets at the station, in May 1894, to prevent them from falling into 'undesirable hands'.[80] He paid the sum of £1580 for the improvements and livestock, and then offered them back to UELCA. The offer was rejected, so Heidenreich made the same offer to the Immanuel Synod, who bought the assets for £1500 in September 1894. The South Australian government gave permission to continue occupying the land as a reserve for Aboriginal mission purposes for a further twenty-one years.

UELCA's rejection may well have been influenced by the state of the Hermannsburg missionaries at the time, for the last of these men had recently left the station. Discord, disappointment and continual sickness had plagued them. Dysentery, inflamed eyes, the common cold virus, pulmonary infections, influenza and typhoid epidemics had sapped their health and energies. The last missionary to remain at the station, Kempe, severely ill himself, gathered his few possessions and took his children south in 1891, after the death from illness of his wife. The Horn Scientific Expedition visited the station in July 1894, three years after its abandonment, and reported that the only evidence of mission influence among the Aranda people was the wearing of scraps of European clothing and their German and biblical names. Most of the Hermannsburg Aborigines had reverted to their own culture and traditional lifestyle.[81]

The early 1890s had seen 'bumper' seasons at the stock station at Killalpaninna, and the Immanuel Synod's confidence in the enterprise was at its peak. After Hermannsburg was purchased, Reuther and Strehlow were sent to Central Australia to survey the station and to organise the takeover.[82] Strehlow stayed on as missionary until his death in 1922. (After twenty-eight years among the Australian Aborigines, and at the age of just fifty-four, he died a slow, agonising death from dropsy and pleurisy. Strehlow was buried at the lonely outpost of Horseshoe Bend, on his way south in the mission buggy, in an emergency attempt to obtain medical help.)

Other Mission Staff at Killalpaninna, 1890s
'Harry' Hillier
In June 1893 a fresh-faced young Englishman arrived at Killalpaninna for a brief period of recuperation and to act as temporary English teacher. He and William Hunt were exceptions to the employment of German staff. Henry (called Harry) James Hillier, son of a deceased English doctor, had been sent to Australia to recover from a respiratory complaint. His widowed mother had not wanted her frail son to work while in the colony, but in Adelaide Hillier had been introduced to Reichner, when it was suggested that he spend the winter months in the dry north. Reichner obligingly gave him a job teaching English to the Aboriginal pupils at Killalpaninna.[83] Hillier was to serve over a period of twelve years at Killalpaninna, and for four years at Hermannsburg.

Harry Hillier was cured of his respiratory illness. He was a gifted artist and linguist, and was interested in the collection and drawing of insects and other biological and botanical specimens native to the Killalpaninna area. His collection and finely drawn, detailed map of the country east of Lake Eyre, containing some 2500 place-names (collated by Reuther), are in the South Australian Museum. Hillier also drew and painted the 'toas', the small totem sculptures made by the Killalpaninna Aborigines and collected by Reuther.

During the year of Hillier's appointment a new two-roomed school building was constructed. Two classes could now be given at the same time. The German children were taught in one room, called the 'colony school' (or the 'German school'), and the Aboriginal pupils in the other, the 'natives' school', with the sexes segregated.[84] Both German and English languages were taught to the Aborigines, and an emphasis was still placed on catechism classes and scriptural education.

In 1903 the visiting Russian scholar, Yashchenko, observed an English lesson given by Hillier in the 'natives' school. Both young and old pupils were in the class, including a one-legged elderly Aborigine. Hillier taught from a blackboard on an easel, after beginning the day's instruction with a prayer. His pupils ranged through several levels of competence in language, and while one dictation class was proceeding, the younger students were loudly spelling out other words, letter by letter! 'All were evidently quite accustomed to this teaching method, and the yelling did not confuse anybody', reported the Russian.[85]

In 1905, after several absences from the station to visit his homeland, Hillier at last resigned to return to England permanently. He believed there were no career prospects for him at Killalpaninna, and besides, felt duty-bound to return to an ageing mother.[86] But he was soon drawn to the Australian desert again, and in 1906 took a position as teacher at Hermannsburg Mission Station, under Strehlow, becoming the translator of hymns into the Aranda language.

Otto Siebert
Reuther requested a third missionary for Killalpaninna in 1893, when he and Strehlow were occupied with the translation of the New Testament into Diyari. It was a period of optimism and confidence, if only in the stock station enterprise, and in March of the following year, 23-year-old Otto Siebert arrived from Neuendettelsau. Siebert was to become a brilliant scholar and ethnographer, and just three months after his arrival preached his first sermon in the Diyari language. Carl Strehlow, however, had rather quickly become disenchanted with missionising at Killalpaninna, writing that: 'Mission work is not very impressive at Bethesda. Compared with other missions our gains are very modest. We can't ever expect large numbers of converts.'[87] Siebert, on the other hand, was new and enthusiastic and wrote, 'The church service made a big impression on me. What I have missed in many German congregations is the careful listening. I found it here.'[88]

But, like other missionaries before him, Otto Siebert was soon to face the realities of life at this mission station. He visited the camp blacks with Reuther one afternoon, and while chatting with a group of Aboriginal wood-gatherers, heard that only one of the nine had never killed a man. One busy gatherer related how he and his brother, on orders from his father, had cut off both legs of an enemy, then an arm, before decapitating the victim. Siebert paled and 'thanked our Lord that He has turned these monsters into Christians', as he wrote sanguinely.[89]

Shortly after Siebert's arrival, Carl Strehlow was transferred to the Hermannsburg Station. Siebert's job was to act as bush missionary, travelling the 750-square-mile Aboriginal reserve, preaching and teaching 'in the field'. A year after he joined Killalpaninna he married Anna Maria Magdalene, at Point Pass. The couple had a house at the mission settlement, but Siebert was away often, sometimes for lengthy periods. He would camp on his travels, or sleep in a small outhouse far from the station, but close to Aboriginal camp settlements, possibly the stone house at Murrapatirrinna. He would bring 'willing' Aborigines back to the station, either for instruction from the school, or for medical treatment for their illnesses. It was hoped that those successfully treated would stay on to receive instruction in the new faith. In reality, however, it was only very ill people who were desperate enough to accompany Siebert, and these people often died soon after arrival.[90] In his search for converts, the bush missionary spent much of his time in the field treating the ill.

An extract from one of Siebert's letters to Neuendettelsau describes nocturnal bush missionising:

> An absolutely beautiful evening, so characteristic for Australia, has passed and a

Otto Siebert and his wife, Anna, with mission girls Ida and Susanne

deep darkness has covered this rather treeless barren countryside. I am on my way to a heathen's camp on the outskirts of the mission run—late at night—because during the day most blackfellows are mainly hunting and only those who are physically unable, or are plain too lazy, remain at the huts. Only a short walk and I am at my destination. Among the darkness the campfires burn to keep the kootchie (devil) out. They burn the whole night. The wood is sometimes carried by very old women from treeless places far away. Paying no attention to the barking of the dogs I enter the camps and say hello to one after the other. In front of the door ahead are four Aborigines (two men and two women). They are rather busy roasting a couple of rabbits and large lizards, a meal which is quite good. A group of half-starved dogs stand around the fires waiting for left-over food to be thrown to them. I take up my place and talk to the four people.[91]

During his nine years at Killalpaninna Siebert collected a large volume of material on the customs and culture of the Diyari people. In 1901 he became ill and was looked after by Vogelsang at Kopperamanna. He was vomiting severely, could not sit, lie or sleep and had abdominal and back pain.[92] During the following year the 32-year-old's health had so deteriorated that he took a year's rest. These were years of prolonged drought, exhausting for the Germans in their length and severity. Siebert, his wife and 2-year-old son left South Australia in May 1902 for recreation leave in Germany. They never returned. Johannes Bogner, then at Hermannsburg with Strehlow, took Siebert's place. 'Bush missionising' had obviously not been fruitful, for Bogner's task was to act as station manager, while Reuther concentrated on mission work and on his endless translating and documenting.

Nathaniel Wettengel
Missionary Wettengel graduated from Neuendettelsau to join Killalpaninna in 1896 as a replacement for Carl Strehlow. Wettengel taught the school pupils and instructed the baptismal candidates. A year later he was married at the station to his German fiancée, Nicole, in a ceremony with six Aboriginal couples, and in the presence of the mission committee who had travelled to the station for the occasion. The twelve Aborigines had been baptised before the committee just a day before the wedding.[93] Wettengel and his bride were the example, and the splendour and importance of the occasion was perhaps a special incentive for the baptisms and the marriages. When writing of that 'main evil', so intolerable to the Lutherans, and still deemed prevalent among the Aborigines, Wettengel reported, 'The only good thing I notice is that those Christians we have married stay relatively faithful and don't seem so often to sin against the sixth commandment'.[94]

Wettengel arranged beds on the verandah of his house for pupils whose parents had returned to camp life, and constructed a small house near his own for these 'deserted Christians'. At one stage he had eight Aboriginal boys living in his own house. He wrote warmly of the characters in his classroom—like one old man who, during a lesson on the Christmas story, would become annoyed whenever Wettengel complained that his answer to a question was wrong and would turn the blame squarely on the missionary. One young man would look sadly at Wettengel, saying he really wanted to ask a question, but he could not get the question out unless the missionary looked directly into his face. Finally the youth managed to dispel his concern, that of whether Mary and Joseph had enough blankets when they were escaping from Jerusalem. 'I have myself learnt to respect these people a great deal since I arrived', Wettengel wrote.[95] And in a report to the mission committee he stated that 'Spiritually and intellectually the black children are in no way behind the white children'.[96]

In the drought crisis of early 1901, with the restructuring of the economics of Killalpaninna, Wettengel was transferred to the Hermannsburg Station. He spent the next two years as assistant to Carl Strehlow before being dismissed, accused of usurping Strehlow's knowledge of the Aranda language.[97]

William Hunt
In June 1896 Reuther advertised in the colony for an English teacher for Killalpaninna, and was answered by a young man then in service as a horse and buggy attendant. Hillier had travelled to England a year earlier and had not yet returned, and Siebert was about to take leave from the station. William Hunt was engaged as a teacher and to perform light work at the station. Hunt very quickly became an admirer of Reuther and of Reuther's work among the Aborigines. To Reichner he wrote:

> He [Reuther] preaches so earnestly for Christ and is so kind to the sick ones here, I never felt God's presence so near as I did three weeks last Sunday. The Reverend Reuther seemed to speak with such great power, moving the whole of the blacks almost to tears . . . I love him because he is so straightforward in all his ways and he lives a Christ-like life every day.[98]

In 1898 Hunt and the schoolchildren accompanied the Reuther family on a journey northwards to witness an unforgettable scene—the sight of floodwaters as they ran through the desert along the watercourses and into the channel to fill Lake Killalpaninna. Back at the station they all sang praises to God while the church-bell rang from the moment the waters surged through the channel and entered the lake.[99]

While at Killalpaninna Hunt's small, neat handwriting changed, with his own metamorphosis, to a heavy, bold script. And within a short period of time he had applied to Reichner for conversion to Lutheranism.

Mission Wives, 1890s
According to Flierl senior, the qualities of a 'good missionary wife' were to be:

> like the female Christians in the very original Christian community, not vain and concerned with jewellery and looks, but to play on the inner decoration of people with the gentle and quiet spirit. Such people then preach and teach without words and have won heathens over because of the lifestyle of the Christian women following the seed of the Lord.[100]

During the 1890s at least four women lived at Killalpaninna and its outstations at any one time. Pauline Reuther, Anna Vogelsang and Elizabeth Jacob endured the full decade (and much longer), as did Jack Ruediger's wife. But, with the many changes of staff, several other wives of missionaries spent time at the main mission station: Emilie Flierl, Anna Siebert, Nicole Wettengel and Riegert's wife, all German-born or descended, except the Lithuanian Riegerts.

Emma Vogelsang (daughter of Hermann) supervising Aboriginal women with their 'mending' at the Kopperamanna Station

All these women were given specific duties at the station, although such duties were never regarded as 'employment' and worth a wage, even for Mrs Riegert, who taught at the school. A missionary's wife was expected to help her husband. Consequently the committee had only male wages to find.

From 1878 Elizabeth Jacob lived the nomadic and isolated lifestyle of a shepherd manager's wife, away from the main station, until her husband's engagement as manager at Etadunna outstation in 1891. Even then she was the only white woman at Etadunna. From 1894 Anna Vogelsang lived at the outstation homestead of Kopperamanna (after the family had endured temporary quarters for two years), 12 solitary miles from Killalpaninna. The Vogelsangs had six daughters and two sons (as well as Hermann's third son), but again, apart from the Aboriginal wives of the black workers at Kopperamanna, Anna was the only European woman at the station. The two sisters, Elizabeth and Anna, would occasionally visit each other, 10 miles ride by buggy, or would meet at the special Sunday services at Killalpaninna. They had grown up with Pauline Reuther in the German community of the Barossa Valley, which formed the basis for a special relationship between the three women during these crucial years.[101]

There are, unfortunately, no known surviving letters from the wives of the mission staff (until the later correspondence of Anna Vogelsang after she had left

The Reuther family, including four of their children and two of Pauline's from her previous marriage

Kopperamanna). But from the diary of Reuther and the letters of the missionaries themselves, there appears to have been a strong bond among the women. Theirs was a lonely lifestyle and undoubtedly harsh and difficult.

The Reuthers were married by the bride's father, Pastor Gustav Reichner, president of the mission committee. Pauline Reuther (called 'Pauli' by her husband), together with her three sons from a previous marriage, arrived at Killalpaninna in early April 1889. Apart from being the wife of Missionary Reuther, her task at the station was to supervise the two black cooks in the kitchen of the Aborigines' eating house. And when Emilie Flierl left the station, her task of teaching sewing and mending to the Aboriginal women was filled by Pauline Reuther and other missionary wives. Sewing and mending had become an important occupation for the Aboriginal women.

The Reuthers' first child together (Gustav Martin) was born on their first wedding anniversary, and Pauline Reuther was to bear a child every year for the next eight years. There was no medical aid within 400 miles of the station, and the pregnant wives were entirely dependent on each other, their husbands and their female Aboriginal house helpers, for assistance with the obstetrics. Anna Vogelsang gave birth to her eldest child at Bucaltaninna, a further six at Killalpaninna, and her youngest, Helene, at Kopperamanna. It had been planned that Elizabeth Jacob would travel to Kopperamanna when the last child was due, but the baby came early and Hermann Vogelsang himself helped with the delivery.[102] Surprisingly, none of the missionary wives died in childbirth. There are, however, documented accounts of Aboriginal mission women dying—like Fanny, the wife of Derilinas, who died in childbirth in July 1892.[103]

The Reuthers' second son, Richard Arthur, was born when Pauline was in her thirty-seventh year. Then came a further four sons (Albert Ewald, Oscar, Georg Edwin, and Ludwig Wilhelm) in successive years, a daughter (Anna Maria Alma) in July 1896, and finally a last child, another son (Rudolph Berthold) in August 1897. Pauline was generally strong enough to be working again three days after the deliveries. With so many babies to attend and so much domestic and mission work to carry out, she could not afford the luxury of a lengthy recovery period.

But tragedy struck for the fifth son, Georg Edwin Reuther. Born in June 1894, he was baptised a week later in the Killalpaninna church. The Cooper had recently flooded, after considerable rain, and it was a buoyant season for the stock station. In August Pauline was cited as being 'unwell', and a month later, after the busy shearing season had finished, Reuther and Strehlow left for Hermannsburg in Central Australia. The Immanuel Synod had just taken control and the two missionaries were required to survey the station and assess its requirements. Young Georg Edwin was just three months old. Pauline was already encumbered with four small children under five years of age, as well as her three children from the previous marriage. Furthermore she had her mission duties to fulfil.

While Reuther was at Hermannsburg, young Georg Edwin fell ill with dysentery, and for eight days his tiny body gradually weakened until he finally died. Reuther did not hear the news until he arrived at Herrgott on his return from Hermannsburg, a week after the baby's funeral. He made a northward dash and on arrival 'found Pauli in deep sorrow'. 'It was very hard for me not to see him here on earth again. My dear Pauli had experienced severe trials, which she had to meet on her own. The Lord in Heaven gave her strength to bear it.'[104]

But Pauline was already two months pregnant again, and there was much to command her attention. Her two eldest sons were preparing to leave Australia for Germany.

In 1891 Reuther had added two more rooms to his original home to accommodate his growing family. He had laid the foundation stones and Flierl had made the wooden framework. But the family soon outgrew that house, and in December 1895 moved to a new home set high on a sandhill at the northern end of the settlement with a view across the lake. There had been a house on the site, previously occupied by Meyer seventeen years earlier, and with help from Ruediger and Jack Irrgang, Reuther built a replica of the original and joined the new with the old by a full-length hallway. Like the other buildings at Killalpaninna its construction was of clay bricks over a wooden frame. The inside walls were lined with wooden boards.

In 1898, after the successes of the stock station, many of the original buildings were demolished and more substantial and comfortable dwellings erected in their place. Wettengel and the schoolchildren built two small houses for the Aboriginal children, with the children themselves making the bricks, plastering walls and constructing a garden.

A description of the Vogelsangs' Kopperamanna house has survived in the memoirs of their youngest daughter, born at the homestead.[105] It, too, was built of mud-bricks on a stone foundation, with a rush-thatched roof over galvanised iron, and cooling verandahs. Initially the house had two bedrooms, one for the girls and one for Vogelsang and his wife (the three boys were older and independent). Later, two more rooms (guest rooms) and a cellar were erected near the homestead. The main house had a large dining–living room with a small harmonium, which all the children learnt to play and which served as the main source of family entertainment. Against one wall was a hard-backed sofa, where guests would sit, or where Hermann rested when ill. Beside the harmonium stood a large bookcase, for both Hermann and Anna were keen readers. Nearby stood Hermann's special table where, particularly in his last years, he could sit for hours reading and writing. Beside this was Anna's cotton-reel-legged sewing table, the handiwork of her son Theodore. During cold winter evenings the room was heated by a small stove. At night the house was lit by candles and kerosene lamps.

Most of the furniture in the German mission homes, such as dressers and tables, was handmade from pieces of scrap wood and large wooden packing cases. Behind the dining-room door at Kopperamanna a large shelf held bowls of goat's milk, resting for separation of the cream to make butter or cheese. Goatskins were used as scatter rugs on bedroom floors, and walls were whitewashed with lime each year. These limed walls would leave a powdery mark if brushed against with the dark clothes popularly worn for formal occasions, particularly annoying for the men in their dark Sunday suits. There were no bathrooms in the houses, and on Saturday nights a washtub would be brought into the kitchen for weekly baths. In the summer months an outside 'shower' (a drum with holes in the bottom) provided a cooling cleanser. But the German children would prefer to run to the edges of the lake for a cleansing swim, or to the channel of the Kopperamanna bore to frolic in the gushing artesian water. When water filled Lake Kopperamanna they loved to swim there.[106]

Water suitable for drinking was frequently in short supply. Each mission house had a water storage tank to collect precious rainwater from gutters on the roofs. When the lakes were full, lake water was made drinkable by putting it in a water sack which was hung from the verandah until foreign matter and heavy sediments settled at the bottom.[107] In dry weather the mission staff depended on soakage wells dug by the Aboriginal schoolboys. They were a last resort for water during severe drought periods and were generally only used for the vegetable gardens. One such life-saving well was located at the bottom of the sandhill upon which Reuther's 1895 house stood.[108] During droughts a 40-gallon water container stood in the Reuthers' kitchen, and every day the Aborigines would fill it from the soak. The water was then passed through a fine sieve to discard marine life before being boiled for drinking purposes. There was also a soak on the shore of Lake Kopperamanna, near the Vogelsangs' garden. Anna

Vogelsang would dip a bucket into the reinforced square soakage well and water her precious vegetables. But there were times when the Vogelsangs, too, had to rely on this for their own consumption.

The need for fresh, familiar vegetables was important to the Germans, and consequently discussions about vegetable gardens featured regularly in reminiscences and correspondence, in which vegetable gardens proudly served as a backdrop to group photographs. The mission station and two outstations all had vegetable gardens, generally tended by the women. They were fenced to keep out goats and small native animals. Hungry birds became pests, and hard work was required to grow and tend such foreign plants as cabbage, spinach, lettuce, carrots, and occasionally potatoes in this harsh environment. Cabbage grew reasonably well, and was made into sauerkraut (for storage), and potatoes were made into dumplings. Fruit trees did not survive. Precious water could not be wasted on flower-growing, and the only flowers were the wild variety.

During periods of prolonged drought the Germans would sustain themselves on native plants. Educated by the Aborigines at the station, they ate munyeroo (that grew in the sand and could be eaten as a salad), yowa (small wild onions eaten either raw or boiled), and winkara or bladder saltbush. By consuming these plants the Lutherans prevented scurvy and maintained health. (As late as the 1930s Aborigines were dying from scurvy during prolonged droughts at Hermannsburg, where pastoral herds had destroyed many of their native plants.)[109]

The diet of the Killalpaninna Germans consisted mainly of mutton and goat meat, with beef occasionally. The goats could live on almost anything organic and could survive longer than cattle and sheep. There was no refrigeration and when an animal was killed the meat had to be salted down that same day. Once or twice a year a pig was killed. A favourite food for the Germans, very little of the animal was not eaten. Large chunks of bacon and ham were cured in the smokehouse, the head of the pig would be cleaned and cooked, the liver and heart kept for a special meal, black pudding was made from the blood, liverwurst and metwurst made and hung in long sausages. The fat was rendered down for lard and the trotters used for making brawn. Rarely did the Germans have the luxury of poultry. There were no fowls at Killalpaninna, as grain had to be sent from the south, which proved too expensive.[110]

The women baked their own bread in large mud-brick ovens, using hop yeast and flour. They made traditional German yeast cake, often in batches of a dozen cakes at a baking. And before Christmas there was a busy biscuit-baking session, traditional in German society. Rock ammonia biscuits, honey cakes and sugared nuts decorated the Christmas tables. Other cooking was done over an open fireplace, a fiercely hot task in the summer months. Coffee was the daily drink, and the beans were made to go further by grinding equal parts with roasted barley and oat grain and adding chicory. Eggs from the black swans and ducks on the lake, as well as emu eggs, were used instead of fowl eggs. Emu flesh was not popular with the Germans, who considered it too oily for their taste. In fact no wild animals were eaten by them with the exception of the introduced rabbit.

Goat's milk was used for all dairy needs. The cream was beaten into butter in large wooden butter churns, and kept in the coolest part of the house. Anna Vogelsang was renowned for a cheese called 'quark'. Prepared from thick goat's-

The vegetable garden at the Kopperamanna settlement, planted after the 1906 flood. Hermann senior, Anna and her daughter, Helene (lounging), are to the right

milk whey hung in a calico bag to drain, to which salt, carraway seeds and cream were then added, the mixture was rolled into balls and stored in earthenware jars until ripened.[111]

Diseases and Accidents

With drinking water often contaminated (having been taken from the lake or the general soak or even the roofs of the houses) and with the heat, flies and fatigue of the summer months, regular outbreaks of typhoid erupted at the station. The infectious fever claimed the lives of several German children and an unknown number of Aborigines. Koch was the first German to die from typhoid, in 1871; baby Georg Edwin Reuther died in 1894. A year earlier young Albert Reuther had suffered from dysentery but had recovered, and in June 1897 Pauline (seven months pregnant at the time) and four of the Reuther children were stricken with the fever. All miraculously recovered. Anna Vogelsang contracted typhoid during the 1890s and a child from Hermann's first marriage died from the fever in the late 1860s. One of Pauline's sons from her first marriage was visiting the mission station from the south when he contracted typhoid and almost died. Prayers were said for him and the other Reuther children paid a last visit, but the young man slowly recovered. Reuther buried several children from surrounding stations who had died of the dreaded fever, and in July 1892 the Ruedigers' second-born child, a daughter, died. The cause of death was not recorded, but it may well have been typhoid again.[112]

Hermann Vogelsang, who suffered from asthma, took an interest in medical cures, especially in homeopathic form. He read prolifically on the subject, and collected small pills and potions. When sick mission people (white or black) came to him, Vogelsang would study their condition in his books, make a diagnosis and formulate what he considered a suitable treatment. As there was no medical practitioner at hand, this amateur approach was perhaps better than nothing. When Aborigines at Kopperamanna presented with a cold, he would administer eucalyptus drops on a teaspoon of sugar. As a localised painkiller, he would saturate a piece of cottonwool with his own homemade substance and apply it to the affected area.[113] Influenza, the common cold, stomach ailments, eye infections and, of course, typhoid were the main illnesses at the station. Jack Irrgang acted as dentist, extracting troublesome teeth with a pair of dental forceps.

Accident victims would be brought to Kopperamanna for treatment, or even to Killalpaninna, where the missionaries had a stock of medicines for such emergencies. Stockmen with infected minor injuries would call at the station for treatment. One man, badly injured after catching an arm in the machinery of the Kopperamanna bore, arrived at Kopperamanna Station after an agonisingly slow journey by horse and buggy.[114] One September evening in 1891 an unconscious Afghan whose head had been split open by a camel, was brought to Vogelsang. Vogelsang could do nothing for the man and three days later he was taken to Herrgott by Jacob.[115] His fate was not recorded.

Entertainment
There was little diversion from home life for the German women. The main entertainment was hymn-singing around the family harmonium, and reading. But in September 1899 a piano arrived at the station, carried by the mission teamster and organised by Reuther while he was in the south giving evidence at the Select Committee for the proposed Aborigines' Bill of that year. Pauline Reuther was an accomplished pianist and thenceforth Sunday evenings were spent at the Reuther home, singing hymns and listening to Pauline play. Mission Aborigines would join the German staff at these gatherings, for they loved to sing. 'Little John' was described as 'small in structure' but with a 'beautiful deep voice'.[116]

The Vogelsangs (whose family name means 'birdsong') were also musical. They spent hours at the family organ. Old Hermann taught the children German folksongs, like 'The Three Roses', 'The Lorelei' and 'Wooden Heart'. The girls loved to sing while rowing on the lake: 'Peace Be Still', 'Master of the Tempest', and Black American songs like 'The Old Folks at Home'. The Vogelsang children sang in choirs both at the Killalpaninna church and later in the south. Hermann junior played violin and clarinet, and purchased a Thomas Edison phonograph. The family would sit on their verandah at Kopperamanna on hot summer evenings, listening to recordings of German brass bands, light classics and waltzes emanating from the large funnel. Hermann junior later became choirmaster at Killalpaninna for an all-black choir. Helene, the youngest daughter, learned to play the zither and mouth-organ, which a few of the Kopperamanna Aborigines also mastered.[117]

Long walks were a regular activity, and picnics with honey cakes, bread and meats were enjoyed under the few spreading gums. Sometimes the picnics

Cake (Kuchen) and tea outside Reuther's house after a baptimal service

included mission Aborigines, who would take the families to distant sandhills and perhaps give a lesson in digging for wild vegetables. Blonde-haired, blue-eyed German children ran in wild abandonment across a sea of sand-dune waves with their dusky, shoeless counterparts. Visits to outstations and other European families were made, and wildflowers gathered along the way. The Reuthers and Vogelsangs were friendly with the Neylon (sometimes spelt Neaylon) family from a nearby station; Reuther baptised the Neylons' children and also buried a Neylon child at Killalpaninna.[118] Ernst Jacob was a keen star- and planet-gazer, and on a clear black night would spend hours lying on his back, telescope to the eye, searching the star-strung sky. When asked whether he would like to travel to a foreign country, he replied he would rather go to Saturn.[119]

On Sundays there were the church services at the various stations, and on Communion Sundays, when the outstation families rode to the Killalpaninna church, there was always cake and coffee together afterwards. The German families would visit each other. Visitors came to the stations, and Elizabeth Jacob would proudly exhibit her vegetable garden 'with her ankle-length skirt very gracefully draped over one arm so as not to have it trailing in the dirt'.[120] Police officers patrolling the north paid frequent visits to the various families, the

Mission boats on Lake Killalpaninna

mailcoach called regularly at Kopperamanna, and there were occasional trips to Herrgott and the south.

In August 1902 the Vogelsangs celebrated their silver wedding anniversary. Kopperamanna played host to the Germans from Killalpaninna and Etadunna, with even the shearers joining in the festivities. Anna Vogelsang was presented with a silver wreath for her hair, and Hermann a silver button-hole, the pair ceremonially seated on chairs decorated with green leaves. Hymns were sung and a service read by Reuther before the party began. The Kopperamanna Aborigines joined the later festivities.[121]

Boating, swimming and fishing were favourite pastimes when the lake was filled, especially for the children. They would fish with the Aborigines in small wooden boats, catching bream or yellow-belly. If night closed in before they returned, their singing and stifled laughter would echo across the still, silent water. At the lake's edge a wooden fishing platform, called 'paroowolpa' (meaning 'big fish camp') was erected by the Aborigines. They would spend hours holding grass fishing lines and dangling bare feet in the cool water. The German children sat with them, chattering in Diyari, until a violet twilight was mirrored in the lake and the crying and restless twittering of masses of budgerigars, plovers and cockatoos quietened and the birds settled into gum trees beside the channel for the night. The children would amble home as kerosene lamps were lit and mosquitoes swarmed in their thousands. On hot summer days, when the lake was dry, Reuther would take his children by buggy to Clayton Dam to swim. There, in the warm shallow water, with the sun beating on unclothed bodies, an infinite expanse of clear, blue sky overhead, the family picnicked to the mournful cry of the black crow and the screeching of white cockatoos.

The German children had few, if any, conventional toys. They made pets of goats, magpies and cockatoos, and ran wild in the sandhills with the Aboriginal children, playing imaginary games. But they loved the arrival of an Afghan hawker, with his box of trinkets and cheap nicknacks. He would arrive in a camel-drawn wagon, and would often unhitch the animal and give the children camel rides.[122]

In one of his reports to the mission committee outlining requirements for the next supply of goods for the station, Reuther, in jest, added 'one monkey' to the end of the list. Either because they took this seriously, or to continue the joke, the committee at Tanunda procured a monkey and cage from the Adelaide Zoo. The creature was sent to the mission station with the next consignment. One evening Ruediger arrived at Killalpaninna with a heavily loaded wagon. Everyone crowded around, as usual, to view the new purchases. When the monkey was produced from its position under the wagon Reuther was astonished. Squeals of excitement came from the children, and murmurs of disbelief and amazement from the Aborigines, who had never seen any animal like it before. The monkey was traumatised from its rough journey, and lunged menacingly at the crowd. Reuther scratched his head and wondered what to do with this alien and unneeded creature.

The monkey lived in a large cage beside Reuther's house for several years before it died. It created quite a stir when it escaped from its cage every now and then, causing riotous chases by the children and Aborigines at the station. It would run from one house to another across the roofs, and would tease the pursuers by clapping its hands as they tried to coax it down. Sometimes, on escaping, it would jump through the Reuthers' kitchen window and terrify the Aboriginal women working there. Headscarves were tossed away as the women ran from the room, or, if braver, gave chase. The cheeky animal would emulate the women by wiping the kitchen table in the manner observed from its cage outside. At times it stole cakes by reaching through an open window. Once Reuther stood too close to the cage while talking to a group of visitors. He had an important letter in his pocket which the monkey snatched before running to the far corner of the cage and tearing to shreds.

The mission Aborigines grew very fond of this creature, with its mischievous personality, and when it died, torn to pieces by pursuing dogs after yet another escape, were very distressed. 'They were determined to give it a proper funeral, even if (they told the lifeless body) it could not expect to go to heaven. "No", they said, "You are damned; you are damned", as they wrapped it in a blanket, and buried it at the bottom of the sandhill, carefully marking the place.'[123]

Fun chases, when they occurred, were a great relief from the formality of mission life for the Aborigines, and were duly relished. During snake plagues at the station, they embarked on snake hunts—searching, creeping, stalking and finally chasing and beating a snake to death while screaming in delight. The

Germans feared these often deadly reptiles, so biblically synonymous with temptation and the devil, and encouraged their extermination.

When the mission committee announced a visit in 1897 Reuther resolved to repay the monkey farce by playing a joke on them. He conspired with 'Jack' Ruediger to give the 'cityfied Germans' a true experience of Killalpaninna. When the well-dressed and dignified gentlemen expressed a desire to inspect the mission run, Reuther and Ruediger saw their opportunity. Reuther winked at the teamster as the buggy was brought out on the morning of inspection. The Aborigines were instructed to bring the 'freshest' (liveliest) of the mission horses. Enthusiastically they joined the mood of conspiracy, for they loved to play pranks, and fetched a couple of half wild brumbies. The horses were placed in shafts and hobbled, while Ruediger climbed into the buggy seat to take the reins. The Aborigines held the horses back tightly as the committee members boarded. One sat beside Ruediger, the other three on a seat behind him. At a given signal, the hobbles were loosened and the Aborigines sprang aside. The buggy gave a great lurch and the horses sped for the open plains. Ruediger gave them full rein. Their pace did not slacken even when negotiating a narrow creekbed. The buggy bounced heavily over the embankment, so that the passengers on the back seat were forcibly ejected from the vehicle. The horses raced on, and when Ruediger saw through his rear mirror that his back passengers were missing, he turned the still galloping animals back to the scene of the ejection. There he found the dazed trio still sitting in their seats, unhurt but with racing hearts. On the next day it was suggested that the committee view the western part of the run. Unanimously they declined.[124]

Demise of Reuther

During the 1890s Killalpaninna was host to important visitors, notably scientists and ethnographers from Europe studying the Aboriginal people and the local flora. Reuther was influenced by these men and their work, and began collecting ethnographic material and artefacts himself. As the Killalpaninna missionaries became fluent in the Diyari language, the Diyari world view came into focus. At about this time the international spotlight of the newly emerging European sciences was directed at Australia, with the social evolutionists in particular looking at Australian Aborigines as isolated survivors of Stone Age man. Aborigines were seen as relics from a past age, and became test cases and the focus of studies for the new Darwinian theories that *Homo sapiens* evolved from apes. The Killalpaninna missionaries would not have shared the basic premise of these irreligious hypotheses, but they did play an important role in the collection of ethnographic material and the development of anthropological debate.

Reuther and Strehlow had completed their translation of the New Testament into Diyari, and Siebert was collecting information on local Aboriginal culture and customs, some of which was published by Howitt. From the time of Strehlow's period at Killalpaninna, Reuther began spending more and more hours in his study and with his Aboriginal informants. However, his responsibility was still as head of the station, that of manager and overseer to the two stock stations, as well as spiritual leader. He spent exhaustingly long periods at his duties.

Living and working in the north was draining in itself, but Reuther had suffered the anxiety of witnessing a fellow missionary's expulsion, the death of a baby son, the struggles of the stock station, yet another severe drought as the century turned and the resultant increasing debt, and constant disappointment at low Aboriginal conversions to the Christian faith. He agonised over the continual breaking of the sixth commandment, and fought the negative influences and the violence of Europeans in the area. It always seemed a losing battle. He had a large family to attend and support, and had become obsessed with writing tomes on the language and culture of the Diyari. Like many others of the time he believed the Aborigines were a dying people and theirs a dying culture, and that it was imperative, his God-given duty perhaps, to document as much as possible before it was too late.[125]

Reuther suffered periods of unspecified illness during his last years at Killalpaninna. He went south for medical attention and to recuperate in 1901, and again in 1904. He was an emotional man who, it seems, may have suffered bouts of severe depression during some periods of his life. In 1889 he wrote in his diary: 'Today I am very sad and do not know why. Dear God give me joy and fidelity in my dear calling and grant that I may work with blessing for time and eternity.'[126] And nearing the end of his life, in late 1913, he expressed depression and a death wish in the last entries of his diary.[127]

In April 1902 Johannes Bogner was sent from Hermannsburg to Killalpaninna as stock station manager to assist the overburdened Reuther. Siebert had recently left the station, also suffering ill-health. But Reuther was to write that 'Brother Bogner is only sitting half in the saddle because he can't bring his wife up here ... the work is too much for just one'.[128] In 1902 Bogner spent only five months at the station, for his sick wife was now living at Tanunda. But Reuther continued his frenetic collating of Aboriginal material, and in October 1904 completed his massive work, the four-volume Diyari dictionary.

A year later, in October 1905, he was to perform his last baptismal and confirmation services in the Killalpaninna church. On that day, Reuther was feeling unwell, reporting to his superiors:

> That my strength is not returning, I am noticing again. My nerves evidently are getting the best of my willpower. Two services one after another in two languages didn't used to affect me much. Now one sermon and one address seems an effort. The partaking of the community dinner in my house with the brethren and sisters woke again the weakened spirits and an hour of quietness afterwards was welcome.[129]

The service had begun at 9 o'clock on Sunday morning. Baptismal and confirmation candidates had met in Reuther's study, while the Aboriginal congregation had assembled outside his door. After a short prayer, the procession of Reuther leading the candidates, followed by the mission Aborigines, walked to the church as the bell rang triumphantly from the tower. The mud-brick chapel was decorated with wildflowers and gumleaf branches, and just three baptismal candidates sat beside the font. The two confirmees stood in front of the altar. The services proceeded, with the lesson being on death, and that sin produces death (for recent news had arrived of the death, in the south, of a local Aboriginal youth). The baptised were named Walter, Arthur and Wilhelmine, and the confirmees were the black children Andreas and Selma.[130]

In late 1905 Reuther was to suffer a grievous blow to his reputation and his career, one from which he would never fully recover and which shadowed him until his death just eight years later. Rumours associated him with fathering a child to a young part-Aboriginal girl called Frieda who was employed as a domestic at the Reuthers' home. Reuther was unable to prove his innocence.

When the baby was born to his unmarried domestic assistant, Reuther was at first accused, by the mission committee, of neglecting his moral and spiritual duties by always being shut in his study, and obsessively focused on his writings. He was deemed indirectly responsible for encouraging immoral behaviour at the station. But soon the accusations deepened and Reuther himself came under suspicion.

Rumours of various kinds had surrounded the station over the years. In 1891–92 certain 'rumours' circulated, their nature unclear, causing Reuther to write in his diary, '[In] The months of January, February and March [there] were rumours on the Station and also among the heathens. It was, as it were, as though the Devil tried to destroy the whole of the mission with all his power and strength but it should not be a success, for the kingdom ours remaineth.'[131] Rumours reached the south about Meyer's drinking problem at Bloomfield, and it seems more than rumours caused the downfall of the younger Flierl.

Rumours had also circulated of 'immoral' activities and violence perpetrated by white settlers and station hands against Aborigines in the area, with the Lutherans as vocal opponents to such activity. Perhaps, given the Germans' opposition to most whites in the area, their attitude of staunch moral rectitude, and perceived moral, religious, even cultural, élitism, such white workers were only too ready to add fuel to rumours about the Lutherans if a hint was to arise. Reuther may well have testified against white station workers during the 1899 Select Committee of Inquiry into the conditions of Aborigines. Whatever the nature of the rumours of 1905, Reuther was suspected of being the father of the almost white child born to his live-in domestic. At the time, young Frieda allegedly had been having sexual relations with a mission Aborigine named Hermann, who was already married to a baptised Aboriginal woman, but from its colouring the baby was obviously not Hermann's child. Consequently rumour began associating the conception of the baby with a white man at the mission. With the girl in service at the Reuther home, the assumption grew that the father was in fact the missionary himself.

During a committee meeting at Tanunda in January 1906, Bogner told shocked members of Reuther being implicated as father of the child. Reuther, by letter, denied the rumours, claiming the girl to be virtually a member of the Reuther family. His admission of knowledge that she had been involved with a married mission Aborigine caused outrage among the committee members because of their missionary condoning this sort of activity. Reuther was then accused of using his privileges in a contemptuous way, of encouraging immoral behaviour by being so closeted with his writings as to be blinded to the activities around him: 'because you are not leaving your cell and don't know what is going on at the station. You cannot condone such depravity.'[132] 'This has gone too far ... In your extensive work that you wish to bring to print ... you have not been driven to further God's word, but to a large extent by your ambition. The immorality has to go to your account', wrote Kaibel to Reuther in early 1906.[133]

The committee conducted an immediate investigation into the matter. The girl

Missionaries Bogner and Reuther not long before their bitter estrangement, c. 1905

was ordered to name the father of her baby 'to save all white station workers', for a 'white seducer' of a black mission woman had, the committee felt (no doubt fearing governmental repercussions), an economic responsibility towards the child. 'Would it have been a white girl then she would be paying herself ... but under these circumstances it is our duty.'[134] Reuther claimed that Frieda had already given him the name of the father in a private and confidential 'confession'. But Kaibel urged him to make the secret public on this occasion, otherwise 'innocent people are in danger of being accused of a crime', adding: 'She has spent time so freely with blacks and whites, no court will convict a white man'.[135]

Soon after the birth of her child Frieda died of a lung infection. But Reuther continued refusing to attend committee meetings of investigation. There, however, Bogner reported that Kokegai, a German labourer employed at the station, had in fact fathered the child of a mission Aborigine called Paula, and that Reuther had told the woman to name an Aborigine as the father and not Kokegai.[136] In anger Kaibel wrote to Reuther, still entrenched at the station and refusing to move, 'If you are the father [of Frieda's child] the outside world will be outraged'.[137]

Reuther immediately stopped conducting services in the Killalpaninna church. Vogelsang complained of this to Kaibel, who responded with suspicion that this 'shows Reuther in strange light'. 'It is dreadful that our mission station is a place for whores and gigolos instead of a place where the light shines in the darkness.'[138]

Kaibel, fearful of the reflection on himself and the committee, and anxious to dispel the rumours surrounding the mission station and its prominent missionary, demanded that Reuther face his accusers and answer the charges, as parishes in the south were now alive with innuendo: 'Reconsider what you are doing. Think of your wife who has stood by you and is the best jewel in your crown. Think of your future. And God light up your mind.'[139]

In late February 1906, after Reuther had written the committee a letter of response considered to be 'unsatisfactory' and 'unclear', Kaibel again demanded that he face them himself or hand in his resignation, which would be accepted immediately: 'The rumour would then condemn you despite your innocence'. But, implored Kaibel, 'If you can clear it up with the committee you can leave for health reasons—to give you an honourable farewell'.[140]

Reuther did not go south, and by early April Kaibel was refusing to accept the resignation letters of both Reuther and his wife. Reuther had written:

> By nature I was endowed with a resilient constitution. But the mental effort, and worry have affected it. Already at the time the New Testament was completed I had attacks, but didn't pay much attention to them. However the recent nervous palpitations, which have left me unconscious and still do, tell me that it is now time to hold myself in check ... Dr Stirling [director of the South Australian Museum] said to me, 'If you don't want to be in the asylum you had better clear out of the North immediately'.[141]

To Neuendettelsau he wrote that: 'My nerves suffered ... so that I often could not sleep ... but I slowly recovered ... Two years ago sleepless nights returned. I had fits which caused me concern, and which often recurred. My body trembles with the slightest excitement . . . Here is my doctor's certificate.'[142]

Again the committee requested that Reuther attend a meeting of 25 April, for 'in order to give you an honourable farewell we need a clear picture'.[143] And they suggested he have a six-month break from the station to regain his health. But Reuther refused.

On 17 May 1906 the Reuther family left Killalpaninna. Ten days later they arrived at the small settlement of Anlaby in the south, to a modest landholding of 400 acres (part of the Dutton Estate) granted to the missionary by the South Australian government for his services to the colony. Reuther had privately applied for the land grant, to the fury of the mission committee, to which he responded: 'We don't want to be a burden to the mission fund, or eat mission bread without paying for it. It will be difficult for me and my large family to make a living. I trust in God and chanced this.'[144] The landholding was sufficient to run only about 500 sheep, and Reuther named his new home Gumvale.

In July 1906 he chronicled an explanation of his departure for the Lutheran newspaper that circulated in South Australia, again citing ill-health to be the only reason. He also stated:

> I don't want to be estranged from the mission friends but I will spend as much time as I can on the written work and on this mission paper regarding the Aborigines of our country . . . If I look over the past eighteen years of my work I can say I have strived for peace with my brothers at the mission. There I had very hard days of work—it was a stony field of work full of human bones. I have stood at about 200 heathen graves and have preached to the living. My courage often sank when I saw the heathens dying and I said to myself that I helped bury a people. But I can with thanks look to God and say that I have experienced some joy. I have taught and Christened about 100 heathens. They still love me today and thank me.[145]

Income from the small farm was not enough to keep the large Reuther family, and the 45-year-old missionary found work as a clerk with the local council.[146] In January 1907 Reuther wrote to the committee that just before her death young Frieda had told him and Pauline that the father of her almost white child was the Frenchman Charles de Pierre, of Cannatulkaninna Station. Commonly referred to as 'Wireyard' Station, this was a pastoral run that adjoined Killalpaninna mission. Frieda allegedly told the Reuthers that she had been afraid to name de Pierre earlier for fear of the violence he may inflict.[147] The two French brothers (Charles and Baptiste de Pierre) were reputed to be cruel and repressive towards Aborigines in their employ.

When they went south, Reuther and Pauline took with them the baby of the dead Frieda, who 'grew up in our house'.[148]

7

Old Rites, New Order and Mission Decline

For two years, from May 1906 until March 1908, Killalpaninna Mission Station was virtually abandoned. With the hasty retreat of Reuther—'Reuther left here like a refugee', Bogner was later to report[1]—there was no permanent authority to maintain the strict control of previous times and to guide the lives of the black Christians. Bogner remained as stock station manager, but spent much of his time in the south with his sick wife. There was no school, no Sunday services, no mission routine, no vigilant patrol at night. Reuther relinquished his post in such haste that he did not even take his beloved riding mare, called May.[2]

The committee at Tanunda struggled to hold the vital stock station. Those time-honoured stalwarts, the Kolonisten, were old men now, and barely able to fulfil their station duties. Hermann Vogelsang was sixty-eight years old, Ernst Jacob seventy-one. Jacob was weak and ill, and died a year after Reuther's departure. But Vogelsang relentlessly persisted at Kopperamanna with morning and evening devotions for the Aborigines while struggling to maintain mission ethics and order. And Theodore (Jack) Ruediger continued as a lifeline for the station, his wagon and horseteam maintaining a supply of rations for the Aborigines.

Mission Aborigines, however, were in a state of confusion, directionless after years of reliance and dependence, where the strict hand of Lutheran discipline had guided their every action. They felt abandoned and lost, and many went back to the camps nearby, attempting to integrate with their own people and the fragmenting culture. Some moved freely between the mission station and the more traditional camp life, searching for identity and perhaps authority.

In 1907 Bogner was made 'missionary' at Killalpaninna until a more permanent appointment could be assigned. But his concerns were largely with the stock station. He and Reuther remained estranged from each other, Reuther embittered over Bogner's implicating him to the committee, and Bogner complaining that Reuther had fled like a fugitive, leaving no instructions at all for him as successor.[3] 'I am not in correspondence with Reuther and I don't answer his letters . . . I would not shake the hand of a man who secretly wants to destroy my harness'.[4] Bogner was requested to learn the Diyari language as quickly as possible (he had obviously learnt little in past years), for he was expected to act as pastor to the Christian Aborigines.

Little was documented from the time of Reuther's departure until Bogner's reports of 1907. His early correspondence, not surprisingly, was filled with accounts of Aborigines returning to old practices, like those of 'adultery', 'prostitution' and 'corroborees', and of the 'failure' of the Christianised Aborigines. It was imperative that the first three, above all, again be subverted.

By 1908 the station was to receive a young, new missionary, a self-confessed and not immodest intellectual by 'culture', who not only implemented a new and rigid order but, by his nature and action, aided the demise of the ailing station. Together with a rapidly declining economic situation and an uncertain political atmosphere, his six-year-period heralded the end of Killalpaninna as a mission station. Disillusionment beset the new missionary; droughts and debts plagued the mission committee. The Aboriginal population was declining, the new missionary clashed with the committee over policy and control, and a Royal Commission into Aboriginal matters statewide (for South Australia had now become one of the states of the federated nation) was launched in 1912, with Killalpaninna a target for investigation. And, just two years later, came the greatest severance between the German community in Australia and the largely British-descended colonial population, with the outbreak of the First World War on 1 August 1914.

These unmitigating factors came together over this final six-year-period, from 1908 to early 1915. Wolfgang Reidel was to be the last Lutheran missionary among the Diyari Aborigines. The venture, so impenitently endeavoured, was to be sold into private hands. After a fifty-year struggle and perhaps a baptismal count of less than 200 restless souls, Killalpaninna Mission Station was to become yet another cattle station in the north of South Australia.

Missionary Bogner, Stock Station Manager

Three months after Reuther's resignation, and after years of prolonged drought, one of the greatest floods ever recorded in the area filled Lake Killalpaninna in just twelve days. Native food in plenitude followed and mission Aborigines scattered to reap the abundance. Perhaps an omen, they may have thought, for now, with their new-found freedom, many of their traditional needs were again met. The desert transformed into a green carpet, the air of excitement pervasive, and spirits were activated and energised. For a time it was almost as if a cathartic metamorphosis was occurring after the preceding defiling events.

The flooding gave fresh hope to the stock station, which now took precedence. Cattle from the Finke River Mission (as it was increasingly called after severance with Hermannsburg in Germany) were mustered and driven south to restock the Killalpaninna outstations. By 1907, with Bogner's appointment as temporary missionary, a debt of £3000 was paid.

Johannes Matthias Bogner was forty-six years old in 1907. He was the son of a Bavarian miller, and a graduate of Neuendettelsau who had dreamt of serving as a missionary in the New World of America. Instead, he was urgently sent to a colony of Australia, to the steamy tropics of northern Queensland to replace Meyer at Bloomfield. Bogner's Nürnberg-born fiancée, Maria Goetz, courageously followed, and the couple were married at Cooktown. But the tropical climate and the conditions at Bloomfield, over the four years she spent there, caused Maria's health to deteriorate. The couple left Queensland for South Australia, leaving behind Maria's German dowry in their haste for medical attention. Bogner was then posted to Hermannsburg in Central Australia, where he acted as stock station manager, with Strehlow taking charge of the missionising and spiritual activities. At Hermannsburg, however, Maria's condition worsened. And when he was sent to Killalpaninna, in April 1902, to assist the overburdened Reuther, Bogner left his fragile wife in the family home at Tanunda.[5] But the missionary was only ever 'half in the saddle', as Reuther had described Bogner dividing his time between his activities at Killalpaninna and his constant travelling to the south,[6] and his expertise had developed for stock station management.

When Bogner took control at Killalpaninna, the mission settlement was in a neglected state, its abandoned buildings shabby and in dire need of repair. Two sons of Hermann Vogelsang were employed: Theodore, twenty-nine years old and unmarried, became general manager and carpenter, repairing buildings and distributing rations to the Aborigines; and Hermann (junior), two years younger and married, was engaged as schoolteacher. Both were, of course, fluent in the Diyari language. But when the school reopened in 1907 the Lutherans could attract only seven pupils. 'Our blacks will never be scientists', wrote Bogner in his first report, 'but the main thing is they are taught the Bible and learn to read and write in their language.'[7]

Few Aborigines were now living at the station and Bogner tried to induce more to return. Perhaps from concern for the contentious reserve land (AL 145), he wrote in that first report that 'We have a duty to the government (to teach and preach) as long as we use the Reserve of the blacks and receive rations'.[8]

Bogner threw his energies into the pastoral pursuits. He had experienced the precariousness of climate and countryside in the north, and it was evident, by May 1907, that the green countryside was again reverting to desert. Correspondingly, the market price for cattle was fluctuating. Bogner was faced with the difficult decisions of when to sell stock and when to risk driving cattle. Nearly 400 head were taken from Hermannsburg to Killalpaninna for fattening before the green feed subsided. Jack Irrgang, stepson of old Jacob, was in charge of mustering, and his Aboriginal stockmen were promised a bonus for their efforts.

Other stock station industries were reactivated. Rabbit skins were gathered piecemeal by the Aborigines and horses were bred and sold as work animals, while wild horses (introduced escapees) were herded and sold for their meat. Revenue was gathered from meals supplied by the Vogelsangs at Kopperamanna to passing passengers on the mailcoach, and from the watering of stock at the Kopperamanna bore. Old Hermann, however, was having difficulty catching shrewd drovers who would slip past the homestead to water their stock without paying. At Etadunna over 7000 sheep were still held, and black shearers and shepherds were again closely supervised. Ernst Jacob had been pensioned from active work a year earlier, and Jack Irrgang became manager. Jacob became restless in his enforced idleness, and early in 1907 Bogner wrote: 'He is old and can't do what he wants to do. When here he thinks the south may be better; when in the south it is not as good as expected.'[9]

While Bogner was allegedly learning the Diyari language he relied on the Vogelsang sons (Hermann, in particular) to conduct Diyari services in the

Cattle mustering and droving at Killalpaninna. In 1909 'Jack' Irrang and two Killalpaninna Aboriginal stockmen brought 600 cattle from Hermannsburg to be fattened at Kopperamanna before being driven to the railhead at Herrgott Springs (Marree) for trucking to the markets in the south

church. In effect, Hermann virtually functioned as sole missionary until the arrival of Reidel in 1908, as Bogner rarely taught or preached. However, there were certain spiritual functions that the unordained Kolonist's son could not perform. In 1907 Bogner officiated at three Aboriginal marriages and, with his limited Diyari, he held the 1907 Easter communion. But at this Easter Day service the missionary turned the usual jubilation sermon, of the resurrection of the Christian Saviour, into a disquisition, warning and threatening the Christianised Aborigines. Just a few weeks earlier the mission Aborigines, who were now beginning to come back to the station, had left one evening to participate in their own rituals (presumably of circumcision). Even those from Kopperamanna had travelled to the ceremonial grounds near the mission station (probably Ngarlangarlani). Bogner was determined to punish all, and refused communion to those previously confirmed. On the following Sunday he again took the service and again chastised the Christian Aborigines with Corinthians 1:10:20 and 21 and Corinthians 1:7:18 and 19; whereupon 'They hung their heads and finally agreed that it wasn't proper'.[10]

Although 'converts' had never completely forsaken their own religious rituals for the new faith, after the two years of relaxed authority they were now engaging more frequently in their own culture. One example of the confused crossing of the two cultures occurred in 1893, when an Aborigine called Sambo lay dying at his camp. He refused hospitalisation, unable to endure the confinement, saying that 'he firmly believed his illness was entirely owing to the Bone being pointed at him by another native, with whom he quarrelled many years ago; he said the Government ought to pass a law to prevent it, and punish all those who break it'.[11]

Aborigines were operating within two sets of laws, with two sets of expectations. The decreed and imposed European law now applicable to them was often quite unknown, yet it could have devastating effects on their lives if transgressed. Living within their own law, Aboriginal people were often unaware that they had transgressed the European system; often, that is, until it was too late. In the case of a pinya execution (the Aboriginal law for 'murder' or 'bone pointing') on mission land, in 1888, the entire pinya party of fourteen men were tried at Port Augusta. It was decided by the European court that the Aborigine who struck first was guilty of 'wilful murder', and he was sentenced to death, while the other thirteen were found 'not guilty'.[12]

Four months after Bogner's refusal of the Easter communion, Theodore Vogelsang reported that nearly all mission Aborigines disappeared again to participate 'in the games of the devil', telling lies to the mission staff that they would not be attending. Theodore (with perhaps Bogner in tow) presumably followed the Aborigines at night, for he described the rituals as 'dirty dances', with 'even the baptised Christian women completely undressed and dancing naked'.[13] And in November of that same year Bogner was still refusing communion to confirmed Aborigines whom he considered not 'serious' about their Christianity, and giving it only to those he believed worthy.[14]

After Reuther's departure the old Kolonisten began privately taking the 'confession' instigated as a public condemnation by the missionary. Bogner, however, put a stop to this practice; 'There would also not be a private confession. The blacks don't know anymore who their confessional father is.'[15]

Bogner described his first year as holding 'little Joy' and 'much pain', with 'storms raging and not only sandstorms'. 'If I had known what I know now nothing would have made me go back to Bethesda.'[16] The Bavarian complained of the difficulty of performing the functions of both missionary and stock manager, and as early as April 1907 was writing: 'We expect the new missionary soon. The sooner the better. Young blood is necessary. They can take a lot more. I am tired.'[17] But according to Theodore Vogelsang, 'Bogner is not doing any work at all', and the station 'looks pretty deteriorated, with everything in a mess and nothing in order'.[18] Certainly the following incident suggests inattention and neglect, but more than a hint of religious preponderance.

In his 1907 report to the mission committee, Bogner discussed the black deaths at the station for that year (of which there were five), and went on to describe one, the death of a young mission girl called Susanne. He wrote: 'Susanne didn't really belong to the good people', and 'I am afraid her sin caused her death.'[19] Susanne was thought to have died on 23 December and was to be buried in the graveyard beside the church. Her body was presumably left in a crude coffin inside the mortuary.

Missionary Johannes Bogner with his wife and children at Killalpaninna. This was a rare visit from Bogner's family, as his sick wife was almost always in the south

On Christmas Eve, usually an event of great excitement for the mission Aborigines, as the great ritual of gift-giving by the missionaries followed, a mopish black congregation gathered in the church for the burial service. The new ritual of 'viewing the body' was insisted upon. Displayed in virginal white, Susanne's body lay lit by an orange glow from a brilliant sunset slanting through the narrow openings of the old mud church. As the solemn procession of black mourners passed the girl's corpse, one Aborigine noticed that the body was still soft and flexible. Rigor-mortis had not yet set in, and the girl had been dead for more than twenty-four hours. He shouted excitedly to the missionary.

All preparations had been made for the burial that evening, but, as Bogner said, 'I couldn't bury her with a clear conscience'. As Susanne lay motionless in her coffin, the German placed a piece of burning ember on her lips to check for breath. 'After a while we saw that you could see her breath on the ember. We could make a cross on it.' Whatever events followed this revelation were not recorded by Bogner, simply that 'the next day she was dead. The ember proved that.' Bogner buried the girl on the day after Christmas Day.[20]

Wolfgang Reidel and a New Mission Order

Wolfgang Reidel arrived at Killalpaninna in March 1908. He was seconded to the position of missionary by request, in letter form, from Kaibel. To this calling, the young German's reaction was one of crushed disappointment; 'I want to shout, "Please spare me heavenly Father".'[21] Reidel had hoped for missionary work in New Guinea, but a year after joining Killalpaninna he reluctantly reported to his superiors, 'This also was God's plan for me . . . But He has girded and led me where I did not want to be. I will be thankful.'[22]

Like his predecessors, Reidel was a graduate of Neuendettelsau. He had arrived in South Australia in 1905, had been appointed assistant to Pastor Leidig at Point Pass and, during the first few months, had been miserably homesick for 'beautiful Franconia in Bavaria'. On arrival in Australia, and much to his chagrin, Reidel was subjected to a *colloquium orthodoxiae* by the Lutheran fathers at Tanunda, ceremoniously engaged in a formal, theological debate over whether or not the Pope was the Anti-Christ.[23] Ten days later he was ordained by the venerable Pastor Johann Christian Auricht, assisted by Leidig and Kaibel, both mission officials for the two Immanuel Synod mission stations, Hermannsburg and Killalpaninna.

Reidel spent the next two-and-a-half years conducting services in the Point Pass region. Of one small parish in his area, a place aptly named World's End, Reidel wrote, 'a tiny building with mud-walls, situated in utter loneliness in a mighty desert-like plain'.[24] A taste, perhaps, of what was to come, for the 'desert-like plains' of the Barossa Valley were veritably lush compared with the desert plains of the Far North.

During his time in the south, Reidel was guest at a German wedding, a traditional, provincial ceremony conducted in a foreign colony some 12 000 miles from the Fatherland and in a manner long forgotten in the homeland. It was the ceremony of the 'Kranzabnahme', the removing of the wreath from the bride's head and replacing it with a 'Häubchen' (lady's cap), and the welcoming of the bride 'in die Mann und Weiber Reih'n' (in the company of husbands and wives). Reidel described the ritual as 'queer' and 'in bad taste', as the guests emotionally sang a poem throughout the ceremony, some with tears running down their faces.[25]

Reidel himself was soon to marry in the colony. His young Viennese-born fiancée travelled to Australia to wed a pastor whom she had previously only met for two hours in Germany before he had sailed for Australia. The Reidels were married at Tanunda, and the Reuthers attended the ceremony.[26]

Reidel was surprised at his calling to Killalpaninna. He had not previously considered the possibility, although he had heard about the northern station, writing. 'It was not of a nature to make a man feel drawn to the place.'[27] Urged by his mentor, Leidig, Reidel accepted the post somewhat reluctantly, later stressing in his memoirs that it was conditional on his role as missionary in the strict sense, and not as stock manager as well. But at a meeting between Reidel and the mission committee over details of his acceptance, 'Good old "father" Linke, a prominent committee member of long-standing', had said with a knowing smile, "I know better; that will come automatically . . .".' 'If anything this

Young mission girls, Susanne and Ida, c. 1907

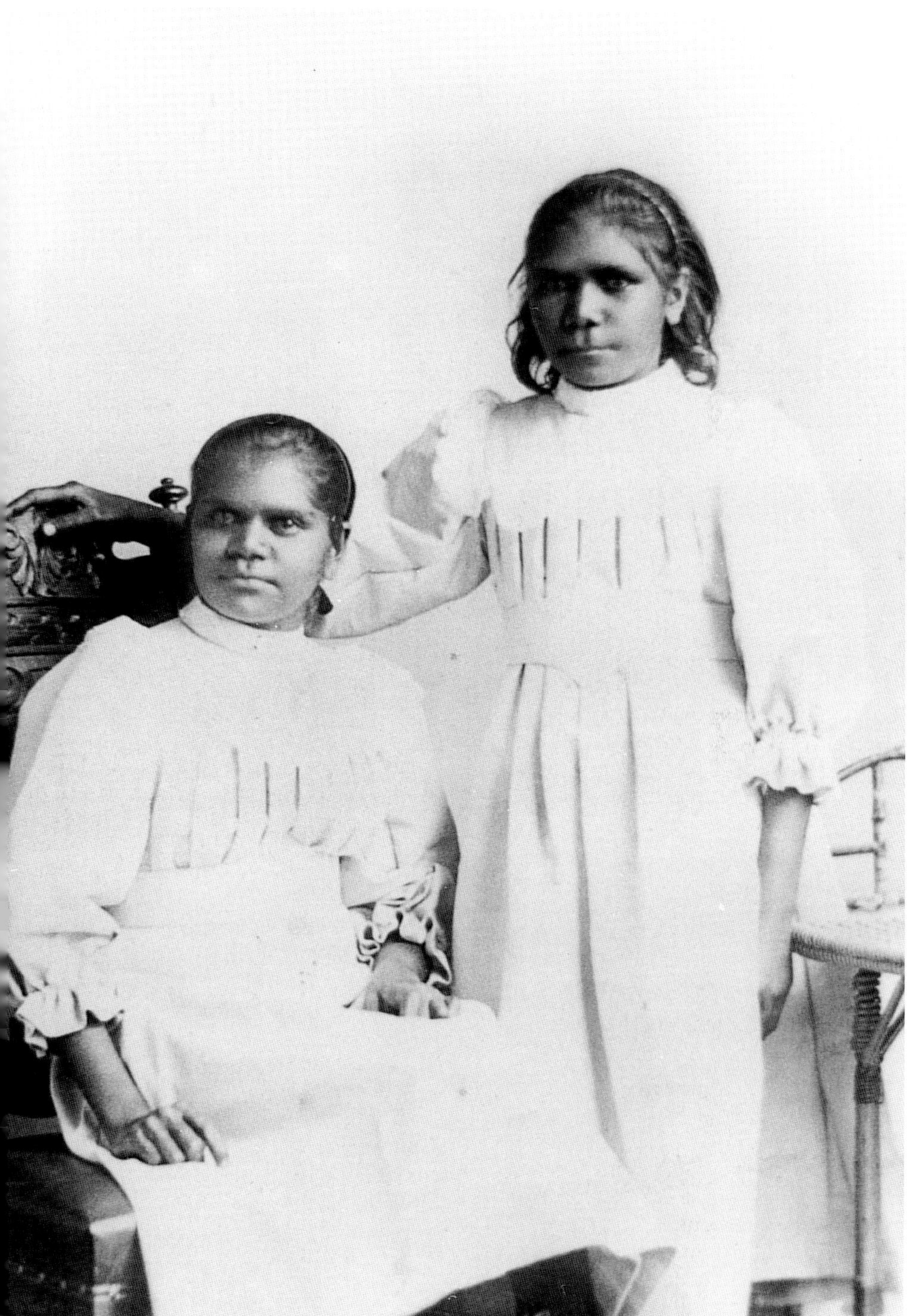

remark strengthened my resolution', wrote Reidel. And, of the mission's later demise: 'I stuck to my resolution and never regretted it'.[28]

The Reidels travelled northwards by train, 'the atmosphere both in the physical as well as the cultural and moral sense becoming more and more northern'.[29] From Herrgott Springs they rode in the mission buggy driven by the mission Aborigines Hermann and Walter, from whom they learned their first Diyari words; 'nilanila!', 'nilanila!', the word for 'mirage' was shouted, as 'the phenomenon of wonderful phantom sheets of water in the far distance which disappeared into the air as we approached'. The Diyari word reminded Reidel of the Latin word 'nihil', meaning 'nothing'.[30]

As they approached the station, beyond the looming bell-tower to their left a still, fine sheet of water lay across the lake bed. All that remained of the 1906 flooding, it gave the incongruous mud-brick settlement an air of tranquillity. But any enthusiasm remotely harboured by the Reidels quickly turned to disillusionment at the shabby conditions at the station. Theodore Vogelsang had laboured to prepare Reuther's old house. Doors and windows were mended, the walls of the study and dining-room were freshly wallpapered and the house on the highest sand-dune was given its most thorough cleaning for two years. But when the young pastor stepped inside he was appalled: 'I don't feel like living in this unkempt way daily'. Reidel immediately ordered flyscreens and new doors and windows of only the best quality to be sent to Herrgott by rail. And he insisted that gutters, cellar windows, fireplaces and the storehouse all be repaired. 'The living quarters of the missionary must be an example. Appearance is a matter of principle to the blacks.'[31]

Barely two months later Reidel wrote to Neuendettelsau of his despair with Killalpaninna, and of his desire to be sent to the mission fields of New Guinea:

> But God's intentions were different. Instead of sending me to those places where there were many people to be converted and where I was longing for the service, He sent me to serve a people that are slowly dying out and are living in the most remote part of the world. It is not an easy job here.

To make things worse,

> The prestige and respect of the missionary has also suffered by what my predecessor has done, in particular as Missionary Reuther was not able to clear the suspicion which was circulating among the black people that he had sinned against the sixth commandment . . . It seems to me that anybody who works here longer than ten years is susceptible to the general deterioration here.[32]

The Reidels arrived in the north at the beginning of a cold and dry winter, with many of the Aborigines suffering respiratory problems. Soon the lake had dried completely, leaving dead and dying fish in an ever-shrinking pool of stagnant water. The stench could be smelt throughout the settlement, and the Reidels were forced to sprinkle their bodies with eucalyptus oil to make breathing less odious.

Killalpaninna was now at its most vulnerable since its first decade. The committee had sent two ill-suited missionaries, of whom one was unfitted for the harsh physical conditions and had little sympathy with Aborigines, and the

Wolfgang Reidel with a confirmation group. Ben Murray is in the front row on the left

other was interested almost solely in the stock station. It was a precarious time, when convert numbers were small, and interest in Christianity had to be re-established.

Wolfgang Reidel, it seems, was a most unlikely candidate for mission work in the 'dreaded north'. He knew little, if anything, of the Aborigines and had no desire to work among them (not that this had been a criterion in the past). He was, however, trained at Neuendettelsau. Reidel was arrogant, xenophobically German, intellectually élitist (even snobbish), and had a sharp tongue and direct and cutting manner when roused. Perhaps these last characteristics gave him the fire and seeming energy needed for the job. But he was a self-confessed scholar, an intellectual at heart, and with, it seems, little practical knowledge or interest. As he himself wrote: 'Fancy me, a booklover and ardent student of theology, exhibiting myself to the cattlemen of the North . . .'[33] He had no interest in or taste for 'external matters' on the station, that essential economic base that must be constantly monitored, considering these matters a hindrance to the real work of missionising. Even external missionising was too distasteful for his sensibilities. He would send his trusted Christian Aboriginal, old Joseph, to the camps on the other side of the lake to read from the Diyari New Testament and to preach for him.[34]

Reidel, however, found time at Killalpaninna to pursue his hobbies of old Greek and Latin, which gave him 'such pleasure'.[35] He ordered specialised books on such subjects as the history of Germany, German philosophy, and 'the best German biographies' to be sent to the mission station for his 'leisure and pleasure'. 'Everyone in the desert is such a peasant. I haven't anyone at my intellectual level . . . Reading and training the brain keeps up my studies and stimulation. It prevents me from mentally decaying out here in the desert among all these savages, black and white.'[36] And, 'At Bethesda there is no opportunity for any analytical work.'[37] Of the Aborigines, he was to write that 'Our black fellows have the brains of little children', and 'I am their highest authority as missionary.' Even Reidel's brother in Germany, with whom he corresponded, accused him of 'being too self-centred, too self-opinionated and too proud and arrogant'. 'Yes, I am aware that I suffer from such traits, but I am trying to keep it under control and struggling against it', he responded.[38]

One visitor to Killalpaninna, a theologian, described Reidel as, 'a man of culture and refinement, who with his young wife, is fighting bravely in the face of great discouragement'. And he reported the Reidels' hospitality as 'true German cordiality' where 'none can exceed the Germans'.[39]

With Wolfgang Reidel in charge, on a salary of £75 a year, and after the embarrassment and neglect of the past, the mission committee placed a tighter control on the Far North enterprise. Reidel was expected to give a fortnightly account of progress and problems, as well as submit the customary lengthy annual reports. All ordering, accounting and documentation was submitted to scrutiny and the smallest details were argued. Reidel implemented a 'new mission order', bringing back old mission rules and regulations and introducing new ones. He was resolute about quality, complaining even when cheaper cloth was sent for petticoat-making for the black women. 'Proper petticoats were thought to assist with the keeping of the sixth commandment', he argued.[40]

With Reidel's scholastic inclinations he became conversant with the Diyari language in just four months, after Theodore Vogelsang's evening tutoring sessions. When Reidel gave his first Diyari service, in August 1908, more than a hundred Aborigines gathered in the church, many no doubt from curiosity

Mrs Reidel with a group of Aboriginal mission children and one German child

about the new missionary. To the 'Mission Friends' in the south, those crucial benefactors, Reidel confidently wrote of his sermon: 'It was a wonderful view as blacks came from all corners . . . I felt elated and small at the same time, as I preached God's Word in a strange language . . . I preached on "God's Word is the Bread of Life" '. And at tea and cake after the service, 'I wiped tears of happiness from their eyes'.[41]

The rigorous new order introduced a formality and rigidity unparalleled in the past. Strict attention was given to the daily prayer periods, to grace at the table, and to the attendance at church three times on a Sunday. Any person who did not appear at morning or evening prayers received no breakfast or supper. And in 1911 a visiting Presbyterian minister from nearby Leigh Creek criticised Reidel's ardent proselytising. 'Here I might say that, though I have the greatest regard and respect for the Lutheran missionaries, I fear they are perhaps not quite practical enough, and insist a little too much on the religious side.' When the minister asked one young Aboriginal boy why he had run away from the station, he was told, 'Too much Jesus Christ yabber'.[42]

The Aboriginal children were subjected to corporal punishment, certainly by Reidel's wife, and probably by Reidel also. One account of Mrs Reidel 'administering bodily punishment to one of the native children' records that her wedding ring came off and fell into the sand. Next day it was found and returned to her by one of the Aboriginal men.[43]

Reidel launched an attack on the dogs from the camps nearby, threatening to have them eradicated, and causing great consternation at the plight of the Aborigines' favourite animal. Alcohol was forbidden on mission leases, and Reidel clashed with Bogner over the private breeding of horses on mission land for commercial purposes.[44] He considered the stock station manager 'had not his soul in the enterprise and was more interested in his family down south', complaining that Bogner was 'virtually useless', had learnt no Diyari, and had worked mainly with the outstations and stock in the years before his own arrival.[45] He accused the Bavarian of having contributed to the decline of the station.

Reidel also complained that the committee itself was attaching too much importance to the stock enterprise and not enough to the 'real work' of missionising. 'The only thing that gives me some joy is my study room, and of this I cannot do much at all.'[46]

The new order imposed and upheld by the young, insolent missionary was based on keeping all Aborigines busy with work, hoping they would be less inclined to drift back to the camps and their old ways. Even schoolchildren were put to work, assisting with buildings and repairs. Every Monday morning the black women were each given a piece of soap by Reidel's wife and were supervised while they washed the family clothes. On Tuesday and Friday afternoons Mrs Reidel supervised the sewing and mending groups. The visiting Presbyterian minister observed:

> the old gins make some pitiful attempts at sewing ... Some of the efforts are startling. One hoary gentleman ... had evidently found his nether garments too tight about the seating portion, and had got his 'widlin' (wife) to insert a strip of cloth. The trousers were dark moleskin, and the strip was pink flanelette [sic]. A rear view of the old gentleman gravely walking about and displaying a streak of flame behind, was really laughable.[47]

Saturday afternoons were the only free time allowed mission Aborigines. Consequently, it became the favourite day of the week, when the men and women would go hunting and gathering in the sand-dunes with their boomerangs and digging-sticks. Aboriginal children followed, the boys with their arms full of small boomerangs, imitating the adults and making onslaughts at sticks and small mounds, imaginary beasts of attack.[48]

New Church, Symbol of Change

The last service to be conducted in the old mud church at Killalpaninna was held by Reidel in September 1909. This unique sacred building, European-styled and primitively constructed, had stood for nearly thirty years. But now the mud bricks were crumbling with the ravages of rain and wind. No attempt was ever made to restore it, and Reidel, in his request for its destruction and replacement, indicated no sign of sentimentality over its distinctiveness. Early in 1909 he requested that a new church, a new school and a new guest house replace the mud-brick buildings, complaining that 'We have a heap of rubble for a station ... Let us show the renewal of the station by erecting a new church as a symbol'.[49]

A new church fund was launched among the Mission Friends in the south and by the end of September the Reidels and the mission Aborigines stood on the dusty track that ran through the settlement for a last glimpse of the old place of worship. It took just minutes for construction workers to push down the walls, and the 40-foot-tall bell-tower jerked to the ground. A new church—of functional, inexpensive galvanised iron cladding over a wooden framework—was quickly erected. This was a common form of utilitarian building material, used mainly for station sheds and some temporary or cheap housing. It is odd that a man so intent on quality and solidity should be the instigator of such a structure. The building was plain, functional and characterless, without a bell-tower and without German features.

The new church was dedicated on 5 December 1909. At its first service Ludwig Kaibel gave the opening discourse, drawing the Aborigines' attention to the generosity of the Mission Friends, and asking them to make donations themselves towards the construction and upkeep. Black shearers and shepherds agreed to donate from their wages, and to earn their extra living expenses from dingo scalps.

Killalpaninna Aborigines, Early 1900s

By the turn of the century the last groups of tribal, nomadic people were emerging from remote parts of the inland deserts, probably—with expanding pastoral pressures—from lack of resources and food, and encouraged by stories of another way of life on the desert fringes. Aborigines collected on the 750-square-mile mission reserve where rations and work were available at the mission station and at stations nearby.

For the two years between Reuther and Reidel, when Killalpaninna Aborigines more freely engaged in their traditional lifestyle, some of their men continued to work at the stock station. Hermann Vogelsang (senior), however, struggled to keep the Kopperamanna Aborigines 'faithful', and relentlessly persisted with prayers and monthly Bible classes, punishing his black employees for gambling with travelling Afghans, and insisting they sleep at their own Kopperamanna quarters and not in the Aboriginal camps nearby.[50] During this period the Aborigines employed at Kopperamanna earned few or no wages, Vogelsang's policy being that 'They must earn enough from killing rabbits for pelts to buy other than their meals. They get meals and prayer at Kopperamanna.'[51] One reason for withholding wages was Vogelsang's paranoia about the Aborigines being indebted to the shrewd Afghans who passed through mission land. These crafty Orientals would take an Aborigine's wage at card-playing, and when he could no longer pay his gambling debts, or for goods purchased from the Afghans, the Aborigine would offer his wife for sexual purposes as payment. This often suited the Afghans, who were generally without women of their own.[52]

Sick Aborigines, accustomed to medical aid from the missionaries, would travel to the Kopperamanna homestead for Vogelsang's homeopathic treatments. After 1906 the old Kolonist began to see a considerable increase in Aboriginal patients, many of whom died. He complained bitterly of the delay of the next missionary, accusing the committee of procrastinating while Aborigines were dying at an alarming rate. 'We don't know what the Lord wants us to do but He has given up on a large part of you ... You hope things will be different when the next missionary is here. It is only hope. Could it really get better?'[53] Trusted Kopperamanna Aborigines Samuel and Thomas had been caught engaging in corroborees, and Vogelsang was angry and disillusioned.

In 1905 the South Australian government dedicated 20 acres of Flinders Ranges land to Aborigines for red ochre pigment collection.[54] The gathering parties were considered disruptive by the local pastoralists, and friction arose between the two cultures. The land grant, near Parachilna, was intended to give all indigenous peoples of that state access to the resources for their traditional corroborees. Consequently red ochre was no longer a commodity of the Diyari for trading purposes. But by 1905, with the fragmentation of their culture, the traditional economics of the tribes had virtually ceased. The Lutherans, however, may not have approved of the government 'dedication', and certainly it seems the government of the time was confused over its intentions for the Christianising and 'civilising' of its Aborigines.

When Wolfgang Reidel arrived at Killalpaninna he was appalled at the degenerate state of the station, and not only with regard to the Aborigines. White mission workers were blatantly engaging in sexual relations with Aboriginal women, and Reidel immediately dismissed several. He wrote that there were 'all kinds of shady and shaky characters . . . around the enterprise' and that these men had been 'most detrimental to the enterprise'. Reidel described the Ruediger household as 'a real bordello', for there he found a young, unmarried black girl working as a domestic servant, already with a part-European baby in tow, and pregnant again. When questioned, the girl admitted having sexual intercourse for money. And when Reidel asked her to name the father of her child, she allegedly answered that she was having intercourse with six young men, all 'Christians', and could not be sure which was the father. After which, Reidel reported, the girl simply smiled. Reidel spoke to the men involved; 'Nobody denied it at all. Nobody seemed upset in any way. Only when I took away their Christmas presents did they look a bit upset.'[55]

At least one Aboriginal woman, married and the mother of two children, was punished during this period for 'being a danger to the men'. In his report to a now circumspect committee, Reidel disclosed:

> It seemed the bad spirits were in her. Nothing could stop her so we finally had to lock her in a dark cow shed. She had seduced too many and would not listen to any advice. Her husband spent the entire night in front of her prison door, talking to her to calm her . . . It is very difficult to help these people. The moral level is like that of animals. They know only the pleasures of the flesh.

The couple were sent to Kopperamanna to work, under the vigilant eye of old Hermann Vogelsang, and away from further corrupting at the mission station.[56]

No mention of pitjiri chewing was made in the letters of the missionaries from the 1890s. Tobacco, readily obtainable by all adults eligible for government rations, had largely taken its place. By the turn of the century, tobacco addiction was widespread. No alcohol, however, was permitted on the mission station, but it was not difficult to obtain from neighbouring stations or from European stockhands and travelling drovers, provided it could be bought either with money or women. One young black horsebreaker at Killalpaninna was caught on a drinking spree with the European mail contractor, who was locally 'their honourable J.P.!'[57] An Aborigine known as Charlie Napier of Clayton Creek was caught offering his Aboriginal wife to passing drovers for money, perhaps to

Three 'old greybeards' (as the Lutherans called them), tribal elders dressed in European clothing. They maintained their status and power and continued to monopolise the 'marriage stakes' to young girls even after 1900

buy alcohol. When Reidel heard of this he wrote to the protector of Aborigines requesting the Napiers' 9-year-old daughter be taken away lest she be corrupted by her parents. He refused to have the girl and her 14-year-old brother at Killalpaninna, stating that 'morally he's corrupted', and the mission station was 'not the right place in this case. The children are not Charlie's. Their fathers are whites.'[58] The State Children's Council took the girl to Adelaide, 'to save her from her obvious fate'. The girl's mother was distraught and threatened suicide.[59]

In the case of a man named Thomas prostituting his wife at the Kopperamanna outstation, Reidel demanded that their child be left at Killalpaninna, away from the corrupting influence of her parents. Thomas refused and, telling Reidel to find another man for Kopperamanna, immediately left for the 'heathen camp'. 'There', wrote Reidel, 'whores and the exchanging of women was in full swing.'[60]

In 1909, 135 Aborigines were living at the station. Their diet consisted primarily of dry bread and meat, with Reidel complaining to the committee of its inadequacy, and instructing his wife to give them more food variety from the German stores. Rations for the Aborigines comprised second-grade flour, sugar, tea and tobacco, hardly an adequate diet to maintain health. The Aborigines were given meat from the station, presumably as part payment for labour. Those at the station fared better than those at the camps, and would have been the recipients of some small food variety from the German stores.

When Reidel arrived, during the cold winter of 1908, he found many of the Aborigines suffering illnesses, from the common cold to tuberculosis, with one mission Aborigine declining fast from tuberculosis. The man, Paulus Tarilinna, was sent in the wagon to Port Augusta hospital (to a special ward set aside for blacks), and before he left was presented with a Diyari New Testament. Paulus was advised to read it diligently for he was not expected to live. Reidel warned him 'God would probably call him up'. But when news reached Killalpaninna that Paulus had indeed died, 'an electrical charge went through the mission'. A dark silence descended, before the mission Aborigines started to cry and wail. Paulus' father, whom Reidel described as 'still a heathen and a defender of the pointing of the bone', lived among the camp blacks. It was decided that the 'murderer' of Paulus must be punished, that a pinya must be mounted. When Reidel heard of this he allegedly managed to calm the father and persuade him against such actions.[61]

Old Rites, New Rites

Traditional Aboriginal rites and customs operated at Killalpaninna, in propinquity to, and concurrent with the new European rituals. Mission Aborigines could never really be described as 'converted' and even the most faithful and trusted regularly reverted to traditional custom, especially when death was involved. Bone-pointing and revenge rites were embedded in their convictions and the new Christian system seems not to have held the same power or fear. In 1909 alone Reidel was to experience at least two pinya encounters at the station, the first as described earlier, the second of a more intimidating nature.

When the second pinya occurred, Reidel himself spotted a party of naked Aborigines in the dry bed of the Cooper about half a mile from the mission station. The party was led by the 'mudla-kutya', elaborately decorated and wearing the distinctive feather head-dress and pubic tassel. The men were armed with spears and shields. Reidel quickly alerted the Germans at the station, before striding boldly across the sand-hills for the camps on the other side of the lake, the destination of the forthcoming pinya. Reidel's wife ran after him, her stout Aboriginal housemaid, Clara, jogging at her side and imploring her not to go. But the missionary's wife refused to turn back and Clara quickly returned to the station, gathered a bundle of boomerangs, and ran after the Viennese woman, tucking her arm into that of the missionary's wife for comfort.

On reaching the camps, Reidel found the opposing groups in the preliminary stages of encounter. He stood between them, and in Diyari forbade any fighting. The atmosphere was tense, the pinya members angry, and a spear was pointed at Reidel's chest. But he grabbed it and broke it in two. The pinya had come from Kopperamanna to kill one of the Killalpaninna Aborigines accused of pointing the bone to cause the death of a man from their group. Reidel argued with the pinya men and eventually they withdrew (perhaps after the manner of earlier

Joseph Ngantijilina ('old Joseph'), Bible in hand, his wife, Rebecca, and their daughter, Katarina (on the right)

female intervention). The mudla-kutya approached the missionary after the matter was settled and, according to Reidel, told the German that he was relieved to have been stopped from fulfilling his duty. He knew that as a consequence of his actions he would be arrested by the white police. He was known to them, and had previously spent time in the Port Augusta gaol. 'By coming to the fight and being prevented by the missionary, he had satisfied the code, and was not particularly sorry to save his own neck as well', rationalised the Europeans.[62] Pinya, by now, was governed by new fears and new laws.

With the arrival of Reidel the power of the pinaru, both at the camps and even at the mission settlement itself (after perhaps a two-year period of renewed status), was again vigorously challenged. When the traditional authority again began to be discredited, old sorcerers started testing their powers and demanded prerogative and regard. In 1910 one old mission Aborigine walked along the sandy track that ran through the settlement, shouting loudly and creating terror among the other Aborigines at the station. He carried a bundle of boomerangs under one arm and a small saddlecloth-bag in the other hand. The bag was filled with 'pointing bones', some 'loaded'. He appeared greatly excited. Lydia Vogelsang (Hermann junior's wife), in a breathless jumble of part German and part Diyari, alerted the missionary to the chaos created by the old man, but by the time the Germans located him the sorcerer was ensconced among a large group of Aborigines. Reidel once again engaged in a verbal battle, allegedly subduing the hoary pinaru and obtaining a promise to formally hand over the 'bones' that night.

> Soon after, a knock announced the bone pointer's arrival. He came in, and, in the kneeling–squatting position of the Aborigines, proceeded to empty his bag upon the floor. Several bundles of dirty rags were unwrapped. The rags—a surprisingly large quantity—were unrolled, and at last disclosed the awsome [sic] weapons concealed within—a roll of hairstring, with a lump of pitch (obtained from the roly-poly bush) at each end. The string being unrolled, we finally arrived at the bone itself. In all, this old magician had five bones: two made from human fibulae, two from camel bones, and one from a spear point.[63]

While the bones were being sorted Reidel maintained a constant exhortation in Diyari of the wickedness of the old man now squatting on his floor. A visitor, present at these events, was later to write:

> Secretly I was more interested than shocked, and really admired the old man who was guilty of such bloodthirsty designs upon his fellows—two of the 5 bones were loaded, or had been pointed, which meant that, without the missionary's interference, 2 men were soon to die. In spite of his crime—and to himself probably, it did not appear as a crime, but merely a custom—the old man had a face full of power and a certain dignity, together with a fine physique, which, if they could be properly directed, would surely do much good. Yet when I learned more of the people, I understood and sympathised with Mr Reidel's anger. Shortly before one of the mission's most promising young men had died from no complaint, but merely because he believed himself to have been boned, and all this after 40 years' mission work among this tribe, must certainly be disheartening; more so as the present offender was a professed Christian.[64]

Lake Allallinna (Ngarlangarlani), just 2 miles south-west of the mission settlement, was the traditional site for the Storm History, an important ceremonial ground for the Diyari. The small lake retained water for some time after flooding and was a favourite Aboriginal camping place, out of sight of the missionaries.[65] Baptised mission Aborigines would sneak away at night to engage in their traditional rituals at this site, but they were often discovered. And in mid-1910 Reidel forced every Aborigine at the station to fast for one day for such violation.[66] One Christian was expelled for 'continuous heathen ways'; and Reidel tried a system of monetary reward for good behaviour: 'We will pay them 9 shillings in future per pair'.[67] However, a few supposedly innocuous rituals were conceded, like the swan hunt, where Aboriginal men were dressed as waterbirds and swam stealthily towards the swans on the lake. They would cap-

Last adult baptism, 1911. Nine Aboriginal candidates (marked with numbers) with Reidel and his wife on the verandah of the missionary's house

ture the birds, later to be eaten in a feast at the station.[68]

The oldest Diyari man, in 1911, was Martin, the 'Rain-maker'. He had been living at the camps, but during the long, severe drought of 1911, when his rites went unresponded and no rain fell, he was persuaded by the women to steal bread from the mission station for his hungry group. He managed to procure a couple of loaves which he concealed in the bag that held his rain-making stone. But Martin was detected, the bread, bag and stone confiscated and the rain-maker returned to the camps disconsolate. His angry wife beat him with her digging-stick for his failure, and the other women joined the thrashing. Battered and bruised, poor Martin left for refuge at the mission station. Several days later his small, avaricious wife, dressed in a red scarf, a belt and a man's shirt that reached her thin knees, arrived to live with her husband.

One hot Sunday morning, during a service in the church, a small bird flew through the open doorway but was unable to escape. It fell exhausted to the floor. Martin seized it by the tail. Old Joseph cried out to him to let it go, but Martin held tightly. The trembling bird had been injured by the fall and died in Martin's hand. Soon afterwards rain fell. The relating of this story implies an omen of the imminence of rain, an omen fortuitous for the old rain-maker. However, when rain did fall in the winter of 1911, many of the Killalpaninna

Aborigines fell victim to an influenza epidemic. Ironically, two of the victims were old Martin and his wife.[69]

As the Aborigines at Killalpaninna moved confusedly between two cultures and two sets of religious principles, even unbaptised people would seek 'absolution' from the missionary when they knew they were dying. They were a strongly spiritual people by tradition, highly sensitive to what Europeans called superstition, and may well have needed to appease the power of the new religion, as well as fulfil their own religious requirements for death. 'Absolution', however, was not always readily given, even to those baptised. It would be withheld if the missionary felt the case was not genuine, and sometimes given only just before death. In one such case a man named Paulus, expelled from the station when it was discovered he was suffering from venereal disease (as was the policy at Killalpaninna), was denied absolution until he was very close to death. Reidel then rode out to his miserable, lone camp some distance from the station to where Paulus' relatives would take food for the sick old man. The German crawled into his wurley, later writing that 'the stink was hardly bearable', and ministered the Eucharist. The 'bread' he offered from a cracked saucer, the 'wine' from an egg-cup, but the smell and the stale air he found so nauseating that he cut the service short. The next day Paulus died. Reidel wrote, 'I am sure his remorse was genuine. He went in peace',[70] and, 'What an adorable condescension on the part of our glorified Redeemer!'[71]

When the wife of a baptised black shepherd called Jacob fell ill, the couple also sought absolution from the missionary. But when she died, Jacob left the mission to give his wife a traditional Aboriginal burial.[72] And when the only child of the trusted old Joseph became ill, he and his wife Rebecca disappeared from the station to search for the 'bone pointer' and pay the price for her release. Joseph (whose tribal name was Ngantjalina)[73] was an informer for Reidel, reporting on acts of 'heathenism', including bone pointing.[74] But it was a second black informer who alerted Reidel to Joseph's treachery. In her parents' absence, Reidel visited Joseph's sick daughter and, according to the missionary, the 13-year-old asked for absolution and Holy Communion, which was duly given. When her parents returned, Reidel called them into his study, and 'When Joseph saw that he was discovered and betrayed (by Samuel, who had informed), he behaved like a savage'. Angrily Joseph shouted, 'Get away from here, you only torment us; let Mr Flierl or Strehlow come back!' A few days later Joseph penitently went to Reidel: 'Should I now commit suicide like Judas, or act like Peter after his fall?'[75]

The young girl lingered, but eventually died. It was not until six months later that Reidel granted absolution to the old informer—in a church ceremony, and before the whole mission congregation. 'Most [black] Christians live worse than heathens because the latter don't pretend', wrote the missionary.[76]

Reidel rarely visited the Aboriginal camps, instead sending Joseph to check on activities or to proselytise. With Bible in hand, the elderly man would walk across the sand-dunes, gather a group around him and read passages from the Diyari New Testament. Reidel found visiting the camps distasteful and unhygienic. He was appalled at conditions inside wurlies, where dogs and people slept in a small hermetically sealed space open only at one end. And he attributed illnesses to such living conditions. When a camp black died Reidel did not minister to the corpse, nor attend the funeral. These people were given a traditional burial.[77]

During the first decade of the twentieth century the enthusiasm and excitement over traditional ceremonies began to be replaced by the festivities and excitement of some of the new rituals at the station. Christmas was especially anticipated. It was celebrated as an exceptionally joyous Christian occasion, in contrast to the usual emphasis on sin, chastisement, punishment and a vengeful God. For weeks mission Aborigines were busy with present-making. Sewing groups worked long hours preparing clothes for Christmas distribution, honey biscuits were baked, the church transformed with decorations. On Christmas Eve a special service was held in the church, with lively hymn-singing among the Aborigines. To their great delight Reidel ordered a special Christmas tree for the 1909 celebrations—a large, German, artificial tree that rotated around a music-box base. A year earlier old Hermann Vogelsang had complained to the committee that he had, 'tried to explain to the blacks the importance of Christmas. But the blacks here in their life of sin have never seen a Christmas tree'.[78]

The German tree was purchased in part from Aboriginal wage donations. On Christmas Eve and Christmas Day parcels of gifts were exchanged. The annual distribution of clothing was made by Reidel and his wife—the shirts, moleskin trousers, dresses, scarves and pinafores made by the Aboriginal women at the station from material supplied by the mission committee. Other small gifts were presented, perhaps a clay pipe, a trinket, a box of German biscuits. Dozens of dolls-heads and balls were distributed to the Aboriginal girls and boys as presents from the south. Reidel wrote, 'How much those people think of such small things, so important to them'.[79] Christmas Day was spent feasting on European food.

However, the excitement of the 1909 Christmas, with its musical, revolving tree, was marred by the punishment meted out to the young Aboriginal girl at the Ruedigers' house, and her multiple black lovers. They were banned from attending the Christmas sermon with its Holy Communion, not given presents and did not receive new clothes.

Singing was a great joy for Aborigines at Killalpaninna, and Hermann Vogelsang junior conducted an Aboriginal choir. The choir enthusiastically displayed its talents at Sunday services, with Hermann accompanying on the organ and the black congregation passionately joining in the performance. At one time a black brass band existed at the station.[80]

Christian weddings were another exciting ritual, with the black brass band playing, photographs being taken, and feasts enjoyed. During the early 1900s several of the Vogelsang children were married at the station, and Aboriginal couples were married in emulation of these glamorous occasions. Confirmation and baptismal ceremonies were similarly seductive and enchanting. There was a reverence for the occasion, the boys dressed in suits, the girls in long white dresses, their heads circled with wreaths. Although they were confirmed and baptised in separate services, the ceremonies were the same for black and white. At baptismal ceremonies Aborigines chose new Christian names, and many named themselves for their German employer or an admired German at the station—names such as Hermann, Luise, Theodore, 'Pauli', Johannes, Heinrich and

'Siebert's Mary'. Others named themselves (or were named) for favourite biblical characters—Joseph, Paulus, Jonathan, Daniel. Small memorabilia were handed to the confirmees, like a passage of personal prayer in ornate handmade envelopes. Everybody was given a Diyari New Testament. After the ceremony the Germans would walk to the missionary's house for coffee and cake. The Aborigines sat on the sand-hills nearby and drank tea and ate cake.

It was a new initiation process, difficult in a disciplinary and educational sense (with the learning of Luther's catechism and biblical study), but without the painful trials that Aboriginal males traditionally endured. As traditional ways were diluting, with the loss of land and scattering of people, the new initiation and rituals offered some replacement and some acceptance into the new culture, at least at a superficial level.

The missionary, whose domain was power and control, was now unequivocally the supreme pinaru (traditional elder). The venerable committee in the south were also pinaru, and with the introduction of the camera (from the 1880s) mission Aborigines were conscious of their images frozen in time and space. Although wary of the mysterious object of the camera, dignity and respectability were instilled into them as virtues admired by the new pinaru. Accordingly, photographs of mission Aborigines were always studied, posed, serious and unnatural. Aborigines felt judged by these images. And Reidel used this phobia as an effective tool to stop physical fighting among the station Aborigines. By simply pointing the small black box in the direction of the affray a fight was instantly over. Women hurriedly tied headscarves over their hair, men quickly straightened shirts and trousers, and everybody went solemnly about their tasks trying to look dignified.

It was often difficult for the old men to make the transition to the new culture, but some did try. One old pinaru, known as Dicky, was in Reidel's 1909 baptismal class. Dicky was hard of hearing, especially in deciphering the consonants, and had the equivocal memory of the ageing. When Reidel was giving a lesson on the Flood Story, and mentioned the biblical Japhet, Dicky thought he said 'David'. When the missionary gave the name again, he interpreted it as 'Rabbit'. Of Capernaum, the New Testament location, Dicky declared it to be 'mita madlentju', a 'bad place', because he was unable to pronounce the word. When asked, during a lesson on Genesis, whether Eve ate the forbidden fruit, the inimitable Dicky answered triumphantly, 'Adam ate the fruit too, and here it sticks', pointing to his throat (his Adam's apple), 'a piece of knowledge I had not imparted but which he must have picked up somewhere else', wrote the missionary.[81]

Before his baptism Dicky was asked whether he had ever killed a person. He answered: 'No, I was the defender and protector of the hunted and when a man at last stood at bay, I stepped forward and stood at his side and, strong as I was, broke all the spears to pieces, then I took the man who was at death's door aside and when I defended him the attackers did not fail to withdraw.'[82] Dicky's head, apparently, was badly scarred and bore the evidence of terrible gashes from repeated blows.[83] The old pinaru's face then changed, his features hardened and his eyes flashed. He put the end of his long beard into his mouth, a gesture that the Diyari made when about to attack to kill. He said, 'Only one man did I kill, because he had killed my eldest brother; I ran the spear right through his body so that he died.' When Dicky showed no remorse at all to his confession, Reidel retorted, 'Our Lord Jesus protects and defends us against Satan, although we do not see Him'.

To this Dicky replied. 'No, the seeing Him will come up there in Heaven.'

'There you will no more help me to learn Diari [sic]; the men there will all understand one another without that', Reidel responded.

'What language is spoken up there; Diari [sic], hey?' Dicky asked.

Reidel replied, 'You may be sure you will be able to understand the others and be understood by them'. 'What language does the devil speak, Wonkungurru [sic]?'

'Yes', the old man said wickedly, 'I think he speaks Wonkungurru [sic].'[84]

Dicky was coached by old Joseph for his baptismal tests. He was baptised on 15 January 1911. Although it was not then known, this was the last adult baptismal service held at Killalpaninna. It was a massive attempt at consolidation, a gathering together of all hoped-for Christian blacks.[85] Young Aborigines, baptised in infancy, were confirmed at this ceremony, and black couples were married. When the missionary's wife asked Dicky, just before the ceremony, what his Christian name would be, the old pinaru answered, 'He', pointing to Reidel, 'will know that alright'. And when Reidel's wife asked him where the old Dicky would then be, he answered, 'Oh him I will chase out to the bullocks, away with you, da, da'.

In later years, after the closure of the mission station, Dicky returned to his home country near Lake Hope. When the next good flooding arrived at the lake, with its abundance of birds and birds' eggs, it was reported that Dicky had overdosed on the delicacies and died as a consequence.[86]

One evening, in September 1909, the mission Aborigines woke Reidel in great agitation: 'God is showing great signs in the sky'. The Reidels gazed in wonderment as various points in the black firmament suddenly lit to resemble a brilliant cloud moving backwards and forwards across the sky. The movement was as swift as lightning, and here and there the sky lit to a bright crimson. The Reidels were fascinated, the Aborigines both excited and frightened. According to Reidel, the 'Christians among them thought the world was ending, that perhaps the Judgement Day of the new religion was upon them. Pieces of the Lord's Prayer mixed with 'table grace' and bits of the ten commandments were muttered in an effort to placate the Christian God. Reidel was later to describe the experience as an 'unforgettable spectacle and a revelation of God's almighty hand in nature'.[87]

The phenomenon was an aurora australis. The Aborigines traditionally knew it as 'pilliethilloili'. They feared it deeply, for it was believed to be a forewarning from the kutchie (evil spirits) to keep a strict vigilance for a pinya. A ceremony of appeasement would traditionally have been performed.[88] Certainly at least some mission Aborigines would have had knowledge of the portentous warning. But its warning may now have held a different fear.

Killalpaninna Aborigines Demand Higher Wages

Wages at Killalpaninna were both tightly controlled and sparingly distributed. With no government aid (apart from rations for Aborigines) the committee relied entirely on donations from South Australia and Germany and on the successes of its station enterprises at Killalpaninna and Hermannsburg. The stations, however, did not always prosper, especially after the severe drought of 1901–02 and the nationwide drought of 1911. A decision had been made during the 1880s to pay wages to black workers at Killalpaninna. But at Hermannsburg, operated by the South Australian Synod until 1894, black workers were not paid, and received only rations and shelter.

During Reidel's time at Killalpaninna, a period of economic hardship, most black stockmen received money only three or four times a year. These payments took the form of bonuses after a muster or when special work was required. Reidel himself did not support wages for Aborigines, considering the blacks lazy and requiring white supervision.[89] At Kopperamanna, Vogelsang senior was loath to hand money to his employed blacks lest they gamble it or spend it on 'sinful' activities. Those who were earning independently, from the sale of dingo scalps, were expected to pay for their own strychnine poison.[90]

The few Killalpaninna Aborigines receiving regular wages were paid at a lower level than Aborigines on other stations in the district. In 1914 shepherds received 5 shillings a week (plus rations and clothing for their families), while a few other workers were paid 7 shillings 6 pence a week. One 'full-blood' received 15 shillings, and one 'half-caste', who worked at Etadunna a full £1 a week. However, Aborigines working at nearby Mount Serle Station were paid £1 and 5 pence per week, plus 10 shillings a week ration allowance. And those employed at Beltana Station were paid £1 and 5 shillings a week (as well as rations).[91] But Reidel was to testify that 'If we put everyone on regular wages we would soon fail'.[92]

The Kolonisten were also lowly paid, with Hermann Vogelsang senior receiving only £1 and 5 shillings a week in 1914. And due to the economic crises of the first two decades of the twentieth century the missionaries themselves were suffering salary reductions; Reidel's, in 1914, just £75 a year, some £5 a year less than Reuther was paid eight years earlier. Kaibel's salary had been reduced by half after the 1901 drought (from £150 to £75).[93] In 1909, after a bad season for the sheep enterprise, there was an attempt to lower the wages of the German labourers at the station from £1 a week to 18 shillings 9 pence.[94]

By 1910, with money perilously short for employing white station hands and supervisers, and with higher wages paid in the area, the mission station was finding it difficult to obtain sufficient workers. Aborigines employed from outside demanded wages in accordance with what was being paid at other stations. This recalcitrant attitude was new to the Lutherans, and Reidel complained that one such employed Aborigine, a man called Theodore, who had lived for years among whites and was now employed at Blazes Well with mission stock, 'has learned mainly from whites how to get into debt and to drink. Now he wants to be paid in advance for the Finke mustering trip. His tone already shows the way he thinks'.[95]

The mission station had trained black shearers and stockmen in the past in order to avoid the need for white labourers. Now, when the mission station could ill-afford current wages, their skilled people were in demand on other stations. Kopperamanna was now the fattening station for Hermannsburg cattle, and many and differently skilled stockmen were required. But when they started demanding the wages paid at other stations, an increase to £1 per week,

Reidel grumbled, 'They can't and won't believe that we only live here to look after their souls and lives. They presume we've come to make profits.'[96] And, they 'think they are doing us a favour when we allow them to work here. It really was a mistake that we started paying them a few years ago in the first place— which was arranged by Jacob—because things are now getting out of hand. At Hermannsburg they are still not paying and there seems to be more law and order up there.'[97] In another letter to Kaibel, Reidel reiterated, 'One shouldn't give money to the blacks because they don't know how to handle it . . . they get ever more demanding and difficult. If you give the Devil your finger he wants your whole hand! They don't pay them at Hermannsburg in the north—but as we've started it it would be very difficult to stop.'[98]

With the expectation of better wages and a knowledge of the demand for black labour, Killalpaninna Aborigines began to abandon their reliance on the missionaries and even the station itself. Their demeanour became less servile, and after one incident, when a mission Aborigine called a German employee a 'bloody so and so', Reidel wrote, 'That is what happens once they are being paid. The blacks are getting too cocky.'[99]

Camel Cartage

In the year 1909 there was an exceptionally dry and poor season for the sheep enterprise. Breeding was severely reduced, stock was dying, and rams were hastily agisted on adjoining Cannatulkaninna Station in an effort to save them. There was little open feed for the team horses, and hand-feeding was costly. At this crucial time, fifteen camels were offered to the mission enterprise at £20 a head as an alternative form of transport. For some years Afghans with camel teams had been assisting with the transport of mission wool.[100]

Camels with supplies from Herrgott Springs (Marree) for the Killalpaninna Mission Station

Camels were eventually purchased by the mission station and a mission cameleer, the part Aboriginal–allegedly part Afghan, Ben Murray, placed in charge of the cartage beasts. Ben was a young man who had been at the mission station since 1908. He and his brother Ern had previously been employed by the de Pierre brothers of Cannatulkaninna Station but, with the assistance of Walter (an ex-Killalpaninna Aborigine), they escaped from the control of the Frenchmen to neighbouring Killalpaninna. Charles de Pierre came looking for the boys stockwhip in hand and accompanied by his two 'kangaroo dogs', but the young Hermann Vogelsang refused to release them.[101]

Ben Murray arrived at Killalpaninna just a few months before Reidel. He was baptised by Reidel and became a loyal member of the mission station, reliable and hardworking. He was taught camel work by an Afghan called Akbar Khan and a part-Aboriginal, Tom Davies, probably around 1912. In November of that year the Ruedigers left the station after fifteen years of service, and horse teams were no longer used. Both the fast riding camels and the sturdy pack camels were purchased for the station. Akbar Khan and Ben, with their pack camel team, carted baled wool from Etadunna to Herrgott, and returned to Killalpaninna with supplies and mail. It was hard work, with long hours of walking under a fierce sun beside loaded camels. Ben received the nominal 5 shillings a week, the same wage as a shepherd. Later it rose to 7 shillings 6 pence a week.[102] Reidel, however, found camels distasteful and claimed never to have ridden one.[103]

Twentieth-Century Illness and Deaths
From about the turn of the century the majority of the Aborigines at Killalpaninna were old people, and Aboriginal deaths began to exceed Aboriginal births. In 1900 Reuther reported that 'We are working among a people who are dying out.'[104] And five years later, 'it [missionising at Killalpaninna] was a stony field of work full of human bones'.[105] And when Kaibel visited Killalpaninna for the first time, in 1902, he commented that the station was aptly named, 'because there are so many blind, lame and ill'. 'Bethesda' was the biblical pool of healing.[106] From 1910 to 1916 there were fifty deaths and only twelve births at the station.[107] Young Aborigines were leaving to seek work elsewhere, often for better wages and with less rigid rules. Born into a changing culture, the young were not so steeped in traditional ways and found it easier to make the transition into a marginal area of the prevailing European society.

In 1915 there were approximately 650 Aborigines living between Lake Eyre and the Queensland border, the so-called Far North of South Australia. Of these people, surprisingly, only 100 to 130 now lived on mission land, with the rest primarily at the various stations in the area. All land, except the Kopperamanna Reserve, had been divided into pastoral runs, owned and controlled by Europeans. The Kopperamanna Reserve, part of mission land, was the largest Aboriginal Reserve in South Australia, and covered an area of 470 000 acres of a total of 502 838 acres of reserve land in that state.[108] Yet relatively few Aborigines now chose to live there—perhaps due in part to the available work elsewhere, and the abatement of outer violence, but undoubtedly also because they were deterred by the rigid restrictions imposed by the Lutherans. Of those living on mission land (including the Kopperamanna Reserve), only seventy-two were baptised, and most of these lived at the mission station. The rest, the camp blacks, lived in groups of about thirty people, close enough to the station to receive rations, government blankets and medical care.

Introduced European diseases had caused immense mortality rates among the Aborigines of the Far North, as they had all over Australia, and by the turn of the century many were suffering tuberculosis and syphilis, with syphilitic blindness common. But sufferers of venereal disease were not tolerated at Killalpaninna. Toleration would denote acceptance of 'immoral' behaviour, and the afflicted would pose a bad example and perhaps be a bad influence on other Aborigines at the station. Besides, expulsion could be seen as punishment, a deterrent perhaps, and could be justified as preventing the spread of the disease. Reidel told the Royal Commission of Inquiry in 1914, that 'We simply tell them they cannot have their wurlies on the station. We had a case here and I placed the patient (Paulus) half a mile away from the others: he was allowed to have his friends to look after him.'[109]

By the turn of the century government ration depots had been established at nine stations in the Far North, one of the earliest being at Killalpaninna. The annual cost to the government for the Killalpaninna rations for 1913 to 1915 was approximately £140 to £150.[110] This amounted to between three and five deliveries each year; of flour in 6000-pound lots, rice in 112-pound lots, tobacco in 20-pound lots, and soap in 112-pound lots. However, between 1913 and 1915 only one issue of blankets was delivered, and that was in March 1914, after news had reached the Lutherans that during the following month, commissioners from the current royal commission would be visiting the station to interview its missionaries.[111]

Reports of widespread illness, and a rapid decline in South Australia's Aboriginal population had prompted the governmental inquiry, in late 1912, into 'conditions' for Aborigines in South Australia. The commissioners were attempting to understand why 'the evidence showed that the aborigines in the Far North are gradually dying out'.[112] Bogner and Reidel were interviewed at Killalpaninna in June 1914, and Kaibel a month later in Adelaide.

No specific explanations could be given for the serious decline. After visiting Killalpaninna the commissioners decided that Aborigines 'lived under better conditions at the mission stations than they would if left to their own resources'.[113] And it was concluded that in the Far North there was a greater proportion of disease among Aborigines on the 'outlying stations'.[114]

Over a decade earlier the Lutherans, in their determined efforts at destroying the belief system of the Aborigines, reported mission Aborigines 'now happily assisting the missionaries with this work . . . [and] progress is being made and the cult and culture of the heathens is disappearing, but unfortunately it seems also that the population is disappearing too. We are working among a people who are dying out—but every soul we save is worthwhile.'[115].

And in 1907 Kaibel had stated:

> Although our efforts may have been at times faulty, and we may have shown sometimes more zeal than discretion, no one can dispute the fact that we have honestly and manfully grappled with the difficulties that beset our path, and that we have not worked quite in vain. If we cannot point, in view of the large financial outlay, to

great numbers, we grant that the nomadic life of the Australian natives, and their being split up into so many tribes, have greatly hampered our labours. Death has removed many of the earlier converts, and it is evident that we labour among a decaying people, whose days of existence, as a people, are numbered. Nevertheless, we are thankful to have been the means of conveying some light and love into the miserable life of an Australian black, and do not repent of the anxieties and untold worries this work has sometimes laid on our hearts.[116]

The Deaths of the Kolonisten

Ernst Jacob died in 1907. Unpropitiously, the old Kolonist, who had supported the Diyari for forty years, died while visiting the south. He was an asthma sufferer (like Vogelsang), had been ill for years with stomach and heart problems, but had retired just one year earlier. Jacob had often reiterated his wish to be buried in the Killalpaninna cemetery, among the graves of the Diyari Christians. But fate decreed that his health worsened while he was absent from the station, and for five weeks he lay ailing at Tanunda. One of his last requests was 'Be good to the poor natives!' He died on 8 July, at the age of seventy-two, and was buried in the Lutheran cemetery beside the Langmeil church. His last words were, 'So, das wird nun reichen bis an's Ufer der Ewigkeit' (There, that will suffice till I have reached the shores of Eternity').[117]

At Killalpaninna the news was unexpected. Bogner wrote, 'One of the bitterest experiences of the past year was the passing away of "Father" Jacob. Not one of us here at the station had any idea when he left us that it should be his last trip to the South. He left us with the intention of returning before long.'[118] His death sent the Killalpaninna Aborigines into deep mourning for their favourite German pinaru.

Jacob's fellow Kolonist, Hermann Vogelsang, outlived him by six years. Neither of the tenacious laymen, who had been part of the enterprise since its inception, lived to see the closure of the station. In March 1912 old Hermann celebrated his eightieth birthday with a service held in his honour in the galvanised iron church. The old man lived for almost a year longer. But just three days before his eighty-first birthday, after suffering a respiratory infection, he died in the early hours of 14 March 1913. For a week he had been listless and weak, but had forced himself to attend to his tasks with the Kopperamanna-employed Aborigines.

'Black Hermann' (employed at Kopperamanna) rode frantically to Killalpaninna for the two sons of the Vogelsangs. Later the Kolonist's body was carried by dray to Killalpaninna, with the Vogelsang family and the Aborigines of Kopperamanna following in buggies. It was a sad, slow journey. Black Hermann was again dispatched to the nearest police station, at Mungerannie, to summon George Aiston for examination of the body and the issuing of a death certificate. The news spread along the Birdsville Track like wildfire. Black Hermann left Killalpaninna on the Friday afternoon. He was back at the mission station by the next afternoon, 104 miles of riding in sixteen gruelling hours. When George Aiston arrived the funeral service had already begun. It was Palm Sunday 1913, late summer and temperatures were still very high. The burial could not be delayed.

Old Hermann Vogelsang with Anna towards the end of his life

Aborigines from near and far poured into the mission settlement. Their old, white pinaru had been like an eternal figure—powerful and immortal. Blacks and whites crowded into a hot iron church, where the corpse, laid inside a rough wooden coffin, was displayed in the aisle for all to view. 'He looked so peaceful and many a tear was shed quietly, but some people also gave vent to their feelings more loudly', wrote his youngest daughter.[119] Timotheus and Gottlieb cried 'like a couple of children'. Reidel conducted Holy Communion, and afterwards a stream of traditional wailing broke forth, as black bearers carried the dead man to the cemetery beside the church. The resurrection hymn was sung in Diyari as the loyal Kolonist was lowered to eternity, into the desert soil of the foreign land to which he had yielded his life; 'Ngaiani jurakokani Jesu nanaiajurna'.

The mourners then moved back to the church, and in the memorial service in Diyari that followed, Reidel told the Aborigines that Vogelsang was not a missionary, but for the love of his Saviour had left his German home and family and had come to them, concerned for their eternal welfare.[120] Reidel then 'admonished the natives to lead such a life that some day, in eternity, they would see their pinaru again'.[121] During the service there was a strange disturbance. Black Johannes' rush-hut suddenly erupted into flames and burnt to the ground in minutes. No explanation could be found.

Of Vogelsang's death, Reidel wrote: 'On the native Christians his passing evidently made a deep impression. Would that this proves to be permanent and that it encourages them to be just as faithful . . . May our Lord replace our friends who have passed on with others who have the same love for our natives and a spirit of sacrifice.'[122] The mission Aborigines donated towards a headstone for Vogelsang's grave. It was carved and inscribed by a Tanunda stonemason, carefully conveyed to the station and erected above the burial place. There it still stands, a last, preserved survivor of the Killalpaninna settlement—Vogelsang, stalwart to the end.

Missionary Reuther's Death

Almost a year after Hermann Vogelsang's death the Reuthers were preparing to celebrate twenty-five years of marriage with a silver wedding anniversary party at Gumvale, their small farm in the south. Seventy guests were invited from various parts of Australia. Some were missionary colleagues.

On the evening before the celebration, Georg Reuther was travelling by horse and buggy to the Eudunda railway station to collect guests when a thunderstorm struck. Reuther had stopped to give a ride to a local Point Pass farmer walking the same route. As the buggy, with the pair riding inside, lurched down the rough dirt bank of Julia Creek, an unseen, unheard wall of water sped towards them. The buggy tilted and rolled to one side, overturning with the power of the flash flood. Water came so fast and so forcibly that it swept the two men from the open carriage and propelled them along its course. Perhaps in these fleeting moments Reuther flashed back twenty-five years, to August 1889, at Killalpaninna. He was then a 28-year-old, a year into his term at the mission station, and had written in his diary:

> I got up early. The flood had already entered the lake though the water was still fairly salty in the lake; we could notice the flood waters. I then saddled the horse to go to the shearing and to stay there for a few days. While riding out I was nearly caught in the flood. Praise to Thee Lord Jesus, that Thou hast protected me from danger and harm and brought me safely to my destination.[123]

But on that February day in 1914 Georg Reuther did not reach his earthly destination, but his eternal domain. Both he and the farmer were drowned. Reuther, just fifty-three years old, was described by his friend, H. Homburg, then attorney-general in South Australia, as 'a fine, big, strapping man, with square shoulders ... ready to face any trouble or hardship'.[124] His body was found near the buggy, the farmer's two miles along the creek. What was to have been a joyous gathering was transformed into a sombre funeral.

The two men were buried at services held simultaneously in the small town of Eudunda. A cortege of sulkies and riders stretched behind the buggy bearing Reuther's coffin as party guests became mourners.

During the eight years since leaving Killalpaninna, Reuther had continued to work on his Diyari material, pressing for publication, but without success. He had held hopes of Moritz von Leonhardi (director of the Berlin Museum, in Germany) eventually publishing his work, and had sent him a completed dictionary of Diyari words, and a volume dealing with Aboriginal weapons and their uses, just a short time before he had drowned. However, von Leonhardi, an old man himself, died soon after Reuther had posted the material and not long before the missionary's own death.[125]

Reuther's last entry in his diary for the year 1913, less than two months before the tragedy, contained more than a tone of depression and a note of prophecy:

Reuther and Pauline in their later years

May the year 1914 be my last year. I am yearning for my heavenly home. After all there is no peace on earth, for with all the joys of this earth there is much sorrow. Mother [Pauli] is very worried; her nerves and heart are causing this. Besides the many earthly blessings, may God grant us a blessed end, through the merits of Christ and the grace of the Holy Spirit. A long-wished-for death would be my release from this earthly sorrow.[126]

Debts and Decline

Because Killalpaninna had become more accessible due to the railroad from the south to Herrgott, its missionaries were subjected to more control and interference from the mission headquarters than were those at Hermannsburg, twice the distance and difficult to reach.[127] Certainly after Reuther's demise, and the perceived state of anarchy during his last years, the station came under close scrutiny. Reidel was instructed to give a full account of activities every fortnight, and committee members visited the station more regularly.

> The church men come here for a few days, have a look around and then think they know all about what is wrong. It takes a lot of time to really get into the depths of what is going on here. From such short visits they come to a judgement about the whole enterprise. The church people in the south have no idea about missions and mission life.[128]

Reidel clashed with committee members, Kaibel in particular. The missionary had a sharp way with words and at times a cruel, sarcastic manner. He once wrote of old Hermann Vogelsang's mode of welcoming committee members as 'the fat little fellow from Kopperamanna [Vogelsang] had already rounded his mouth for a brotherly kiss because you probably would have been the only person other than myself who would have denied him such a happy experience'.[129] Reidel's letters irritated the president, who interpreted the caustic words as attacks on himself and his work. Reidel's attention to quality and insignificant detail annoyed Kaibel, who told him to concentrate on bigger issues. And the missionary constantly resisted pressure to act as manager for the stock enterprises, a point that was to become a salient factor in the last few years of the mission. 'Almost every letter I write down south has been misconstrued or misunderstood', wrote Reidel, who considered committee members to be 'very old with old bones' and 'hard to deal with'.[130] In late 1909 he penned: 'Things have got so bad lately that I will no longer report to the committee down there'. He also planned to attend the next synod conference to argue a case for reforms at the station and more independence.[131]

But the committee resisted any change in mission management and a year later Reidel complained that he felt like the victim of a pinya, surrounded on all sides and unable to escape. 'We've been running this enterprise now for forty-four years and all we can account for is a number of *baptised heathens.*'[132]

Morale at the station was not high during these years. Reidel was interested only in the spiritual side of the enterprise; the stock station he considered the domain of others. Begrudgingly, however, he was forced to act as general manager, but this took the form of weekly consultations with Irrgang, manager of the sheep station, and Ruediger, who ran the cattle enterprise. Reidel complained that his Monday morning discussions were 'enormously time-consuming' and the station badly needed a second missionary.[133]

Johannes Bogner, who had left Killalpaninna soon after Reidel's arrival, to some degree did act as that second 'missionary' (albeit itinerant). But his involvement seems to have been only at times of special stock operations, such as the mustering of cattle from Hermannsburg and their droving to Killalpaninna. The route south passed through Horseshoe Bend and Oodnadatta, and when there was a drought in the north, as in 1912, the cattle arrived in poor condition. 'We often feel depressed about these large dealings in stock, that there should be no detrimental repercussions', synod members wrote apologetically to their supporting Mission Friends in 1913, when the station had become dangerously indebted.[134]

The 1880s and 1890s were boom years for Killalpaninna and saw the expansion of the stock stations. But during the first decade of the twentieth century the station faced continual economic crises. The severe drought in 1901–02 had crippled the enterprise, leaving it short of stock and without income for some time. It managed to survive by drawing on past savings, and by donations from Germany and South Australia. But it never fully recovered. In 1908 the committee was having difficulty paying for mission blankets, and in 1909 was late with its accounting and unable to pay wages.[135] The German employees were desperately overworked, and in 1909 Jack Rohrlach was engaged as overseer. Black labour was in short supply, especially black shepherds, and Reidel suggested reducing the sheep enterprise, claiming it had become 'completely unmanageable'.[136] Apart from economic concerns, he was haunted by the prospect of black shepherds reverting to traditional custom in their isolation. But white labourers, employed from necessity, were still viewed with suspicion: 'All kinds of shady and shaky characters are around the enterprise'.[137]

Reidel even suggested giving up all stock enterprises: 'The most important reason for giving up the sheep and cattle stations is to make proper missionary work possible'.

The severe drought of 1911 again crippled the station. No income at all came in that year, until the mission's stock agents, Coles and Thomas, advanced the enterprise £1800 without security.[138] The advance, however, was not enough to keep the station viable. A further £600 was borrowed privately from Sir J. Coles himself, and as much as possible gathered from German charity (£160) and South Australian donations. A grant of £500 from the South Australian government was raised.[139] Killalpaninna and Hermannsburg stations were operated from a joint mission account and by 1912 the combined debt to Coles and Thomas, on the two stations, was £4000–£5000. That same year the station lost Theodore Ruediger, who retired, exhausted, to the south.

The financial position of Killalpaninna, in particular, was so serious that the committee called a meeting for 1 May 1912 to discuss its future. Reidel travelled south to attend, and Kaibel gave a grim account of the rising debts and limited income from the two stations. It was despondently declared that mission work, at least at Killalpaninna, could no longer be continued.[140] Reidel was informed that he was free to seek another post. He received an offer from a parish in Queensland that, surprisingly, he refused: 'although the fate of Bethesda was trembling in the balance, I did not feel justified in leaving this field and thereby probably hastening the end. I declined the call. The Mission was somehow kept going precariously.'[141]

At one point Reidel suggested the station be moved to a more suitable place— which may even provide benefits, such as training for other than the contemptible station work!—rather than be abandoned: 'Our young people are artificially kept on a lower level in life than that for which they have the capabilities to be trained.'[142]

Apart from the skilled stockmen (many of whom were moving to other stations) and the few employed shepherds, there existed a perennial problem of finding occupation and employment for unskilled Aborigines. Agricultural pursuits were impossible in the desert, and the standard occupation in earlier decades had been brick-making and building—useful, but to no financial advantage. Women not employed as domestics bided their time making baskets and mats from scraped rushes, which they decorated with hair cut from their heads. However, Reidel made it clear to the committee (in his inimitable, disparaging way) that those few Aborigines that were gainfully employed were given no responsibility at all in their endeavours, so understandably had little interest in their work. Independence, he noted, was definitely not encouraged among them, and even at this late period the committee insisted on Diyari being their language at the station. It was a language that locked mission Aborigines to the mission station, with English not taught during Reidel's time. Indeed, the second language was German, useless beyond the mission confines.

Killalpaninna managed to survive for a further two years. But these were two years fraught with continual problems. By late 1912–early 1913 Bogner was again at Killalpaninna, as stock station manager, while Reidel was absent for long periods, arguing with the committee in the south. After Ruediger's resignation of that year, an advertisement was placed in the church newspaper for his replacement, but there was no response at all. Furthermore, in 1912 the Commonwealth government began enquiries into conditions for Aborigines at Hermannsburg after accusations of forced detainment were made by the anthropologist Professor Baldwin Spencer.[143] In defence, the Lutherans at Hermannsburg allegedly asked their black Christian congregation to decide for themselves whether black children should be locked in at night—the issue in question. They allegedly 'voted unanimously' for 'keeping the former order'. Fearing for the future of the Central Australian station, Kaibel then attempted to place the synod's case before the inquiring Commonwealth minister of the Aborigines' Department (newly established under the 1911 Act) during one of his official visits to Adelaide. But the minister refused to see the president, after which Kaibel reported:

> If we are compelled to stop this authority, we may as well give up Hermannsburg... Should the minister's decision be against us I shall inform him of the decision made by the congregation (at Hermannsburg) which has more insight than the learned Professor. Obviously we are a thorn in the flesh for the gentlemen from the ministry.[144]

He added:

> Where the intentions of the Government will lead we will find out when our lease expires (for the Finke River land) in two years time. Then they can, under cover of their rights, put us out of the door as the lease says nothing about a right to renewal, but that after 21 years, all that we have done there in building and improvements, without any compensation, must be left to the Government.[145]

The dejection over Hermannsburg cast further pessimism over Killalpaninna. And, unpropitious for its fate, 1913 was a poor period for the stock stations (cattle now being the primary stock). During that year Coles and Thomas, whose unsecured loans were still outstanding, requested the mission leases as security. Dry conditions persisted in the north; no rains or floods came to rescue.

Reidel and Kaibel continued their discordance, particularly over Reidel's continued refusal to manage the stock stations. And in September 1913 Reidel received a letter from the president, stating his position at Killalpaninna to be 'unsatisfactory'. In later attempting to defend himself against accusations of causing the collapse of the station, Reidel was to write:

> This was exactly what I in the beginning had declined to take upon myself; and the committee had agreed... The years out there never changed my attitude, least of all now, when the work appeared to be on the point of collapse. This attitude of the Committee expressed through its chairman, actually amounted to a breach of contract. It was this attitude of the Committee which finally decided me to resign my post of missionary and look for another place of duty. I sent in my resignation in January 1914.[146]

After receiving Reidel's resignation Kaibel appealed to the South Australian government for financial assistance as 'we were in such frightful straits'. He received a grant of £500, 'until such time as the Aborigines' Royal Commission should make its report'. The synod managed to raise a further £500, and £1000 was reduced from the mission account's bank overdraft. Kaibel must also have appealed to Reidel to stay longer, for the Reidels did not leave the station for another eight months, on 25 September 1914. 'If rain would set in', wrote a desperate Kaibel, 'the mission work would have a new life.'[147]

Bogner was appointed caretaker missionary and manager of the stock station after the eventual departure of the Reidels.

Killalpaninna Sold Into Private Hands

In 1912 a Royal Commission was instigated by the South Australian government to report upon the control, organisation and management of all Aboriginal institutions in the decade-old state (after federation in 1901). The inquiry took over three years to complete. Part of the commissioners' task was to visit the various Aboriginal institutions in the state, and Killalpaninna, as one, came under close scrutiny.

On the morning of 15 June 1914, two weeks before the assassination of Archduke Ferdinand in the Austrian province of Bosnia (Serbia), the single event that heralded the outbreak of the First World War, Reidel and Bogner were interviewed by the commissioners at Killalpaninna. A month later Kaibel was interviewed in Adelaide, and informed that 'we find your institution doing good work, and we want to bring it under the control of this department so as to do the least injustice to you and the best possible for the aborigines'.[148] Kaibel was told to discuss this proposal with his board and report back. In despondency and desperation the president responded that 'the increase (in Aborigines) is so low . . . it is a matter of time when these blacks will disappear altogether'. And he questioned the government going to the expense of taking over the enterprise. But his protestations were to no avail.

Soon afterwards synod members met unofficially—'on account of the political state of the country we did not call a synod'—and decided to surrender at least one of their mission stations, 'if we would not lose both'.[149] The members had long considered that 'the Commonwealth government still have their eyes on our Station Hermannsburg', and doggedly refused to relinquish it.[150] Consequently, with so much weighed against it, the station fated to be renounced was Killalpaninna.

But on 19 November 1914, three months after Britain and France declared war on Germany following Germany's invasion of Poland, Killalpaninna and its pastoral leases were hurriedly sold to the missionary Johannes Bogner, and a German farmer, Johannes Gottlieb Jaensch. At the time of the sale the liabilities of the station were just over £4500, and debts exceeded £5000. When they bought Killalpaninna for the sum required to clear its debts, Bogner was fifty-four, and Jaensch sixty-six. Stigmatised by the divisiveness of national loyalties and a rising anti-German sentiment, the recalcitrant committee was now determined not to allow the station to fall into government hands. At least with this arrangement Killalpaninna was still in Lutheran hands, in German hands. One very specific condition was applied to the sale: that the committee reserved the right to buy back the station for the same sum as it was sold (namely £5000) within a period of ten years. With this arrangement Killalpaninna was considered safely in reserve for future assessment. And with an ex-missionary as purchaser surely no better alternative could be found, considering the dire financial condition of the previous situation and the current international crisis.

A second condition was also applied, namely that the purchasers 'continue the mission work to the satisfaction of the synod'.[151] However, no vigilance could now be kept over this condition and it seems that once the transfer was finalised, on 12 January 1915, the synod prorogued Killalpaninna for a further thirty years.

The station was sold as a 'walk in–walk out' proposition. A deposit of £500 was paid, with an additional £2000 to be paid within the next four months. The remaining £2500, in the form of various debts, was to be taken over by the purchasers. Livestock assets were set down as 1200 cattle, 1500 sheep, 300 horses and 45 camels, although no full-scale muster had been done for some years.[152]

After the sale the committee had a credit of £1800 in the joint mission account with which to manage Hermannsburg. Aboriginal Lease 145, the 470 000-acre Aboriginal Reserve, could not be officially transferred to the new owners. But it was taken for granted that, as part of 'mission territory', the reserve belonged to mission land. The Lutherans had traditionally relied on grazing stock on that land, as boundaries were non-existent across their leases and authorities had never patrolled or interfered in the past. But after January 1915 Killalpaninna was a private enterprise and no longer officially a mission station, regardless of later Lutheran argument. The polemics of Aboriginal Lease 145 were to cause virtual economic ruin for Bogner and Jaensch.

At a recall to appear before the commissioners in April 1915, Bogner defended the sale by stating that 'We only took the station for the sake of the natives and to keep on the mission'. And Jaensch claimed, 'It is simply to keep the mission carried on. I have been connected with the mission all my life, and my father before me. I agreed to assist Mr Bogner. I put up 2000 acres of freehold unencumbered to start us. I handed this over to the committee to allow us to start selling stock . . .'[153] The commission members could do nothing to recover Killalpaninna for the government. And with the sale sealed, Kaibel officially informed South Australia's protector of Aborigines, W. G. South. The protector, who tried unsuccessfully to persuade Kaibel against his actions, responded to the commissioners with:

> The Aborigines have long been led to regard Killalpaninna as their home, many of them having been born there. If they are now turned off they will suffer great hardship, and probably some of them will die. I am sure the synod, who I know have the interests of the Aborigines at heart, would deeply regret doing anything hurtful to them.

He recommended that the new owners, 'gentlemen [who] will do their best to continue the mission work as hitherto', be allowed to persist until such time as the Royal Commission made its final report. 'I cannot recommend that they or any other private person or firm have permanent control of Aborigines. The synod have collected and spent on the mission work, £11 040 between 1901 and 1914.'[154]

Kaibel also reappeared before the commissioners in April 1915, the same month as Allied troops landed on the Gallipoli Peninsula, Australia's momentous blood sacrifice for the Motherland. He pleaded financial difficulties for the hastened sale.

In its final report, published in 1916, the Royal Commission declared that the 'care of the Aborigines is a national matter' and that it was the duty of the government to acquire possession of mission properties and take direct responsibility for Aborigines. The commissioners recommended that the Aborigines' Bill be amended to allow the government to assume control at Killalpaninna and Koonibba, and to acquire possession of the two properties. They pointed out that in South Australia there were 504 759 acres of Aboriginal Reserve land of which 470 000 lay within land occupied by the new owners of Killalpaninna (Aboriginal Lease 145). All earlier Reserve land had been resumed by the government, with revenue from it fetching £73 433 to Treasury. The commissioners recommended that 'this be borne in mind when considering any increase of Government expenditure for the benefit of the comparatively few Aborigines who remain'.[155]

8

Linguists and Ethnographers

The languages of the indigenous people of Australia have been solely oral. By all accounts these 260 or so languages were diverse, rich, complex and descriptive. Aborigines could speak some of the languages of neighbouring groups—essential for trade and ceremonial communication—and many of the groups had an extensive sign language by which they could communicate in silence—useful during hunting or when silent communication was socially more effective (such as conveying a death or when mourning). But none had a written form, although drawings were made as messages or special sacred symbols.

The people who had occupied the north-eastern deserts of South Australia belonged to a number of different linguistic groups that constituted part of the one large language family, Pama Nyungan, which covers most of Australia.[1] These groups were further divided into sub-groups whose languages were not mutually comprehensible. Fortunately for the Killalpaninna missionaries the languages of the area that came under their control were closely related to each other in grammatical and semantic structures, although the words themselves often differed. To proselytise among these people the Lutherans first had to learn to speak the local language. With the progressive dispossession of Aboriginal land and the resulting disruption of their culture, Aborigines from different language-speaking groups gathered near the mission settlements for food and protection. Providentially for these groups, regional language structures were similar, for under such disrupted conditions many were forced to become multilingual.[2]

When the German missionaries first arrived at the Lower Coopers Creek area, the dominant Aboriginal group were still the traditional owners, the Diyari. Consequently Diyari became the language that had to be learned by the Lutherans, and mastered by other Aborigines who came to live at or near the mission station. Thus it was that the Diyari language became so widely spoken in the Far North of South Australia, and that, as the greatest translators of any Aboriginal language, the Killalpaninna missionaries turned a millenia-old oral language into a written form and produced the only group of Aborigines (apart from Strehlow's efforts at Hermannsburg in Central Australia) comprehensively literate in their own tongue. A hunting and gathering society literate in its own vernacular language was a rare phenomenon,[3] but this literacy was confined to Aborigines educated at Killalpaninna Mission Station. There is no evidence that it spread beyond the mission school.

The Killalpaninna missionaries published vocabularies and grammars, and translated Christian works into an Aboriginal language that they had carefully transcribed into a near phonetic form which served the practical function of educating and converting. As a consequence the Diyari language has been rescued from the fate of many Aboriginal languages and preserved in works that are now resting in archives.

In the 1860s, when the Lutherans first ventured into the Killalpaninna area, there were estimated to have been about 3000 to 5000 people living in the Lake Eyre region, with about a dozen different languages spoken among them.[4] A hundred years later their languages were all but extinct, with only a handful of aged descendants capable of speaking any of the indigenous tongues. In the early 1990s there were only two known native speakers of Diyari still living (and one European-descended academic), one known speaker of Thirrari, a few elderly speakers of Arabana and Wangkangurru, and no speakers of Karanguru, Ngamini, Kungardutji, Yadliyawara, Kuyani or Yandruwantha.[5]

As the Killalpaninna missionaries became fluent in the Diyari language, the Diyari world view came more into focus. The Lutherans sent accounts of Diyari customs and beliefs in their letters to the mission headquarters in Germany and to the committee at Tanunda, and these were published in mission journals. At about this time the international spotlight of the newly emerging European sciences was directed at Australia, with, in particular, the social evolutionists looking at Australian Aborigines as isolated survivors of Stone Age humans. Aborigines were seen as relics from a past age, and became test cases and the object of studies for the new Darwinian theories that *Homo sapiens* evolved from apes. The Killalpaninna missionaries would not have shared the basic premise of these irreligious hypotheses, but they did play an important role in the collection of ethnographic material and the development of anthropological debate.

Diyari Language Learning
In early 1867, after being appalled at the customs of ritual cannibalism and polygyny practised among the newly encountered 'heathens', and disturbed at their diminishing numbers due to European diseases, Homann reported an urgency to learn the local language. These Aboriginal people, he perceived, were desperately in need of the Christian message.[6] And as friendly local Aborigines aided the heat-exhausted Germans with constructing rough shelters against the ferocity of their first summer, they began to teach the foreigners a few words of their language.[7]

It was, of course, necessary that missionaries sent to the New World learn the languages of those they sought to convert. But it was also the determined policy of Ludwig Harms that a writing system be devised to facilitate a Christian education using Christian works translated into these languages.[8] Harms, who himself had studied ancient and modern languages extensively, required high standards of literacy and linguistic knowledge from his missionaries.[9] Consequently, literacy became a central feature of mission policy and practice at Killalpaninna during its entire fifty-year history.

Samuel Gason, police trooper stationed at Lake Hope, was the first European to take an interest in the language of the Diyari. He published a vocabulary in 1879, noting the Diyari sign language as 'a copious one [where] all animals, native man or woman, the heavens, earth, walking, riding, jumping, flying, swimming, eating, drinking and hundreds of other objects or actions, have each their particular sign, so that a conversation may be sustained without the utterance of a single word'.[10] Alfred Howitt, on encountering the Diyari and neighbouring tribes in 1861, during his search for the missing Burke and Wills party, also made reference to the complex Diyari sign language.[11] The Lutherans, however, did not trouble with this silent form, and made no reference to it in their many reports. It was not until 1910 that a visiting Presbyterian minister again described Diyari sign language, indicating that it was still practised among the Aborigines at the mission station.[12] If the Lutherans were not intent on learning the complexities of this silent form, it may well have served the interests of mission Aborigines not to encourage them. Information about matters at the camps, impending traditional ceremonies, grudges at the mission, and other forbidden communication could be discussed at virtually any time and any place without the knowledge or interference of the missionaries.

By May 1868 Homann was reporting progress in learning to speak the Diyari language.[13] In February of that year the Lutherans had befriended a local Aborigine whom they named 'Picalli' (sometimes written 'Pickally'). The old man attached himself to the Germans, becoming their first 'disciple', and in return giving intensive lessons in the Diyari language. As Pickally was told about the 'Big Father' (or the 'Big Master'), translated as 'Aberipila' in Diyari, words were exchanged and the Lutherans, by listening to the words spoken, wrote them phonetically to compile their first dictionary.

Schooling and Conversion

The mission school, centre for educating, hence converting (as most mission education was Christian indoctrination), was the focus around which the mission station revolved. It was the first structure to be built (after domestic shelters), and it persisted, as a condition of the sale into private hands, for some years after Killalpaninna ceased to be a mission station.

Wilhelm Koch was the first designated schoolteacher. In the early years, before a schoolhouse was built, classes were resolutely conducted in the open air, under the cool shade of a eucalypt in summer, or among scrubby bushes sheltered from cold winter winds. In the winter of 1868 the open-air class boasted twenty-two pupils. At that time, with drought persisting in the area, Aborigines were gathering around the settlement at Bucaltaninna for the food rations distributed by the Germans, with Homann reporting that 'food suits our purpose'.[14] That same year a schoolhouse was built and a Diyari grammar prepared for the pupils. Pickally was 'still working well with us', and young Koch demonstrated a gift for the language. As Homann became more fluent, also late in 1868, he began regular church services for the Aborigines in Diyari (held in the schoolroom), which were 'attended fairly well by the natives'. Proceeding slowly so that the right words were spoken (otherwise, such was the language structure, the opposite meaning might be conveyed) he began twice daily to hold a 'short sermon and prayer with those Kerna who worked with us' in language learning.[15]

In late 1868 Koch and Homann began work on a Diyari dictionary and translation of Christian works into written Diyari. With twenty-eight pupils now in the school, 'We soon hope to be in a situation to teach them the first major part of the Catechism. If we had the words I could immediately commence baptism of old Pickally and some of the boys, but it is not a simple task to get the words across and find a paper translation for everything', wrote Homann with a mixture of enthusiasm and frustration.[16] Koch and Homann were finding that words essential to the Christian message had no equivalent in the Diyari language, words and concepts such as 'sin' and 'Heaven' and 'Hell' causing enormous difficulties with translating and teaching.[17]

Koch, like most of his Killalpaninna colleagues throughout the mission's history, considered Aboriginal languages to be inferior to those of Europe ('fallen' languages from a time of greater culture) and to be similar to one of the ancient European liturgical languages: 'I realise that the language, although very badly distorted, still has some good points and besides there is a similarity to the Greek language, not so much in words as in style'.[18] The younger Flierl deduced that the Diyari language originated from a lost, higher culture by its 'sophistication' and its 'wonderful relatives system', the 'rather strange mordu [sic]'.[19]

On first encountering Aborigines, with their nature–land based culture and philosophies, the Killalpaninna missionaries consistently perceived them as materialists in the absolute sense, as having no religious life at all in their culture. Consequently they viewed their own task of translating European religious works into a language without words to deal with abstract moral and religious concepts of those words both daunting and near insuperable. But after some language knowledge these narrow perceptions became marginally tempered. Koch noted that there seemed more to Diyari culture: 'There is no language expression for anything other than every day life. But after six months now there is evidence to the contrary. Their language is a colourful one. To someone not familiar with the habits of the people it seems laughable. But that is why it is so difficult to understand their culture and language.'[20]

Homann, at his Sunday sermons in faltering Diyari, battled with alternative words for Christian concepts such as 'mercy', 'sanctity', 'justice' and 'injustice'. For the word 'sacred' he used 'clean' or 'obedient'. He reported that he delivered his messages 'very simply, very childlike. They are not like the people of the Essenes, or the Greek past, nor are they Hindus. But they are "natural people" '.[21]

In 1870 a primer, catechism (with hymns), and a Bible history written by Koch and Homann in Diyari and entitled *Nujanujarajinkiniexa—Dieri Jaura Jelaribala* was published by the mission committee at Tanunda.[22] Copies were sent to Bucaltaninna for use in the school.

After Homann's resignation in 1872, Carl Schoknecht, during his two-year period as missionary at Bucaltaninna, compiled a Diyari–German and German–Diyari dictionary and a grammatical statement setting out the noun and verb inflections.[23] But this was never published, for in 1873 Schoknecht was recalled. Two years later the Immanuel Synod commissioned Carl Meyer to act as teacher at the Bucaltaninna 'open-air' school, and to continue the education process until a suitable missionary could be sent from the new recruitment centre of Neuendettelsau. Again the school was the focus of concern for the missionaries. Before he had sufficient Diyari language Meyer used English in the school, as by the mid-1870s many Aborigines in the Far North had acquired some English from interactions with local pastoralists and the visiting sub-protector of Aborigines. During this period Vogelsang, now fluent in Diyari, was instructed by the committee to assist in the school, and both layhelpers began construction of a schoolhouse building. By the late 1870s, with the new school building showing promise, and Meyer—now more familiar with the Diyari language—using the printed works of Koch and Homann as teaching aids, 'some pupils were able to read fairly well'. The Diyari version of Luther's *Small Catechism* was to be learned by heart by the pupils, with explanation by Meyer, 'according to their ability to understand'.[24]

But the severity of the forthcoming drought forced the reluctant Lutherans to dismiss their precious few school pupils to life at the camps. Provisions at the station were precariously low and the mission wagon was grounded due to the drying of the land. In January 1877 the drought broke, the wagon was again back on the road and food hurriedly carried northwards. The school was immediately re-established: 'Naturally the preaching of God's Word, on account of the little knowledge of their language, was far from perfect, but still it was better than previously'.[25]

A year later Flierl senior arrived. Determined to master the Diyari language quickly, Flierl attended the classes conducted by Meyer and Vogelsang in the Bucaltaninna schoolhouse. Under Meyer's influence, English was now well used among the pupils. Meyer stayed on as schoolteacher, and the mission station was moved back to Lake Killalpaninna. Just before the move, however, the first group of 'educated' pupils, who had been instructed by Meyer and Vogelsang, were baptised by Flierl. The baptismal ceremony was conducted in Diyari,[26] but the newly baptised were presented with a copy of a Bible in English as there was not yet a Bible (or New Testament, as it became) translated into Diyari. Under Meyer, the pupils probably became reasonably literate in English so the presentation seemed appropriate and 'Lame Henry' spent 'a lot of time reading it [the Bible]'.[27]

According to Flierl the Diyari language was understood by all neighbouring tribes. He reported that Aborigines spoke very quickly, and used many word shortenings when talking among themselves, describing this as 'loses all its nice sounds and sounds like somebody walking down a ladder'.[28]

In his first year Flierl described the Diyari language:

Like all languages here it is very vocal, with a nice sound, and the simplicity of it all is wonderful. It contains an extraordinary completeness. But there are no words for anything abstract or anything spiritual . . . It is not easy for blacks to learn our cultured languages. They formed a striking contrast when transferred into their own language. Their language, although nice, is poor in words and covers only one tenth of our language.[29]

But later in his life, after seven years with the Killalpaninna Aborigines and many years missionising in New Guinea, Flierl was to write of the Diyari language that: 'One gets to know all kinds of strange things . . . they aren't particularly well endowed with expressions for spiritual things, but what they see and touch, and of nature they have a much richer vocabulary than in the language of we cultured people'.[30]

At the Lake Killalpaninna settlement a schoolhouse was built as a priority. Like that at Bucaltaninna it also functioned as a church (even for the first weddings of baptised Aboriginal couples), until the mud-brick church was built in mid-1880. As Flierl mastered the Diyari language he removed English from the curriculum, translating hymns and further Christian works into Diyari. In the early 1880s he had a reading book entitled *Wonini-Pepa Dieri-Jaurani Worpala* printed for use in the school. Its content not only carried the Christian message but also embodied European cultural values. When the new books arrived at the mission station they were issued for use in the schoolroom.[31]

The erratic interest of the Aboriginal pupils during confinement in the classroom with its formalised, strict, European-style teaching, their habit of 'going walkabout' at a moment's notice, and their seeming 'laziness' frustrated the Lutherans, anxious to convert through education. By the mid-1880s the fifteen to eighteen pupils at the school were a mixture of children and adults, with Flierl writing:

> Learning progress cannot compare with Europe. Those who stay on for a while learn quite well and know how to read and write. The older ones manage to do some reading and understand some teaching of the catechism and Bible stories. Arithmetic is beyond them and they have little talent for geography. They are not interested in foreign countries and people.[32]

In his work on the Diyari language Flierl senior proved an 'excellent linguist', reforming the earlier spelling system by recognising the initial velar nasal pronunciation in the spoken language, which he wrote as 'ng'. Furthermore he substituted 'tj' for an earlier 'x', to represent the lamino-palatal stops in the language. Flierl refined Schoknecht's grammatical statement, adding a parallel grammar of the Wangkangurru language, for by the 1880s Wangkangurru people were coming southwards and settling near the sanctuary of the mission station. Flierl translated the catechism and the epistles and gospels into Diyari for Sunday use in the Killalpaninna church. The translations were bound into the title *Christianieli Ngujangujara-Pepa Dieri Jaurani* (or 'Epistles and Gospels for Sundays and Holy Days of the Christian Year'), and printed in 1880. The orthography developed by Flierl remained the standard for all subsequent mission writings and translations.[33]

The schoolroom and its Aboriginal pupils became a measure of the success of the mission, and consequently a centre for success propaganda. Visiting committee members would be taken to the classroom to question pupils about their biblical and secular knowledge, and Aboriginal pupils were set assignments of letter writing to committee members or to missionaries on holiday in the south. These letters, carefully constructed and containing the most promising hope and harvest of education and conversion, were written (over the years) in both Diyari and English, and were designed to be proudly circulated among the Lutherans.[34] Letters written in the schoolroom at Killalpaninna were sent to Germany and some were published in the journals of the Neuendettelsau Mission Institute to demonstrate educational success both in literacy and in Christian conversion.

Perhaps the initial impetus for this form of propaganda came from the 1881 and 1882 letters of Henry Tipilanna ('Lame Henry') and 'Rosalee'. One was possibly

Outdoor Bible class at Killalpaninna given by Missionary Wettengel (centre right)

spontaneous (Henry Tipilanna, 1881), the other (Rosalee, 1882) perhaps initiated by the missionaries as a European convention of gratitude for a rescue by the visiting committee members from a violent incident at the camps. But more importantly they were demonstrations of mission success. These letters from baptised Aborigines caused a suitable response from the mission headquarters, both in South Australia and in Germany, so that other letters were also initiated, far less spontaneously or genuinely, to demonstrate mission success and seek response.[35]

During the 1890s the Killalpaninna school again had English added to its curriculum, with Henry Hillier engaged as a teacher. By 1893 the schoolhouse boasted two teaching rooms, enabling different classes to be held simultaneously. During one prolonged absence of Hillier, Reuther advertised in the south for an English teacher to fill the vacancy and engaged William Hunt. It was during Hunt's time that class letters, expounding wistful, yet somehow questionable, Christian sentiments, were written in English to the president of the mission committee.[36]

During his first decade Reuther spent much of his time teaching at the mission school, describing it as 'plenty of joy and misery'.[37] The missionary encouraged older pupils simply to learn the catechism by heart, considering it too difficult to teach these old people to read, write and understand arithmetic, as 'they never get beyond the letter D in the alphabet, or past the number 3 in numerals'. 'They manage to understand most of my daily prayer, which I keep very simple, and learn it by repetition.'[38] Siebert's view was quite different: 'pinaru ... are not as stupid as is sometimes made out. Some can read after a month'.[39]

Strehlow's first impression at Killalpaninna was of an Aboriginal population diminishing alarmingly and of the decreasing life-expectancy of Aborigines in general.[40] Aborigines needed the patronage of the Lutherans for sanctuary, jobs and, in particular, food, and, by the early 1890s had begun to take an interest in what the Lutherans had to offer them—cultural 'gifts', compassion and direction (relative to other encounters with Europeans)—enabling them to cope with the imposed national cultural changes and decrees. When he was first learning Diyari, Strehlow reported that 'They particularly like it when I speak to them a little in their language . . . They try hard to speak as slowly as possible so as to make themselves understood to me.'[41] And when he started teaching in the school, 'several heathen youngsters aged between 14 and 20 were making good progress, one was writing well after 6 months at the school, one had a good memory and understood, was perfect in English and could pick up foreign languages and Bible stories'.[42]

By the late 1890s Reuther was no longer in the classroom. Wettengel taught in one, with Hillier or Hunt in the other. Three languages were now instructed: German (for the children of the missionaries), Diyari (for the Aborigines, and mainly for New Testament study), and English (for both German and Aboriginal pupils). In 1898 Wettengel wrote:

> Spiritually and intellectually the black children are in no way behind the white. An eight-year-old boy has learnt more than 20 hymns and the catechism by heart without anyone ordering him. He sits among the children at night and tells them what to do. Most of them like to learn. But when they reach 12 to 14 years many become disinterested, which lasts for several years. The education task is not easy for missionaries because 'education' is a term the Papua themselves don't know.[43]

Mission Masterpiece: Translation of the New Testament into Diyari

In 1893, a year after Strehlow's arrival at Killalpaninna, Johann Georg Reuther and Carl Strehlow embarked on the most ambitious translation attempted at the mission station. They began work on translating the entire New Testament (Luther's sole manifesto for Christianity) into the Diyari language. To date the Lutherans had baptised a total of seventy-nine Aborigines.[44] The new two-roomed schoolhouse had been built, a mud-brick church stood on a high sanddune, and there was an urgency about conversion, with Aboriginal people dying prematurely and their children dangerously influenced by partly 'heathen parents', Strehlow reporting that 'the apple does not fall far from the treetrunk'.[45] Reuther had returned from a two-month holiday in the south, and during his absence Strehlow had perhaps perceived a need for a New Testament translation. On 10 April 1893 Reuther entered in his diary: 'We began to translate the Gospels. God grant that we have the health in the body and soul that this may rebound to His glory and become a blessing to many.'[46]

Progress on the massive work was slow, with mission duties and schoolwork taking precedence. In the evenings Reuther would walk to the top of a sandhill beside his house and call, 'Cooee, Cooee!', cupping his hands to his mouth and swaying to the left and right. He would then stride into his study and wait until a group of four or five Aboriginal male elders approached his house, entered the study and sat patiently and quietly on the floor. Reuther, at his cluttered desk, presumably with Strehlow nearby, would take up the translating task. Whenever a troublesome word arose the Germans would turn to the old men for discussion.[47]

It has been postulated that Strehlow was the mainspring of the work, that Reuther was 'a good practical man, but lame at languages', and only an average

Reuther and Strehlow with Killalpaninna Mission people. Some of the older men were probably assistants in the missionaries' translation of the New Testament into Diyari

speaker of Diyari.[48] In fact, in his 1892–93 report Reuther had stated he was 'still not in full command of Dieri [sic] language'.[49] And soon after the translation task began Reuther requested a third missionary to assist with the schoolwork. His plea was successful, for that same year the graduate, Otto Siebert, was sent from Germany to Killalpaninna.

The translation of the New Testament took almost three years to complete. It dominated the time and passion, certainly of Reuther, and perhaps too of Strehlow. When the task was barely half completed Strehlow was transferred to the Hermannsburg Mission Station in Central Australia. Reuther laboured on alone at Killalpaninna. The translation, when it was finally published in 1897, was attributed to both authors. It is possible that Siebert also assisted with some of the work. He proved a scholarly missionary, taking just four months to deliver his first sermon in Diyari, and demonstrating an academic approach to ethnography and anthropology.[50] But it is also highly probable that Reuther contributed the major portion of the New Testament translation, possibly corrected in parts by Strehlow, perhaps after completion and before publication. It was on 29 October 1895 that Reuther entered in his diary: 'Thank God I finished the translation of the Dieri [sic] testament, Soli Deo Gloria'.[51]

Copies of the Diyari version of the near 2000-year-old Semitic document were proudly distributed among the baptised Aborigines at Killalpaninna and presented to new converts after baptismal ceremonies. The 600-page achievement must have brought accolades to Reuther and Strehlow from their peers in the south and in Germany. It allegedly impressed church circles in Australia for it was the first complete translation of the New Testament into an Aboriginal language.[52] The accomplishment had taken the Killalpaninna enterprise thirty years of hardship and frustration, and it held the hope and promise of the Christian Word among Aborigines. The heavily bound books were titled *Testamenta Marra* and subtitled *Jesuni Christuni Ngantjani Jaura Ninaia Karitjimalkana Wonti Dieri Jaurani* ('Words Praying to Jesus and Translated into the Diyari Language').[53]

Reuther continued to translate Christian works into Diyari, and for one allegedly 'lame' in languages he was certainly prodigious. He translated the Orders for Common Prayer, Baptism, Confirmation, Holy Communion, as well as hymns and psalms. In July 1899 he completed a new Diyari Grammar, followed, in 1901, by similar Wangkangurru and Jandruwonta grammars, 300 pages of manuscript, accompanied by a parallel vocabulary of eight contiguous languages of South Australia and Queensland.[54] In 1903–06 Reuther compiled his dictionary of the Diyari language in four volumes.

Reidel and the Diyari Language

When Reuther left Killalpaninna, most of the teaching and preaching material used at the station had primarily been translated by him. Reuther's replacement was the scholarly, fastidious Reidel who used Reuther's work to learn the Diyari language. He also learned from the sons of the old Kolonisten, 'Jack' (Johannes) Irrgang, now station manager at Etadunna, who 'grew up with the Dieri [*sic*] and knew their language best and most thoroughly', and Theodore Vogelsang, who was now manager at Killalpaninna.[55] Reidel relished theoretical challenges and requested that the committee retrieve Reuther's thick manuscripts of grammars and dictionaries, and of ethnographic material, which his predecessor had doggedly taken with him on leaving the mission station. 'I find it necessary and prudent to thoroughly read the language', Reidel wrote to the committee, 'let us have at least sometimes the dictionary—the Dieri [*sic*] languages and customs and to use his example . . . it is his duty with his God. I will hold this weapon under his nose'.[56] He also wrote to Siebert in Germany. 'You have heard of our difficulties, two years without a missionary. During your time you have worked on a translation of psalms. Could you send me your material?'[57]

Reuther eventually obliged Reidel in late 1908. Within the parcel he included a letter for one of the Aboriginal girls at the station. Reidel, in his disparaging way, refused to pass it on to the girl, yet in this first of correspondences with Reuther was surprisingly praising of Reuther's manuscripts: 'The books have arrived undamaged . . . Their content is . . . a treasure of words and too good for the work I do here. That you haven't sorted the words alphabetically, makes the looking up for somebody else but you very time consuming and difficult . . .'[58]

Reidel arranged Reuther's dictionary into alphabetical order and condensed the work into one volume, returning the manuscripts in May 1909: 'So now I have a wonderful handbook. I have given it to Kaibel . . .'[59] He continued to correspond with Reuther over the translations throughout 1909, stating that he felt the earlier missionaries had been hasty in their versions 'before anyone had a good look at the people', and that they tended to substitute 'foreign words' before they 'found the Mura'. Reidel corresponded with Reuther partly in Diyari and partly in German, and like a select club the two were rare communicators in a written Aboriginal language.[60]

To Strehlow at Hermannsburg, during that same year, Reidel again hinted at past inaccuracies, declaring he would not dare have anything put into print 'unless I have lived with the Dieri [sic] for a few years . . . First the spirit of the language and the people have to become one's own, don't you think so?'[61]

As his language and comprehension skills improved Reidel began the ambitious project of translating the Old Testament into Diyari. He would teach Old Testament stories from an illustrated (German) version of the Bible at baptism classes, the pictures holding the interest of the class and Reidel picking up Diyari words and concepts for his own explication.

In translating the various Christian works the Lutherans continually wrestled with Diyari cultural alternatives for the European understandings of Semitic concepts. In translating the New Testament, Reuther and Strehlow used the Diyari word 'Neyi', with its embodied Diyari connotations, for 'Christ'. 'Neyi' meant 'older brother', the one who was duty bound to stand by, help and protect, even unto death, his 'ngadada' or 'younger brother'. It was considered one of the more successful subrogations, as such sentiments as 'Christ (Neyi) dying on the cross for our (ngadada) sins' was 'a usage thoroughly understood by the blacks'.[62] Even old Dicky, for long a traditional protector of others who might be victims of a pinya, as elder brother had killed the man who had, in his words, 'killed my ngadada'.[63]

While Reidel was translating the Old Testament he searched for a powerful alternative word-concept for 'soul'. He finally settled on the Diyari word 'tepi', which denoted a circumstance that bordered between material and immaterial, between (as it was interpreted by the Germans) the realm of physical and spiritual. An example of 'tepi' as understood by the Diyari was the shadow of the shadow of a stick lying on still water, its shadow's shadow (tepi) thrown on the bottom of the water pool.[64] The word for this shadowy phenomenon was deemed that most suitable as a description of the Christian soul. And in discussions with Aboriginal elders, including old Joseph, Reidel searched for an alternative word for 'grace', a missing word-concept that had long haunted the Lutherans. He asked the old men what word they would use when, on closing in for a pinya execution, they felt sorry for the victim. After a long silence, one man replied, 'We never let the man go. We would hurry up and kill him, but our livers become soft and we let him go.'[65] The Diyari word for 'pity' was 'kalumilcha', literally translated as 'liver soft'. The liver was considered the seat of emotions in Diyari culture, 'softening' towards a person to produce pity. Reidel, however, found the word 'liver' too indelicate for such a sacred Christian concept as 'grace', and presumably a translation remained elusive.[66]

As he furthered his work on the Diyari language and continued to translate the Old Testament, Reidel revised what had become standard mission orthography. This had previously tended to over-differentiate vowels and under-differentiate consonants. Reidel removed many of the 'e' and 'o' vowels, replacing them with the more correct low vowel 'a', for (according to Austin) Diyari has only three vowels, 'a', 'i' and 'u'. And he corrected consonant stops, the many 'r's' to 'rr', 'nk' to 'ngk' and 'ntj' to 'njti'.[67]

Reidel's translation of the Old Testament into Diyari was never published. The end of the mission was too near, economic problems weighed heavily, and Reidel and Kaibel were continuously at variance. Furthermore, the committee was still insisting that Diyari be the language of mission education, while Reidel argued for English. Although circumspect, he rationalised its importance for an Aboriginal future and survival beyond the narrow confines of the mission station itself; 'I am not a great fan of introducing English, but it might just be better for the black people. The Dieri [sic] should have their mother tongue as long as possible.'[68]

In 1914 Reidel and Bogner were interviewed by the commissioners of the 1912–16 Royal Commission. It was reported, unfavourably, that at Killalpaninna the Diyari language was taught, with German as a second language and English a poor third.

Reidel's translated Old Testament was never used at the Killalpaninna school, nor in Killalpaninna church services, as intended. Entitled *Ngujangujarra Pepa Diari Talini* (literally translated 'Paper For All Of Us In The Diyari Tongue'), the massive handwritten manuscript lies in the Lutheran Archives at Adelaide.

Nineteenth-century Theories Regarding Australian Aborigines

William Dampier, in the late fifteenth century, was the first Englishman to observe (from a distance) and publicly describe the indigenous people of Terra Australis Incognita, that vast southern mass of mysterious land on the other side of the world from Europe. He caricatured them as a degraded race who were not fully human, assuming they had no religious beliefs at all.[69] The Old 'known' World of the Europeans was coming into contact with another half of the planet, these xenophobic European societies for the first time confronting very different cultures. Most of Europe had developed philosophically and theologically along Graeco-Roman and Judeo-Christian thought. And with the emergence and proliferation of a dominant Christian ecclesia there had arisen a notion of religious exclusiveness, that Christianity was in fact the one true religion of God's special creature, man. As the Genesis account relates, the first man, Adam, was created by God, the first woman created from Adam's rib, and from these two special creations the rest of humanity was descended. Although banished from a utopian environment of nature, created by God for man's benefit and enjoyment alone, yet humans were given, by God, dominion over the entire realm of nature. Man had only to worship the one true God and obey His rules. This basic hierarchy and relationship of God–man–nature was the basis of European thought for over 1200 years.

As the world of Europe came into contact with the world of the Australian Aborigines various theories arose to explain the social, religious and cultural differences between these disparate peoples. At about the time of William Dampier, a time of very early contact with people of the New World, some European theorists (known as polygenists) proposed that not all men were descended from Adam. The origin of some of these new people, it was thought, was uncertain and obscure. Others, known as Deists, saw every group of humans as part of the one natural creation that was being revealed in the emerging sciences of people such as Copernicus, Galileo and Newton. But essential to this, for the Deists, was that each human group, no matter how 'savage', had a common sovereign deity, the one monotheistic God. They believed that man's reason and logic, no matter how 'primitive', led to the inevitable common notion of God's existence.[70]

From this Deist conception came the idealisation of what was seen to be 'natural man', 'naked man', unashamed and uncorrupted, who became a utopian ideal in the sentiment of the Noble Savage. With the rapid growth of industrialisation in Europe during the eighteenth century, and the development of science and technology, the simple life of 'natural man' in the New World seemed an attractive alternative to modern society, and the doctrine of the Noble Savage became popular among Europeans. James Cook was of this notion and, disillusioned with orthodox Christianity, he attacked Dampier's view of Australian Aborigines, claiming them, after he had landed in Australia in 1770, to be 'in a pure state of nature' and 'far more happier than we Europeans'.[71]

Not surprisingly, the Noble Savage doctrine did not survive beyond the early nineteenth century. The theories of Darwin and the other social evolutionists took a firm hold globally, and the European world became divided over the biblical Genesis theory. The idea that humanity, like other living forms being determined scientifically, evolved from primitive to sophisticated, from a lower to a higher state, with many stages in between, was articulated by the social evolutionists. Its proof was being determined by the ever-growing bulk of ethnographic evidence from the New World. The tools and weapons of living hunter-gatherers were deemed 'primitive', those from Australia deemed the most primitive of all, indeed Stone Age, and extrapolation was extended to non-material aspects of the New World cultures. The theories of the social evolutionists suited the exploitative purposes of the Old World in colonising the New, growing wealthy from relatively untapped resources, with land in plenitude and a ready pool of cheap labour. In the case of Australia the governing European bodies and large pastoral and mining enterprises justified their appropriation of land, convinced they were merely fulfilling the destiny dictated to them by the evolutionary process. The indigenous Stone-Age relics of inferior peoples, it was believed, had reached their zenith and must either integrate into the higher culture (believed impossible by most) or become extinct.

As Australian Aborigines were seen as perhaps the least developed culture encountered in the New World, semi-nomadic hunters and gatherers without agricultural tendencies, they were perceived as the most evolutionarily backward, relics from contemporary man's past, the earliest surviving species of man and perhaps a link between ape and man. The perceived poor physical conditions of landscape in Australia were thought by some to be a likely reason for the 'primitive' state of its human inhabitants, their intellects considered too 'childlike' and sluggish for the evolution of a religion. (Both views were held by the missionaries, though for reasons other than pure social evolution, namely the regressive corruptibility of 'heathenism'.) Aboriginal beliefs and ceremonies were presumed vague, superstitious imaginings.[72] Aborigines were deemed materialists, claiming full control over the world, with no God and no recourse to a final morality.

German Missionaries and Australian Aborigines
It was with this general view (tempered with the Genesis account of Creation) that Killalpaninna's first German missionaries encountered Aborigines in the Far North of South Australia, just eight years after publication of Darwin's *Origin of Species*. Theories of social evolution had been well received in Germany, with the rise of nationalistic groups and Pan-Germanism seeking

German unification under Bismark and Wilhelm I, particularly after de Gobineau's essay on supremacy of the Teutonic race.[73]

When the first Lutherans arrived at the Lake Killalpaninna area, in 1867, several Britons (notably Howitt, Gason and Buttfield) had already encountered the local Aborigines, learnt aspects of their language, and had some knowledge of their customs. The Lutherans were to acquire their first understandings from communicating, in their limited English, with two of these men. Howitt, six years earlier, had recovered the bodies of Burke and Wills and found the emaciated John King sheltering with the Aborigines of the Cooper. He had engaged Aboriginal guides, one a Yantrawanta man, the other a Diyari, to conduct his party through the unknown countryside, and these guides had taught Howitt some language, some survival methods and something of the local customs. Howitt, who was initially disgusted by Aborigines and despised them, later became a major figure in the development of anthropology in Australia.[74] His first published paper, descriptive and non-analytical, concerned these Cooper people. Howitt was to describe them as 'in many ways just like children'.[75] One of his guides on the expedition, a Narrinyeri boy whom Howitt named 'Charlie', was later killed by the Diyari for taking the Europeans through their tribal territory, probably after the fear of the first wave of violence from pastoralists taking up land in that area.[76]

In the wake of this first wave of violence, too, came the first police troopers stationed at Lake Hope to defend the pastoralists and their stock from Aboriginal attack. Samuel Gason spent nine years in Diyari country, and during that time observed local customs, descriptions of which he included in his 1879 publication. Although he spoke Diyari effectively Gason had limited comprehension of Aboriginal society and belief, heading sections of his account with such titles as 'Superstition on Trees', where he claimed 'there are places covered by trees held very sacred, the larger ones being supposed to be the remains of their fathers metamorphosed', and 'Indescribable Customs', a section devoid of descriptive content and relating to those particular increase ceremonies that involved sexual freedom, too terrible for the police trooper to describe. Gason perpetuated the notion of a pagan, immoral society, impulsive and untrustworthy: 'A more treacherous race I do not believe exists. They imbibe treachery in infancy, and practise it until death, and have no sense of wrong in it.'[77]

By the mid- to late 1860s the first sub-protector of Aborigines, John Buttfield, was following the proposed policy of learning the language of his territory and gaining knowledge of local customs. But when arguing for legal punishment for offending local Aborigines, instead of pastoralists taking the law into their own hands, Buttfield reported, 'The Aborigines are children alike in intellect and knowledge, and I am of opinion that the same kind of treatment which a Christian parent deems necessary to meet [sic] out his wayward and erring children should be in the same spirit and with similar motive administered to offending Aborigines by a parent Government.'[78]

As they gained a knowledge of the Diyari language, the Lutherans began to glimpse Aboriginal culture. Images of the 'kutchie', interpreted as the biblical Devil, took shape, although this 'bad spirit' was believed by the Diyari to be present in such mundane things as flies, bad eyes and poisonous snakes, a kind of physical badness as opposed to the spiritual badness of the Christian Devil.

As cross-communication between Aboriginal school pupils and German Lutherans began, Homann declared them to be 'a people who have sunken very low and have terrible sins in their culture . . . these young people have dirty souls which they express without shame and with a smile . . .'.[79] And as there was no word for 'sin' in the Diyari language the Lutherans considered this to be symptomatic of their godless state. Aborigines were seen as depraved people in the darkness of sin, godless and religionless, evidenced by their 'terrible' ceremonies and customs, the eating of parts of a dead corpse, infanticide, the 'awful' painting of the body with blood for ceremonies, and the 'indecent dancing' and 'other unmentionable incidents'. They were seen as 'childlike', intellectually backward, and as interested only in fulfilling their physical requirements, a full stomach, a little tobacco, a ration-issue blanket and perhaps a warm shirt:

> then all their wishes are satisfied. They sing and dance and seem happy in this enormous misery of theirs, and their animal-like state of depravity . . . Of God they have only the darkest imagination, and the bad spirits (devils they fear) that is just the king of fright which often changes like their singing and dancing into a terrible misery and frightful complaining howling. They are real materialists in their ways.[80]

These were the images sent back to Germany and perpetuated in the colony; certainly not a Deist conception, nor a perception of the Noble Savage. Regarding the Noble Savage theorists, Flierl senior, after three years with the Aborigines, and following a tirade on the perceived immorality and backwardness of these people, rather disparagingly reported: 'From all this we can gather our black people are not as harmless as our nature freaks here claim, because those nature freak imagemakers seem to envy these children of nature. Only people who have no knowledge of the depths of the depravation can think like this.'[81] Flierl described Aborigines as 'people who only live for the moment, with no concept of the past and no concept or hope of the future'. He reported that they had 'no folklore, no sagas, no remainders of the stories of the past or ancestors'.[82] To lead this dying race of primitive heathens to salvation through introducing the Christian God was the paramount intent of the Killalpaninna missionaries.

The harsh landscape of the Australian interior was considered a powerful factor determining the perceived backwardness of Aborigines, with Flierl senior, in the early 1880s, reporting that: 'It is understandable that people who live in such a poor country where the land yields so little for their bodily needs are naturally living on a very low cultural level. And actually the Australian Aborigine, if not as regards the body, but morally, has such a low standard as anyone created in the image of God could possibly have.'[83] Flierl, however, by the early 1880s understood that there were two kinds of what he described as 'super-human (transcendental) "human beings", the muramura', which he described as 'a kind of beginning of the biblical Creation Story', and the 'Kutchie, about which the blacks have a great fear'.[84] Aboriginal beliefs and culture did not conform to those of the known world, and could be described by the Germans only through known patterns of thought, patterns of good and evil, morality and immorality. They were not even like the patterns of thought and behaviour of the black Africans being encountered on other mission fields. Baffling was the rite of circumcision practised among Australian Aborigines, the Lutherans' only explanation being that it was 'without any religious meaning, although in earlier years this may [not] have been so'; these people may, they thought, have had a 'higher' culture lost in some distant past.[85] Flierl junior certainly came to this conclusion, deduced from 'the wonderful relative system (kinship) and the strange institution of the mordu [sic]', which he understood to mean 'sects'. Furthermore, he considered their language to be uncharacteristically sophisticated.[86]

By the late 1870s, with the official recognition of the Aboriginal population fast disappearing (after the 1860 Select Committee of Inquiry), sub-protectors, missionaries and police in frontier parts of South Australia were encouraged to document Aboriginal 'folklore' in their areas and send their papers to the Department of Crown Lands for editing by George Taplin, missionary of Point McLeay.[87] Gason's work was perhaps part of this project. But Flierl senior did not enter the fray of ethnographic collecting and documenting in Australia, his interest in Aboriginal culture being minimal, and his impressions of Australian Aborigines as 'poverty stricken, just like their whole life.'[88]

Reuther, Collector and Documenter

Reuther spent eighteen years as missionary at Killalpaninna. After he and Strehlow had worked on the translation of the New Testament, and Reuther had spent many hours with Aboriginal male elders searching for Diyari words and concepts to replace Christian ideas, the ex-railway and postal worker gained a greater insight into Aboriginal culture than did any of his missionary predecessors. During the 1890s Reuther was influenced by two compelling factors: visits to Killalpaninna of a scientific nature made by overseas scholars, and the increased recognition that the Australian Aborigines were doomed to extinction. Before the New Testament translation, Reuther had planted informers among mission Aborigines to report on any planned traditional ceremonies to enable him to interfere and stop the heathen practices. He had also instigated 'confessions' for erring mission Aborigines, with pre-confession talks, stating that 'This is worthwhile. We can really get into the thinking and believing of these people.'[89] At this time knowledge gained by such means was simply intended for mission control.

However, by the time of Siebert's arrival in 1894 Reuther was beginning to take the Aboriginal religious system more seriously, describing, with obvious interest, mythological stories in some detail in his reports. Aware of the concept of 'many muramuras' and interpreting them as allegories for good and evil, he now considered the Aborigines to have 'the laws (of good and evil) written in their hearts', as described in Romans 2:14–15 of the New Testament. He even equated Aboriginal social law and rules with the social morality embodied in the biblical ten commandments. He attested, however, that 'only a small part of such recognition can be detected among these people who have sunken to such low depths'.[90]

In 1894 Reuther described his first muramura song story, that of the Karkakordana muramura, the 'old man who is able to produce rain or water' and whose speciality was to create trees and waterholes, obviously a most vital muramura to the desert Diyari. But, he related, 'It is not a particularly sophisticated interpretation of a Higher Being, and it is easily gathered that any depth or proper development of Creation and the proper recognition of how the world was created, could not really be developed, or was completely forgotten, among the Australian Aborigines'. Of the rite of circumcision, Reuther declared in 1894 that it carried no religious significance, but simply indicated that a boy had reached the age of manhood.[91]

By the late 1890s Reuther had become immersed in ethnographic collecting and describing, the missionaries frantically documenting traditional Aboriginal life:

> The way of life of the heathens is slowly collapsing, and because of that Siebert and Wettengel have begun to collect the old sagas and stories, legends and myths of the Dieri [sic]. From all that there emerged ever more clearly that there were spiritual images among the Dieri. Indeed one sees now that there are creation stories—stories of the Flood, stories which are also predicting the end of the world ...[92]

Siebert, as 'bush missionary', had opportunities to observe ceremonies and lifestyle, and to talk with Aboriginal people less inhibited about their customs. Liberating them was their distance from the constraints of the mission station. Reuther, on the other hand, had to rely on Aborigines attached to the mission station for his information, men like 'Joseph', a loyal Christian who would preach the biblical message to other mission Aborigines and felt ashamed of his peoples' sinful ways.[93] As a result, Reuther probably received a sanitised version. There is some evidence that he was jealous of Siebert's extrication of material, and that he poached Siebert's informants when they came to the station, at times adopting Siebert's findings as his own.[94]

Reuther became ever more obsessive, compiling vast inventories of names and meanings, descriptions, myths, stories and vocabularies. He would 'cooee' the old men into the unfamiliar confines of his cluttered study, and question them intently, all the time scribbling in his untidy hand. His main informants had been old Diyari men, but by the turn of the century he had Wangkangurru men ensconced on the floor of the study. The Wangkangurru, newly emerged from the Simpson Desert, were the last Lake Eyre Basin Aborigines to come into direct contact with Europeans.[95] Hence they had the least interfusion and were the most traditional, and Reuther felt he might gain undefiled material from them.

Not surprisingly, this passing on of traditional information to European strangers, men who already held great power among Aborigines in the area, created intense suspicion and unease among some of the elders at the camps. Mission Aborigines, in particular, came under bitter imputation. Furthermore there seems to have been a polarisation of views among Aboriginal groups over the handling of traditional knowledge during this period of disintegration. It was obvious that their culture was collapsing with the dispersal of people, the loss of land and spiritual base, and the attractions of the new culture. Some elders freely chose to pass on information to the Lutherans (and others who came into the area for that purpose), recognising it as the only future preserve. Most who held this view were mission Aborigines confused over cultural and spiritual affiliations. In 1901, for instance, one Killalpaninna man, a Thirrari named Emil Kintalakadi, who was engaged to guide Professor Gregory and his geological team to the northern edge of Lake Eyre, took the party to the base of a boxtree, and dug from the ground a sacred stone, presenting it to Gregory claiming, despondently, that it would not be wanted again. He explained that it was a 'Womma gnaragnara', 'the heart of the Snake'. The stone had been used in increase ceremonies for 'Womma', the dark, olive-brown carpetsnake.[96]

It seems there were also elders from outside the confines of the mission station proper prepared to divulge religious knowledge, as evidenced from Siebert's work. Other elders chose to withhold information, even from their own young people. They felt they might retain the traditional power by protecting sacred knowledge, adjudging the young, who were invariably drawn to mission offerings, no longer worthy. Some of the informants at the mission station were allegedly 'boned' by elders at the camps for transferring such knowledge, especially knowledge that did not belong to them.[97]

During this time the Germans discovered a fossilised sacred tree near the edge of a lake to the west of the settlement. Reuther ordered the fossil tree broken into three separate parts and carefully carried by horsedrawn mission wagon the difficult 25 miles of sandhill country to Killalpaninna. The tree was erected in front of Reuther's house, a tangible muramura (in the missionary's understanding), and Reuther persuaded the baptised mission Aborigines to enact their old rites before the sacred fossil. In stereotyped manner, these rites were thus later described: 'They danced around it in an excited and frenzied manner, blood dripping from torn flesh.'[98]

Artefacts were perhaps given over in the same spirit and faith as traditional knowledge. It was unlikely that the missionaries, or their visitors, paid for these objects with hard currency, as the use of money among Aborigines was discouraged at Killalpaninna. They may have been traded for valued consumables such as tobacco, perhaps a clay pipe, new clothes or some household item. Certainly Yashchenko paid some of his Aboriginal helpers with sticks of tobacco.[99] But mission Aborigines, in the quest for approval and favour with the missionary, may well have freely given artefacts to Reuther as a symbol of renunciation of their old life. They may even have secretly been proud that their material culture was now being valued and collected by Europeans.

Reuther compiled a repository of thirteen volumes of information on the Diyari and their neighbours, and collected a total of 1308 separate items and artefacts which he displayed in the large passageway of his house at Killalpaninna.[100] One visiting journalist described Reuther's 'Killalpaninna museum':

> The interior of Mr Reuther's dwelling is a veritable museum. The passage contains over a thousand pieces of native weapons, ornaments, and apparel, including 100 boomerangs suspended from the ceiling. Four hundred symbols, composed of almost every kind of material available, form an interesting collection.[101]

Visiting Ethnographers

During the 1890s anthropological interest in Australia gathered momentum. The Australian Aborigines, threatened with imminent extinction, had become an anthropological enigma to some and, for the social evolutionists, test cases for their theories. There was an international rush to study these people before they were no longer living specimens.

In November 1892 a policeman stationed at Port Augusta, while on routine patrol in the north, discovered the bones of a prehistoric diprotodont in the dry, salt-crusted bed of Lake Callabonna.[102] This spectacular discovery increased scientific interest in the north of the colony, and two years later a large privately financed scientific expedition (the Horn Scientific Expedition) travelled through the north of the colony as far as Central Australia collecting specimens, surveying the land and studying the Aboriginal people. The party comprised six eminent scientists, including Dr E. C. Stirling (later director of the South Australian Museum, to whom Reuther sold his collection), and Professor W. Baldwin Spencer, who was to feature prominently in Australian anthropology.

The expedition did not pass through Killalpaninna, but took the westerly route through Oodnadatta and on to the MacDonnell Ranges. At about the same time, Strehlow and Reuther were travelling to Hermannsburg for Strehlow to take control as missionary. During that same year, too, occurred the momentous meeting between Baldwin Spencer and the Alice Springs telegraph operator, later sub-protector of Aborigines in Central Australia, Frank Gillen, with whom the professor was to form a long and significant professional partnership. Gillen was to spend nearly twenty years in Central Australia, and as sub-protector had extensive contact with the Aborigines of the area, particularly the Aranda tribe. This was invaluable to Spencer, who spent long periods with Gillen in Central Australia studying the Aborigines. The two Europeans became accepted by the Aranda, undergoing full initiation into the tribe over their years of contact.

Jealousies and rivalry developed between the Hermannsburg missionaries in the same area (most of whose Aboriginal people were Aranda) and the anthropologists, with Gillen slighting the missionaries at the 1899 Select Committee. He testified that in his opinion the Lutherans were 'making the natives' path to extinction easier', destroying 'all that was good in their organisation and [giving] them nothing in return'. Having just finished his joint publication with Spencer (*Native Tribes of Central Australia*), Gillen stated he was 'anxious to see the old habits of the blacks kept intact. The black fellow in his savage state is infinitely superior to the semi-civilised natives who haunt towns all over Australia.'[103] Strehlow, who became fluent in the Aranda language, criticised Spencer and Gillen for their deficiency, and consequently their interpretation of the anthropological material.[104] The two groups, with Reuther entering the fray, were to compete and polarise, particularly over religious interpretations.

Spencer and Gillen were to receive international recognition for their work on the Aranda, with James Frazer, in his epitath to Baldwin Spencer, praising him for his 'full, detailed, and exact description of a people living in the Stone Age', a people whose 'material condition', Frazer declared 'the simplest and lowest consistent with the existence of human life on earth'.[105] Gillen, although prone to the Noble Savage image of Aborigines, in 1899 testified to their being 'the lowest in the scale of barbarian races, as well as the lowest in human intelligence', and that 'Scientific investigation goes to show that the Aboriginal race began to decay many years before the white man set foot in Australia'.[106]

Spencer and Gillen have been credited with an immense contribution to the understanding of Aboriginal totemism, and with articulating the absence of the worship of gods among Aborigines.[107] This appeared to fit well with current anthropological theory in Europe, with Frazer, in the preface to the publication,

Reuther and Pauline working in the missionary's study at Killalpaninna

writing that 'When we contrast the universality of magical rites among the Australian tribes, with the conspicuous absence of the worship of gods among them, we may fairly conclude that these facts lend some support to the theory first broached by Hegel that in the early history of humanity the Age of Religion has been preceded by an Age of Magic'.[108]

The urgency of such work as *Native Tribes of Central Australia* was well heeded among international anthropologists aware of the evanescence of these 'relics of primitive man'. In their introduction to *Native Tribes* the authors also made this precipitancy clear:

> The time in which it will be possible to investigate the Aboriginal native tribes is rapidly drawing to a close, and though we know more of them than we do of the lost Tasmanians, yet our knowledge is very incomplete, and unless some special effort be made, many tribes will practically die out without our gaining any knowledge of the details of their organisation, or of their sacred customs and beliefs.[109]

It was almost a plea for immediate, impetuous study of these people. Australian Aborigines had become a popular theme of academic scrutiny in Europe, and of general curiosity, with public lectures on the peculiar habits of these primitives and displays of their material culture, even their skulls and skeletons. Both professionals and amateurs became interested in visiting Australia and taking back ethnographic knowledge and artefacts from these unique Stone Age remnants.

Dr Erhard Eylmann, a German medical practitioner with an interest in ethnography, visited Australia in 1900 (one of three visits he made) and spent twelve days at Killalpaninna. He relied on Reuther for much of his information on the Aborigines, collected artefacts, and returned to Germany to write his account, entitled *Die Eingeborenen der Kolonie Südaustralien* ('The Aborigines of the Colony of South Australia'), published in 1908. Eylmann took back a collection of 263 Aboriginal artefacts, not all from the Killalpaninna area, which were sold to the Bremen Overseas Museum in 1926.[110]

A year later, during the Australian summer university break, a Melbourne professor of geology, J. W. Gregory, arrived at Killalpaninna with five students.[111] Doubtless inspired by the diprotodont find of nine years earlier, the party were searching for the bones of extinct, prehistoric animals, combing the dry, desert lake beds of the Lake Eyre region in the blazing heat of December and January. They stayed at Killalpaninna for one week, and during that time one of the students became lost in the miles of sandhills and short scrub nearby. A Killalpaninna Aborigine tracked the young student from footprints on the parched ground. And when the party left the mission station, Emil Kintalakadi guided them safely towards Lake Eyre. From this expedition Gregory produced his well-known book, which helped coin the descriptive phrase for arid Australia, *Dead Heart of Australia*, published in 1906.

In the winter of 1903 a Russian professor of ornithology, and amateur ethnographer, Alexander Leonidovich Yashchenko, arrived at Killalpaninna by mailcoach and stayed for ten days. The Strehlows, from the Hermannsburg Station, were also visiting the Reuthers, perhaps prearranged for the eminent international visitor.

It was after lunch on a wintry afternoon, when Reuther, Yashchenko and Strehlow were deep in discussion in Reuther's study, that Reuther showed the Russian his voluminous documentation of Aboriginal material 'in several ledgers'. According to Reuther, Yashchenko was the first to have seen the ledgers, although 'German societies had more than once asked him for these notes, but he had always refused to surrender them'. The Russian professor was impressed and 'tried in vain to persuade the pastor that they should be published. He asserted that he had noted all these things down purely for the sake of preserving what would otherwise have vanished without a trace, within the past few years'.[112]

Perhaps flattered by Yashchenko's interest and attention, and impressed by his profession, Reuther offered to sell his museum collection to the Russian scholar for just £10 sterling, 'assuredly a trifling price, considering the scientific value of the collection', wrote Yashchenko. The Russian agreed to the purchase, but postponed the arrangement until after his return to Russia. The purchase, however, was never made. Yashchenko did return to Russia with Aboriginal artefacts, some of which were given to him by the Killalpaninna staff: stone tools from Hillier's own collection, locally woven baskets from Bogner, Reudiger sold him a necklace, and Reuther gave him 'a gift of crocodile bones'.[113] Yashchenko also collected from other parts of Australia.

In the nineteenth and early twentieth centuries the anthropological world had become infatuated with questions over the origins and evolution of man, with the skulls of Australian Aborigines postulated as bearing the greatest resemblance to those of Neanderthal man. These physical anthropologists (phrenologists) thought that the measuring of the form of the skull and the face would be scientifically informative relative to the evolutionary process and its consequence, the development of the human brain. Darwin himself wrote of the female Australian Aborigine, in his *Descent of Man*, that she was a creature 'who uses very few abstract words, and cannot count above four, exert her self-consciousness, or reflect on the nature of her own existence'.[114]

One of the central quests for nineteenth-century ethnography and anthropology was the search for the missing link that would connect humans with apes. Australian Aborigines were suspected as being that link, consequently 'specimens' of Aboriginal skulls, whole skeletons, even preserved heads and preserved bodies were keenly sought for scientific study. It has been ascertained that thousands of specimens were sent from Australia to Europe.[115] The method of acquiring such human skulls, skeletons and preserved bodies is generally unknown. Allegedly one leading German anthropologist, Hermann Klaatsch, in 1906 'amused his lecture audiences with his experiences of stealing a corpse from amid a group of Aboriginal mourners. He later exported that skeleton to his university in Germany, where it still forms part of the extensive collection held throughout Europe.'[116]

There is no evidence, however, that any such specimen collection was undertaken by the Killalpaninna missionaries. Quite apart from their moral scruples, the missionaries' theological commitment to the biblical Genesis account of Creation would have negated any involvement with social evolutionist theories. The only specimen collections undertaken by the Lutherans at Killalpaninna were those of a weapon, utensil or tool variety, or of local plants, animals and birds.

Siebert and Howitt

Alfred W. Howitt, who (with W. Baldwin Spencer and Frank Gillen) became one of the fathers of Australian anthropology, corresponded with the major European figures of nineteenth-century anthropology—Lubbock, Tylor, J. G. Frazer, Andrew Lang, Adolf Bastian, Arnold van Gennep, as well as with Darwin, offering assistance for their international pursuits with material from Australia. Darwin advised Howitt to take special note of Aborigines' 'capacity of abstract reasoning . . . quasi-religious beliefs . . . their curious marriage laws . . . you could certainly write a very valuable memoir or book, in the course of a few years'.[117] Howitt also corresponded with various people in the field in Australia, including Reuther and Siebert, from whom he received much of his material.

Otto Siebert spent eight years at Killalpaninna, many of these as 'bush missionary'. Reuther, however, was suffering health problems, frequently apologising to Howitt for his correspondence (or lack of it) and his inability to undertake field trips.[118] Howitt's collaborations with Siebert resulted in several joint articles on the legends, customs, beliefs and social organisation of the Aborigines from the Lake Killalpaninna area.

Reuther and Siebert may well have become rivals over their willingness to supply Howitt with material. Both were impressed with the public figure's status and flattered by his need for their knowledge.[119] It was at about this time that Reuther began seizing Siebert's Aboriginal informants when they came to the station, taking them to his study to extract information. Siebert, in later years, complained:

> But then, every time after the old men had been at my place, he [Reuther] got them immediately to come over to his place and made them tell him everything that I had obtained from them at great trouble previously. I could tell you a lot more about it, but I suppose this will be sufficient. Please do not tell others about it, Reuther had ended most tragical [sic]; therefore it is not our place to judge.[120]

Siebert later also accused Reuther of plagiarism. He claimed to have allowed Reuther to read his material, but that Reuther would copy the notes and read them to others, such as the mission committee, as his own investigations.[121] Moreover, Siebert claimed part authorship in the *Diyari Grammar* published by Eylmann in 1908, which Reuther had attributed only to himself.[122] Apart from his own aggrandisement in this case, Reuther may well have been jealous of the attention given his junior missionary, particularly considering his own difficulties with recognition for his years of documentation work.

Otto Siebert was also to differ from Reuther on theorising about Aboriginal religion. Reuther claimed a monotheistic God (a grand muramura) at the centre of the muramura concept, a theory that well suited the Lutheran position. But when he began to argue vehemently against the current orthodox anthropological hypotheses, Baldwin Spencer wrote to Howitt in 1905 suggesting Siebert's disregard for the Lutheran position had caused Reuther to harden his own line: 'Possibly the fact that your friend Mr Siebert's work was not altogether approved of by the Lutheran authorities may have incited him (Mr Reuter [sic]) to action in this particular direction'.[123]

Regardless of the anonymity often attributed to him, Siebert willingly supplied Howitt with material for presentation and publication, generally under Howitt's name only. And although rivalry with Reuther caused resentment and secrecy with material, Siebert saw his own vocation as missionary, seemingly unconcerned in these ministering days about public acknowledgement. Among other material, he sent the anthropologist precise, detailed information on the complex marriage rules and kinship system of Aborigines (about which Howitt lectured publicly and published), and material on the legends of the Lake Eyre tribes.[124] Siebert did publish one article in German, describing and discussing the 'mudlugga' (anti-European) ceremony which he observed in 1901.[125]

After Siebert became ill and left Killalpaninna in 1902 Howitt was sent material by Reuther, who claimed Siebert's whereabouts to be then unknown.[126] By this time, however, Reuther's health was seriously faltering, his letters scrawled, messy, laboured attempts at English but lapsing into almost unreadable German. It seems that Howitt was not able to use Reuther as a source of information.

In 1904 Howitt published that 'very valuable book' suggested by Darwin. Entitled *Native Tribes of South-Eastern Australia*, it relied on much of Siebert's material, but was published only under Howitt's name. Later in his life Siebert was to explain: 'I was corresponding with Mr Howitt, he translated my notes into English and wanted to publish the book in my name and his. But as I on

In 1901 Otto Siebert documented and photographed the mudlugga ceremony, the non-secret, anti-European dance, at Lake Allallinna (Ngarlangarlani), 4 kilometres south-west of Killalpaninna Mission Station

account of my illness could not trouble any more about the conclusion of the book, Mr Howitt published the book in his name.'[127]

Aboriginal Religion—One God? Reuther versus the Prevailing Orthodox View

As anthropologists and ethnographers gleaned some knowledge about Aboriginal rites and ceremonies, international debates raged over understanding this so-called 'primitive religion'. Articles and counterarticles appeared in England, Germany and Australia. Anthropologists became divided between a majority who believed Australian Aborigines to be relics of an earlier age of human development without a religion or a supreme god, simply with a set of beliefs and superstitions, and those who considered they did have a supreme god. Reuther and Strehlow fitted the second category, providing the main opposition to the views of Spencer, Gillen, Howitt and Siebert. Strehlow asserted that the 'Altjira' of the Aranda represented an all-powerful supreme being (like the Christian God), Reuther claiming this concept among the Diyari to be the 'Mura', both missionaries clashing with Spencer and Gillen's analyses that Aboriginal religion was very different from the monotheism of Christianity, and demonstrating that it was based on a system of totems, not a system of deities with a single godhead. It suited missionising supposition that there be points of contact between Christianity and Aboriginal religion, a one-God concept that was true for all humankind. Reuther had written:

> Feeling my way into the mental world of these people, I searched through their legends and the god-and-spirit world of heathendom in an attempt to discover points of contact with the Christian faith and thereby destroy their pagan concepts. Indeed it cost me much time and labour to become a Dieri [sic] to my Dieri people, for in my opinion a missionary without a thorough knowledge of the language and customs of his people, is, in the best instance, like a watch that works without hands.[128]

However, the debate between the Lutherans and the anthropologists did not become public in Australia, at least, as neither missionary published in English. Apart from a small paper, in English, in 1905, Reuther was not published at all during his lifetime.[129] In fact, when Spencer and Gillen's book was first released, Howitt sent a copy to Killalpaninna. In shaky handwriting Reuther had acknowledged the gift, adding: 'I am too weary on my return from a journey to see after my black sheep to do more at the time . . . your kind present . . . with heartfelt thanks. I have had but little time to glance over the work . . . but I can say that in many respects it will be a standard for our work. A more complete critical opinion can only be formed later on . . .'[130]

Certainly Reuther's beliefs did differ from those of the Spencer and Gillen work, but he lacked an arena for expression of his views beyond the Lutheran body. He sought to publish in Germany, sending material to Moritz von Leonhardi, some of which the director of the Berlin Museum published under his own name. One such piece was Reuther's provocative supposition (considering the international acclaim of Spencer and Gillen's theories) of the Diyari's belief in Mura as God. Von Leonhardi, however, was criticised for his assertions, and in his defence cited his own informant:

> the former missionary, G. J. Reuther, who claimed to have found such a belief in God among the Dieri [sic] people. I was well aware that I was pronouncing an assumption that could well be contradicted, and that I ought to make a claim only as far as the possibility of such a belief is concerned, the actual existence of which could only be verified after further research . . . The only thing that matters is whether Reuther can come up with proof for his assumption . . . He [Reuther] brings forward yet another piece of evidence which at first glance seems remarkable . . . Reuther . . . has no satisfactory response to this objection [of his making mistakes] so it seems to me that his proof of the existence of the Dieris' belief in God has completely failed.[131]

Reuther's Mura-godhead did find support among a few German and Austrian scholars (like Rene Hoffmann and Wilhelm Schmidt), but in Australia his views found little, if any, support among Australian scholars. Reuther attempted to have his theories published by the Royal Society of South Australia, but was unsuccessful. When Baldwin Spencer heard of the missionary's attempt, he wrote a deprecatory letter to Howitt:

> Rev Mr Reuter [sic] a Missionary at Kopperamanna [sic] . . . describes the mura as originally 'a great God' or something of this kind, and says that the ceremonies concerned with the muras are really of the nature of invocations to them to assist the natives, but adds that at the present time the latter do not understand what they

really mean. So far as I can gather from Gillen's account, Reuter says that the native of the present day performs certain ceremonies which have a significance unknown to the native. How the Rev Reuter arrives at the conclusion that originally they had a certain meaning I cannot understand.[132]

Reuther's main writings on the subject are contained in volume 11 of his massive thirteen-volume manuscript. He cites religion as 'the fundamental basis of all human thought', stamped upon every person, and draws a distinction between the Mura and the muramuras (one God and many deities), claiming the Mura to be 'shrouded in dark mystery', and not articulated by the 'primitive' Aborigines. Muramuras, on the other hand, he deemed lesser deities, 'nothing more than the alleged forefathers and ancestors of the human race to whom however in the course of time, honour has been assigned'. Reuther, however, misunderstood that the Aboriginal informants he used (some of whom were Wangkangurru and with whose language Reuther was less skilled) were so familiar with their stories of ancestral wanderings, creations and totemic affiliations that they sometimes abbreviated names or used nicknames in their close familiarity. Reuther simply interpreted this as greater and lesser names, related to the realm of what he perceived as deities.[133]

It was during this same year, 1909, that Reuther was allegedly requested from Germany to undertake a comparative study of Aborigines across Australia. Undeterred by his critics, the now retired missionary-turned-farmer enthusiastically responded, claiming to be 'the proper man to be sent', and contacted the director of the South Australian Museum for support with mounting an expedition along the lines of that undertaken by Eylmann:

> If I would travel I would contact with unknown tribes and would require at least two or three years only to travel the six winter months and to have Queensland or Western Australia as the starting point . . . Would it not be something great for the completion of the world's history and to know something about the ancient race of Asia? . . . I shall appeal to your justice for the investigation of our people living in the state of nature. You do what you can and your name shall have an everlasting value in regard to the Aborigines.[134]

The expedition was not realised. The director of the South Australian Museum was perhaps reluctant to endorse the unorthodox Reuther–Strehlow view on Aboriginal religion. Reuther continued to press Stirling for publication of his manuscript material, especially that relating to artefacts deposited with the museum, telling Stirling that he was 'doubtful that Baron von Leonhardie [sic] on account of old age and overloaded with work will be able to finish the copy'.[135]

But neither Stirling nor von Leonhardi published Reuther's massive manuscripts. The director of the Berlin Museum died a short time before Reuther himself. Little interest was taken in Reuther's manuscripts, deposited with the South Australian Museum after the missionary's death, until Theodore Vogelsang was engaged to begin translation of the work from German into English in the 1930s. During that time Theodore Vogelsang began a correspondence with Otto Siebert in Germany. Siebert was to write that 'A German ethnologist acquainted with me told me that Reuther had sent him his work, but he had to send it back to him, he couldn't do anything with it'.[136]

Reidel, Non-Ethnographer

After the frenetic ethnographic compilation of Reuther's period, the theorist Reidel showed virtually no interest in collecting or documenting. His preoccupation became perfecting the written Diyari language in order to correct and add translations. By now many of the mission Aborigines were old people, with death continually reducing their numbers, and Reidel would have had access to material already gathered, including the borrowed Reuther manuscripts.

In 1909, less than a year after he took control, Reidel received a request from von Leonhardi for artefacts and ethnographic material, with von Leonhardi offering to arrange the sale of these artefacts for the missionary. Reidel pleaded overwork and promised only to keep the suggestion in mind: 'Unfortunately nothing can be done by me in this direction as yet. That the people are dying out is clear. In a few weeks we have in close proximity ten old [?dying] people. It will be to my gratification if it would be possible for me to do some of my real work and to send you in this direction something that would serve science.'[137]

A year later an amateur ethnographer, the young Presbyterian theological graduate John Love, stayed with the Reidels at Killalpaninna. He produced a substantial handwritten manuscript documenting Aboriginal culture at the mission station in this first decade of the twentieth century.[138] The manuscript portrays Aboriginal beliefs and culture as threatened, diluted and underground, the people holding a fear of the power and authority of the missionary figure Reidel. It portrays traditional tasks, such as basket- and mat-making, as relegated to handicraft activities, whereas 'real work' now had become mission tasks—domestic chores and sewing for the women, and station work for the men. Saturdays were the only days that Aborigines were permitted to engage in hunting and gathering trips, and this had become their 'best day of the week'.

Love described the Aborigines' array of tools and weaponry, now rarely used, claiming that 'the men and women would part freely with old carved boomerangs and spears, but were unwilling to part with the everyday roughly made wona, as it was of more practical uses'. By this time, too, pieces of discarded metal station-equipment were being formed into useful tools by the Aborigines:

> A favourite utensil was formed from a piece of shear blade, hoop iron, or any old iron, ground to a chisel edge, and fastened to a small Kaudri-shaped handle about one foot in length. It is interesting to see the way in which the Dieri [sic] cling to the boomerang curve in making modern implements. I saw it used in chopping out the handle of a shield and was amazed to see the dexterous way in which a difficult piece of work was executed with such a clumsy weapon.[139]

In 1912 a curator from the Museum of Dresden, which housed a specialist ant collection, requested from Reidel a selection of ants from the Killalpaninna region. The museum sent tweezers and glass tubes filled with preserving fluid, and Reidel surely felt compelled to comply. Several previously uncatalogued ant species were discovered from the collection that he posted to Saxony, and one particularly interesting specimen was named for the missionary *formica Reidelii*.[140]

Publications, Artefacts, Museums: Aborigines as Artefacts

The mission works, of Christian religious translations into the Diyari language, were all published by the Lutheran Church of South Australia. Copies of these works, such as Reuther and Strehlow's translated New Testament, are held in the church archives in Adelaide. There, too, was lodged Reidel's unpublished Old Testament translated into Diyari. Reuther's thirteen-volume handwritten manuscript was deposited with the South Australian Museum by Pauline Reuther soon after the missionary's death. It has now been translated from German into English, an enormous task occupying four years of labour and completed in 1978 by an Adelaide Lutheran pastor, Philip Scherer.

Reuther's collection of artefacts and botanical specimens, over 1300 items, were sold by the missionary to the South Australian Museum in 1907. Just four years earlier he had offered it to Yashchenko for £10 sterling. He now wanted the grand sum of £450, offering the collection to museums in London, Berlin and Adelaide. Reuther had become aware of the growing international market for Aboriginal artefacts, and after negotiation with Stirling, sold the collection for £400. In October 1907 the artefacts and specimens left behind at Killalpaninna after Reuther's hurried retreat had been packed into saddlebags and carried by camelback to the Herrgott Springs railway depot for freighting to Reuther's Gumvale property. From there the artefacts were carried by horsedrawn buggy to Adelaide. Consequently many arrived at the museum in a damaged state.[141]

In 1914, with the closure of Killalpaninna as a mission station, Reuther's manuscripts were also added to the museum's collection, at a cost of £75.[142] In the words of two contemporary curators at the museum, 'The unusual scientific value of this great collection [Reuther's artefacts] lay in the fact that a large proportion of its contents was documented in meticulous detail by Reuther'.[143]

Among the artefacts sold to the South Australian Museum was the 'fossil tree', that sacred ancient relic around which the missionary had urged mission Aborigines to dance in the manner of old, and that Reuther had reconstructed from sawn sections beside his Killalpaninna house. Today it is mounted and stands like a symbolic sentinel beside the entrance to the South Australian Museum steps.

Another controversial facet of the Reuther artefacts are the 385 contentious toas. These are small sculptures, each allegedly representing geographical sites in the Lake Eyre region, and containing encoded messages. The toas, Reuther declared, told the stories of the muramuras and their exploits at each geographical place. However, the question remains over their traditional nature, as no knowledge about toas can be found among the Aboriginal descendants of the Lake Eyre people today.[144] Accompanying the toas are watercolour miniatures of the sculptures painted by Hillier. The English teacher and artist also drew and painted watercolours of Reuther's collection of Aboriginal weaponry, and assisted Reuther with the Reuther–Hillier Map, which allegedly gives 2468 significant Aboriginal locations recorded by the missionary.

Hillier also made collections of Diyari, and later Aranda, artefacts, which he shipped to England. His collections are now held in the Horniman Museum, the Museum of Mankind, and the Cambridge University Museum. Part of his collection is lodged with the Australian Museum in Sydney.

Otto Siebert's collection of Diyari artefacts is held in the Völkerkunde Museum in Frankfurt, Germany. The artefacts collected by Eylmann are housed in the Bremen Museum in Germany. Yashchenko's artefacts form the largest collection of Australian material at the Peter-The-Great Museum of Ethnography at the NN Mikhlukho-Maklay Institute of Anthropology and Ethnography in

St Petersburg. Diyari artefacts also found their way to the Staatliches Museum für Völkerkunde at Stuttgart, and museums in Munich and Hamburg, as well as the Canterbury Museum in Christchurch, New Zealand.

Reuther's collection of artefacts and plant specimens, nevertheless, and the wide scope of Reuther's ethnography—far wider than that of Siebert and Strehlow—provides an unequalled record of traditional Aboriginal life in the Lake Eyre region. Today he has been accredited with making 'a major contribution to the knowledge and understanding of Aboriginal mythology and sites in the Lake Eyre Basin'.[145] In the words of today's scholars: 'The great work of the missionary Reuther'[146] and 'There was nobody who could rival the achievements of the Rev Reuther in documenting the languages and traditions of the Lake Eyre Basin. Without his great work of fourteen volumes . . . much information would be totally lost.'[147]

9
'A Scattered Homeless Flock'

Killalpaninna closed as a mission station at the outbreak of the First World War to become an ordinary cattle station. The mission Aborigines were released back to the more traditional lifestyle at the camps, a few staying on to work for the new station owners, while the families of the missionaries went south to establish new lives. These turbulent war years were a time of deep insecurity for Germans in Australia. With divided loyalties themselves, they became targets of acrimony and suspicion, and feared the humiliation of internment, with its separation of family members.

Later Killalpaninna history, from the years after the First World War to the present day, was dominated by the children of the old Kolonisten, and in particular the Vogelsang descendants. Just like their fathers of sixty years earlier, when Killalpaninna was threatened with closure after the establishment of the Hermannsburg Mission in Central Australia, the sons and daughters of Hermann Vogelsang and the stepson of Ernst Jacob continued contact with the scattered Killalpaninna Aborigines, and fought a painful conscience over their abandonment. These sons and daughters had spent their childhood and youth at Killalpaninna Mission; their playmates had been Aboriginal children. They had formed close emotional ties with the people and the countryside for they had had the longest continuous contact. Hermann Vogelsang junior had stayed on as schoolteacher after the closure of the mission station, and his brother, Theodore, had stayed even longer, as overseer at the cattle station. Other Kolonisten sons and daughters had taken former mission Aborigines south to work in their homes or in their new enterprises.

The first direct contact with those ex-mission Aborigines scattered in the north was made by Theodore Vogelsang in 1931. And between 1932 and 1940 Hermann junior made many visits to the north, eventually advocating a further mission reserve for the Killalpaninna people. The conscience of the Lutheran church body gradually felt the abandonment of religious responsibility towards the black Christians, and the visits north became closely linked with the performance of Lutheran religious services at Aboriginal camps and the ritual of Christmas gift-giving. These visits, often with a Lutheran pastor in charge, took the form of 'adventure journeys' into the remote north. However, they were also poignant reminders of an only partial past success. A few enthusiastic and seemingly faithful Christians remained among the fragmented camps, now mainly small groups of family units, or groups of station workers, but these seemed very few—old Katarina, Bertha, Alec Edwards, Ben and Ern Murray, Gottlieb and Frieda Maltilinna and a few others being the main stalwarts. After fifty years of conversion struggle, these were modest numbers indeed.

The small, sad pockets of ex-mission people encountered on such visits, perhaps marginalised even more than their non-mission counterparts by their conditioning into German Lutheran ways, had become nostalgic for the old mission lifestyle and its protection from the outside world. These people were now ageing, but spent their time moving about the north-east in search of station and domestic work, or ration depots for basic sustenance, their camps havens of poverty and ill-health. This was still a dark period for Aborigines. Although they were expected to conform to European laws and cultural patterns, even European religion, none were recognised as citizens within their own country until the late 1960s (although some would say they are still not fully recognised).

The Years of the First World War

The sale of Killalpaninna had been conditional upon unofficial missionary work continuing among the Aborigines there. This was certainly a naive expectation, irrespective of a Killalpaninna missionary being part of the new ownership (particularly as he had shown considerably more interest in stock management than in missionary activity).

For the first two years the mission school was continued and services were held by Bogner at the Killalpaninna church, undoubtedly irregularly, as Bogner would, of necessity, have been absent with stock duties and station problems. As part of the sale conditions Bogner was expected to write the quarterly reports of past committee control. In other words, the Tanunda headquarters expected the privately owned cattle station, which was still an established ration depot, to function as a missionising centre remaining under their specific direction, but without being seen as such by an antagonistic government. The committee members were, however, relieved to leave the expensive and troublesome stock station to the control of the new owners.

The year 1915 saw potent anti-German feeling in Australia, aggravated by mounting losses on the battlefields. During that year three Lutheran churches in South Australia were burned to the ground, Lutheran pastors became targets of suspicion, and nearly 6000 of some 100 000 German people in Australia at that time were interned.[1] A War Precautions Act had been passed the year before, which took from Germans living in Australia both civil and national rights. The Act forbade 'persons of enemy origin' (including descendants) the right to vote, and denied them the right of action for libel or slander, or the right to board any ship in harbour. It also empowered employers to dismiss Germans (including those naturalised), fellow employees to refuse to work with them, clubs to cancel membership, and local policemen to direct any restrictions put upon such 'alien enemies'. After a petition was presented to the mayor of Adelaide, all Germans who held positions within government departments were forced to resign.[2]

Some of the ex-mission staff remained employed at Killalpaninna Station after its sale to Bogner and Jaensch; Hermann Vogelsang junior as schoolteacher (complying with the conditions of the sale), Theodore Vogelsang as overseer of the Killalpaninna leases, and Jack Rohrlach (now husband to Hermann and Anna Vogelsang's daughter, Bertha) as manager at Kopperamanna, with old Anna Vogelsang still living at the Kopperamanna homestead. Some of the Killalpaninna Aborigines also remained employed, both on the stock station and in the homes of the Germans.

The summer of 1914–15, the first months of private ownership, saw a devastating drought. There was little feed for the stock, little water at the station, and little money to run the enterprise. The new owners tried growing grain (a failed experiment during Flierl's time), with 2000 acres sown with wheat, and an unspecified acreage sown with oats. But the prospects did not look hopeful. As stated in Bogner's first quarterly report, 'Unfortunately we can't give the men the full pay for their work, as all three treasuries (Farm, Mission and Store) are not only empty but have an overdraft. As we are not allowed to send our natives away and don't want them to suffer hardship, and as they don't respect handouts, but are pleased to keep themselves and their children with honest work...'[3] Aborigines had been put to work 'stump picking' (collecting the gnarled roots of the stunted mallee trees after the land had been cleared for crop sowing).

In this first desperate year Bogner requested a donation from the Lutherans in the south—a time-honoured reliance of Killalpaninna as a mission station— 'either as free gifts or else as a loan with or without interest'. He was hoping for some economic recovery after two failed harvests. Considering his continuation of missionary activity (for which he was not paid or financially supported), Bogner pleaded, 'there surely are a good many members in our Synod who have something to spare for our Mission, and when they read this, surely will gladly do it, so that the work of the Lord may prosper'.[4]

But money and enthusiasm were scarce among the estranged Germans in the south, while the cruel, relentless, northern climate devastated the landscape with hot, dry winds and whipping sandstorms, pushing man and beast to the very edge of existence. Stationers were forced to move their horses to feed and water, with the result that stations became isolated from food supplies beyond those they could provide themselves. At Killalpaninna, with seventy Aboriginal children to feed, 'The stores can't give them [the Aborigines] any more credit... our baptised members are dissatisfied and complaining about meals... receiving only very plain but nourishing food... There is no chance of much variety during these times.'[5] Services in the Killalpaninna church very likely centred not only on the hardships of the current drought, a concept close to the hearts of the Aborigines themselves, but also on the difficult times of the war raging on the other side of the world, the cause of much alienation and anxiety among the Germans at the station, but a concept likely to have been little understood by the Aborigines listening to these services. Nevertheless, 'These sad times are surely also a means in the hands of God, to make the hearts of our natives more willing to hear His Word and trust in it completely and to help them in practising all Christian virtues... Formerly there were various complaints about this and that as regards their meals; now however they are much more content.'

Although food was in short supply, and money for wages in even shorter supply, the busy task of running the station required at least two sets of boundary

Anna Vogelsang with her house help at the Kopperamanna homestead

riders and patrolling stockmen, whose task was to prevent stock from straying or being incorporated into the herds driven down the Birdsville Track. Such vigilance required skill and continuity, and Aboriginal men were employed. Although their wages were considerably less than those a European expected, they often received only food rations during these hard times. But with the Germans unable to pay even minimal wages, and ex-mission Aborigines now much older, while their children were moving away to seek work at other stations, Bogner, like Reidel before him, found the engagement of sufficient able Aboriginal stockmen increasingly difficult.

The war in Europe intensified during 1916, with the horrific battles of Verdun, of Jutland and of the Somme, and the surrender of 10 000 British troops at Kut-al-Amara. Australians were warned by their prime minister, Billy Hughes, to be on guard against German spies and the espionage network known to be operating in the Pacific. As a consequence, employees of German consulates and others within official German institutions, like Lutheran churches, were interned. In August 1916 a resolution was passed in the South Australian House of Assembly that German-sounding place-names be changed, with the governor, Sir Henry Lionel Galway, stating: 'the German spy system has worked hard during the last century in this State to strengthen the chances of the Kaiser one day becoming the Ruler of Australia. The system of nomenclature of towns was one of the methods employed.'[6] Sixty-nine such names were changed in South Australia alone, including the nearest town to the Killalpaninna Station, Herrgott Springs (named for the German botanist who had explored with John McDouall Stuart), which thereafter became Marree.

In December 1916 Bogner discussed with Hermann Vogelsang the possibility of the station being confiscated by the South Australian government, suggesting Vogelsang close the school and leave for the south. Apart from his fears of government interference, Bogner was having difficulty maintaining the Vogelsang family at the station. Anna Vogelsang and her youngest daughters also left with Hermann and his wife for the south. One daughter claimed Anna had suffered 'a nervous breakdown' after her husband's death, and that the family had become 'very subdued' in these later years.[7] As the Vogelsangs packed their possessions into a camel-drawn buggy and lurched away from the Kopperamanna homestead where Anna had spent twenty years of her life (nearly forty years in total at the mission station), she realised, looking back at the mud walls and thatched roof with its overhanging verandah, that she would never see the place again. Nor would she again travel across these bare desert plains.

Ironically, 1916 had seen good rains in the north of South Australia, with 7.05 inches for that year. Furthermore, the South Australian government had sunk another well near Etadunna, at Cannuwaukaninna, which yielded 276 000 gallons of boiling artesian water each day, greatly easing the local water supply problem. In 1917 a further 6.93 inches fell in the north, and the higher prices gained for stock—due to the food shortages of wartime—enabled Bogner and Jaensch to clear their property-purchase debts.[8]

However, in 1917 the United States of America entered the European war, allegedly after German submarines sank unarmed passenger ships. The South Australian government closed all Lutheran day schools, including the school at Killalpaninna. And Killalpaninna was also closed that year as an official post office. By the end of 1917 the dry season was again gripping at the purse strings of battling stationers, and Bogner and Jaensch were again unable to pay debts. Jaensch withdrew from the partnership (and died within a few years), leaving the ex-missionary to manage the station alone. Only Theodore Vogelsang had stayed on after the exodus of his family the previous year. Bogner lived alone at Killalpaninna, visiting his wife and family at Tanunda whenever station duties permitted (and sometimes when they did not). The loneliness of his life, the isolation from local company because of his German origins, and the continual burden of pressing debt perhaps underlie the rumours of his drinking 'plenty of whisky and wine' and his 'involvement with Aboriginal girls'.[9] Bogner would travel to Marree for stores and for company. It seems he found at least some of that company among another alienated and marginalised group, for the German would visit the old Afghan ex-camel merchant, Moosha Balooch, at the Ghantown there. Moosha, who did not drink alcohol, as his religion forbade it, poured tea, and the two men would sit at Moosha's kitchen table, drinking the hot sweet substance and talking for many pleasant hours.[10]

The war of 1914 to 1919 aroused remarkable patriotism towards Mother England from Australia, none more extraneous than that of the 300 to 400 Aborigines who found a way around the discriminatory ban regarding enlistment in the Australian forces. Many others were turned away after travelling for days to army centres.[11] Ben Murray, the young part-Aboriginal, part-Afghan who had been the mission station's cameleer, was one who succeeded in enlisting with the Australian forces. His seems an unusual patriotic gesture considering his protection by the German missionaries and his loyalty to the mission station and to Lutheranism. He says he joined for the adventure. He became a veteran of Gallipoli, vividly recalling the trenches, the dashes for higher ground and the shooting of a Turk at close range.[12]

The war ended in November 1918, with Germany defeated and signing the armistice. That year had witnessed the death of Kaibel and the appointment of J. J. Stolz as his successor. It had also seen good rains in the north again, with Bogner beginning to make slow progress, although plagued now by a rabbit infestation that followed the greening. Over the past few years Bogner had been able to keep only the Christmas rituals for the ex-mission Aborigines still working at the station and those living in camps nearby. With war paranoia creating the need for a low profile for Germans, the quarterly reporting to the mission committee had not been demanded by Tanunda. However, in November 1918 the secretary of lands reviewed Bogner's pastoral holding and the conditions of the 1915 agreement. He found that Aboriginal Lease 145, the contentious 470 000 acreage, could not be transferred to the private owners (as the station was no longer a charitable institution), and that use of the land should have been reviewed after the publication of the 1912–16 Royal Commission report. Aboriginal Lease 145 was immediately withdrawn from Bogner's holdings.

The final blow had been struck against the struggling ex-missionary. His station was now far too small to be economically viable.[13] Bogner argued for maintaining between fifty and 100 Aborigines on the leases, but by April 1919 the secretary of lands declared the lease not renewable. The South Australian government subsequently transferred it to an ex-soldier under the Returned Soldiers' Land Settlement Scheme.

Ironically, just as the rains had again revived the countryside, Bogner could no longer continue at Killalpaninna. Although relationships between him and the mission committee had progressively deteriorated over the past three years, he offered the station back to the Immanuel Synod, as agreed, in February 1920. A month later the synod held its first official meeting for six years—since before the outbreak of war. It had been forbidden for Germans to hold meetings, and during those years no contact was made between the Neuendettelsau Mission Institute and its Australian connections. Furthermore, the missionary son of Johannes Flierl ('Flierl the First'), Wilhelm Flierl, was interned, together with a visiting mission inspector from Neuendettelsau, when Australia took control of German-held New Guinea.[14]

Bogner, however, would not attend this 1920 meeting. The ex-missionary had been unable to repay the debt owed the synod, and had refused to continue mission work and reporting. As a response to his offer of sale the committee demanded he face them over breach of the missionising agreement, arguing that the station still belonged to the synod. Bogner responded with: 'I have not stolen the station, I have the lease [?] and will use it as a weapon. Your [accusation?] that I have acted in my interest, while the station still belongs to the Synode [sic], I refuse to accept...'[15] Bogner simply wanted to be freed of the burden of the station, and refused to argue the ethics of his outstanding debts.

The meeting took place without Bogner. The new president, Stolz, justified the actions of 1914–15, when Killalpaninna was sold in some haste and somewhat unofficially by Kaibel. After sharp debate the synod members finally vindicated the 1914 committee members who, it was declared, 'acted conscientiously under most difficult circumstances'.[16] The synod resolved to purchase the station from Bogner on condition that the South Australian government financially maintain the Aborigines there.[17] Government authorities, however, declined, possibly for several reasons. Germans were still not well accepted in this patriotic British colony. Germany itself had just been declared solely responsible for the First World War at the 1919 Treaty of Versailles, and was forced to pay dearly.

Bogner decided his only choice of action was to sell the unworkable property on the open market. The country had never looked so well, with water in the lake, birds in countless numbers, wattle bushes and broom-brush blooming, and wildflowers in profusion.[18] In October 1920 the station was sold for the sum of £11 000 to a 33-year-old ex-British Army major who had served in the war with the Indian Imperial Forces, Lance Kaye MacHattie Powell, and his 19-year-old English bride, Beryl. The sale price included the transfer of the Killalpaninna leases (excluding AL 145), now some 690 square miles of mainly sandhill country, 800 head of cattle, 350 horses, 300 sheep, 300 goats and 50 camels, and the five houses that remained on the property. Bogner owed £7000 to the land and stock agents, and it was agreed that he pay this debt on completion of the sale. It appears that the debt was not paid, for it was later transferred to Lance Powell, whose own capital assets were only £1700.[19]

Bogner continued to owe money to the mission committee, which he never repaid, insisting that the committee still owed money to Hermann Vogelsang for teaching at the Killalpaninna school.[20]

The Lost Years

During the years of Bogner–Jaensch and the Powell ownership of Killalpaninna, the station continued as a government ration depot for local Aborigines. After the official closure of the mission station about fifty Aborigines remained for a period for such rations and for the regimented, protected and ordered life to which they had become accustomed, presumably continuing to live in the mission buildings. But as the mission community quickly transformed into an ordinary stock station community, many began drifting to the camps and visiting the empty station only for ration supplies. Those who were young, fit and willing to work under the prevailing economic conditions (certainly a minority by the second decade of the twentieth century) stayed on at the station.

There are no records attesting to the problems of assimilation between camp Aborigines and ex-mission Aborigines. Hostilities, resentments, punishments, cultural conditioning, spiritual teachings, integration and confusion would have divided the two groups. Both, however, were united in their landlessness and their reliance on welfare from the ruling interlopers. The mission station had operated for fifty years, and some of these mission Aborigines had known little beyond mission life with its European culture and values. The traditional Aboriginal world had to be discovered and learnt. Hunting techniques, reliance on bush food, participation in ceremonies and rituals, the severity of initiation rites, bone-pointing and pinya retribution would all have required formidable adaptation.

For camp Aborigines the lifestyle was still traditionally semi-nomadic, as they moved between hunting grounds and water sources. Basic ration supplies of flour, sugar, tea, and perhaps tobacco were available from several stations as supplementary food, but the groups moved about this general area in constant search of sustenance and water. During 1916, after the rains in the north, many ex-mission Aborigines were camped at the Murrapatirrina block, north of the Killalpaninna settlement, for its hunting potential, and would collect their ration supplies from the depot at Mungerannie Station.[21] These semi-traditional Aborigines had to compete with the introduced animals for water and plantlife, and with the European eradication of their hunting game (seen as stock pests). By 1917 many ex-mission Aborigines were camped with non-mission Aborigines at Lake Allallinna (Ngarlangarlani) and at Cannuwaukaninna Bore.[22] After a large corroboree at the Ngarlangarlani site, the group was terrorised with threatened sorcery and violence by a kurdaitcha (a sorcerer) from near Innaminka who was camped among them, a man known as George. George claimed the Darana muramura had given him magical powers to kill by means of lightning or meteors. In premonitory manner, George began boasting that he had earlier killed a white man and his Aboriginal woman by this sorcery, and it transpired that the woman happened to have been the mother of one of the women (Agnes) present. (At about this time, a white man and Aboriginal woman were allegedly hit by a meteor near Murnpeowie Station.[23]) Agnes' husband (Ned) then bravely fought and killed George in retribution, and buried his body. Ned subsequently became legendary among the local groups, his heroic success against the feared kurdaitcha incorporated into a song-cycle about the Ngarlangarlani area.[24]

The ex-mission Aborigines, who had adapted to eating only European food, and were conditioned to a daily cleansing of the body before covering it with freshly washed and ironed European-style clothing, now had to contend with largely bush food, often irregularly available, rare bathing in the lakes, and scraps of dirty clothing. They had been taught that traditional Aboriginal ways were 'bad' and 'un-Christian', that they would be forsaken by Jesus if they reverted, and they would suffer in Hell as a consequence. But now, with pressure from non-mission Aborigines with whom they had to integrate, these Christians were forced to again adopt their former beliefs and rituals. Already a breakdown of transference of information was occurring between elders and young Aborigines as the new culture intervened and suspicion arose. According to one traveller–writer of the 1940s–1950s, pressure was brought to bear on many of these eastern Lake Eyre people by Aborigines from further west, beyond Oodnadatta:

> They tried to persuade Dieri [sic] blacks to return to tribal ways of life. Some went with them. Most having been brought up within the orbit of white man refused to go. They refused to submit to initiation rites and many of them were never seen again. First one would be kidnapped, then another. The pressure was put especially on the women, as potential mothers of the new generation of tribal blacks.[25]

Certainly by 1918, some 200 Aborigines, many of whom had come from Oodnadatta, Marree, Mundowdna, Murnpeowie and Kanowa, spent twelve months camped with ex-mission Aborigines at Kopperamanna. According to the local police officer (Aiston) the large group became self-sufficient, living from the sale of dingo scalps and rabbit skins.[26] However, by 1919 many ex-mission Aborigines had moved southwards to Marree, and were living in camps on the outskirts of the town.

During 1919, with soldiers returning from the battlefields of Europe, a deadly infection, known as Spanish Influenza, was carried to Australia. An epidemic swept the country, and Aborigines, with no resistance to European viruses, a poor diet and virtually no ready medical aid, died in their hundreds (there are no records of most of these deaths). The epidemic killed several million people worldwide and hit hard at the area in the north-east of South Australia. Three years earlier there had been a severe outbreak of typhoid in the area.

So serious was the Spanish flu epidemic for Aboriginals in the north-east that an Adelaide physician, Dr Herbert Basedow, organised a series of medical relief expeditions into the area. In 1919 he spent four months travelling along the Strzelecki and Birdsville tracks, examining and treating Aborigines and attempting to determine the Aboriginal population loss. He contacted 380 Aborigines in this area, in contrast to South's (the protector of Aborigines) figure of 650 just five years earlier.[27] The decrease, however, may also have included other mitigating factors, such as the movement of people to other parts, and the effects of other diseases. Basedow found the Aborigines living in highly contagious, unhygienic conditions, no longer the traditional airy brush dwellings or open-air camps. They huddled into congested, sealed 'humpies', with shared clothing and shared domestic utensils, unrestricted sexual practice and stock-polluted water, all elements that favoured the spread of infection. These people suffered bronchial and tubercular illnesses, gastric and intestinal conditions, hydatids (contracted through contact with dogs infected from water fouled by sheep), glaucoma, cataracts, blepharitis, leukoma, the 'alarmingly high incidence' of syphilis, gonorrhoea 'rampant in both males and females', and gonorrheal conjunctivitis. Basedow concluded that sexually transmitted diseases 'contributed more than any other (factor) to population loss throughout the region' and 'The decline in birthrate is no doubt largely due to sterility following upon the unchecked ravages of this disease in either sex'.[28]

During his 1919 expedition Basedow encountered several ex-mission Aborigines living in such camps—Jacob, Walter (the rescuer of Ben Murray), Mick (the rescuer of Mrs Reidel's hat), the inimitable Dicky, Gottlieb and Frieda Maltilinna and their children (including Susie Kennedy), Gertie, Albert, Selma, Anna and Timotheus Maltilinna (Flierl the First's protégé, who later changed his name to the European Merrick, attempting to rid himself of all Aboriginality) and Johannes (who was later trained as an evangelist). He also examined several Aborigines who had come to Killalpaninna Mission from Hermannsburg, including Bertha and Katarina. There was no mention of old Joseph, Reidel's informant and proselytiser, but there were other Aborigines with German or biblical names on Basedow's list, and these were probably also ex-Killalpaninna people—Ruth, Hildegard, Rudolph, Sarah, Hesikel, a second Johannes, Wilfred and Ewald among them.[29]

Old Timotheus Maltilinna (Merrick) had lived for many years at Blazes Well during his employment as a stockman by the mission station. One of the Vogelsang daughters described him as an 'extremely honest and reliable man, [who] could easily have been classed with the white man, and was superior to many of them'.[30] His sons, Martin and Gottlieb, were also considered loyal Christian Aborigines and when the mission station closed, Martin and his wife, Florrie, went south with the Vogelsang family to work at the home of Luise and

Gottlieb Schmidt at Lowbank. Gottlieb Maltilinna (Merrick) and his wife, Frieda, stayed in the north, lived in an extended family camp and travelled from station to station following employment. The family would travel to Kopperamanna by buggy to join the large gatherings for traditional ceremonies still held there, with 'great excitement . . . no segregation of the women . . . grandmother (Anna) and all there'.[31]

When the Killalpaninna leases were first sold to the Powells, Gottlieb and Frieda were employed by the new owners—Frieda as a domestic in the station homestead (the old Reuther–Reidel house, then known as 'Government House'), and Gottlieb as a stockman and shearer. Their daughter, Susie, became a playmate for the Powells' own daughter. Aborigines had become excellent stockmen, and with these skills, and with Aboriginal wages being considerably lower than those for European workers (allowing sufficient men to look after stock spread across huge tracts of arid country at relatively inexpensive outlay to the stationers), Aboriginal stockmen were highly sought after at the northern stations. One manager at Clifton Hills Station in 1950 claimed that 'This country couldn't have been settled without them . . . without them it still couldn't be worked. You can't get good stockmen these times.'[32]

The Powells employed Aboriginal ex-mission stockmen, but Lance was forced to spend long periods of time away from the station homestead mustering, and checking fences, stock and stockmen. His young English wife spent days and nights alone at the station, surrounded by measureless sandy plains, the immense silence and isolation terrifying and paralysing. From her refuge within the house, Beryl looked down upon the abandoned mission settlement; mud buildings, the iron church and, most depressing of all, the countless crosses marking the graves of dead mission people. Portions of human skeletons protruded from the sand, as the ever-eroding wind beat at the ground to change the surface contours. At night the silence was broken by the howling of dingoes. Before the births of her three children, Beryl had only the company of her two enormous and elegant staghound dogs (that had been brought from England) during these absences.

When the Powells first arrived they were appalled at the state of the building in which they were to live. The missionary's house had deteriorated during Bogner's time, and then had been occupied by local Aborigines. There was no bathroom and few comforts or furniture. After sweeping and cleaning, the couple removed pews from the church and a trestle table from the schoolroom, and arranged them as dining furniture. Further pews were given an English-style high back to become comfortable sitting-room furniture. 'The natives came to see what they could do, or pick up, as the case might be; but they were hastily dispatched elsewhere, for they had lived and spat in the house too long to be tolerated without complete reformation.'[33]

Monday was 'ration day' and either Beryl or Lance would ring the bell beside the storehouse and wait for the Aborigines to leave their camps or mud houses and form a queue for the issue of their weekly portions of government-supplied tea, flour and sugar. With the new owners, at first

> They were wary of strangers and took a long time to place trust in them. But when those in the background saw the others in front receiving their portions, they came

up slowly, one by one, until all were served. Everything was weighed and the amounts entered on forms, which also stated the number of natives who received rations. Beryl felt they neither approved nor disapproved of her and she sensed she was on probation. A few old gins sucked pipes unemotionally, as they stared at her through eyes clustered with flies. Not many natives were about, for the season being so good, they had gone far afield to hunt. This they really preferred to do, even down to the western waters.[34]

Soon after arriving Beryl wandered through the abandoned mission buildings, with their old German papers and books, dust-covered and strewn about, and a forsaken New Testament in Diyari. She walked the grounds and was startled to come upon a tombstone enclosed in an iron fence on a lonely sand ridge.[35] As she wiped sand from the inscription, Beryl incredulously read that here lay the remains of a woman from Bromley in Kent, the very same town as hers! It was the grave of Mrs Milner, of Bucaltaninna Station, who had been nursed for weeks by Luise Homann, but who had died of the effects of heat exhaustion at the fledgling mission station during the severe drought of 1868.

Lance Powell was assisted by Theodore Vogelsang as his overseer. Theodore encouraged the Powells just once a year to provide personally for the Aborigines of the area by keeping the Christmas festivities as close as possible to mission tradition. Although there were no religious services possible in the church (without a missionary), no communion and no sermon in Diyari, Christmas carols and simple Lutheran prayers could accompany the beloved revolving Christmas tree and excitement of gift-giving. These elements of the ritual, he felt, may remind the ex-mission Aborigines of the Christian message and teachings.

At the first settled Christmas for the Powells, in 1921, more than seventy Aborigines suddenly arrived at the station on Christmas Eve. Word had circulated about the festivity, the first for six years. Beryl had worked for weeks making small gifts, sand was swept from the church floor, the German 'musical tree' was dusted and oiled, lanterns were filled and lit in the church, and gifts were hung on tree branches. As excited Aborigines poured through the doorway of the modest iron building, and stood about in expectation of the formal service of old, Lance Powell wound the big music box tightly and the tree began to revolve to the sound of German carols. The Aborigines tentatively started to sing the words in their native language, and soon the magic of this special ceremony again enchanted and captivated. The Powells were touched.[36]

On Christmas Day the adult Aborigines had chosen curry for their traditional feast (having probably acquired a taste from interaction with the Afghan cameleers servicing the area). Lance had killed a bullock, and meat curries had been prepared in empty, washed kerosene tins. There were no vegetables, but huge dampers mopped the curries, the feast and festivities being the topic of conversation among the Aborigines for weeks afterwards.

Theodore Vogelsang, who had managed the ration store and collected dingo scalps from the Aborigines for their sale,[37] had left the employ of Lance Powell and went south just weeks before the planned celebrations.

His day of departure was a memorable one, and his leavetaking of the natives most pathetic. Some had known him from birth, others had grown up with him. It took them a long while to realise that he was leaving forever, that he would never return and that they would not see him again. When they did understand, many of them wept bitterly and openly.[38]

After Theodore's departure—the last link with the German missionaries—many Aborigines left Killalpaninna for Mulka, Mungerannie or Cooraninna Bore as 'they did not readily take to the strange, new order'.[39] Only three young males stayed, as station hands, and two Aboriginal women, as domestic help for Beryl. The women were Katarina, a part-European from Hermannsburg who had worked for a time as a domestic at Tanunda, probably in the Bogner home there, and Bertha (who had worked in the Vogelsang home at Kopperamanna). Bertha, it was alleged, had been captured by local Aborigines from a passing tribe in earlier days and, after forcibly resisting her captives, had eventually settled to marry and become a baptised mission Aborigine. Katarina and another ex-mission Aborigine, named Alec, wanted to marry 'properly', in the Christian manner of the mission station. As there were now no means to do this at Killalpaninna, they determined to travel to Tanunda. Katarina travelled ahead of Alec but, unhappily, her husband-to-be reached no further than Marree. Resplendent in his new suit of clothing and new hat, Alec had visited a friend's camp on his first evening, there to be enticed to an all-night game of poker. The train for Tanunda did not leave for another day, so Alec spent a second night trying to recoup losses and increase his future prospects. By the morning of his proposed departure he had lost all his money, his new suit, his new hat and even the shirt he was wearing. The winners, however, graciously gave him enough for a telegram to Katarina that requested her return to Marree. The couple were subsequently married at a civil service at the railway town before returning north to Killalpaninna.[40] Both Katarina and Bertha were to feature in the later contact between the Lutherans from the south and the remnants of mission Aborigines living in the north.

When the Powells attempted to repeat the Christmas celebrations the following year an accident caused the last link with mission culture to be finally severed. Many Aborigines had returned to Killalpaninna on Christmas Eve in 1922. The Powells had again prepared for them, and again they filed into the abandoned church to find it lit and filled with the same magic and excitement. But during the hymns and gift-giving a stay at the top of one of the kerosene lanterns that hung suspended from the church ceiling, snapped. The lamp crashed to the floor, and in an instant fire raced through the building sending the terrified crowd clambering, panic-stricken, for the only doorway. Lance Powell tried to control the blaze, but with the passing of time and desert dryness, everything burned perniciously. Like a ghostly lamentation, the solid German music-box continued to play, and the tree to revolve, as flames leaped and consumed. Sand was carried in every possible container and thrown through the smoke and flames. The music-box gradually slowed to a deathly stop, the tree now a charred and blackened pole. The older Aborigines wept. This conflagration symbolised their very last link with mission life; their very last Christmas at Killalpaninna.[41]

The summer of 1922–23 was hot and dry, and Aiston reported very few Aborigines in the Birdsville Track area. They had been driven northwards by the drought, away from the concentration of stations, to Birdsville and remote

Coongy Station near Innaminka, both also ration depots but 'where they can get their natural food . . . those that are left are only those who are too feeble to travel'.[42] Many, accustomed to wearing shoes or boots, now complained that the hot ground hurt their bare feet. When winter rains fell they returned to harvest local, native food, but the winter of 1923 was wet and cold. Chest and lung infections increased, and the Aborigines continued to visit Killalpaninna for rations, government-issue blankets, and medical attention from Beryl. Many would remove their precious few clothes during wet weather in an effort to keep them dry (and possibly clean, after mission expectations), huddling beneath a blanket or two with their dogs on cold, wet nights.[43] The death rate of old people, and those suffering illness, increased. Two old and colourful men, some of the last of the Lake Gregory sub-tribe of the Wangkangurru, died at Mungerannie (a police station and ration depot). They were Mundowdna Jack and Elias, the latter claiming to have been a young man in 1866 when McKinlay camped at Lake Perigundi. Elias (whose name suggests he had been baptised at Killalpaninna) had accompanied the explorer from the lake to Cuttapirrie. Mundowdna Jack's wife, Mundowdna Polly, died a fortnight after her husband.

> She had suffered a fistula in her back passage, and was very weak, but when her man died she insisted on wearing the old fashioned Mung-waroo, or mourning hat. This weighs anything up to 14 lbs, and is made of burnt gypsum. Polly wore this for ten days and collapsed when she took it off and destroyed it according to the old custom.[44]

Aiston argued with government officials for a piece of land for the old people:

> where they will not be interfered with by the whites, and where the cattle will not come, the cattle feeding around a waterhole destroy all the native food plants and destroy the cover for ground game, and there is continual trouble with the whites over the blacks' dogs disturbing the cattle at the watering places . . . [A place to] serve the remnants of the Wonkanguru [sic] and Yaurorka [sic] and Ngameni [sic] tribes . . . (and) the Dieri [sic] tribe.[45]

According to Aiston, young Aborigines still held a reverence for elders and would revert to traditional ways themselves as they aged; 'when they begin to show a little bit of white in their hair, they take to the camp, and gradually forget their white men's ways'. There the old men still ruled, they still monopolised the marriage stakes, and the traditional custom of a young man for an older woman and a young girl for an old man was still practised. According to Aiston, 'they graft what they are taught by the whites on to what they are taught by their own legends, and the result is a secret contempt for the white man's teaching'.[46]

Aiston, it should be remembered, was vehemently against educating Aborigines ('they cannot be educated for any good'), preferring that they be left to their traditional ways, and had testified at the 1912–16 Royal Commission against the practices of the German Lutherans at Killalpaninna. He was however, not averse to interfering in customs of which he disapproved:

> I stopped their bonepointing a lot by allowing them to point a bone at me and go through the usual process of burning it. They kept a close watch on me and when they found nothing happened, they started to ridicule the custom themselves— they have a very broad sense of humour and a very keen appreciation of fair play—

they tried their best to make me 'a little bit sick, not too much' that they were satisfied. The custom still obtains but there is a lot of scepticism, sufficient to rob it of its former deadly significance.[47]

Aiston was not successful in obtaining his proposed reserve for old Aborigines. The Mungerannie police station was closed in November 1928.

As for the Powells, their eight years at Killalpaninna were years of drought, when the lake did not fill and the countryside reverted to aridity. Lance Powell leased the Kopperamanna Bore from the South Australian government, watering his stock and charging fees for all travelling herds. Nearby Cannuwaukaninna Bore, which was on AL 145, was now prohibited for his stock. But water flowed freely from this new government drilling, travelling for miles along the hard dry ground. Lance found it impossible to keep his herds from following the scent and away from the lease they had previously grazed. He eventually made an arrangement with the lease's new occupier and was able to water stock there.

During 1924 no rain fell, dust storms blackened the sky and the cattle lost condition. By 1927 the drought had not broken, only 170 points of rain fell during the entire year, dust storms increased in frequency, and Beryl's health was failing. The Powells were heavily indebted to their stock agents, their cattle virtually worthless in a depressed market flooded with drought-ravaged stock, their income virtually nil. In 1928, with even less rainfall, heat and endless blowing wind, cattle and horses dying as the Cannuwaukaninna Bore stream became a boggy deathtrap for weakened animals (2000 cattle were lost near this bore alone), Lance forced to take healthier cattle northwards across the Queensland border to better country, and Beryl's health worsening, the young English woman, in her solitary endurance, made the decision to leave the station permanently. She now had three children to consider, as well as her own physical condition. Surrounded by death, she felt determined not to meet her own out there. She had watched the hundreds of black crows pecking at carcasses of dead animals, and dingo packs carrying off whatever remained. The continual sandstorms kept uncovering new skeletons in the Aboriginal graveyard beside the church. Old coffins had disintegrated and many of the bodies had been wrapped only in a sheet for burial. From the front rooms of her house, alone at night, Beryl watched as the moonlight eerily lit the bleaching bones, and skeletons grinned and gaped. During one violent sandstorm the landscape was changed so that sand reached to the roof of the homestead and buried one window in the northeast corner.[48]

One day Beryl could take no more. She walked to the Aboriginal camps, informed them of her decision and told them to collect their rations from Aiston, who was now at Mulka. She loaded the Powells' battered car with a few essentials, placed the children on the seats and drove the sandy track. She left behind her English treasures, including her Wedgwood dinner service. There was no money with which to remove them, and nowhere to take them. She had just £10. When she reached Marree, Beryl telegrammed Lance of her decision.[49]

The Powells retained their leases at Killalpaninna for a short while, until they were cancelled through arrears of rent. The rainfall during 1929 was only 70 points at nearby Mulka, and vast areas of South Australia, Queensland and New South Wales were devastated by a drought never before experienced during European settlement. But, as is the nature of this unpredictable country, 1930 saw heavy rains and the landscape again transformed. However, the Great Depression of the 1930s had begun and, besides, the Powells had already lost their leases. By 1937 they were returning to England. Lance, who had suffered recurrent malaria (from his time in India), had by now developed a duodenal ulcer. When their ship was off the coast of Aden, Lance had a sudden attack of appendicitis and died. He was buried in the Aden cemetery. Beryl and the children lived for the rest of their lives in England, where Beryl Powell died in May 1954 of a heart attack.[50]

Missionary Descendants in the South

The children of the old Kolonisten, and in particular the Vogelsang sons and daughters, played a decisive role in the last phase of the history of Killalpaninna Mission. In 1907 Luise Vogelsang was married by Bogner to Gottlieb Schmidt in the old mud-brick church. The couple then travelled south to the Murray River area, 120 miles from Adelaide, where Gottlieb had acquired a block of virgin land. When large tracts of this inexpensive land were released by the South Australian government, a considerable movement of second and third generation German families from the Barossa area left the beautiful rolling hills with their majestic gums and deep valleys, where land occupation was now complete, and travelled to the newly released flat, dry country further east. At twenty-three years of age, Carl Gottlieb Schmidt, in 1899, had taken a stretch of mallee scrub on the banks of the Murray River at Holder (later called Low Bank, after the Schmidt homestead there), and cleared and ploughed, seeding a wheat crop and building a rough hut. He battled to make the land productive and built a substantial stone house at the river's edge before marrying Luise Vogelsang, at Killalpaninna, eight years later.[51]

It was to Gottlieb and Luise's home at Low Bank that old Anna Vogelsang and the unmarried Vogelsang daughters went after leaving Kopperamanna in 1917. Several of the other married children also settled in the Murray River area, but the stone house at Low Bank became the Vogelsang family focus, like the Kopperamanna homestead had been in earlier times. The old mission stalwart, Timotheus Maltilinna (Merrick), joined his son, Martin, and Martin's wife, Florrie, for a short time after they went to Low Bank to work, Martin as a farm labourer, Florrie as a domestic in the Low Bank house. Another Aboriginal domestic from the Kopperamanna homestead, known as 'our Mary', also travelled with Anna Vogelsang to work at the Low Bank home. These people, probably anxious to stay within a familiar situation and fearing extraneity if left to camp life or with the new owners, had paid their own fares to the south from their earnings in the north.[52]

Several other ex-mission Aboriginal women were sent as domestics to the homes of Lutheran pastors in the south: Rebecca Maltilinna to Pastor Leidig's (the friend and colleague of Reidel), accompanying the Leidigs to a parish posting in Victoria. Timotheus Maltilinna (Merrick) worked for a time for Dorothea Vogelsang and her husband Friedrich Paschke, who also took up land near Low Bank. Old Tim lived in a shed near the Paschke home. However, probably through loneliness and isolation, he later returned to the north to live west of Dulkaninna Station (near Mooloorinna) with a group of camp Aborigines.[53] His son, young Tim, grew up with the Paschke boys, but at the age of thirty he died

Timotheus Maltilinna (Merrick), centre, with his son, Tim, and grandson in the Murray River area

in hospital from the effects of alcoholism. It was a lonely life in the river area for these Aborigines far from their home country, their friends and relatives. They were 'not well accepted by locals', and some were desperately poor. At one time Martin Merrick (Maltilinna) found a job collecting wood for steam engines. On his first day he was surprised to be invited to sit with the other employees, all white, during the lunch break. They in turn were surprised that Martin had no lunch; 'One man asked, "What do your people live on?" "Oh, they boil and eat wheat", was Martin's reply.' The next day all the woodgatherers brought an extra sandwich, which they gave to Martin.[54]

Martin's father, old Timotheus, had achieved considerable respect from the Germans at Killalpaninna, and status among mission Aborigines. He did not like being called 'a blackfellow'. When he returned to live in the north, and his camp was visited by Hermann Vogelsang during one of his trips of spiritual goodwill, Timotheus refused to join the Lutheran service with the other camp Aborigines as he was embarrassed at his current affiliation.[55]

When Ben Murray returned from the First World War, he and his brother Ern also worked for the ex-mission families in the Murray River area. Ben, who was employed by the Paschkes for many years, lived in a stone outhouse, although

Rebecca Maltilinna (Merrick), daughter of Timotheus, as a live-in domestic with Pastor Leidig's family in Victoria

'A Scattered Homeless Flock'   247

he was permitted to eat meals with the German family. He worked as a farm labourer, wrote to a girl in the north, although he never married, and taught the Paschke boys to throw the boomerang.[56]

The German community in the riverland mallee country worked mixed farms of cereals and animals. Each home had a smokehouse where pork was cured into sausages, metwurst, hams and bacons. The families would gather in each others' homes when visiting pastors—one of whom was Bogner—arrived to conduct Lutheran services. They spoke German most of the time, and their children had to be taught English before they could enrol at the small, local public school. Luise Schmidt taught her children to read and write in the Gothic-style German of her parents as she knew no other form. She kept a tiny leatherbound and embossed German birthday book, with the birthdates and names of many mission people in their own handwriting. It included that of Ben Murray, carefully written, with a birthdate of 1893.[57] Luise also kept a Diyari boomerang on her mantlepiece. It was characteristically incised with cross-hatched decoration and darkened with bloodstain at one end, a reminder of Killalpaninna days.

Three Auricht sisters: Elizabeth Jacob, Anna Vogelsang and E. Hanische, 1920

After thirty-nine years at Killalpaninna, Anna Vogelsang spent a further thirty years in the riverland area: 'Many a time I longed to be back among the natives. My work among the natives has come to an end . . . I can pray for them that the Good Shepherd may keep each one of them in His fold, that not a single soul of them is lost.'[58] Her view was now of a brown river, tall gums and flat, scrubby plains.

In 1913 the small stone St Paul's Lutheran Church was constructed at Low Bank on part of the Schmidts' property, and Wolfgang Reidel became its first pastor.[59] Every Sunday, with Luise Schmidt as organist, old Anna Vogelsang, dressed in a black jacket, could be seen in its congregation, spritely, alert and pious.[60]

Elizabeth Jacob had moved to Tanunda soon after Ernst's death in 1907. Despite the hard life she had led in the north, she was described as 'elegant' and a 'real lady'. 'Tapa Jakab', as she was called, wore long skirts, elegantly held from the hem, and a small black cap.[61] She spent her last years in her former home, the house she and her first husband had shared. She died in October 1924, at the age of eighty-three years, and at her Tanunda funeral the conducting pastor proclaimed:

> Thus came to an end a plain life, a silent activity in a comparatively small sphere, and yet noble and grand. Those who contacted her were inspired by her simplicity. Her life was a life of service . . . Just to mention one instance. When no-one could grow vegetables on the mission station, 'Mother Jacob' was still able with few water supplies to wrest some green from the desert sands and willingly shared them with the mission personnel.[62]

Elizabeth's son, 'Jack' Irrgang, who as a young boy had grown up with the Diyari children, now had a fruit-growing farm in the riverland area. He was part of the St Paul's Lutheran Church congregation and the German community there.

Bethesda Society and First Contact

In April 1930 Bogner died of heart failure aged sixty-nine years.[63] A year later the Board of the Finke River Mission (Hermannsburg in Central Australia, for there was no longer a mission committee for Killalpaninna), requested that Theodore Vogelsang travel to the north-east to report on 'our deserted Dieri [sic] Christians', and that the last missionary, Wolfgang Reidel, visit them 'as soon as possible' to 'tell them of the Word of God'. (The latter, however, did not eventuate.)[64] This was the first official concern for the ex-mission Aborigines since the closure of Killalpaninna, seventeen years earlier.

By October 1931, Theodore Vogelsang, alone, travelled by train to Marree and by camelback into the country northwards. At Marree he found about twenty Aborigines, some of them former mission people: 'The joy of the reunion was great . . . . How neglected the natives in these camps looked. I inquired after different ones, but was often told they had died. Amongst them also some young people, mostly of venereal diseases.'[65] Theodore, with an Aborigine called Bob, travelled to Mulka Bore. After passing the ruins of the old Killalpaninna settlement, he reported that 'The buildings on this station have more or less become ruins and are no more habitable, excepting one.' At Mulka Bore he found

Hermann Vogelsang junior with a group of ex-Killalpaninna Aboriginal people during one of his trips north, c. 1930s. Many of these men worked as stockmen and station hands, the women as domestics in station homesteads

Katarina and Bertha among the camp. At Mungerannie, 'where the most natives were . . . I discussed God's Word with them, and reminded them of what they had formerly heard on the Mission Station . . . they felt like forsaken children'. One woman asked Theodore why the missionaries had left them: 'My children were good when you were here, now they are dead . . . they died of venereal diseases'. One young girl from the camp, it was reported, had been abducted by a white man and had a child by him. However, he was expected to send the girl back soon as he already had his eye on another girl at the camp. Although he had a wife and two grown daughters in Marree, it was alleged that he had been abducting Aboriginal girls for years.

Theodore was told of hardships during the drought years, of one old man, who used to be a shepherd at the mission station, dying of starvation at the camp while the young were out hunting for food. When they arrived back only his bones remained. The starving dogs had eaten the flesh. The same thing had happened to an old woman near Marree.

When he returned south, Theodore Vogelsang reported forty to fifty ex-mission Christians still alive in the north. His report was published in the *Lutheran Herald* paper, and Lutheran officials endeavoured to somehow 'rehabilitate' the mission Aborigines. For the next ten years journeys were made to these scattered people to hold Lutheran services at their camps.

Susie Kennedy, daughter of Frieda and Gottlieb Maltilinna (Merrick), at Marree in 1991. Then about eighty years of age, Susie was born at Killalpaninna, and after its closure wandered the north with her parents who sought station work

The Vogelsang sons were chosen to make these journeys and be the link because of their fluency in the Diyari language, their knowledge of the countryside, and their strong ties with the ex-mission Aborigines. Wolfgang Reidel was not intent on further direct involvement. In 1932 Hermann Vogelsang made contact, engaging camels and an Aboriginal companion at Marree. The pair encountered 122 Aborigines on their travels, fifty-one of whom had been baptised. Only twenty of the 122 were children.[66] Hermann conducted Lutheran services at the camps he visited, and on his return reported that such visits were of little value, recommending the board take up the old Killalpaninna Station again. The Bethesda Mission Society, with Pastor E. H. Proeve as chairman and Hermann Vogelsang as secretary, was formed to raise money and find voluntary support for the project.[67] And in April 1933 Hermann Vogelsang made a survey journey north to search for an appropriate base for the project. On his return the society approached the South Australian government for the procurement of Mungerannie Station, where the largest concentration of Aborigines were camped. It was a ration depot close to the abandoned Killalpaninna Station, and protection and some medical attention had been available from George Aiston in the past.

The Pastoral Board, however, refused Mungerannie to the Lutherans, suggesting the old de Pierre station of Cannatulkaninna (or Wireyard) as an alternative. In September 1933 Wireyard was inspected by the Lutherans, as was nearby Mooloorinna Station. The government was approached for the acquisition of one of these stations, but the lessee of Cannatulkaninna refused to part with his full property, offering instead that part that now included the old Kopperamanna run. This possibility, of course, excited the Bethesda Society, who dreamed nostalgically of re-establishing a mission station on familiar ground. While the government considered assistance (such as financial aid, a ration depot and the declaration of the run as a 'reserve') the society prepared proposals on how the church might conduct such a revived mission station.

It was postulated that, if granted, the old Kopperamanna run be a mission centre only, and it not also be a stock station as in the past (which must have given Reidel distinct satisfaction). Meanwhile, it was agreed, a qualified person, equipped with suitable literature, should visit these mission 'remnants' twice a year, with expenses paid from society funds.[68] Furthermore, it was decided that control of this work be transferred to the board of the Finke River Station.

Hermann Vogelsang was again despatched to obtain the latest local information. Accompanied by Proeve, and a fellow Lutheran, W. Schilling, he travelled to 80 miles east of Murnpeowie Station, where a group of the now late Timotheus Maltilinna's family lived—Gottlieb, Frieda and his son-in-law, Walter, now living with a 'heathen'. The men worked as stockmen and station hands, but Gottlieb and several others were droving cattle across the Queensland border. The Lutherans had been informed at a nearby station 'that Gottlieb was not living up to his good name. He was not providing any spiritual food for them (his family group) out of the Word of God.' And after prayers around the campfire, young Walter placatingly declared, 'You know . . . I used to be a drunkard. I am free of this now and won't let the whites tempt me again.'

Reports of such encounters were published in Lutherans papers, tailored to inspire a revived mission in the north. They contained anecdotes of small groups of ex-mission Aborigines clinging, in the midst of chaos and paganism, to Christian customs and belief, and accounts of ever-present exploitation of these people by local un-Christian whites. The ex-mission Aborigines themselves would don a guise of guilt, or faithfulness, when visited by these Lutherans, immediately adopting mission customs and Christian rhetoric. Very likely, by now, they quite happily and comfortably lived within their traditional practices, as evidenced by Susie Kennedy's account of Gottlieb and Frieda, and old Anna, and probably even old Timotheus, delighting in the traditional ceremonies on the Kopperamanna plains.[69]

But there would have been times when the old diehard mission faithful would have recourse to their Christian teaching. Walter recounted to Hermann Vogelsang the passing of old Timotheus, claiming that before he died: 'Again and again he would fold his hands and pray aloud. He asked that Jesus would take him to Himself in Heaven.' According to Walter, during Timotheus' last weeks he was visited by an old 'heathen' who had witnessed the death of the mission stalwart old Joseph (Reidel's informant). 'He (Joseph) said he could see a bright light and knew that Jesus would now take him home. Immediately afterwards he fell asleep quietly and peacefully.' The old heathen presumably wanted to be present when Timotheus also died, to perhaps test the 'magic' of this alien belief. He would stay with Timotheus, talking to the dying man, and

A visit by the Lutherans to a camp of ex-Killalpaninna people, c. 1930s. The women dressed for the occasion in the mission style of long European dresses and scarves tied over their hair. The men wore European stockmen's clothing

allowing Timotheus to read to him from his Diyari New Testament. 'The questions this old man would ask him he (the dying Timotheus) would answer as well as he could.'[70] Such stories provided justification and certainly reinforced the intentions of the Bethesda Society and its supporters. When the news of Timotheus' death reached the Lutherans in the south, they wrote: 'We hope and believe God has him home out of this nasty world . . . He commands respect that he lived as well as he has in the wasted north, under conditions as they were for Aborigines. We presume his friends and relatives gave him a Christian funeral.'

The Lutheran trio drove to Marree, where they found 'a number of baptised Christians', and to Mungerannie, 'where there had always been a fair number of natives', to find none at all. But there they found the former galvanised iron church from Killalpaninna re-erected as a storehouse after serving as Mungerannie's hall for a time. The cross that had stood in reverence on its roof now impiously embellished the Mungerannie meathouse,[71] such idolatrous desecration perhaps the work of Aiston, who detested the missionaries' interference with Aboriginal practices.

At Mirra Mitta they found 'Edward and his tribe', and Katarina and Bertha; 'They had seen us coming early and so they all stood appropriately dressed in front of their huts, and greeted us with the hymn "Praise to the Lord Almighty".' One ex-mission woman who lived at this camp hid from the Lutherans, allegedly ashamed that she had left her baptised husband and was now living with a heathen.[72] At each of these camps the Lutherans held a service in Diyari.

On visiting the old Killalpaninna settlement, the trio were shocked and depressed: 'What a sight! Ruins! Desolation! The place has no resemblance to a former Mission Station . . . The crumbling buildings were havens for wild animals, and skeletons lay strewn on the sand . . . The sight of Bethesda, a pointing finger of the Lord. May it be a warning for us.' The men heaped the human bones into a pile and buried them again. As they drove away from the profanity, like a divine chastisement a duststorm suddenly whipped the surrounding desert into darkness, the winds so strong that the paint on the numberplate of the car was erased.

Meanwhile, in the south, the General Synod met regarding the proposed mission project, appointing the Finke River Mission Board in charge and determining proposals for the reactivation of missionary work:
1   the acquisition of a reserve and the stationing of a teacher on it;
2   the appointment of an itinerant white missionary at Marree;
3   the training of one or more Diyari to act as evangelists among their own people;
4   the organising of periodical visits to these people.[73]

However, it was soon after this meeting that the Lutheran Church received the unhappy news that the South Australian government would not be supporting the project. It had declared the site of the proposed reserve unsuitable.

Coincidentally, in Germany a dictator had been elected to power just a year earlier, and the prelude to the Second World War slowly began to take shape.

In January 1935 the board of the Finke River Mission decided that the only course of action for further mission work was to adopt the third proposal, the training of Aboriginal evangelists. They could be instructed at Hermannsburg, where black evangelists were already working among their people, and two ex-Killalpaninna men, Andreas and Johannes, were chosen as the first to be trained. When Hermann Vogelsang arrived to collect them, only Johannes could be found. Andreas, it was later learnt, lay in the Port Augusta Hospital with a broken leg. But by October 1935, all three men were on their way to Hermannsburg Station in Central Australia.[74]

The evangelist experiment failed. Johannes met the daughter of another evangelist at Hermannsburg, old Moses, and when he wanted to marry her, Moses made him promise not to take his daughter away.[75] It is unclear whether Andreas completed his training, for after he returned to the north of South Australia, little more was heard of him.

In the winter of 1937 Hermann Vogelsang again visited the north, taking clothing and dried fruit, needles, cotton, soap and biscuits. Andreas, the failed evangelist, now lived near Marree in a camp of ten people. Again Hermann held services for the few 'faithful' groups: Bertha, Katarina, the relatives of Timotheus.[76] During the winter of 1938 Hermann travelled to Hermannsburg Mission Station to take up a position as teacher. In September of the following year, as he passed through the Marree area on his way south for a short holiday, he visited the ex-Killalpaninna Aborigines for the very last time. Accompanied by Johannes, who was gathering his children to take back to Hermannsburg, Hermann set out on camelback along the Birdsville Track. There had been good rains that year, and Hermann reported: 'I have never seen this country so rich in feed. A beautiful sight.' Seven months later he died at Hermannsburg. At just sixty years of age, after an active life and good health, he suffered a sudden heart attack. He was buried at the Hermannsburg cemetery.

On hearing the news in the south, Wolfgang Reidel, chairman of the Finke River Mission Board, published:

> Mr Hermann Vogelsang proved himself an always willing helper wherever he could. When the gaps in our staff had been filled again, we retained his services, especially with the intention to make use of his services among our scattered Dieris [sic] around Bethesda. We saw in him the only person through whom we hoped to be able to do at least a little for the spiritual welfare of the Dieris [sic] . . . (his widow and children) and also our scattered Dieris [sic] are now more orphaned than ever.[77]

The Years of the Second World War

During the same month and year that Hermann Vogelsang was visiting the Killalpaninna Aborigines for the last time, the Second World War was proclaimed. On 1 September 1939 Germany attacked Poland to win back land taken in the reparations after the First World War. Two days later Britain and France declared war on Germany. Again Australia was subsumed in the conflict as a colonial arm of Britain.

That same year saw the publication of an article about the Diyari tribe by Professor Ronald Berndt and Theodore Vogelsang as joint authors.[78] Theodore, during the Depression years, had taken a job at the South Australian Museum, translating from German into English some of the Reuther manuscripts deposited there. The museum's curator of ethnology, Norman Tindale, was preparing the Reuther material for publication in edited, condensed and illustrated book form. But with museum funding cut by the outbreak of the Second World War, publication was again denied Reuther.[79] Two years earlier a description of several Diyari myths was published by H. K. Fry[80] after Theodore Vogelsang had translated these from handwritten Diyari into English. By request, Theodore had written to Samuel Dintibana at his camp in the north (via a local station), knowing him to be literate from his days at Killalpaninna, and Samuel had duly posted a body of Diyari legends.[81] Interest in documenting Aboriginal cultures was again prominent among scholars. However, during the 1930s Elkin, displaying the same old cultural xenophobia, allegedly wrote that:

> The missionary should know and learn to appreciate the native religious life; this is for the most part secret and consists of myths, beliefs, symbols and rites. These provide the sanctions in moral and social life, and give hope for the present and future. Real success (in converting the Aborigines to Christianity) will only come when they get to understand the old men, with their grip on the secret life, and after much conversation, plus earnestness to convert them towards our view of life, so that eventually the New Testament will take the place of their own unwritten lore.[82]

But the war years again divided Anglo-Saxon Australians from German-descended Australians. Again hatreds and suspicions erupted, even though many German-born or descended people now saw themselves as very definite 'Australians', enlisting in the forces to fight in Europe and defending the imperial Motherland against a once-loved Fatherland. Two sons of Luise and Gottlieb Schmidt served in the Australian Army, and a son of Bertha and 'Jack' Rohrlach serving in the Australian Airforce was killed in England. He had been born at Kopperamanna.[83]

Aborigines also enlisted during the Second World War, despite the discriminatory ban on non-Europeans (in operation until 1951). Some, however, were quickly discharged and sent back to their homes when the ban was realised; others managed to remain enlisted.[84] There is no evidence of any ex-Killalpaninna Aborigines enlisting in Second World War forces.

In 1940, the year after war erupted, Wolfgang Reidel, ever the outspoken critic, published a booklet warning against the evils of 'lodges' (popular secret societies like Masonic Lodges, Buffalo Lodges, Druids and the like).[85] He claimed them to be 'religious societies in opposition to the Church of God', an 'all world religion' that accepted all denominations, even Jews, Muslims and 'heathens', and 'an anti-Christ' religion. During the Depression years these 'lodges' had in fact flourished, with Ben Murray, for one, having joined the Buffalo Lodge in the hope of contacts for work opportunities.[86] Reidel, at this time, was a lecturer at the Lutheran seminary in Adelaide. During one midday meal, when the seminary staff were eating in the dining-room, an unexpected official visit from Australian Army staff singled him out for a summons to court, and a search was made at the seminary for spying operations. In the courtroom the prosecutor kept referring to Reidel's authorship of a booklet against 'lodges'.

The ex-missionary was later arrested, regrettably on the day before his daughter's wedding, and interned for the remainder of the war years as a potential enemy of Australia. Reidel spent these years isolated from his family, in the monotony and indignity of an internment camp at Loveday on the Murray River.

With Hermann Vogelsang now dead, revived Lutheran mission activity quashed in the north of South Australia, and Australia's Germans again under suspicion and threat, no visits were made to the ex-Killalpaninna Aborigines from 1939 until 1944. In October of that year one of Reuther's sons, the 47-year-old Pastor 'Bert' Reuther, with Pastor E. H. Proeve (who had accompanied Hermann Vogelsang earlier) and Gerhard Schmidt set out for the north in a Ford V8, with a trailer attached carrying Christmas gifts. The trio held a service for Aborigines at Marree, and at Finniss Springs (a sheep station that five years earlier had become a non-denominational Christian mission station established by the United Aborigines' Association). Old Katarina and her husband, Alec, now lived at Finniss Springs, but Bertha had died. They sang hymns with Reuther in Diyari and gave 'thank-you' letters to the Lutherans to take south (presumably written in Diyari). 'These letters would be well worth publishing in our church paper', suggested Proeve.[87]

The trio engaged Jimmy Russell ('Little Jimmy', an ex-mission Aborigine) as a guide and travelled to the Killalpaninna ruins. Decades of sandstorms had banked so much gritty earth against the missionary's house that Bert Reuther walked across the roof of the house in which he had been born nearly half a century ago. He had left Killalpaninna when he was five years old.

The establishment of Finniss Springs Mission (near Marree), which was described as an 'oasis in the wilderness',[88] and the presence there of several 'mission faithful', to a large degree relieved the conscience of the Lutherans in the south. And during the remainder of these war years they continued to send parcels north each Christmas. Dilly bags, sewn by the Lutheran women at the

Ruins of 'Government House', the former home of the main missionary at Killalpaninna (the Reuther–Reidel residence), 1940s

Point Pass Sewing Circle, and filled with food gifts, were sent by train to Marree, then travelled with the mailman, Tom Kruse, to the various stations along the Birdsville Track. Jimmy Russell collected parcels from Ooroowilannie Station and delivered them to outlying camps. Each parcel was labelled with the name of a known ex-Killalpaninna person or one of their children. At Mirra Mitta, 'Hannah can read so she will read them out'. The local stationers now nostalgically viewed the Killalpaninna missionaries of past times as 'honourable', even desiring that they 'might still be there', a far cry from the resentment and animosity of the late nineteenth century.[89]

Post Second World War and Adventure Trips
The war in Europe ended in May 1945 with the surrender of Germany. That same year the Lutheran press in South Australia published Proeve's booklet, *A Scattered Homeless Flock*, a testament to the missionaries of Killalpaninna and a travelogue of the last trip north. Its proceeds were to assist Bethesda Mission funds. A copy of the booklet was sent to Otto Siebert in Germany in 1947, together with photographs of Timotheus Maltilinna and his family. Siebert wrote that it had been Timotheus, and Johannes Pingilinna, who had begged him and his

wife to stay at Killalpaninna in 1902, but that he had been at death's door and was forced to leave.[90]

That same year, too, Anna Vogelsang died at Tanunda, at the age of ninety. Active to the end, she had arisen from her bed at midnight on 12 October, lit a lamp and pronounced her end to be near. She was suffering pain around her heart. At 7 o'clock the next morning she died.[91]

In 1946 Theodore Vogelsang approached the Finke River Mission Board regarding a visit to the Killalpaninna remnants for the forthcoming Christmas. Proeve also approached the board suggesting a base for these remnants be established at Murnpeowie Station. But the board had decided that the ex-Killalpaninna Aborigines were to make the mission at Finniss Springs their home, and a Christmas visit was not necessary as the 1946 gifts were to be sent by rail and mail to the northern stations.

It was not until the winter of 1949 that Theodore Vogelsang again visited the north. And this was to be his last trip. With uncle and nephew pastors, E. H. and H. F. W. Proeve, and Bruno Doecke, he set out in a Chevrolet utility, Vogelsang and the gifts riding in the back. Rain had fallen, the Cooper had again flooded, and the Birdsville Track was closed.

At the Clayton River they found the deserted wurlies of the Maltilinna family, with only Ewald nearby, tending cattle at Lake Harry.[92] The Chevrolet passed the woolshed and shearing quarters of Etadunna Station enroute to Kopperamanna. There the old homestead was now roofless, the Aboriginal quarters simply gum-post skeletons. Nearby the men found Vogelsang's boat, used for ferrying across the flooded Cooper, and a mile or so away the site of the Moravian mission of the 1860s.

At Killalpaninna only the shells of half a dozen mud-brick houses and the limepacked floor of the church were discernible. An empty inkpot marked the site of the school. But, immutably and resolutely, the graves of Hermann Vogelsang senior and of the Reuther baby had resisted all desecration of the elements. They stood on a high sand-dune beside the church floor, white sentinels by day, black silhouettes as the sun dipped below the silent lake. It was a journey of nostalgia, the last for Theodore Vogelsang, who died six years later.

During these latter years Theodore Vogelsang had become the nostalgic mission link for the ex-Killalpaninna Aborigines, and during his years as a translator for the South Australian Museum he corresponded with several literate ex-mission people. The arrival of a letter from Theodore created great interest at the camps, and was passed around and read aloud. The Vogelsang daughters also continued to correspond with their old Aboriginal friends, especially with Katarina and Alec. Even Wolfgang Reidel occasionally wrote, particularly at Christmas time. At Proeve's request Reidel wrote a devotional sermon, copies of which were posted to Aboriginal camps.[93] The letter-sermon used the term 'kutschi' (kutchie) for the biblical Devil, and concentrated on God's mystical power and revenge, on the Creation Story, and Jesus' mystical power in the resurrection account, drawing on traditional Aboriginal religious understanding. The stories were presented with child-like simplicity and couched in somewhat degrading colloquial English: 'Now Adam had to work hard for his tucker, for his wife's and for his children's tucker . . . But when the big fellow bosses saw how all the people came to listen to Jesus, they did not like it . . .' He ended the

The scattered ex-Killalpaninna people and the mission ruins in 1949. Vogelsang's Kopperamanna homestead is on the right; Rohrlach's homestead on the left

sermon with: 'To tell you and all Dijari [sic] people this the missionaries came to Killalpaninna, Missionary Flierl, Reuther, Missionary Reidel and others, also Vater [sic] Vogelsang, Mr Jacob, Johannes Irrgang, the sons of father Vogelsang, Hermann and Theodore Vogelsang . . .'[94] Aborigines were still being treated as inferior intellectually, adults given a child-like mental capacity. And fear, of the mighty power of the Christian God, was unremittingly upheld. Proeve had earlier tried to persuade Reidel to visit the ex-Killalpaninna people, but without success. By the mid-1950s he had resiled from further attempts; 'I did not contact Pastor W. Reidel and ask him to come along as I did not have the time to contact him and await his well considered reply. I deemed it hopeless to try to get him along on this trip.'[95]

Proeve continued to visit the mission remnants throughout the 1950s, taking gifts of fruit and honey cakes, second-hand clothing and shoes, and holding Lutheran services wherever sufficient numbers of ex-mission Aborigines were gathered. To the visiting pastor, Ulius Devana claimed he felt sad whenever he passed 'the old mission place', Katarina requested a Diyari New Testament, and Ben Murray promised to read Reidel's Diyari sermon to others at his camp. Proeve erected a monument to old Hermann Vogelsang at the Killalpaninna ruins.[96] On one trip, in 1958, Proeve took with him the octogenarian stepson of Ernst Jacob, 'Jack' Irrgang. When the Lutherans visited Ben Murray's camp near Witchelina Station, Ben walked towards his old friend, hands outstretched and tears rolling down his cheeks. 'Johannes', he said, 'it's been a long, long time I see you.'[97] Ben was fencing and dingo hunting for the station owners, but conditions for Aboriginal employees were extremely poor. Ben's camp had no comforts at all, simply a dirt floor in his hut, a crude bunk-bed and bush-style table and, in an attempt to keep his home mission clean and orderly, Ben had planted a square of struggling couch grass at its front as 'lawn'. Ben was described as 'intelligent' and 'absolutely trustworthy'. The managers of stations along the Birdsville Track 'have high praise for the older men, especially those who came from our mission', Proeve reported. He also declared that the younger generation, those not conditioned by the mission experience, were considered not as reliable.[98]

In 1956 Finniss Springs was temporarily closed as a mission due to drought and water shortage. There had been up to 150 Aborigines living at the station during that year.[99] Two years later a large group of Aborigines had left Finniss Springs to meet another group camped near a creek, and preparing for an initiation ceremony. A few young men from camps at Marree were to be initiated, and several old cars and trucks began arriving, bringing many more for the occasion.[100] Despite the fragmentation of Aboriginal tribal society and the pressure to adopt another culture, many traditional customs and practices were still firmly held, especially among the older people. At a service conducted at Ben Murray's camp, Proeve described an 'old heathen', who still wore his hair in the traditional style, taking off his hat respectfully to listen, with curiosity, to the service.[101] These older people fell into two categories: those who held fast to traditional ways, uncorrupted by mission indoctrination; and those who had undergone mission pedagogy and now led two cultural lives, one among the traditionalists, the other manifested whenever they were visited by Lutherans from the south. On his last visit north, in 1964, Proeve was told that 'old Sandy' the Rain-maker, who for many years had camped near the ruins, had recently died. On an earlier visit Sandy had said to Proeve, 'You know me, I am Sandy, me make rain'. And when Proeve had responded with, 'God makes rain', Sandy replied, 'Me believe in God, too. God and me make rain.' Many years earlier Sandy had run away from the mission school; 'Too much stick at school', he had said. Another old Aborigine, who was camped with Sandy, had declared to Proeve, 'That feller [the missionary] must have been all wrong that Jesus has been here. I have looked everywhere and not found His tracks.'[102]

During the 1950s Britain made a series of tests of its nuclear weaponry in the desert of its colonial outpost. The north of South Australia, some 400 miles south-west of the Killalpaninna area, was chosen for its remoteness and, presumably, its lack of perceived human settlement. The site of the testing of nine nuclear bombs, exploded between 1952 and 1957, was Maralinga, a spot on the map determined to have been 'just desert'. The radiation and force of these bombs was estimated as twenty times greater than that from the bombs dropped on Hiroshima and Nagasaki in August 1945,[103] an extreme act which finished the war in the Pacific. (More than 130 000 people were killed in Nagasaki and Hiroshima as a result of a single bomb dropped on each city, and an unknown number were maimed or mutilated, or died of resulting diseases.[104]) The Maralinga site lay within the tribal territory of the Pitjantjatjara people. No country in pre-colonial Australia was 'just desert'; it all belonged, in a spiritual as well as a tribal sense, to particular groups of people. As stated earlier, some of

'Jack' Irrgang addressing a group of ex-mission people at Finniss Springs, 1958

the ex-Killalpaninna people and others from the north-east of South Australia had allegedly travelled further west, perhaps to escape to areas less settled by Europeans. The numbers of Aboriginal deaths directly or indirectly resulting from the Maralinga testing are unknown.

During the 1960s several of the Vogelsang daughters, now elderly themselves, made nostalgic visits to the Killalpaninna ruins and emotional pilgrimages to their father's grave. Walking alone at the northern end of the lake, on the last evening of her 1965 visit, and looking back at the image of trees and moonlight on the mirror-like surface of water, Helene Vogelsang reflected that: 'Our endeavours [were] to be of help to the natives among whom we had grown up, and between us after the years there was still a bond of deep affection, and I shall never agree with people who say "It was all in vain" '.[105] In that same year Finniss Springs Station was closed as a mission station. Aborigines from there were again homeless.

Aftermath

On the outskirts of Port Augusta in South Australia is an Aboriginal reservation called Davenport. It spreads across a few square miles of red earth, sand-dunes and empty saltpans. Here, paper, glass, plastics and aluminium cans, products of a modern 'throw-away' society, blow and lie untidily against prickly saltbush and bluebush, or in crevices of dry creekbeds. Government-provided rectangular structures house Aboriginal families. Ration depots have been replaced by unemployment cheques as disillusioned and bored Aborigines, many from further northwards, while away their days, some in a dazed and drunken stupor. Within this reservation is a home for aged Aborigines called Wami Cata (meaning 'Snake's Head') and run by the Uniting Church. This clean, orderly complex comprises separate huts for individual old people or couples, and has an air of dignity and serenity. Here, several of the ex-Killalpaninna Aborigines spent their last years or months. In 1970 the faithful Katarina and Alec lived in one such hut, Katarina spending her last years blind, deaf and in a wheelchair.[106] Gertrude passed her final years at Davenport.[107] Florrie (who had worked in the Vogelsang home at Kopperamanna and was the daughter of Samuel Dintibana) was at Davenport in 1983.[108] Century-old Ben Murray, whose tribal name is Palkunguyu (meaning 'One Mass of Clouds'), is still a resident of Wami Cata. Ben retired from station work at the age of eighty-five, after a troublesome horse put him in hospital with a broken leg. He daily sits in the sun on his tubular steel and plastic chair, beside his tidy bedroom-hut, distinguishable by heavy-rimmed glasses, an ever-present knitted hat, and a walking stick that can poke the coals of a winter fire. Tall, straight, always carefully dressed in jacket and trousers, and sporting his Buffalo Lodge badge, he will occasionally lapse into the German language. He speaks several Aboriginal languages, including Diyari. Blinded from trachoma, Ben has periods of acute memory that enable him to relate detailed incidents about his life at Killalpaninna. 'There are not many people that speak Dieri [sic] anymore ... I had a Bible in Dieri. I lent it to a bloke and he never returned it. I had an English Bible, too. I used to read the Old Testament and the New Testament, but I can't read it anymore. I can't see.'[109]

In the early 1970s the last survivor of the Yandruwantha tribe from the Strzelecki Desert area, Murtee Johnny, who was nearly 100 years old, died at Wami Cata. He would regularly pack and repack his battered suitcase, saying to the staff, 'I want to go back to my own country, my country with the red sandhills'.[110]

Jimmy Naylon, whose Wangkangurru tribal name was Arpulindika (meaning 'Sweeping the Ceremonial Ground'), was always homesick for his own country, which he left in 1899. Shortly before his death in 1965 he took his favourite grandson from Birdsville into the Simpson Desert to look at 'kilpatha' ('tjilpatha'), one of nine special wells traditionally used by his people, and its traditional camping spot. The site was associated with the eastern Simpson Desert rain cycle, which was sung by Mick McLean and Johnny Reese (whose tribal name was Njanpika), who is now spending his last years at Wami Cata. Johnny Reese, for many years a horse-breaker on stations in the north, has been suffering the effects of syphilis for most of his life. The Wangkangurru, who belonged to the Kutikutithirinha, or Rain Ancestor myth associated with kilpatha, allegedly walked with a limp to show their affiliation with their ancestors, who had been affected by the power of Kutikutithirinha.[111]

At Marree lives Susie Kennedy, daughter of Gottlieb and Frieda Maltilinna. In the early 1990s about eighty years old, she was the little girl who was kept in the Powells' house at Killalpaninna as a playmate for their lonely daughter. Susie is quietly spoken, gentle by nature, and soft-featured. Dressed in an immaculate cotton frock that would have made the missionaries swell with pride, she shyly spoke of the difficulties her family encountered after the closure of Killalpaninna as a mission station.[112] Susie married a young ex-mission

Aborigine named Rudolf, but they separated later in life after Rudi became hopelessly alcoholic.[113]

There were few Aboriginal people alive in the 1990s who knew the traditional stories, songs, rituals and practices of their past culture. Those who once held custody have virtually all died, and often only fragments of knowledge remain. Much of what does remain of these stories from the north-east of South Australia has been rescued by Dr Luise Hercus (who speaks Arabana, Wangkangurru and some Diyari) with her invaluable documentation.

In the 1980s Hercus took Ben Murray and Jimmy Russell (whose tribal name was Wanga-mirri, meaning 'Many Mornings') in search of the site of Ditji-mingka (the Sun-cave), so important to the Diyari people. Samuel Dintibana (whose tribal name was Kinjmilina) had been the last 'owner' of the Ditji-mingka myth, and had written down the myth for Fry and Theodore Vogelsang. Samuel claimed to have a 'sunbag', filled with light-blue earth from Ditji-mingka, which could be used to 'sing the sun and make it very hot'.[114]

Travelling northwards towards Ditji-mingka's cave, the trio passed Blazes Well, the watering place of much of Killalpaninna's stock and the site of a small depression in the earth where Ditji (the Sun Ancestor) stepped into muddy ground on his travels across the landscape during the great Creation Period. The cave where Ditji lived was on Etadunna Station land. High on the western slope of a ridge that faced the bed of Ditji-mingka Creek, a soakage had traditionally sustained the Diyari people camped there for Ditji-mingka ceremonies. Ben Murray and Jimmy Russell, although not Diyari themselves, had nevertheless heard about this important place, and Jimmy had once been inside the cave. It had sparkled with sunshine. There were circles that symbolised the sun, rock carvings, and, as the sun began to set each evening, the walls and ceiling reflected its last rays. The men grew excited at the prospect of seeing the sacred cave, the home of the sun.

But when the trio at last found the difficult site, all that remained was a pile of stones. The European owners of Etadunna Station had found the troublesome cave a haven for snakes and a trap for animals. During the 1970s they had dynamited it and razed it to the ground.[115] They did not know of its significance, but even had they, there is no reason to believe the site would have survived. This ignorance of a once-flourishing Aboriginal culture bonded spiritually to the Australian landscape is widespread. The intricacies and subtlety of Aboriginal religious thought was never heeded nor understood until recent times. Furthermore, until recently there has been a conspicuous absence of Aboriginal presence in the annals of Australian history. For nearly 200 years the original occupiers featured as a mere footnote. By the time of real interest in this unique culture, the last custodians of the oral myths and histories, dances, songs and rituals had virtually disappeared. Much of this knowledge had not been passed on to the younger men and women, due to the fragmentation of family and tribal units, the interference of alcohol, distrust of the young by elders, and the fear of repercussions for betraying spiritual secrets. A 'Christian half-caste' (probably a Killalpaninna person) gained possession of the Diyari's 'two hearts of the Darana Mura-mura's sons' (sacred rain-making stones) and sent them to Theodore Vogelsang at the South Australian Museum after the last elder of the Diyari tribe died. The elder took with him many of the secrets of the Darana totem. The precious 'hearts', and the pointing-sticks that were used to kill betrayers of Darana's secrets, now lie in a glass case in the museum.[116]

But some of these myths and rituals, and some understanding of the culture, can be found in the documentation undertaken by the Killalpaninna missionaries. Their works form a unique body of material about the Aborigines of the north-east of South Australia. The documenting of the Diyari language by these missionaries, and to a lesser degree the Wangkangurru language, ironically also ensure the survival, at least in written form, of this centuries-old language. In 1986 the South Australian Museum held a major exhibition of the contentious Killalpaninna toas (marking sticks), made by the mission Aborigines during Reuther's time.

Flying in an aircraft over the Channel country of the Cooper Basin in the early 1990s, the landscape appears like reddish-brown marble, mottled and cleaved by surface fissures, channels for water from the mighty river systems that gush across the vastness of the desert only after prolonged monsoonal rain in tropical North Queensland. The landscape is awesome, immense. Huge empty expanses stretch in all directions. Waves of regular ridges from the ever-blowing winds sculpt the earth into a brown seascape. People must live closely within nature to exist in this environment.

In the late 1980s Lake Killalpaninna once again filled from the overflow of flooding in the Cooper Basin. I made a pilgrimage to the ruins of Killalpaninna Mission Station to view the lake filled with water. Such a pilgrim turns from the Birdsville Track onto the sandy path that runs through Etadunna Station land, at the site of a huge iron cross which stands like a stoic sentinel beside the gateway to the mission ruins. It was erected on the centenary of the arrival of the first missionaries at Lake Killalpaninna.

The sandy track winds past Dead-Man's Waterhole, past foreboding bare limbs of swamp gums, past undulating sand-dunes; a track deeply carved by Jacob's wagon. The screeching of cockatoos and the mournful caw of black crows are the only sounds, soaring wedgetail eagles, a flash of bright green finches the only lifeforms. One magestic red dingo loped beside the vehicle, crossed leisurely in front, and recrossed playfully again before loping off into the desert distance. Rounding a corner of box-gums the track suddenly splayed to a vast sandy landscape, the path running between crumbling mud-brick ruins of the old mission settlement barely visible. The lake to the left shone silver as the sun sat low in the sky. Irregular undulations of heaped sand and wooden posts, like bleached skeletons, marked mission structures; the missionary's house, high on the farthest sand-dune, easily discerned.

On the right-hand side of the track, on top of a sand-ridge, stands the grave of Hermann Vogelsang, dominant, immutable, presiding over the remains of Killalpaninna. Beside him is the tiny headstone of the Reuther baby, and nearby are the mounds of an unknown number of Aboriginal graves. Rabbits have burrowed into this loose earth, and tourists in four-wheel-drive vehicles have compressed the mounds and the mud-brick remains while pitching tents and collecting souvenirs.

The Killalpaninna experience of nineteenth- and early twentieth-century Australia is a microcosmic example of the wider European colonial occupation

Ben Murray beside the grave of Hermann Vogelsang senior at the Killalpaninna ruins, c. 1960s

of Aboriginal Australia. The Judeo-Christian thought of this European culture, where God occupied the centre stage of the cosmos, and humans the centre stage on earth, was diametrically opposed to the nature–land based philosophy of the indigenous hunters and gatherers, whose very existence depended on sustaining a harmonious balance between themselves and nature, considered one and the same. The European culture was sustained by excess productivity and exploitation of resources to provide material wealth, justified philosophically by God's special creatures, humans, who had dominance of the earth. Theirs was a culture of individuality. Conversely, in Aboriginal society, a community culture, there was no ownership, either individually or collectively, beyond necessities for simple daily existence, no productivity or exploitation for material gain or wealth.

The Killalpaninna missionaries maintained their enterprise by exploiting vast tracts of Aboriginal tribal land for material gain, money with which to operate their mission station. As a result, they too both occupied and raped the landscape and, like other European colonists, contributed to the environmental degradation that has been a result of the 200 years of European habitation in Australia. The primary task of the Killalpaninna missionaries was to impose the

European philosophical and religious view on the local Aborigines, an aim well supported in principle by other colonists in Australia, irrespective of local rivalries or national affiliations. Like their British compatriots, the Germans at Killalpaninna were largely oblivious to the Aboriginal 'sacredness' of the Killalpaninna landscape, and to Aborigines' totemic affinity with animals for spiritual and conservation purposes.

The Killalpaninna Mission ruins are silent and eerie. The sand-dunes are reflected in a death-like stillness on the stagnant lake. Here occurred a unique experience of history. A group of post-industrial Christian Europeans and hunter-gatherer Australian Aborigines interacted for the very first time. The lives of both cultures were to be unequivocally affected, though none more profoundly than the lives of the displaced indigenous people. It is a poignant place, one of convergence of two elements of thought from two diverging cultures, elements that had, and may still have, a profound effect on the history of humankind.

Notes

Introduction
1. G. Smallwood, 'Aboriginal Health by the Year 2000', paper for the Australian Tropical Health and Nutrition Conference, October 1990 (copy sent to me by the author).
2. ibid.
3. *Weekend Australian*, 24–25 November 1990.
4. ABC Radio news broadcast, 13 May 1992.
5. G. Smallwood, 'Impact on Indigenous Women', paper given at conference on World AIDS Day, November 1990 (copy sent to me by the author); 'Aboriginal Health by the Year 2000'.

1 German Altlutherans
1. A. Brauer, *The 100th Anniversary of the Lutheran Pilgrim Fathers and the Establishment of the Lutheran Church in Australia*, Lutheran Printing House, Adelaide, 1938, p. 9.
2. ibid.
3. D. Pike, *Paradise of Dissent: South Australia 1829–1857*, Melbourne University Press, Melbourne, 1967, p. 130. See also M. Hartwig, 'The Progress of White Settlement in the Alice Springs District and its Effects Upon the Aboriginal Inhabitants, 1860–1894', 2 vols, PhD thesis, University of Adelaide, 1965, p. 154.
4. Brauer, map, p. 13.
5. Norman L. Auricht, Reg. S. Munchenberg & the Christian Auricht Family Reunion Committee, *From Persecution to Freedom: Christian Auricht and Descendants, 1806–1980*, Lutheran Printing House, Adelaide, 1980. See also *Australian Lutheran Almanac 1934*, pp. 60–4, and Brauer, p. 15.
6. Auricht et al., p. 24.
7. J. Tampke & C. Doxford, *Australia, Willkommen*, New South Wales University Press, Sydney, 1990, p. 31.
8. Brauer, pp. 18–19.
9. Auricht et al., p. 25.
10. Brauer, p. 27.
11. ibid.
12. ibid., p. 28.
13. Hartwig, p. 158, citing J. Lyng, *Non-Britishers in Australia: Influence on Population and Progress*, Melbourne University Press, Melbourne, 1935, p. 35.
14. Brauer, pp. 28–30.
15. Tampke & Doxford, p. 32.
16. Brauer, p. 34.
17. Auricht et al., pp. 20–1.
18. Tampke & Doxford, p. 26.
19. Brauer, p. 30.
20. ibid., p. 37.
21. Kathleen Hassell, 'History of Port Lincoln', MS, Library Board of South Australia, Adelaide, p. 74, Port Lincoln Library, South Australia.
22. ibid., p. 77.

23 ibid.
24 ibid.
25 Leigh, W. H., *Travels and Adventures in South Australia, 1836–1838*, Elder Smith & Co., London, 1839, p. 170.
26 ibid., pp. 171–2.
27 Hassell, p. 77.
28 Brauer, p. 59.
29 Hartwig, p. 162.
30 ibid., p. 163.
31 ibid., p. 164. See also Brauer, pp. 223–4.
32 Hartwig, p. 164.
33 Christobel Mattingly & Ken Hampton (eds), *Survival in Our Own Land: Aboriginal Experiences in South Australia Since 1836*, Wakefield Press, Adelaide, 1988, from GRG 5/2, box 13, 55/66 PRO, Adelaide.
34 ibid.

2 The Diyari

1 F. J. Bradman, B. K. Arnold & S. L. Bell (eds), *A Natural History of the Lake Eyre Region*, South Australian National Parks and Wildlife Services, Adelaide, 1991.
2 P. Veth, G. Hamm & R. Lampert, 'The Archaeological Significance of the Lower Cooper Creek', *Records of the South Australian Museum*, vol. 24, no. 1, 1990, pp. 43–66.
3 R. Brough Smyth, *The Aborigines of Victoria*, vol. 2, Government Printer, Melbourne, 1878; A. Howitt, *Notes on the Aborigines of Coopers Creek*, p. 302.
4 Howitt, p. 302.
5 ibid., p. 303.
6 L. Hercus, 'Ned Palpilinna, the Last Wadikali', paper, p. 9.
7 ibid., p. 10.
8 Howitt, p. 302.
9 J. R. Love, 'A Visit to the Lutheran Mission Station at Killalpaninna, Coopers Creek, South Australia, 1911', Lutheran Archives, p. 36.
10 Samuel Gason, 'The Manners and Customs of the Dieyerie Tribe of Australia', South Australian Museum Archives, 1879, p. 259.
11 ibid., p. 31.
12 Brough Smyth, p. 303.
13 E. H. Proeve & H. F. W. Proeve, *A Work of Love and Sacrifice*, privately printed, South Australia, 1952, gives four divisions. P. Austin, *A Grammar of Diyari*, Cambridge University Press, Cambridge, 1981, gives five divisions.
14 P. Jones & P. Sutton, *Art and Land*, South Australian Museum & Wakefield Press, Adelaide, 1986, p. 23.
15 ibid.
16 Proeve & Proeve, p. 51; Love, p. 1.
17 Howitt, p. 302.
18 A. P. Elkin, *The Australian Aborigines*, Angus & Robertson, Sydney, rev. edn, 1976, p. 124.
19 Adapted from Austin, with assistance from L. Hercus.
20 Reuther MS, vol. 10, 1981, AIATSIS Archives, Canberra, trans. p. 1.
21 A. P. Elkin, 'Cult Totemism and Mythology in Northern South Australia, *Oceania*, vol. 5, 1934–35, p. 176.
22 R. M. Berndt, Fascicle 1, 1974, p. 23; R. M. Berndt, *Australian Aboriginal Religion*, E. J. Brill, Leiden, 1974, p. 7.
23 Elkin, 'Cult Totemism'.
24 Berndt, *Australian Aboriginal Religion*, p. 6.
25 Elkin, *The Australian Aborigines*, pp. 248–9.
26 Reuther MS, p. 190. Gilbert Mant, 'Letters Recount the Death of a Tribe', *South West Pacific*, no. 7, 17 April 1946.
27 Reuther MS, p. 189.
28 Gason, p. 280.
29 Reuther MS, p. 196.
30 Mant, 'Letters'. T. Vogelsang, 'The Hearts of the Two Sons of the Muramura Darana', South Australian Museum, n.d.

31 Reuther MS, p. 17.
32 Elkin, 'Cult Totemism', p. 177.
33 Reuther MS, p. 43.
34 Elkin, 'Cult Totemism', p. 176.
35 Berndt, *Australian Aboriginal Religion*, p. 3.
36 Howitt Papers, box 8.
37 ibid.
38 Berndt, *Australian Aboriginal Religion*, p. 3.
39 R. M. Berndt & C. Berndt, *The World of the First Australians*, Rigby, Adelaide, 1985, pp. 152–3.
40 Howitt Papers, box 8.
41 J. Flierl, *Dreissig Jahre Missionsarbeit in Wüsten und Wildnissen* (Thirty Years Mission Work in Deserts and Wilderness), Germany, 1910.
42 Berndt, *Australian Aboriginal Religion*, p. 4.
43 Howitt Papers, box 8.
44 Berndt, *Australian Aboriginal Religion*, p. 4.
45 ibid., p. 19.
46 J. Isaacs, *Australian Dreaming: 40 000 Years of Aboriginal History*, Lansdowne Press, Sydney, 1986, p. 239.
47 P. Jones, 'Red Ochre Expeditions: An Ethnographic and Historical Analysis of Aboriginal Trade in the Lake Eyre Basin', *Journal of the Anthropological Society of South Australia*, vol. 22, no. 7, September 1984.
48 ibid.
49 ibid., p. 8.
50 ibid., p. 7.
51 ibid.
52 Proeve & Proeve, p. 66.
53 Howitt Papers, box 8; notes, 'Initiation Ceremonies of the Dieri'.
54 Elkin, 'Cult Totemism'.
55 ibid., p. 185.
56 ibid.
57 ibid.; Howitt Papers, box 8.
58 Elkin, *The Australian Aborigines*, pp. 1601–1.
59 Gason, p. 280.
60 Howitt Papers, box 8.
61 Berndt, *Australian Aboriginal Religion*, p. 14; L. Hercus, 'The Status of Women's Cultural Knowledge', in P. Brock (ed.), *Women's Rites and Sites: Aboriginal Cultural Knowledge*, Allen & Unwin, 1989, p. 111.
62 Hercus, 'Blanche Ned'.
63 Hercus, 'A Pirlatapa Myth'.
64 Reuther MS, p. 14.
65 Gason, p. 263.
66 ibid., p. 283.
67 Berndt, *Australian Aboriginal Religion*, p. 9.
68 Gason, p. 276.
69 R. M. Berndt & T. Vogelsang, 'Notes on the Dieri Tribe of South Australia', *Royal Society of South Australia Transactions*, no. 63, 1939, p. 168; A. Howitt, *The Native Tribes of South-East Australia*, Macmillan, London, 1904, p. 799.
70 Reuther MS, p. 15.
71 Otto Siebert, 'Legends and Customs of the Dieri and Neighbouring Tribes in Central Australia', *Globus*, vol. 97, no. 3, 20 January 1910, pp. 44–51; R. M. Berndt & C. Berndt, *The World of the First Australians*, pp. 267–8.
72 Gason, pp. 275–6.
73 Berndt, *Australian Aboriginal Religion*, p. 5.
74 Berndt & Vogelsang, p. 169; Berndt, *Australian Aboriginal Religion*, p. 5.
75 Gason, p. 274.
76 Siebert, p. 26.
77 Vincent Serventy, *The Desert Sea: The Miracle of Lake Eyre*, Macmillan, Melbourne, 1985, p. 48.
78 Berndt & Vogelsang, p. 170.
79 Berndt, *Australian Aboriginal Religion*, pp. 5, 9.

80 Elkin, *The Australian Aborigines*, p. 160.
81 Gason, pp. 263–5.
82 Berndt & Berndt, *The World of the First Australians*, p. 273.
83 Love, p. 22; Reidel's Reminiscences, South Australian Museum, Adelaide, p. 26.
84 Siebert.
85 Howitt Papers, box 8; Letter Siebert to Howitt, 19 May 1897.
86 ibid.
87 Elkin, *The Australian Aborigines*, p. 158.
88 ibid.
89 ibid., p. 149.
90 R. M. Berndt, *From Black to White in South Australia*, Cheshire, Melbourne, 1951, p. 35.
91 Elkin, *The Australian Aborigines*, p. 161.
92 ibid., p. 162.
93 Berndt & Vogelsang, p. 168.
94 Elkin, *The Australian Aborigines*, p. 160.
95 Berndt & Vogelsang, p. 168.
96 Berndt, *Australian Aboriginal Religion*, p. 10.
97 Hercus, 'The Status of Women's Cultural Knowledge', pp. 108–9.
98 ibid.
99 Berndt & Berndt, *The World of the First Australians*, p. 158.
100 Berndt, *From Black to White in South Australia*, p. 103.
101 Gason, p. 258.
102 ibid.
103 ibid.
104 PRO, Adelaide, GRG 48/1 PG20.
105 ibid.
106 Berndt, *From Black to White in South Australia*, p. 61.

3 First Contact

1 P. A. Scherer, 'Looking Back on a Hundred Years, Bethesda Mission', *Lutheran Herald*, 24 September 1966.
2 E. H. Proeve, *A Scattered Homeless Flock: Mission Among the Dieri*, privately printed, South Australia, 1945, p. 10.
3 Proeve & Proeve, *A Work of Love and Sacrifice*, p. 55.
4 ibid.
5 'The Pilgrim's Earthly Journey', *Chronicle*, 24 May 1972, p. 33.
6 Goessling's first letter to Hermannsburg, *HM*, 1867.
7 Proeve & Proeve, *A Work of Love and Sacrifice*, p. 56.
8 Letter from Goessling to Hermannsburg, *HM*, 1867.
9 ibid., no. 3.
10 Proeve & Proeve, *A Work of Love and Sacrifice*, pp. 46–7.
11 Georg Haccius, *Hannoversche Missionsgeschichte*, 3 vols, Missionshandlung, Hermannsburg, Hanover, (1905) 1909–20, p. 36.
12 Proeve & Proeve, *A Work of Love and Sacrifice*, p. 45.
13 ibid., pp. 46–7.
14 Accounting Book, 1866, Lutheran Archives.
15 Letter from Goesling to Hermannsburg, *HM*, no. 3, 1867.
16 Proeve & Proeve, *A Work of Love and Sacrifice*, p. 62 (from DAC, July 1862, p. 36).
17 ibid., p. 63 (from DAC, July 1866, p. 28).
18 ibid., pp. 64–5 (from letter H. Walder to Protector of Aborigines, 6 December 1866, in PRO, Adelaide, 259/66 Aborigines Department).
19 ibid., p. 66 (from petition by Walder to Chief Secretary, 18 March 1867, in PRO, Adelaide, CSO 625/67).
20 *Advertiser*, 29 April 1968 (from that same date of 1868).
21 Proeve & Proeve, *A Work of Love and Sacrifice*, p. 87 (from Pastor P. J. Oster to Aborigines Department, 29 April 1867, in PRO, Adelaide, 191/67, Aborigines Department).
22 ibid., p. 69 (from letter from Homann, 3 February 1867, reprinted in *KMZ*, 28 July 1914, p. 238).
23 Second letter from Goessling to Hermannsburg, *HM*, 1867.
24 ibid.

25 ibid.
26 Proeve & Proeve, *A Work of Love and Sacrifice*, p. 70 (from letter from Homann of 3 February 1867, reprinted in *KMZ*, 28 July 1915, p. 238).
27 ibid. (from letter from Goessling written from Manuwakaninna, 9 March 1867, reprinted in *KMZ*, 4 August 1914, p. 245).
28 ibid., p. 74.
29 ibid., pp. 75–6 (from letter from H. Walder to Chief Secretary, 18 March 1867, in GRG 52/1/1867, no. 137, PRO, Adelaide).
30 Letter of 25 March 1867, Police Archives, Hindmarsh, GRG 5/2/1867, no. 633.
31 Letter Oster to Aborigines' Office, PRO, Adelaide, GRG 52/1/1867, no. 146.
32 Letter from Goessling to Hermannsburg, *HM*, 1867.
33 Letter from John Morton, 1 May 1867, Police Archives, Hindmarsh, GRG 5/1867.
34 Report, April 1872, Police Archives, Hindmarsh, GRG 5/1872.
35 Petition by H. Walder from Kopperamanna, 18 March 1867, Police Archives, Hindmarsh, GRG 5/1867.
36 Letter of 1 May 1867, Police Archives, Hindmarsh, GRG 5/1867.
37 Report from Police Journal of Lake Hope Police Station, 6–9 May 1867, Police Archives, Hindmarsh, GRG 5/1867.
38 Proeve & Proeve, *A Work of Love and Sacrifice*, p. 81 (from Report of J. P. Buttfield, 10 May 1867, in PRO Adelaide, 233/67, Aborigines Department).
39 Harms' Report on the Mission in Australia, *HM*, 1867.
40 Letter from G. Hamilton, 22 May 1867, Police Archives, Hindmarsh, GRG 5/1867.
41 Proeve & Proeve, *A Work of Love and Sacrifice*, p. 88 (from letter from P. J. Oster to Aborigines' Department, 29 April 1867, PRO, Adelaide, 191/1867, Aborigines' Department).
42 ibid., p. 90 (from letter from E. B. Scott to P. J. Oster, 9 September 1867, in PA 1322, 252/67, PRO, Adelaide).
43 ibid.
44 ibid., p. 90 (from Minute, 16 December 1867 to Walder's letter of 17 June 1867, in PRO, Adelaide, 305/67, Aborigines' Department).
45 Luise Homann, 'Journal of a Life of Many Moves', Adelaide, 1965, p. 22.
46 ibid.
47 ibid.
48 Olga Hardy, *Like a Bird on the Wing*, Lutheran Publishing House, Adelaide, 1984, p. 67.
49 Letter from Koch to HB, 26 October 1867, Lutheran Archives.
50 Homann, p. 24.
51 ibid.
52 ibid.
53 ibid.
54 ibid.
55 Letter from Homann to Hermannsburg, *HM*, 31 April 1868.
56 'The Life of H. H. Vogelsang: Pioneer Missionary on the Coopers Creek', typed booklet, Lutheran Archives.
57 Letter from Koch, 21 April 1868, Jericho Material.
58 Letter from Homann to Hermannsburg, *HM*, 5 May 1868.
59 ibid.
60 Letter from Reichner to Commissioner, 9 August 1869, PRO, Adelaide, GRG 52/1/1868, no. 428, Aborigines' Department.
61 Proeve, *A Scattered Homeless Flock*, p. 25.
62 Homann, p. 25.
63 Letter from Homann to Hermannsburg, *HM*, 6 February 1868.
64 ibid., 5 May 1868.
65 Homann, p. 25.
66 Letter from Homann, published in *HM*, 13 February 1871, Jericho Material.
67 Letter from Homann to Hermannsburg, *HM*, 14 January 1869.
68 ibid.
69 ibid.
70 ibid.
71 ibid.
72 ibid., *HM*, November 1869.

73 ibid., 23 November 1868.
74 Letter from Koch, n.d., Jericho Material.
75 Letter from Homann to Hermannsburg, *HM*, 2 February 1871.
76 Newspaper cutting, 1871, Lutheran Archives.
77 Homann, p. 26.
78 ibid.
79 Letter in *KMZ*, 27 October 1914, Jericho Material; 'The Life of H. H. Vogelsang', typed notes, Lutheran Archives.
80 Typed notes taken from *The Almanac, 1872*, Jericho Material.
81 Hardy, p. 74.
82 Homann, p. 26.
83 Loose notes, Lutheran Archives; typed notes, Jericho Material.
84 Homann, p. 26.
85 Letter from Homann to Hermannsburg, *HM*, 5 May 1871.
86 ibid.
87 Homann, p. 27.
88 Letter from Homann to Hermannsburg, *HM*, 5 May 1871.
89 ibid.
90 Homann, p. 27.
91 ibid.

4 Bucaltaninna and the Kolonisten

1 P. A. Scherer, 'Mission Among the Diyari, Looking Back on 100 Years, Bethesda Mission', *Lutheran Herald*, 24 September 1966, Lutheran Archives.
2 Obituary of Schoknecht, typed notes from DAC, 2 February 1905, South Australian Museum.
3 ibid.
4 Letter from Schoknecht to Hermannsburg, *HM*, 8 February 1872.
5 Draft letter, 1872, to Commissioner of Police, South Australia, Lutheran Archives.
6 *Lutheran Herald*, 24 September 1966; Homann, p. 30.
7 Letter to Commissioner of Crown Lands, 1873, Lutheran Archives.
8 Eric Bonython, *Where the Seasons Come and Go*, Gillingham Press, Adelaide, 1972, p. 11.
9 Letter from Schoknecht to Hermannsburg, *HM*, 8 February 1872.
10 Letter from George Hamilton, Police Commissioner of South Australia, 8 July 1873, Police Archives, Hindmarsh, GRG 5/73.
11 Letter from Schoknecht to Hermannsburg, *HM*, 3 June 1872.
12 Uncatalogued notes, Lutheran Archives.
13 Annual Report from Hermannsburg, *HM*, June 1873.
14 Uncatalogued notes, Lutheran Archives.
15 ibid.
16 Letter from Schoknecht to Hermannsburg, no. 22, 1873 (unpublished), Hermannsburg Mission Institute Archives, Germany.
17 *Lutheran Herald*, 24 September 1966; DAC 2 February 1905.
18 *Lutheran Herald*, 24 September 1966.
19 Uncatalogued notes, Lutheran Archives.
20 Notes of letter, n.d., Lutheran Archives.
21 *South Australian Government Gazette, 1874*, Lutheran Archives, Adelaide.
22 P. A. Scherer, *Venture of Faith*, Lutheran Printing House, Adelaide, 1963, p. 3.
23 ibid., p. 4.
24 ibid.
25 ibid.
26 'The Life of H. H. Vogelsang, A Pioneer Lay Missionary on the Coopers Creek', typed booklet, Lutheran Archives.
27 Flierl's first letter to Neuendettelsau, *KMZ*, 1878.
28 Letter from Reichner to Nuriootpa branch of the National Bank of Australia, 1875, uncatalogued material, Lutheran Archives.
29 Uncatalogued material, Lutheran Archives.
30 E. H. Proeve, *Three Missionary Pioneers*, Lutheran Printing Office, Adelaide, 1946, p. 18.
31 George Farwell, *Land of Mirage*, Rigby, Adelaide, repr. 1971, p. 152.

32 Letter from Vogelsang to Hermannsburg, Germany, 18 May 1875 (unpublished), Lutheran Archives.
33 ibid.
34 Letter from Hermann Vogelsang to his parents in Suelz, Germany, 18 October 1854, Jericho Material.
35 'How Father and Mother Vogelsang of the Bethesda Mission Traced God's Footsteps in Their Lives', booklet, Lutheran Archives; Proeve, *Three Missionary Pioneers*, pp. 17–19.
36 Farwell, p. 151.
37 'Lost—An Old German Sword'. *Chronicle*, 21 July 1966.
38 Scherer, *Venture of Faith*, p. 7.
39 ibid., p. 17.
40 ibid., p. 19.
41 ibid., p. 20.
42 Letter from Meyer to Protector of Aborigines, 7 January 1878, PRO, Adelaide, GRG 52/1/1873, no. 13.
43 Uncatalogued notes, Lutheran Archives.
44 Flierl, *Dreissig Jahre Missionsarbeit*, ch. 4.
45 Private material lent by Veronica Copeland (of the Vogelsang family), Wakefield, South Australia; typed MS of Helen Jericho (née Vogelsang).
46 Letter, 1 April 1873, Lutheran Archives.
47 Letter, 31 March 1873, Lutheran Archives.
48 Scherer article, *Lutheran Herald*, 12 November 1966.
49 Uncatalogued notes, Lutheran Archives.
50 Farwell, p. 152.
51 Mission Committee, *History of the Evangelical Lutheran Mission in South Australia*, South Australia, 1886, Lutheran Archives.
52 Auricht et al., *From Persecution to Freedom*, Lutheran Printing House, Adelaide, 1980, p. 22.
53 *Lutheran Herald*, 12 November 1966.
54 Flierl, *Dreissig Jahre Missionsarbeit*, ch. 4.
55 ibid.

5 Flierl the First

1 Flierl senior's first letter from Bucaltaninna Station, *KMZ*, 1878.
2 ibid.
3 Flierl senior's first letter; also handwritten notes by 'Jack' Irrgang, n.d., Lutheran Archives, Adelaide.
4 Flierl's first letter.
5 ibid.
6 ibid.
7 ibid.
8 Report from Flierl, *KMZ*, no. 6, 1879.
9 ibid.
10 ibid.
11 Meyer to Protector of Aborigines, PRO, Adelaide, GRG 52/1/1880, no. 39.
12 Letter from Flierl senior, *KMZ*, 30 June 1879.
13 Report from Flierl, *KMZ*, no. 6, 1879.
14 'Jack' Irrgang's handwritten notes.
15 Letter from Flierl senior, *KMZ*, April 1880.
16 Jericho Material. Private collection of Fay Story, Tumby Bay, South Australia.
17 Letter from Flierl senior, *KMZ*, April 1880.
18 ibid., *KMZ*, 26 July 1881.
19 J. Flierl, 'Mission Among the Heathen Papuans in Australia', (lead article) *KMZ*, 1881.
20 ibid.
21 Letter from Flierl senior, 26 July 1881, 'News From Australia', *KMZ* 1882.
22 Report from Reichner, July 1882, Lutheran Archives.
23 ibid.
24 ibid.
25 Letter from 'Rosalee' to Mission Committee at Tanunda, 30 August 1882, in 'The History of the Bethesda Mission of Lake Killalpaninna: On the Birdsville Track', typed notes, Lutheran Archives.

26   Flierl, *Dreissig Jahre Missionsarbeit*, ch. 4.
27   ibid., ch. 1.
28   *Report of the Lutheran Mission at Kopperamanna, Coopers Creek in South Australia: From the Beginning in 1866 to 31 December 1884*, Scrymour & Sons, Adelaide, 1885, Lutheran Archives.
29   Letter from Besley to Hamilton, PRO, Adelaide, GRG 52/1, no. 21, 1888.
30   ibid.
31   Letter from Flierl senior to Mission Committee at Tanunda, 1883, Lutheran Archives.
32   Typed notes from German paper of 1 May 1933, p. 4, Lutheran Archives.
33   Flierl, *Dreissig Jahre Missionsarbeit*, ch. 4.
34   Notes from German paper, 1 May 1933.
35   ibid.
36   ibid.
37   Flierl, *Dreissig Jahre Missionsarbeit*, ch. 4.
38   L. Hercus & P. Sutton (eds), *This is What Happened*, AIATSIS, Canberra, 1986, pp. 182–92 ('The End of the Mindari People').
39   Timotheus Maltilinna, typed notes, p. 11, Lutheran Archives, 354Sa.
40   Notes from German paper, 1 May 1933.
41   Flierl, *Dreissig Jahre Missionsarbeit*, ch. 4.
42   Letter from Flierl junior, *KMZ*, mid–1884.
43   ibid., *KMZ*, 26 January 1884.
44   Letter from Flierl senior, *KMZ*, 1883. Translation of Flierl's letters, n.d. (1883–84?), Jericho Material.
45   Translation of letters, n.d. (1884?), from Flierl senior(?).
46   Flierl, *Dreissig Jahre Missionsarbeit*, ch. 2.
47   Letter from Flierl senior, *KMZ* 1885.
48   'Report of the Lutheran Mission at Kopperamanna', Lutheran Archives.
49   Last letter from Flierl senior, *KMZ*, 1885. 'The History of the Bethesda Mission of Lake Killalpaninna', typed notes, Lutheran Archives.
50   Last letter from Flierl senior, *KMZ*, 1885.
51   'The History of the Bethesda Mission of Lake Killalpaninna' typed notes.
52   Scherer, 'Looking Back 100 Years'.
53   'The History of the Bethesda Mission of Lake Killalpaninna', typed notes.
54   Letter from Flierl senior, *KMZ*, 1885.
55   Last letter from Flierl senior.
56   First letter from Flierl senior, 1878.
57   Flierl, *Dreissig Jahre Missionsarbeit*, ch. 4.

6   Reuther and the Glorious 1890s
1   First letter from Reuther, *KMZ*, 1888.
2   Reuther's Diary, 1888–1914, p. 2, trs. from the original German by R. D. Reuther, Nuriootpa, 1970.
3   ibid.
4   ibid., p. 20.
5   P. A. Scherer, 'Donor of Aboriginal Heritage', *Lutheran*, 9 July 1979.
6   Jones & Sutton, p. 13.
7   Letter Reidel to Kaibel, 1910, Reidel's Letterbook, South Australian Museum.
8   'A Brief Biography of John Georg Reuther, His Family and Work', typescript, South Australian Museum.
9   Letter from Reuther, *KMZ*, 1889.
10   Reichner's evidence, Report of the Select Committee for the Aborigines' Bill, 1899, Parliamentary Papers of South Australia, 1899, nos 77A and 77, PRO, Adelaide.
11   Letter from Reuther entitled 'News from Bethesda', *KMZ*, 1891; Letter from Strehlow, *KMZ*, 1892; and letter from Strehlow, *KMZ* 1894, no. 2.
12   Letter from Reuther, *KMZ*, 1889.
13   Letter from Flierl junior (lead article), *KMZ*, 1889.
14   ibid.
15   Letter from Reuther entitled 'News from Bethesda', *KMZ*, 1891.
16   Letter from Reuther, *KMZ*, 1892.
17   Letter from Reuther entitled 'News from Bethesda', *KMZ*, 1891.

Notes 275

18 Reichner's evidence, Report of the Select Committee, 1899, pp. 11, 13.
19 Letter from Flierl junior, *KMZ*, 1886.
20 Letter from Strehlow, *KMZ*, 1894, no. 2.
21 Letter from Siebert entitled 'Death of Two Dieri Children', *KMZ*, 1895.
22 Letter from Reuther entitled 'News from Bethesda', *KMZ*, 1891.
23 Reuther's Diary, p. 9.
24 Letter from Reuther entitled 'News from Bethesda', *KMZ*, 1891.
25 Copy of the 'Synod Report', 23–25 February 1913, Jericho Material.
26 P. Austin, L. Hercus & P. Jones, 'Ben Murray: Parlku-Nguyu-Thangkayiwarna', *Aboriginal History*, vol. 12, 1988; Jones & Sutton, pp. 36–8; Reuther's Diary, p. 10.
27 Letter from Reuther entitled 'News from Bethesda', *KMZ*, 1891.
28 Bonython, p. 28; Scherer, 'Donor of Aboriginal Heritage'.
29 Reuther's evidence, Report of the Select Committee, 1899, p. 53.
30 *Lutheran Herald*, 9 July 1979.
31 Reichner's evidence, Report of the Select Committee, p. 13.
32 Letter from Flierl junior, *KMZ*, 1886.
33 Reuther's evidence, Report of the Select Committee, p. 53.
34 Letter from Reuther, *KMZ*, 1893.
35 Letter from Wettengel, *KMZ*, 1896.
36 Reuther's Diary, p. 22.
37 Letter from Reuther entitled 'News from Bethesda', *KMZ*, 1891.
38 Report to the Commission, 1 June 1889, Lutheran Archives; Records of Justice Samuel Way, 1889, Supreme Court Records, Adelaide.
39 A. Yashchenko, *Puteshestviye po Australii* (A Journey Through Australia), Moscow, 1959, ch. on Killalpaninna.
40 Letter from Strehlow, *KMZ*, 1894, no. 2.
41 Letter from Sergeant Dittmer, 25 August 1887, PRO, Adelaide, GRG 52/1/1887.
42 Letter from Flierl junior (lead article), *KMZ*, 1889.
43 Second letter from Reuther, entitled 'Reuther to a Friend', *KMZ*, 1890.
44 Reuther's Diary, p. 9.
45 ibid., p. 10.
46 Letter from McMahon to Hamilton, July 1887, PRO, Adelaide, GRG 52/1/1887, no. 272.
47 ibid.
48 ibid. Report of M. C. Dittmer of Marree Police Station to B. C. Besley, Inspector of Police/Sub-Protector of Aborigines for Far North of South Australia, stationed at Port Augusta, 25 August 1887.
49 Reuther's Diary, p. 12.
50 Protocol of the Commission held at Bethesda, 1–9 June 1891, Lutheran Archives, box 306.510.
51 Reuther's Diary, p. 12.
52 Protocol of the Commission, 1–9 June 1891.
53 Reuther's Diary, p. 7.
54 Christopher Anderson, 'The Political and Economic Basis of Kuku-yalanji Social History', PhD thesis, Bloomfield Mission, Queensland, 1984, p. 190.
55 Protocol of the Commission, 1–9 June 1891.
56 Bonython, p. 31.
57 Second letter from Reuther, entitled 'Reuther to a Friend', 1890.
58 Letter from Reuther entitled 'News from Bethesda', *KMZ*, 1891.
59 ibid.
60 ibid.
61 Letter from Reuther, *KMZ*, 1892.
62 Reuther's Diary, p. 13.
63 Bonython, p. 21.
64 Notes of Helen Jericho, Mortlock Library, Adelaide, PRG 355.
65 Agreement letter, n.d., Lutheran Archives, uncatalogued material.
66 J. W. Gregory, *The Dead Heart of Australia*, John Murray, London, 1906, pp. 60–1.
67 Wages and Salaries Books and Notes, Lutheran Archives, uncatalogued material, box 306.510.
68 Letter fragments, Lutheran Archives.
69 Helene Jericho, *Down Memory Lane*, privately printed, repr. 1983, p. 4.
70 Bonython, pp. 31–2.

71 Proeve, *Three Missionary Pioneers*, p. 23.
72 ibid.
73 ibid.
74 Bonython, p. 26.
75 Letter from Reuther, *KMZ*, 1899.
76 Bonython, p. 32.
77 ibid.
78 Letter from Reuther, *KMZ*, 1893.
79 Hartwig, p. 541.
80 ibid., p. 542.
81 Everard Leske (ed.), *Hermannsburg: A Vision and a Mission*, Lutheran Publishing House, Adelaide, 1977.
82 'History of the Lutheran Church in Australia, 1830–1925', Lutheran Archives, AA:CA948, AP308, 20418/5.
83 Letter from A. W Gosnell to Reichner, June 1893, Lutheran Archives.
84 Yashchenko, p. 14.
85 ibid., p. 15.
86 Letter from Hillier to Lohe, 13 March 1905, Lutheran Archives.
87 Letter from Strehlow, *KMZ*, 1894.
88 Letter from Siebert, *KMZ*, 1894.
89 Report from Siebert, *KMZ*, 1894.
90 Letter from Wettengel, *KMZ*, 1898.
91 Letter from Siebert, *KMZ*, 1898.
92 Letter from Vogelsang to Kaibel, 30 October 1901, Lutheran Archives.
93 Reuther's Diary, pp. 21–2.
94 Letter from Wettengel, 1896.
95 ibid.
96 Report on the 'Three Missions in Australia', *KMZ*, March 1900.
97 Leske, p. 27.
98 Letter from Hunt to Reichner, 10 September 1896, Lutheran Archives.
99 Letter, 1898, Lutheran Archives, box 306.510, file 1900–1904.
100 Flierl, *Dreissig Jahre Missionsarbeit*, intro.
101 Jericho, p. 19.
102 ibid., pp. 1–2.
103 Reuther's Diary, p. 14.
104 ibid., p. 19.
105 Jericho, p. 23.
106 ibid., pp. 23–6.
107 Letter from Reuther entitled 'From Reuther to a Friend', *KMZ*, 1890.
108 Bonython, p. 24.
109 Leske, pp. 46–7.
110 Jericho, p. 11.
111 ibid., p. 25.
112 Reuther's Diary, p. 14.
113 Jericho, p. 15.
114 ibid., p. 14.
115 Reuther's Diary, p. 13.
116 Jericho, p. 41.
117 ibid.
118 Reuther's Diary, pp. 4, 13, 14.
119 Handwritten notes, 25 March 1972, Jericho Material.
120 Jericho, p. 18.
121 Letter from Luise Vogelsang to Dora Vogelsang, 1 September 1902, Jericho Material.
122 Jericho, p. 8.
123 ibid., p. 19; Bonython, p. 30.
124 P. Stolz, J. Irrgang, F. Vogelsang & K. Smith, 'Bethesda', handwritten notes lent by Brian Oldfield.
125 Letter from Reuther (trs. from German by Helene Vogelsang), *KMZ*, 25 October 1905, Jericho Material.

126 Reuther's Diary, p. 6.
127 ibid., p. 29.
128 Letter from Reuther to Mission Committee, 1 June 1904, Lutheran Archives.
129 Letter from Reuther, 25 October 1905, Jericho Material.
130 ibid.
131 Reuther's Diary, p. 4.
132 Letter from Kaibel to Reuther, 7 December 1905, Lutheran Archives.
133 Letter from Kaibel to Reuther, early 1906, Letterbook of Kaibel, president of Mission Committee, p. 107, Lutheran Archives.
134 ibid., p. 117. Letter from Kaibel to Reuther, January 1906.
135 ibid. Letter from Kaibel to Reuther, 4 January 1906.
136 ibid. Letter from Kaibel to Reuther, 18 January 1906.
137 ibid.
138 ibid. Letter from Kaibel to Vogelsang, 18 January 1906.
139 ibid. Letter no. 125, Kaibel to Reuther, n.d., labelled 'private'.
140 ibid. Letter from Kaibel to Reuther, 27 February 1906.
141 Scherer, 'Donor of Aboriginal Heritage', pp. 12–15.
142 Letter from Reuther, 14 January 1907, Lutheran Archives.
143 Letter from Kaibel to Reuther, Letterbook of Kaibel, 11 April 1906, Lutheran Archives.
144 *KMZ*, no. 8, 11 July 1906.
145 ibid.
146 'A Brief Biography of Johann Georg Reuther, His Family and Work', typed notes, Lutheran Archives.
147 Letter from Reuther to Kaibel, 14 January 1907, Lutheran Archives.
148 Reuther's letters, 1907, Letterbook of Kaibel, pp. 6–7, Lutheran Archives.

7   Old Rites, New Order and Mission Decline

1 Letter from Bogner to Kaibel, 20 May 1907, Letterbook, Lutheran Archives.
2 ibid.
3 Letter from Bogner to Kaibel, 20 May 1907.
4 ibid.
5 'Johannes Matthias Bogner', *Lutheran Herald*, 1930, p. 188, Lutheran Archives.
6 Letter from Reuther to Kaibel, 1 June 1904, Lutheran Archives.
7 Bogner's Annual Report to Mission Committee for 1907, Lutheran Archives.
8 Letter from Bogner to Kaibel, 11 September 1907, Lutheran Archives.
9 Letter from Bogner to Kaibel, 24 April 1907, Lutheran Archives.
10 ibid.
11 Letter from Besley to Hamilton, 17 March 1893, PRO, Adelaide, GRG 52/1, no. 93, 1893.
12 Letter Besley to Hamilton, PRO, Adelaide, GRG 52/1, no. 356, 1888. Transcripts of Port Augusta Circuit Court under Judge Samuel Way's Records, p. 117, Supreme Court Records, Adelaide.
13 Letter from Theodore Vogelsang to Kaibel, 14 August 1907, Lutheran Archives.
14 Letter from Bogner to Kaibel, 26 November 1907, Lutheran Archives.
15 Bogner to Kaibel, 24 April 1907.
16 Bogner's Annual Report, 1907.
17 Letter from Bogner to Kaibel, 10 April 1907, Lutheran Archives.
18 Letter from Theodore Vogelsang to Kaibel, 22 May 1907, Lutheran Archives.
19 Bogner's Annual Report, 1907.
20 ibid.
21 Letter from Reidel to Leidig, 1 March 1906, Letterbook, South Australian Museum.
22 Letter from Reidel to Inspector at Neuendettelsau, 9 June 1909, South Australian Museum.
23 Reidel's Reminiscences, typed MS, p. 4, South Australian Museum.
24 ibid., p. 5.
25 ibid., p. 11.
26 Letter from Reidel to a friend (Kurts/Kwietz?) in Germany, 16 October 1909, South Australian Museum.
27 Reidel's Reminiscences, p. 14.
28 ibid., p. 20.
29 ibid.

30 ibid., p. 21.
31 Letter from Reidel to Kaibel, n.d. (only p. 3 found), Lutheran Archives.
32 Letter from Reidel to Inspector at Neuendettelsau, 9 June 1908, Lutheran Archives.
33 Reidel's Reminiscences, p. 20.
34 Author's interview with Ben Murray, Port Augusta, 1990.
35 Reidel to a friend in Germany, n.d., Letterbook, South Australian Museum.
36 Reidel to Brother Ottenburger at Tanunda, n.d., Letterbook, South Australian Museum.
37 Letter from Reidel to a friend (Kurts/Kwietz?) in Germany, 16 October 1909.
38 Letter from Reidel to Hans, New Year, 1910, Letterbook, South Australian Museum.
39 'The Record: Sabbath School Missionary Magazine of the Presbyterian Church of South Australia', 1 October 1910, p. 14, AIATSIS Archives, Canberra.
40 Letter from Reidel to Kaibel, 5 October 1909, Letterbook, South Australian Museum.
41 Reidel's Report to the Mission Friends, 24 August 1908, Lutheran Archives.
42 J. R. Love, 'A Visit to the Lutheran Mission Station at Killalpaninna, Coopers Creek, South Australia', handwritten notes, pp. 8–9, Lutheran Archives, box 306.510 (and from PRO, Adelaide, GRG 214/3, series 3).
43 Jericho, pp. 33–4.
44 Letter from Reidel to his former superior at Neuendettelsau, 20 October 1909, South Australian Museum.
45 Letter from Reidel to C. Strehlow, end 1908, South Australian Museum.
46 Letter from Reidel to a member of the Mission Committee, 2 February 1909, South Australian Museum.
47 Love, p. 11.
48 ibid., p. 12.
49 Letter from Reidel to Kaibel, 26 January 1909, Letterbook, South Australian Museum.
50 Letter from Hermann Vogelsang senior to Kaibel, 4 January 1907, Lutheran Archives.
51 ibid., n.d. (1908?)
52 Christine Stevens, *Tin Mosques and Ghantowns*, Oxford University Press, Melbourne, 1989.
53 Letter from Hermann Vogelsang senior to Kaibel, 13 January 1908, Lutheran Archives.
54 Report of the Royal Commission . . . 1912–1916', p. 44, PRO, Adelaide.
55 Letter from Reidel to Leidig, n.d. (end 1908, beg. 1909?), Letterbook, South Australian Museum.
56 ibid. Reidel's Annual Report, 1909, *KMZ*, early 1910.
57 Letter from Reidel to Sabel, 26 May 1910, Letterbook, South Australian Museum.
58 Letter from Reidel to Kaibel, 29 November 1910, Letterbook, South Australian Museum.
59 Love, p. 2.
60 Letter from Reidel to Sabel, 26 May 1910.
61 Reidel's Report to Mission Friends, 24 August 1908, Lutheran Archives.
62 Reidel's Annual Report, 1909; Love, p. 15.
63 Love, pp. 6–7.
64 ibid.
65 Austin et al., 'Ben Murray'.
66 Letter from Reidel to Sabel, 26 May 1910.
67 Letter from Reidel to Kaibel, 29 November 1910.
68 Letter from Reidel to Leidig, n.d., Letterbook, South Australian Museum.
69 Love, pp. 26–7.
70 Letter from Reidel to Kaibel, 7 September 1909, Letterbook, South Australian Museum.
71 Reidel's Reminiscences, p. 34.
72 Letter from Reidel to Sabel, 26 May 1910.
73 Love, p. 23.
74 Reidel's Reminiscences, p. 37.
75 ibid.
76 Letter Reidel to Sabel, 26 May 1910.
77 Author's interview with Ben Murray, 30 March 1991.
78 Letter from Hermann Vogelsang senior to Kaibel, 30 December 1908, Lutheran Archives.
79 Letter from Reidel to Kaibel, 2 November 1909, Letterbook, South Australian Museum.
80 Jericho, p. 42.
81 Reidel's Reminiscences, pp. 25–6.
82 ibid.

83 Love, p. 23.
84 Reidel's Reminiscences, pp. 25–6.
85 Jericho, p. 42.
86 Reidel's Reminiscences, p. 26.
87 ibid.
88 Gason, p. 298.
89 Letter from Reidel to Kaibel, 26 January 1909, Letterbook, South Australian Museum.
90 Hermann Vogelsang senior to Kaibel, 3 November 1909, Lutheran Archives.
91 South's evidence, Report of Royal Commission, 1912–1916, p. 24.
92 ibid., p. 17.
93 ibid., p. 26.
94 Letter from Kaibel to Kokegai, 6 October 1909, Lutheran Archives.
95 Letter from Reidel to Sabel, 26 May 1910.
96 ibid.
97 Letter from Reidel to Kaibel, n.d. (1910?), Letterbook, South Australian Museum.
98 ibid.
99 Letter from Reidel to Strehlow, n.d. (1911?), Letterbook, South Australian Museum.
100 Letter from Reidel to Kaibel, 15 September 1909, Letterbook, South Australian Museum.
101 Austin et al. 'Ben Murray'; also author's interviews with Ben Murray over many years.
102 ibid.
103 Reidel's Reminiscences, p. 46.
104 'Report on the Three Missionary Stations: Queensland, Hermannsburg and Bethesda', *South Australian Lutheran Newspaper*, March 1900, Lutheran Archives.
105 Letter from Reuther, *KMZ*, no. 28, 11 July 1906.
106 Letter from Kaibel, *KMZ*, 1902.
107 Report of the Royal Commission, 1912–1916, p. iv.
108 ibid., p. 44.
109 ibid., p. 18.
110 ibid., p. 44.
111 ibid., p. iii.
112 ibid., pp. iii, iv.
113 ibid., p. iv.
114 *Lutheran Newspaper*, March 1900.
115 J. F. W. Schulz, *Destined to Perish?*, Lutheran Printing House, Adelaide, 1938, pp. 29–30.
116 ibid.
117 Proeve, *Three Missionary Pioneers*, p. 12.
118 Bogner's Annual Report, 1907.
119 Jericho, p. 49.
120 ibid., pp. 49–50.
121 Letter from Hermann Vogelsang junior to his brothers and sisters in the south, 19 March 1913, Jericho Material.
122 Copy of letter from Reidel to Kaibel(?), n.d., Jericho Material.
123 Reuther's Diary, pp. 5–6.
124 'A Good Man Gone: Mr J. G. Reuther's Career', newspaper cutting, March 1914, Lutheran Archives.
125 ibid.
126 Reuther's Diary, pp. 28–9.
127 Letter from Reidel to Neuendettelsau, 20 October 1909, South Australian Museum.
128 ibid.
129 Letter from Reidel to Liebler, Reidel's Correspondence Journal, p. 125, South Australian Museum.
130 Letter from Reidel to Kaibel, 1909, South Australian Museum.
131 Letter from Reidel to Leidig, 12 December 1909, South Australian Museum.
132 Letter from Reidel to Doeffler, 5 December 1910, South Australian Museum.
133 Letter from Reidel to Kaibel, n.d. (1909?), South Australian Museum.
134 Mission report, trs. by Helene Jericho. *KMZ*, February 1913, Jericho Material.
135 Letter from Bogner to Kaibel, 25 June 1908, Lutheran Archives.
136 Letter from Reidel to Kaibel, n.d. (1909?).
137 ibid.

138 Report of the Royal Commission, 1912–1916, p. 27.
139 ibid., p. 21.
140 Reidel's Reminiscences, p. 47.
141 ibid.
142 Letter from Reidel to Kaibel, n.d., trans. by H. Jericho, Jericho Material.
143 Immanuel Synod Report, 23–25 February 1913, trans. by H. Jericho, Jericho Material.
144 ibid.
145 ibid.
146 Reidel's Reminiscences, pp. 47–8.
147 Report of the Royal Commission, 1912–1916, p. 26.
148 ibid., p. 29.
149 ibid., p. 37.
150 Immanuel Synod Report, 23–25 February 1913.
151 Report of the Royal Commission, 1912–1916, p. 38.
152 ibid., p. 40. Scherer, 'Mission Among the Diyari'.
153 Report of the Royal Commission, 1912–1916, p. 40.
154 ibid.
155 ibid., pp. iv–vi.

8 Linguists and Ethnographers
1 Hercus, 'Aboriginal People', p. 140.
2 ibid., p. 151.
3 C. Fergusson, 'Literacy in a Hunting and Gathering Society', *Journal of Anthropological Research*, vol. 43, no. 3, 1987, p. 224.
4 ibid., p. 223.
5 Hercus, 'Aboriginal People', p. 151.
6 Homann's second letter, *HM*, 1867.
7 ibid.
8 Fergusson, p. 228.
9 ibid., p. 225.
10 Gason, p. 290.
11 Brough Smyth, *The Aborigines of Victoria*, vol. 2; Howitt, 'Notes on the Aborigines of Coopers Creek', pp. 308–9.
12 Love, 'A Visit to the Lutheran Mission Station'.
13 Letter from Homann, *HM*, 1 May 1868.
14 Letters from Homann, *HM*, 30 July and 31 August 1868.
15 Translations, n.d., Jericho Material; letter from Homann, *HM*, 31 August 1868.
16 Letter from Homann, *HM*, 23 November 1868.
17 ibid., 14 January 1869.
18 Translations from church newspapers; letter from Koch, 14 January 1869.
19 Letter from Flierl junior, *KMZ*, 26 January 1884.
20 Letter from Koch, *HM*, 14 January 1869.
21 Letter from Homann, *HM*, November 1869.
22 Austin, *A Grammar of Diyari*.
23 ibid., n. 25. Schoknecht MS, trs. by his son in 1947, La Trobe University Library, Melbourne.
24 Hebart, *History of the Evangelical Mission*.
25 *Annual Mission Yearbook, 1883*, Lutheran Archives, Adelaide. Notes, n.d., uncatalogued Jericho Material.
26 Second letter from Flierl senior, *KMZ*, 7 January 1879.
27 ibid.
28 ibid.
29 ibid.
30 Flierl, *Dreissig Jahre Missionsarbeit*, ch. 4.
31 Report of Flierl senior, *KMZ*, no. 6, 1881.
32 'The History of the Bethesda Mission on Lake Killalpaninna', typed notes.
33 P. Austin, 'Diyari Language Postcards and Diyari Literacy', *Aboriginal History*, vol. 10, no. 2, 1986.
34 'The History of the Bethesda Mission on Lake Killalpaninna', typed notes; letter written by Johannes Pingilinna in Diyari to Meyer in the south, 31 March 1886; letter written by Rosalee in

Diyari to Committee Members, 30 August 1882. Letter from Pauline Ninpilinna in English to Reichner, 21 March 1899; letter from Johannes Nguujanakana in English to Reichner, 21 March 1899, Lutheran Archives.
35 Letter from Flierl, *KMZ*, 26 July 1881.
36 Letter from Pauline Ninpilinna in English to Reichner, 21 March 1899; letter from Johannes Nguurjanakana in English to Reichner, 21 March 1899, Lutheran Archives.
37 'Reuther to a Friend', *KMZ*, 1890.
38 Reuther's third letter, headed 'Another Story from Bethesda', *KMZ*, 1890.
39 Letter from Siebert, *KMZ*, 1894.
40 Letter from Strehlow, *KMZ*, no. 17, 6 September 1892.
41 ibid., *KMZ*, 6 September 1892.
42 Strehlow's second letter from Bethesda, *KMZ*, no. 2, 1894.
43 'Report on the Three Mission Stations: Queensland, Hermannsburg and Bethesda', *South Australian Lutheran Newspaper*, March 1900.
44 Letter from Reuther, *KMZ*, 1893.
45 Letter from Strehlow, *KMZ*, 6 September 1892.
46 Reuther's Diary, p. 16.
47 Jones & Sutton, p. 52, from Tindale interview with Reuther's son, Pastor R. B. Reuther, June 1964, sound tapes 149–53, South Australian Museum.
48 Report of Tindale to Stirling, AIATSIS Archives, Canberra, B1, MS p. 161, 3 May 1937.
49 Letter from Reuther, *KMZ*, no. 11, 1893.
50 Jones & Sutton, p. 50.
51 Reuther's Diary, p. 20.
52 Letter from Siebert, *KMZ*, 1899.
53 Reuther & Strehlow, preface to *Testamenta Marra*, trs. into German from Diyari by Pastor R. B. Reuther, son of Reuther, and into English from German by Dr M. Lohe.
54 Scherer, 'Donor of Aboriginal Heritage', p. 286.
55 Reidel's Reminiscences, p. 23.
56 Letter from Reidel to Leidig(?), Reidel's Correspondence Book, 16 July 1908, p. 53.
57 Letter from Reidel to Siebert, Reidel's Correspondence Book, 4 September 1909, p. 277.
58 Letter from Reidel to Reuther, Reidel's Correspondence Book, 17 December 1908.
59 ibid., 17 May 1909.
60 ibid., 7 July 1909.
61 Letter from Reidel to Strehlow, Reidel's Correspondence Book, 11 March 1909, p. 153.
62 Love, 'A Visit to the Lutheran Mission Station', p. 23.
63 ibid.
64 ibid., p. 32.
65 ibid., p. 20.
66 ibid., pp. 29–30.
67 Austin, 'Diyari Language Postcards'.
68 Letter from Reidel to Br(?) Parps, 13 March 1913, South Australian Museum.
69 T. Swain, *Interpreting Aboriginal Religion: An Historical Account*, Australian Association for the Study of Religions, Adelaide, 1985, p. 8.
70 ibid., p. 11.
71 ibid., p. 16.
72 ibid., p. 29.
73 V. Courto, 'Dr Erhard Eylmann', BA (Hons) thesis, Australian National University, Canberra, 1991.
74 Mary Howitt Walker, *Come Wind, Come Weather: A Biography of Alfred Howitt*, Melbourne University Press, Melbourne, 1971, p. 209.
75 Brough Smyth, *The Aborigines of Victoria*, p. 305.
76 Walker, p. 211.
77 Gason, p. 280; Walker, pp. 257–8.
78 Letter from Buttfield to Protector, 22 February 1867, PRO, Adelaide, GRG 52/1, no. 82, 1867.
79 Letter from Homan, *HM*, 23 November 1868.
80 Letter from Schoknecht, *HM*, no. 728, 3 June 1872.
81 'Mission Among the Heathen Papuas in Australia', lead article from Report from Flierl senior, *KMZ*, 1881.
82 ibid.

83 'The History of the Bethesda Mission on Lake Killalpaninna', typed notes.
84 'Mission Among the Heathen Papuas', Report from Flierl senior, *KMZ*, 1881.
85 ibid.
86 Letter from Flierl junior, *KMZ*, 26 January 1884.
87 Copy of Report of the Sub-Protector of Aborigines for 1878, p. 2, Lutheran Archives.
88 Letter from Flierl senior, *KMZ* 1885.
89 Letter from Reuther, *KMZ*, 1892.
90 ibid., *KMZ*, 1894.
91 ibid., *KMZ*, April 1894.
92 ibid., *KMZ*, 1899.
93 Letter from Siebert, *KMZ*, 1894.
94 Tindale discussion with Siebert, Germany, 1936.
95 Hercus, 'Aboriginal people', p. 157.
96 J. W. Gregory, *The Dead Heart of Australia*, John Murray, London, 1906, pp. 79–80.
97 P. Brock (ed.), *Women's Rites and Sites*, Allen & Unwin, Sydney, 1989, p. 110.
98 Bonython, p. 25, from a discussion between Bonython and 'Jack' Irrgang.
99 Yashchenko, ch. on Killalpaninna.
100 Scherer, p. 286.
101 *Observer*, 20 February 1906.
102 Port Augusta Police Station Letterbook, PRO, Adelaide, GRG 5/1 series.
103 Report of the Select Committee, 1899, pp. 99–100.
104 Courto, p. 40, from Eylmann, p. 181.
105 R. R. Marrett & T. K. Penniman (eds), *Spencer's Last Journey*, Clarendon Press, Oxford, 1931.
106 Report of the Select Committee, 1899, pp. 99–100.
107 Swain, p. 62.
108 B. Spencer & F. Gillen, *Native Tribes of Central Australia*, Macmillan, London, 1899, p. ix.
109 ibid., p. xiii.
110 Courto, passim.
111 Reuther's Diary, p. 23.
112 Yashchenko, ch. on Killalpaninna, pp. 3, 106.
113 ibid., p. 11.
114 R. Glover & D. Langsam, 'Day of Reckoning for Darwin's Bodysnatchers', *Sydney Morning Herald*, 3 March 1990, p. 79.
115 ibid.
116 ibid.
117 Walker, p. 221.
118 Letter from Reuther to Howitt, 1 June 1898, Howitt Papers.
119 Letter from Siebert to Howitt, 13 October 1897, Howitt Papers.
120 Letter from Siebert to Theodore Vogelsang, 21 June 1935, South Australian Museum Archives, AA266/1539.
121 Jones & Sutton, pp. 50–1.
122 Letter from Siebert to Theodore Vogelsang, 21 June 1935, South Australian Museum Archives, AA266/1539.
123 Jones & Sutton, p. 139.
124 Howitt & Siebert, 'Two Legends of the Lake Eyre Tribes, Report for the 9th Meeting of the Australasian Association for the Advancement of Science, 1902; Howitt, 'On the Marriage Rules of Australian Tribes', from material supplied by Siebert that now lies in the AIATSIS Archives, Howitt Papers, box 8.
125 Otto Siebert, 'Sagen und Sitten der Dieri und Nachbarstamme in Zentral-Australien', *Globus*, no. 47, 1910.
126 Letter from Reuther to Howitt, 30 January 1904, Howitt Papers, box 8.
127 Letter from Siebert to Theodore Vogelsang, 21 June 1935, South Australian Museum Archives, AA266/1539.
128 Scherer, 'Donor of Aboriginal Heritage', p. 14. 'A Brief Biography of Johann Georg Reuther, His Family and Works', typed notes, South Australian Museum Archives.
129 The publication being 'A Brief Sketch of the Australian Aboriginals, Notably the Diari [sic] tribe of East of the Lake Eyre District', possibly with the assistance of Dr Stirling of the South Australian Museum, where the article is now lodged.
130 Letter from Reuther to Howitt, 19 April 1899, Howitt Papers, box 8.

131 Moritz von Leonhardi, 'Der Mura und die Mura-Mura der Dieri', *Anthropos*, no. 4, 1909, p. 1065.
132 Jones & Sutton, p. 139.
133 L. Hercus & P. Clarke, 'Nine Simpson Desert Wells', *Oceania*, no. 21, 1986.
134 Jones & Sutton, pp. 139–40, from letter from Reuther to Stirling, 2 March 1909.
135 ibid.
136 Letter from Siebert to Theodore Vogelsang, 21 June 1935, South Australian Museum Archives, AA266/1539.
137 Letter from Reidel to von Leonhardi, 22 September 1909, South Australian Museum Archives.
138 Love.
139 ibid.
140 Reidel's Reminiscences, p. 37.
141 Jones & Sutton, pp. 6, 13.
142 ibid., p. 75.
143 ibid., p. 13.
144 *Adelaide Review*, no. 23, 1986.
145 L. Hercus & V. Potezny, 'Locating Aboriginal Sites: A Note on J. G. Reuther and the Hillier Map of 1904', *Records of the South Australian Museum*, vol. 24, no. 2, pp. 139–51.
146 Hercus & Clarke, 'Nine Simpson Desert-Wells'.
147 L. Hercus, 'Looking for Ditji-mingka', *Records of the South Australian Museum*, vol. 21, no. 2, 1987, pp. 149–56.

9 'A Scattered Homeless Flock'

1 Tampke & Doxford, pp. 185, 189.
2 H. Homburg, *South Australian Lutherans and Wartime Rumours*, privately printed booklet, Adelaide, 1947, South Australian Museum Archives.
3 Bogner Report, 23 July to 14 October, written to Mission Committee, 18 February 1915, Jericho Material.
4 Bogner Report to Mission Committee, 18 February 1915, Lutheran Archives.
5 ibid.
6 J. Praite & R. Praite, *German Place Names in South Australia*, privately printed, South Australia, 1989, Lutheran Archives; information taken from 'More Varieties of Vice Regal Life', *Journal of the Historical Society of South Australia*, no. 9, 1981.
7 Jericho, p. 49.
8 Bonython, p. 44.
9 Author's interview with Fred Vogelsang, Victor Harbour, South Australia, 20 March 1991.
10 Author's interview with Zainie Khan, Marree, 15 August 1991.
11 Robert Hall, 'The Black Diggers', *Sydney Morning Herald*, 10 March 1990, p. 74.
12 Author's interview with Ben Murray, 1983, 1985–86.
13 Bonython, p. 47.
14 'History of the Lutheran Church in Australia, 1830–1925', Lutheran Archives, AA:CA 948, AP308, 20418/5.
15 Letter from Bogner to Immanuel Synod Committee, 17 February 1920, Lutheran Archives, Bogner file.
16 Scherer, 'Mission Among the Diyari'.
17 Thomas Hebart, *History of the Evangelical Lutheran Mission in South Australia*, Mission Committee of the Evangelical Lutheran Immanuel Synod in South Australia, Adelaide, 1886, trans. from the German by Reidel, extract about Killalpaninna, South Australian Museum Archives.
18 Bonython, p. 53.
19 ibid., pp. 53–4.
20 Letters from Bogner to Mission Committee, 4 November 1923, 15 February 1926.
21 Letter from Aiston to South, Mungerannie Police Station, 18 December 1916, PRO, Adelaide, GRG 5/309/2.
22 Letter from Bogner to Aiston, 29 June 1917, PRO, Adelaide, GRG 5/2/1917/570.
23 Mant, 'Letters Recount the Death of a Tribe', p. 27.
24 Letter from Bogner to Aiston, 29 June 1917, PRO, Adelaide, GRG 5/2/2927/570.
25 Farwell, p. 164.
26 Mungerannie Police Station Report, 14 November 1918, Mungerannie Police Station Reports,

1913-23, PRO, Adelaide, GRG 5/309/2.
27 Philip Jones, 'Ngapamanha: A Case Study in the Population History of the North-East of South Australia', p. 167 (copy of paper given to me by the author).
28 ibid., p. 168, from H. Basedow, 'Report Upon the First Medical Relief Expedition Among the Aborigines of South Australia, pp. 68–71, PRO, Adelaide, MS GRG 23/1/1920/144.
29 Basedow's 1919 report, p. 32, lists of individuals, PRO, Adelaide, GRG series.
30 Jericho, p. 44.
31 Author's interview with Susie Kennedy, Marree, March 1991.
32 Farwell, p. 159.
33 Bonython, pp. 58–9.
34 ibid., pp. 59–60.
35 ibid., p. 62.
36 ibid., p. 70.
37 Author's interview with Fred Vogelsang, 20 March 1991.
38 Bonython, p. 70.
39 ibid., pp. 71–2.
40 ibid., pp. 73, 78–9.
41 ibid., p. 76.
42 Aiston's Report, 4 June 1923, Mungerannie Police Station Reports, 1913–23, PRO, Adelaide, GRG 5/309/2.
43 Bonython, p. 83.
44 Aiston's Report, 4 June 1923, Mungerannie Police Station Reports, 1913–23, PRO, Adelaide, GRG 5/309/2.
45 ibid.
46 ibid.
47 ibid.
48 Bonython, pp. 123–5.
49 ibid., p. 126.
50 ibid., p. 235.
51 Private material of Veronica Copeland (of the Schmidt–Vogelsang family), Waikerie, South Australia. Handwritten notes on 'Carl Gottlieb Schmidt' and typed notes of reminiscences of various members of the Schmidt family.
52 Jericho, p. 43.
53 Author's interview with Carl Paschke, Waikerie, 9 March 1991.
54 ibid.
55 ibid.
56 ibid.
57 Author saw this book in 1991, now in the possession of Dora Paschke, Waikerie, South Australia.
58 'How Mother and Father Vogelsang of the Bethesda Mission Traced God's Footsteps in Their Lives', booklet, Lutheran Archives.
59 Reidel's Reminiscences, p. 48.
60 Author's interview with Luise Schultz, Waikerie, South Australia, 8 March 1991.
61 ibid.
62 Proeve, *Three Missionary Pioneers*.
63 'Johannes Matthias Bogner', *Lutheran Herald*, 1930, p. 188, Lutheran Archives.
64 Proeve, *A Scattered Homeless Flock*, p. 21.
65 Report of Theodore Vogelsang, 'A Visit to the Former Mission Field of Bethesda and Vicinity in the Far North of South Australia, 19 September 1932, Jericho Material.
66 Scherer, 'Mission Among the Diyari', p. 2.
67 ibid., p. 3.
68 ibid.
69 Author's interview with Susie Kennedy, Marree, March 1991.
70 Report of Proeve, 'Scattered Like Sheep Which Have No Shepherd', 1 October 1934, Jericho Material.
71 ibid.
72 ibid.
73 ibid., p. 4. Proeve, *A Scattered Homeless Flock*, p. 23.

74 Report, 'Bethesda', 17 June 1935, and Report, 'From Bethesda Mission', 9 March 1936, Jericho Material.
75 Hermann Vogelsang, 'A Journey from Hermannsburg, Central Australia, Through the Former Bethesda Mission District, South Australia', Report, 11 December 1939, Jericho Material. See also Scherer, 'Mission Among the Diyari', p. 4, and Proeve, *A Scattered Homeless Flock*, p. 25.
76 'Again a Journey Into the District of the Former Bethesda Mission Station', Report, 23 August 1937, Jericho Material.
77 Proeve, *A Scattered Homeless Flock*.
78 'Notes on the Dieri Tribe of South Australia', *Royal Society of South Australia Transactions*, no. 63, 1939 p. 167.
79 Jones & Sutton, p. 75. See also 'Jericho Papers', Mortlock Library Archives, South Australia, PRG 355/6.
80 H. K. Fry, 'Dieri Legends', *Folk-lore*, vol. 48, 1937, pp. 87–206, 269–87.
81 Jones & Sutton, p. 23.
82 Schulz, p. 8.
83 Letter from Luise Schmidt, Low Bank, to Bertha Rohrlach, 9 August 1942, Jericho Material.
84 H. Gordon, *The Embarrassing Australians*, Landsdowne Press, Adelaide, 1962; Hall, *The Black Diggers*.
85 W. Reidel, *Lodges*, Lutheran Book Depot, North Adelaide, 1940, South Australian Museum.
86 Author's interview with Ben Murray, Port Augusta, 1986.
87 Proeve, *A Scattered Homeless Flock*, p. 44.
88 ibid., p. 43.
89 'An Echo of Bethesda', *Lutheran Herald*, 6 August 1949, Jericho Material.
90 Letter from Dorothea Paschke to 'Pastor' (E. H. Proeve?), 20 October 1947, Lutheran Archives.
91 Typed notes of letters, October 1945, Jericho Material.
92 ibid.
93 'Caring for the Dieri', typed notes signed E. H. Proeve, 23 January 1951, Lutheran Archives.
94 Typed notes of the sermon, Lutheran Archives.
95 E. H. Proeve, 'Another Visit to the Remnants of the Dieri Tribe', typed notes, 1956, Lutheran Archives.
96 Report of E. H. Proeve, 'Homeless Dieri', 1954(?), Lutheran Archives.
97 'Jack' Irrgang(?), 'Another Visit to the Dieri People', typed notes, 14 May 1958, Waikerie, Lutheran Archives.
98 Proeve, *A Scattered Homeless Flock*, p. 57.
99 Report of Proeve, 'Homeless Dieri'.
100 Proeve, 'Another Visit to the Remnants of the Dieri'.
101 Proeve, *A Scattered Homeless Flock*, p. 61.
102 E. H. Proeve, 'Visit to Leigh Creek and the Marree Area', typed notes, August 1964, Lutheran Archives.
103 G. Smallwood, 'Aboriginal Health by the Year 2000'.
104 *World Book Encyclopedias*, USA, 1981.
105 Helene Jericho, typed booklet, Jericho Material.
106 Letter from Helene Jericho to a sister, 20 August 1970, Jericho Material.
107 Author's interview with Fred Vogelsang, Victor Harbour, 20 March 1991.
108 Letter from Helene Jericho, September 1983, Jericho Material.
109 'Killalpaninna—Ben Murray Remembers', *The Lutheran*, 11 November 1985.
110 L. A. Hercus, 'Aboriginal People', in M. J. Tyler et al. (eds), *Natural History of the North-East Deserts*, Royal Society of South Australia, Adelaide, 1990, p. 159.
111 L. Hercus & P. Clarke, 'Nine Simpson Desert Wells', *Archeological Oceania*, vol. 21, 1986.
112 Author's interview with Susie Kennedy, Marree, March 1991.
113 Letter from Maria Tschirn to Helene Jericho, 23 October 1973, Jericho Material.
114 Fry, p. 193. L. Hercus, 'Looking for Ditji-Minka', *Records of the South Australian Museum*, vol. 21, no. 2, 1987, p. 150.
115 Hercus, 'Looking for Ditji-Minka'.
116 Mant, 'Letters Recount the Death of a Tribe'.

Bibliography

Lutheran Church and Mission Journals
Der Australische Christenbote (*DAC*): Journal published in German in Victoria.
Hermannsburger Missionsblatt (*HM*): Letters and reports written by the missionaries and the South Australian Mission Committee and published in German in the journal of the Hermannsburg Mission Institute, Germany, between 1866 and 1874.
Kirchen und Missionsblatt Zeitung (*KMZ*): Journal (predominantly known by this title), published in German at Tanunda, South Australia, and containing letters and reports from the missionaries and the South Australian Mission Committee.

Hermannsburg Mission Institute Archives
Handwritten letters from South Australia to headquarters in Germany.

Lutheran Church Archives, Adelaide
Uncatalogued material on Killalpaninna Mission held in boxes labelled 306.510. Includes handwritten letters in German from the South Australian Mission Committee to the various missionaries at Killalpaninna, and handwritten letters from the various missionaries to South Australian committee members and others.

Balance sheets and wages.
Bank books.
'Jack' Irrgang's handwritten notes.
Letters and reminiscences of trips to the 'remnants' of mission Aborigines between the 1930s and 1960s.
Letters written by Aboriginal pupils at the mission.
Missionary reports and mission correspondence of Siebert, Reuther, Reidel, Hillier, Wettengel, Hunt, Strehlow, Bogner, Homann, Goessling, Schoknecht.
Private letters.
Public Gazette of Land Leases for 1874.
Reidel's handwritten corpus of his translation of religious works into the Diyari language.
Reminiscences and notes.
Report of the Protocol of the Commission held at Bethesda, 1–9 June 1889.

Australian Almanac, 1934.
Flierl, J. *Dieri-Juanrana*, Adelaide, 1883 (reading book in the Diyari language for mission school pupils).
Hebart, Thomas. *History of the Evangelical Lutheran Mission in South Australia*, Mission Committee of South Australia, Adelaide, 1886.
'History of the Lutheran Church in Australia, 1830–1925', typed MS.
'How Mother and Father Vogelsang of the Bethesda Mission Traced God's Footsteps in their Lives', privately printed, South Australia, n.d.
'The Life of H. H. Vogelsang, Pioneer Missionary on the Coopers Creek', centenary paper, typed MS.
Jericho, Helene. *Down Memory Lane: Memoirs of Helene Jericho*, privately printed, South Australia, repr. 1983.

Love, J. R. 'A Visit to the Lutheran Mission Station at Killalpaninna, Coopers Creek, South Australia, 1911', handwritten notes.
'Timotheus Maltilinna', typescript notes trans. from German and from an account by Johannes Flierl.
'Mission Among the Diyarie: Looking Back on a Hundred Years', typescript MS.
Nitschke, A. *Memoirs*, pamphlet.
Praite, J. & Praite, R. *German Place Names in South Australia*, privately printed, South Australia, 1989.
Proeve, E. H. *A Scattered Homeless Flock: Mission Among the Dieri*, privately printed, South Australia, 1945.
Proeve, E. H. *Three Missionary Pioneers*, Auricht's Printing Office, Tanunda, 1946.
Proeve, E. H. & Proeve, H. F. W. *A Work of Love and Sacrifice*, pt 1, privately printed, South Australia, 1952.
Gustav Julius Rechner, 1830–1900, privately printed booklet.
Report of the Lutheran Mission at Kopperamanna, Coopers Creek in South Australia, from the Beginning in 1866 to the 31 December 1884, Scrymour & Sons, Adelaide, 1885.
Scherer, P. A. *A Venture of Faith*, Lutheran Printing House, Adelaide, 1963.

Newspaper Articles
Lutheran
'Aboriginal Mission in South Australia', 5 June 1967.
'Centenary of a Mission is Remembered', 19 September 1967.
'Donors of Aboriginal Heritage', 9 July 1979.
'Famous Seminary [Neuendettelsau] Closes its Doors', 30 September 1985.
'Helen of the North, 14 November 1983.
'Killalpaninna, Ben Murray Remembers', 11 November 1985.
'Memorial Service at Bethesda', 11 November 1985.

Lutheran Herald
'An Echo of Bethesda', 6 August 1949.
P. A. Scherer, 'Mission Among the Diyari (Dieri): Looking Back 100 Years, Bethesda Mission', 24 September 1966, 12 November 1966.

Clippings
'A Good Man Gone: Mr J. R. Reuther's Career', n.d.

South Australian Museum Archives, Adelaide
Killalpaninna material largely uncatalogued.

'A Brief Biography of Johann Georg Reuther, His Family and Work', typescript pamphlet.
Collection of postcards written in Diyari from mission Aboriginals and to mission Aboriginals.
'Diary of Reuther, 1888 to 1914', trans. from original German by R. D. Reuther (son), Nuriootpa, 1970.
Gason, Samuel. 'The Manners and Customs of the Dieyerie Tribe of Australia', 1879.
Hillier, H. Map of Aboriginal Settlement and Population Concentrations in the North-east of South Australia, 1904.
Homburg, H. *South Australian Lutherans and Wartime Rumours*, privately printed, Adelaide, 1947.
Howitt, A. W. 'On the Marriage Rules of the Australian Tribes', Report of the 9th Meeting of the Australasian Association for the Advancement of Science, 1902.
Howitt, A. W. & Siebert, O. 'Two Legends of the Lake Eyre Tribes', Report of the 9th Meeting of the Australasian Association for the Advancement of Science, 1902.
Letterbooks of Reidel and Kaibel.
Letters relating to the sale of Killalpaninna artefacts to the museum and elsewhere by Reuther.
Reidel, W. *Lodges*, Lutheran Book Depot, North Adelaide, 1940.
Reidel, W. 'Reminiscences', typed MS.
Reuther, J. G. & Strehlow, C. (trans.) *Testamenta Marra* (New Testament in Diyari), G. Auricht, Tanunda, 1897.
Schulz, J. F. W. *Destined to Perish? With Chevrolet to Hermannsburg*, Auricht's Printing Office, Tanunda, 1938.
Schoknecht, Carl. Diary and Autobiography.
South Australian Museum's 'toa collection' (artefacts made at the mission during Reuther's time as missionary) and correspondence relating to the debate over the authenticity of the toas.

Tindale, Norman. Correspondence regarding Reuther's MS (at AA 266/1539).
Tindale, Norman. Interview with O. Siebert, Germany, 1936.
Vogelsang, T. 'The Hearts of the Two Sons of the Muramura Darana', typed paper, n.d.

Public Record Office (PRO), Adelaide
Aboriginal Affairs material, GRG 52/1 series.
Aboriginal Health, GRG 2/13 and GRG 88/2.
Basedow, H. 'Report Upon the First Medical Relief Expedition Among the Aborigines of South Australia', GRG 23/1/1920/144.
Earliest reference to Aborigines' Protection Society, 960/33, vol. 5, p. 6.
First Protector of Aborigines, GRG 48/1 PG20.
Love, J. R. 'Sign Language of the Dieri Tribe, Coopers Creek, South Australia', GRG 214/3, series 3.
McKinlay's Diaries, GRG 24/203.
Police Journals for the Far North of South Australia, GRG 5 series.
Royal Commission on the Aborigines, *Final Report, Together with Minutes of Evidence and Appendices*, Government Printer, Adelaide, 1916.
Select Committee of the Legislative Council on the Aborigines' Bill, *Report, Together with Minutes of Proceedings*, Government Printer, Adelaide, 1899, Parliamentary Papers of South Australia, 1899, nos 77A, 77.

Mortlock Library, Adelaide
Cyclopedia of South Australia, 1907.
Jericho, Helen. Notes, PRG 355/H.

Newspaper Articles
Advertiser
20 February 1890 (Jacky's case).
29 April 1968.

Chronicle
'Bethesda Mission Centenary', 24 November 1966.
'Killalpaninna Mission', 28 January, 1965.
'Lake Killalpaninna Mission Ruins', 20 May 1965.
'Lost—An Old German Sword', 21 April 1966.
'The Pilgrim's Earthly Journey', 24 May 1972.
'Pioneer Days at Bethesda', 24 May 1974.

Observer
4 January 1890.
11 January 1890.
25 January 1890 (Jacky's case).

South Australian Register
16 December 1889.
17 December 1889.
7 May 1890 (Besley's report of 1889).

La Trobe University Library, Melbourne
Original MS of Schoknecht, trans. by his son in 1947.

Supreme Court Records, Adelaide
Transcripts for Port Augusta Circuit Court, Justice Samuel Way, 22 November 1888, p. 117.

Police Archives, Hindmarsh, South Australia (now defunct)
Material from the PRO GRG5 series of police correspondence and journals.

Australian Institute of Aboriginal and Torres Strait Islander Studies (AIATSIS) Archives, Canberra
Howitt Papers
    Box 6   Diyari Customs (Howitt).
    Box 8 (1)   Siebert Correspondence with Howitt.
Reports by Tindale on the Reuther MS to Director of the South Australian Museum, 1937.
Reuther's MS, vol. 10, 'Diari Religion: Myths and Legends', trans. from German to English by Rev. Philip Scherer, Tanunda, South Australia, 1975.
Baldwin, Rev. E. 'A Visit to a Lutheran Mission in South Australia', *Recorder-Sabbath School and Missionary Magazine of the Presbyterian Church of South Australia*, 1 October 1910, p. 15522.
Yashchenko, A. L. *Puteshestviye po Australii* (A Journey Through Australia, trans. M. Barratt), Moscow, 1959.

Interviews and Oral Histories
Interview with Susie Kennedy (née Merrick, the European version of Maltilinna), Marree, 16 March 1991.
Interview with Zainie Khan, who was employed as companion and domestic aid to Mrs Beryl Powell, Marree, 17 March 1991.
Interview with Ben Murray, Wami Cata, Port Augusta, South Australia, 30 March 1991.
Interview with Carl Pashke, Waikerie, 9 March 1991.
Interview with Pastor H. F. W. Proeve, Tanunda, 7 March 1991.
Interview with Luise Schulz, granddaughter of Hermann Vogelsang senior, Waikerie, South Australia, 8 March 1991.
Interview with Fred Vogelsang and Frieda Pascoe, son and daughter of Hermann Vogelsang junior, Victor Harbour, South Australia, 20 March 1991.

Private Material
Material lent by Veronica Copeland, Waikerie, South Australia.
Material of Helen Jericho (deceased), youngest daughter of Hermann Vogelsang senior, held by her family at Tumby Bay and Yeelanna, South Australia.
Handwritten notes lent by Brian and Kath Oldfield, Balhannah, South Australia (previously of Etadunna Station).
Typescript, Obituary of Luise Eleanor Schmidt (née Vogelsang), 1883–1969.

Journal Articles, Papers and Theses
Anderson, C. 'The Political and Economic Basis of Kuku-yalanji Social History', PhD thesis, Bloomfield Mission, Queensland, 1984.
Austin, P. 'Diyari Language Postcards and Diyari Literacy', *Aboriginal History*, vol. 10, 1986.
Austin, P., Hercus, L. & Jones, P. 'Ben Murray: Parlku-Nguyu-Thankayiwarna', *Aboriginal History*, no. 12, 1988.
Berndt, R. M. & Vogelsang, T. 'Notes on the Dieri Tribe of South Australia', *Royal Society of South Australia Transactions*, no. 63, 1939.
Blaess, E. J. H. 'Evangelical Lutheran Synod in Australia Inc. and Mission Work Amongst the Australian Natives in Connection with the Dresden (Leipzig) Lutheran Mission Society, 1838–1900', BD thesis, Concordia Seminary, St Louis, Missouri, 1941.
Boehmer, J. 'Die Südostaustralischen Dieri und Otto Siebert, *Anthropos*, no. 22, 1928.
Cane, C. & Gunson, N. 'Postcards: A Source for Aboriginal Biography', *Aboriginal History*, vol. 10, 1986.
Courto, V. 'The Tragical History of Dr Eylmann', BA (Hons) thesis, Australian National University, Canberra, 1991.
Dodd, R. & Gibson, J. 'Learning Times', *Aboriginal History*, vol. 13, 1990.
Elkin, A. P. 'Beliefs and Practices Concerned with Death in North-Eastern and Western South Australia', *Oceania*, vol. 7, 1937, pp. 275–99.
Elkin, A. P. 'Cult Totemism and Mythology in Northern South Australia', *Oceania*, vol. 5, 1934.
Elkin, A. P. 'Reaction and Interaction: A Food Gathering People and European Settlement in Australia', *American Anthropologist*, vol. 53, no. 2, 1951.
Ferguson, C. 'Literacy in a Hunting-Gathering Society: The Case of the Diyari', *Journal of Anthropological Research*, vol. 43, no. 3, 1987.
Fry, H. K. 'Dieri Legends', *Folklore*, no. 48, 1937.

Hartwig, M. 'The Progress of White Settlement in the Alice Springs District and its Effects Upon the Aboriginal Inhabitants, 1860–1894', 2 vols, PhD thesis, University of Adelaide, 1965.
Hassell, Kathleen. History of Port Lincoln, MS, Library Board of South Australia, Adelaide.
Hercus, L. 'Blanche Ned', (in press).
Hercus, L. 'Looking for Ditji-Mingka', *Records of the South Australian Museum*, vol. 21, no. 2, 1987.
Hercus, L. 'Ned Palpilinna, the Last Wadikali', (in press).
Hercus, L. 'A Pirlatapa Myth', (in press).
Hercus, L. & Clarke, P. 'Nine Simpson Desert Wells', *Oceania*, no. 21, 1986.
Hercus, L. & Potezny, V. 'Locating Aboriginal Sites: A Note on J. G. Reuther and the Hillier Map of 1904', *Records of the South Australian Museum*, vol. 24, no. 2, 1990.
Homann, Luise. 'Journal of a Life of Many Moves' typed MS, Adelaide, 1965.
Howitt, A. 'The Dieri and Other Kindred Tribes of Central Australia', *Journal of the Royal Anthropological Institute*, vol. 20, 1891.
Howitt, A. & Siebert, O. 'Legends of the Dieri and Kindred Tribes of Central Australia', *Journal of the Royal Anthropological Institute*, no. 34, 1904.
Howitt, A. & Siebert, O. 'Two Legends of the Lake Eyre Tribes', *Reports of the Australasian Association for the Advancement of Science*, vol. 9, 1902.
Howitt, M. E. B. 'Some Native Legends from Central Australia', *Folklore*, no. 13, 1902.
Jones, P. 'Ngapamanha: A Case Study in the Population History of Northern South Australia', in P. Austin et al., *Language and History: Essays in Honour of Luise A. Hercus*, Pacific Linguistics, Australian National University, Canberra, 1990, pp. 157–73.
Jones, P. 'Red Ochre Expeditions: An Ethnographic and Historical Analysis of Aboriginal Trade in the Lake Eyre Basin', *Journal of the Anthropological Society of South Australia*, vol. 22, no. 7, September 1984.
Lehmann, H. 'The South Australian Germans in the Second Half of the 19th Century: A Case of Rejected Assimilation', *Journal of Intercultural Studies*, vol. 2, 1981.
Mant, Gilbert. 'Letters Recount the Death of a Tribe', *South West Pacific*, no. 7, 17 April 1947.
Siebert, O. 'Legends and Customs of the Dieri and Neighbouring Tribes in Central Australia', *Globus*, vol. 97, no. 3, 20 January 1910. ('Sagen und Sitten der Dieri und Nachbarstamme in Zentral Australien', *Globus*, no. 47, 1916.)
Smallwood, Gracelyn. 'Aboriginal Health by the Year 2000', 'The Role of the Churches from an Indigenous Woman's Perspective', and 'Impact on Indigenous Women', conference papers for World AIDS Day, November 1990, James Cook University, Townsville, October and November 1990.
Veth, P., Hamm, G. & Lampert, R. 'The Archaeological Significance of the Lower Cooper Creek', *Records of the South Australian Museum*, vol. 24, no. 1, 1990.
von Leonhardi, Moritz. 'Der Mura and die Mura-Mura der Dieri', *Anthropos*, vol. 4, 1904.

Newspapers and Radio
Adelaide Review
'Exhibition of Toas from Killalpaninna', no. 23, 1986.

Sydney Morning Herald
Evans, B. 'Tribal Art Becomes Our Elgin Marbles' (from John McDonald, London), 14 July 1990.
Glover, R. & Langsam, D. 'Day of Reckoning for Darwin's Bodysnatchers', 3 March 1990.
Hall, R. 'The Black Diggers', 10 March 1990.
Hewitt, T. 'Aboriginal Remains From Abroad Receive Enthusiastic Welcome Home', 21 September 1990.
Hewitt, T. 'Back to His Land Still a Mystery', 22 June 1990.
'Time to Return Black Curios', 26 June 1990.

Weekend Australian
Rintoul, S. 'Mansell Wants Shiney's Head', 3–4 March 1990, 24–25 November 1990.

ABC Radio Newsbroadcast, 13 May 1992.

Books

Auricht, N. L., Munchenberg, R. S. & the Christian Auricht Reunion Committee. *From Persecution to Freedom: Christian Auricht and Descendants, 1806–1980*, Lutheran Printing House, Adelaide, 1980.

Austin, P. *A Grammar of Diyari, South Australia*, Cambridge University Press, Cambridge, 1981.

Berndt, R. M. *Australian Aboriginal Anthropology: Modern Studies in the Social Anthropology of the Australian Aborigines*, University of Western Australia Press, Perth, 1970.

Berndt, R. M. Aboriginal Religion, fascicle 1, 1974.

Berndt, R. M. *Australian Aboriginal Religion*, E. J. Brill, Leiden, 1974.

Berndt, R. M. *From Black to White in South Australia*, Cheshire, Melbourne, 1951.

Berndt, R. M. & Berndt, C. *The World of the First Australians*, Rigby, Adelaide, 1985.

Berndt, R. M. & Berndt, C. (eds). *Aboriginal Man in Australia: Essays in Honour of A. P. Elkin*, Angus & Robertson, Sydney, 1965.

Bonython, E. *Where the Seasons Come and Go*, Gillingham Press, Adelaide, 1971.

Bradman, F. J., Arnold, B. K. & Bell, S. L. (eds). *A Natural History of the Lake Eyre Region*, South Australian National Parks and Wildlife Service, Adelaide, 1991.

Brauer, A. *The One Hundreth Anniversary of the Arrival of the Lutheran Pilgrim Fathers and the Establishment of the Lutheran Church in Australia*, Lutheran Printing House, Adelaide, 1938.

Brock, Peggy (ed.). *Women's Rites and Sites: Aboriginal Cultural Knowledge*, Allen & Unwin, Sydney, 1989.

Brough Smyth, R. *The Aborigines of Victoria*, vol. 2, Government Printer, Melbourne, 1878.

Elkin, A. P. *The Australian Aborigines*, 2nd edn, Angus & Robertson, Sydney, 1943.

Eylmann, Dr Erhard. *Die Eingeborenen der Kolonie Südaustralien* (Aborigines of the Colony of South Australia), Dietrich Reimer, Berlin, 1908.

Farwell, G. *Land of Mirage*, Rigby, Adelaide, repr. 1971.

Farwell, G. *Traveller's Tracks*, Melbourne University Press, Melbourne, 1949.

Flierl, J. *Dreissig Jahre Missionsarbeit in Wüsten und Wildnissen*, (Thiry Years Mission Work in Deserts and Wilderness), Germany, 1910.

Gordan, Harry. *The Embarrassing Australians*, Landsdowne, Adelaide 1962.

Gregory, J. W. *The Dead Heart of Australia*, John Murray, London, 1906.

Gribble, J. B. *Dark Deeds in A Sunny Land, or Blacks and Whites in NW Australia*, University of Western Australia Press, Perth, repr. 1987.

Haccius, Georg. *Hannnoversche Missionsgeschichte*, 3 vols, Missionshandlung Hermannsburg, Hanover, (1905), 1909–20.

Hall, R. *The Black Diggers*, Allen & Unwin, Sydney, 1989.

Hardy, O. *Like A Bird On The Wing*, Lutheran Publishing House, Adelaide, 1984.

Hercus, L. & Sutton, P. (eds). *This is What Happened*, AIATSIS, Canberra, 1986.

Horne, G. & Aiston, G. *Savage Life in Central Australia*, Macmillan, London, 1924.

Howitt, A. *The Native Tribes of South-East Australia*, Macmillan, London, 1904.

Isaacs, J. *Australian Dreaming; 40,000 Years of Aboriginal History*, Landsdowne, Sydney, 1986.

Jones, P. & Sutton, P. *Art and Land*, South Australian Museum, with Wakefield Press, Adelaide, 1986.

Leigh, W. H. *Travels and Adventures in South Australia, 1836–1838*, Elder Smith & Co., London, 1839.

Leske, Everard (ed.). *Hermannsburg: A Vision and A Mission*, Lutheran Publishing House, Adelaide, 1977.

Lyng, J. *Non-Britishers in Australia: Influence on Population and Progress*, Melbourne University Press, Melbourne, 1935.

Marrett, R. R. & Penniman, T. K. (eds). *Spencer's Scientific Correspondence*, Clarendon Press, Oxford, 1932.

Mattingly, Christobel & Hampton, Ken (eds). *Survival in Our Own Land: Aboriginal Experiences in South Australia Since 1836*, Wakefield Press, Adelaide, 1988.

Pike, D. *Paradise of Dissent: South Australia, 1829–1857*, Melbourne University Press, Melbourne, 1967.

Reynolds, Henry. *The Other Side of the Frontier*, Penguin, Ringwood, 1990.

Rowley, Charles. *The Destruction of Aboriginal Society*, Penguin, Ringwood, 1986.

Serventy, Vincent. *The Desert Sea: The Miracle of Lake Eyre*, Macmillan, South Melbourne, 1985.

Spencer, B. & Gillen, F. *Native Tribes of Central Australia*, Macmillan, London, 1899.

Stevens, Christine, *Tin Mosques and Ghantowns*, Oxford University Press, Melbourne, 1989.

Swain, T. *Interpreting Aboriginal Religion: An Historical Account*, Australian Association for the Study of Religions, Adelaide, 1985.

Tampke, J. & Doxford, C. *Australia, Willkommen*, New South Wales University Press, Sydney, 1990.

Tolcher, H. M. *Drought and Deluge: Man in the Coopers Creek Region*, Melbourne University Press, Melbourne, 1986.

Tyler, M. J., Twidale, C. R., Davies, M. & Wells, C. B. (eds). *Natural History of the North East Deserts*, Royal Society of South Australia, Adelaide, 1990.

Walker, Mary Howitt. *Come Wind, Come Weather: A Biography of Alfred Howitt*, Melbourne University Press, 1971.

Index

Aboriginal
   artefacts 219, 222, 228, 229
   choir 126, 154
   culture 1, 15
   customs still practised 260
   deprivation by Lutherans 5
   elders (*see also* pinaru) 29, 38, 52, 62, 63
      assisting New Testament translating 209, 217
      death of last Diyari 263
      as informants 218, 227
      suspicion of 218, 219, 238
   evangelists 254
   genocide (*see also* genocide) 1, 2, 3
   girls abducted 250
   graves at Killalpaninna 264
   law and European law 126, 181
   polygyny 203
   population 190
      Lake Eyre Basin 22
   religion 263
      nineteenth-century theories of 214, 225
   resistance at Lake Hope 16
   soaks 134, 151–2
   uprising planned 125
   weddings 95–7, 108, 167, 185, 207
Aboriginal Reserve 55, 56, 57, 60
   advocated by Hermann Vogelsang (junior) 231
   Aiston argued for 243, 244
   on Elim Mission Station 115
   at Hermannsburg 142
   at Killalpaninna (AL145) 119, 133, 166, 200–1, 236, 237, 244
   at Kopperamanna 190
   land at South Australia 201
   mission reserve 74
   Reservation (Davenport) 261, 262
   travelled by Siebert 144

Aborigines
   abandon reliance 189
   and absolution 184
   as artefacts 158, 221–2, 223, 228
   Bill 201
   demand higher wages 187
   desert, last emerging 177
   dispossessed 10, 43, 119, 120, 266
   dying out 110, 118, 119, 159, 165, 177, 190, 191, 203, 208, 219, 243
   enlisting in First World War 235
   ex-Killalpaninna 231, 232, 233, 234, 237, 239, 240–3, 245, 246, 248, 249–53, **250**, **253**, 256–62, 263
   and fossil trees 219
   landless 88, 112
   'laziness' 92, 94, 207
   literate 202–3
   mission 64, 67, 80, 101, 121, 122, 123, 125, 128, 154–8, 164, 168, **171**, 176, 179, 182, 184, 190, 219
   traditional ceremonies 168, 180, 182, 184
   nineteenth-century theories about 213–14, 216, 223, 225
   as 'parasites' 112
   polarised over informants 218
   in Queensland 108, 114, 134
   released to camp life 231
   traditional housing of **21**
   unskilled or unemployed 197
Adelaide Mission 13, 14
Afghans 48, 102, 136, 154, 157, 190, 241
   gambling 177
   mission cartage 141, 189
   Moosha Balooch 235
Aiston, George 192, 238, 242, 243, 244, 251, 253
alcohol 50, 252, 263
   and Aborigines 121, 132

Bogner, Johannes 235
  exchanged in prostitution 178–9
  Flierl the Second 130, 131, 132
  forbidden on mission leases 176, 178
  Maltilinna, Timotheus, son of 245–6
  Meyer, Carl 132, 160
  white labourers 135
Allallinna, Lake (*see also* Ngarlangarlani, Lake) 238
  site of Storm History 123, 182
Allo Allanenni, Lake 57
Altlutherans 2, 5, 81, 82
  connections with Hermannsburg (Germany) 142
  emigration of 6, 11
Andreas (Aboriginal evangelist) 254
Angus, George Fife 6, 7, 13,
Aranda 225
  artefacts 229
  at Hermannsburg 143
  hymns into 144
  Spencer and Gillen, and 220
Augsburg Confession 4, 16
Auricht, Anna Maria 84, **9**, **85**
Auricht, Johann Christian (Pastor) 15, 45, 84, 102, 170
Auricht, J. E. **9**
Auricht, Luise 102
Australian Mission Friends' Society 90

baptism 61, 63, 69, 73, 94, 108, 111, 114, 126, 209, 210
  of babies of Aboriginal couples 112
  ceremonies 112, **155**, 185–6
  of first Aborigines 84, 90, 206
  as initiation before weddings 108, 146
  last adult baptismal ceremony **183**, 187
  of Anna Maltilinna 107
Barossa
  and Aborigines 99, 100–1
  lease of land 10
  Lutherans 58, 74
  valley 11, 45, 46, 148, 170
Basedow, Herbert 239
Beltana 47, 71, 87
  Pastoral Company 133
  Station 188
Bengalee 6, 7
Berlin 5, 11, 114
  cattle station 110
  museum 194, 226, 227, 229
Berndt, Ronald 30, 35, 255
Bertha 239, 242, 250, 253, 254, 256
Bethesda (Killalpaninna Mission) 90, 101, 102, 110, 114, 140, 168, 174, 190, 197, 254
Bethesda Mission Society 249, 252, 253, 257
Bible 49, 62, 166

classes at Kopperamanna 177
English 90, 206, 262
Luther and 3, 4
stories 86, 92, 111, 186, 209, 212, **208**
Biblical first names 86, 90, 108, 112, 143, 186, 239
Biggs, J. H. 82
Birdsville 101, 108, 110, 132, 136, 242, 262
Birdsville Track 17, 84, 101, 121, 132–3, 192, 234, 239, 242, 254, 258, 260, 264
Blanchewater 55
Blazes Well 188, 239, 263
Bloomfield Mission Station (*see also* Elim Mission Station) 115, 132, 140
Bogner, Johannes 146, 159, 166, 167, 168, **169**, 196, 222, 232, 233, 235, 240
  biography 165
  at Bloomfield 142
  death of 249
  of Susanne 168–9
  debts owed 236, 237
  at Hermannsburg 142, 146, 166
  interviewed by commissioners 191, 199, 213,
  as missionary 164–5, 166, 167, 168, 192, 199, 245
  purchase of mission leases 199, 233
  and Reuther 160
  sale of Killalpaninna 237
  sick wife 159, 165–6, 235
  as stock station manager 146, 159, **161**, 164, 197–8, 199
  visiting pastor, Murray River 248
Bogner, Maria (née Goetz) 165–6, **169**
'bone pointing' 36, 180, 182, 184, 219, 237, 243–4
  illness of Sambo 168
  victim of 94
Boucaut, J. P. 74
Bremen 59
Bucaltaninna, Lake 72, 83, 89
Bucaltaninna Station 55, 56, 61, 115, 150, 204, 241
  Aborigines 90
  as mission 71, 72, 73, 74, 75, 76, 79, 80, 82, 83, 84, 87, 89, 90
  school 207
buildings
  and Aborigines 1
  at Bucaltaninna 80, 206
  built by Jacob 86, 139
  first mission 60, 64, 65, 72, 111
  new, at Killalpaninna 88, 90, **91**, 95, 143, 150
  Reuther house, additions to 150
Burke and Wills 15, 16, 50, 51, 119, 204, 215
Buttfield, John 48, 50, 51, 55, 56, 106, 215

Callabona Lake 29, 220
Calvinist 4, 142
camels 48, 84, 102, 136, 154, 157, 229, 235,
    249, 251, 254
  mission cartage 141, **189–90**
Cannatulkaninna Station ('Wireyard')
    163, 189, 190, 251, 252
Cannuwankaninna Bore 235, 244
Cape Bedford 114, 115
Carlsruhe 74
catechism 90, 92
Catharina 6, 7, 10
Catholic
  Luther as 3
  opposition to Luther 4
  wars with Protestants 4
cattle 50, 72, 75, 82, 87, 140
  drives from Hermannsburg 140, 165, 166,
    167, 196
  during drought 87, 110, 132
  Kidman's 136
  Killalpaninna as station 231
  at Kopperamanna 133, 134, 137
  to stock markets 101
ceremonies (*see also* corroboree and
    ritual) 33, **34**, **124**, 167
  Diyari 22, 216
  forbidden by missionaries 122
  for increase rites 35, 219
  near Kopperamanna 240, 252
  Lutheran, pre-breakfast 92
  Mindari (*see also* Mindari) 33
  mission Aborigines engaging in 94, 123
  mudlugga 224, **225**
  rain-making 28, 35
  secret 42
  women's 42
children
  Aboriginal 6, 65, 119, 122, 151, 156–7,
    175, 176, 251
    of Aboriginal Christian couples 112
    after sale of mission station 233
    removed 179
  births, German 62, 66, 67, 69
  deaths, German 65, 67, 69
  Diyari 19, 37, 41, 42, 43, 61, 85
  German 67, 151, 153, 156–7
    at Murray River 248
  of Elizabeth Irrgang 84
  of Lutherans in Germany 5, 6
  part Aboriginal 112, 160, 162, 163
  of Powells 240, 244
  of Pauline Reuther 116, 148–50
  of Vogelsangs 148, 154–5, 231, 245
  of Luise Wendland 58
chiliasm 12, 16
Christ, Jesus 2, 3, 5, 12 ,112, 138, 167, 238,
    252, 258, 260

in death of Simeon 112
as kunkie 122
in pinya rituals 94
Christmas 146, 147, 152, 178, 185
  Day, Lake Hope 16
  Eve 119, 168–9
  for ex-Killalpaninna Aborigines 231, 236,
    241, 242, 256, 257, 258
  first for missionaries 49, 50, 67, 69
  at Killalpaninna 185
  tree 185, 241
Church
  Aboriginal weddings in 108
  bell tower 98, 101, 116, 147, 172, 177
  Catholic 3
  Communion Sundays at 137, 139, 155
  graveyard 240, 244
  at Hahndorf 8
  at Killalpaninna 62, 91, 92, 94, **97**, 98, 126,
    150, 207, 245, 258
  Lutheran, in South Australia 12, 14
  at Low Bank 249
  mission Aborigines in 126
  new church 176, 192–3, 240
  paper 11, 15, 16, 73, 174
  polity 12
  Prussian Calvinist 5
  remains of, at Mungerannie 253
  services
    Aboriginal attendance at 67
    after sale of mission 232, 233
    burial of Susanne 168–9
    conducted by Hermann Vogelsang
      (junior) 167
    last, old 176
    no services in 162, 241
  at Tanunda 15
  use of 'neyi' as Elders of 115
  Wittenberg 3
circumcision 29, 167, 216–17, 218
citizenship
  for Aborigines 232
  for German settlers 8
conversion 98, 159, 207
converts
  Aboriginal 61, 94, 98, 112, 114, 116, 167,
    173
  potential Christian 74
Cook, James 1
Cooktown 114, 165
Coondambo Station 106
Coongy Station 242
Coopers Creek
  Aborigines 16, 17, 19, 22, 29, 31, 50, 106,
    119, 202, 215
  Basin 264
  flooding of 98, 121, 134, 136, 139, 140,
    150, 258

Cooraninna Bore 242
corroboree (*see also* ceremonies and rituals)
   grand 24, 30, 35
   grounds, Lake Perigundi 17
   intertribal 53, 54, 67
   at Killalpaninna 165
   large, (uprising) 125
country (*see also* land)
   Aboriginal knowledge of 83
   Australian, familiar to Jacob 82
   as described by Flierl the First 115
   desolate 87
   Diyari defend own 56
   explored by Burke and Wills 16
   at Lake Hope 16
   nature of, (Central Australia) 73
   wild, near Hahndorf 10
creation period (*see also* Dreaming) 25, 27, 29, 31, 263

Darana (muramura), myth of 27, 28, 238, 263, 264
dara-ula 28, 35, 263, 264
dargun 68
Darwin, Charles
   theories of 158, 203, 214, 223, 224
Dean, Henry 16, 53
death
   black deaths at Killalpaninna 65, 66, 168, 190, 250
   Christian hope in 2
   Diyari
      belief in 27, 28, 31, 32, 36, 38
      bone pointing 36
      infanticide (*see also* children) 42, 67, 216
      of last elder 263
   of Frieda, mother of part-Aboriginal child linked to Reuther 162, 163
   of German children (*see* children)
   of old Joseph's daughter 184
   of H. H. Kempe's wife 142-3
   of Wilhelm Koch 65
   of Timotheus Maltilinna (Merrick) 245
   mourning cap **37**, 243
   of Paulus 184, 191
   of Pingilinna's wife 115
   of Maria Pingilinna 122
   reprisals at Lake Hope 17
   ritual state of 29-30
   of baby George Edwin Reuther 150
   sentence for ringleader of pinya 128, 168
   of Susanne 168-9
   of Paulus Tarilinna 180
   of Dorothea Vogelsang 76
   of Hermann Vogelsang (senior) 192-4
Debney, George 70
de-Pierre Brothers 163, 190, 251

desert 2, 5, 49, 83, 101, 137
   culture 2
   German initiation into 48
   people 21
   survival skills, Aborigines 88
   wilderness 52, 67, 170, 260-1
Devana, Ulius 259
Devil (Satan) 63, 85, 97, 99, 160, 189,
   kutchie as 215
Diamentina River
   Aborigines at 102, 108, 110
Dicky 186-7, 212, 239
Dintibana, Samuel 255, 262, 263
diprotodont 29, 220, 222
disease (*see also* illness) 22, 35, 72
   European 191, 203,
   local Aboriginal 36, 50
   on *Skiold* 11
dispossession
   of Aborigines (*see* Aborigines)
   of German immigrants 46
Ditji-mingka (Sun Ancestor, cave of) 263
Diyari
   Aborigines 2, 3, 7
   attempt to oust strangers 53
   at Bucaltaninna 90
   country 17, 24
   dependence on mission 3
   dictionary 159, 204, 205
   feuds 38
   first encounter with Flierl (senior) 88
   head men 22
   interest in, by Europeans 118
   at Lake Hope 16
   language speakers (1990s) 203
   law and customs 24, 26, 36, 40-1, 42, 63, 212
   neighbouring tribes of 22
   patrilocal clans 22, 26, 39
   publications on culture 255
   religious life 26, 28, 29, 31
   translations, vocabularies, grammars 203, 204
   tribal divisions 12
Doecke, Bruno 258
donations
   from Aborigines 177, 194
   appeal to South Australian government for grant 198-9
   Bogner request for 233
   from Germany 102, 114, 141, 196, 197
   from Lutherans in South Australia 114, 141, 196, 197
   for mission 82, 98, 187
   for new church 176, 177
Dreaming (*see also* creation period, Mura)
   association of Henry Tipilanna to Flierl (senior) 100

formation and evolution 26
origin of languages 22
tracks 26, 27, 32, 38
women in the 42
Droegemueller 79–80
drought 42, 50, 52, 53, 60, 61, 64, 65, 66, 67, 68, 69, 70, 71, 83, 140, 146, 147, 151, 152, 159, 165, 183, 188, 196–7, 204, 206, 233, 241, 242, 244, 250, 260
  in Central Australia 140
  Darana myth of 27, 28
  food handouts during 114
  at Lake Hope 16
  repeated 132
  starvation due to 21
Dulkilinna, Benjamin 106, 107
Duvel, Magdalene 57, 59, 65

Ebenezer Mission Station 50
Edwards, Alec 242, 256, 258, 262
Edwards, Katarina 239, 242, 250, 253, 254, 256, 258, 259, 262
Elder, Thomas 16, 47, 48, 56, 82
  lease of Kopperamanna Bore 133
Elim Mission Station (*see also* Bloomfield Mission Station) 114
emigration
  of Altlutherans 2, 6
  of Europeans to Australia 1
  German immigrants 10
  Prussian right of 6
  Skiold Lutherans 11, 12
Emu (*see also* Mindari)
  ancestral (Kuringii) 31, 32, 33
  feathers 30, 36, 39, 46
Enchilina, Joseph 102, 103
Encounter Bay 13, 14
Etadunna Station 131, 156, 190, 235, 264
  Cave of Ditji-mingka 263
  Jacob's house at **139**
  outstation **133**, 138, 166, 258
  shearing season at 134
  waterhole 86
Eucharist (Lord's Supper/Holy Communion) 5, 73, 184,
  banning, by Kavel 11
  Lutheran interpretation of 3, 4, 5
  pinya parallels 38, 94
  refusal to attend 130
European Station Workers 97, 128, 134, 136, 139
  'immoral' activities and violence by 160
  paranoia over 121, **135**, 197
  sexual relations 116, 120, 130, 162, 178
  wages for 136
Evangelical Lutheran Church of Australia (ELCA or Immanuel Synod)
  forming of 12, 15, 16, 72, 73, 74, 75, 79, 87, 140, 147, 157, 170, 196, 199, 200, 205, 236, 237
  mission committee 75, 115, 130, 143, 160, 164, 165, 168, 232, 236, 237,
  clash with Reidel 165, 170, 172, 176, 195
  complaints to 131
  letter from Aborigines 100, 207–8
  published translations 205
  purchase of Hermannsburg 142–3, 150
  Reuther rumours 160, 162–3
  tighter control 174, 195
  visit to Killalpaninna 101, 131, 146, 158, 207
Eylmann, Erhard 227
  collection of artefacts 229
  visit to Killalpaninna 222
Eyre, Lake
  Aborigines 203, 218, 224, 230, 238
  Basin 19, 22, 24, 33, 42, 112, 190, 218
  map of country east of (Reuther–Hillier Map) 143
  region 222, 229

Farina (Government Gums) 88
  railhead 101, 136
  hotel at 102
Farwell, George 76
Finke River 74, 80, 140
  Mission (Hermannsburg) 165
  board 249, 252, 254, 255, 258
Finniss, Colonel Boyle Travers 10
Finniss Springs Mission Station 256, 258, 260, **261**
First World War 165, 199, 231, 232, 234, 235, 236, 239, 255
Flierl, Emilie (née Gallasche) 112, **113**, 125, 126, 147, 149
Flierl (the First), Johannes 84, 87, **95**, 99, 101, 105, 108, 111, 112, 114, 148, 233, 239, 259
  on Aborigines 88, 89, 92, 99–100, 216–17
  arrival at Bucaltaninna 90, 206
  arrival at Killapaninna 92, 94, 97, 98, 106
  first journey 98, 99
  house built 102, **105**
  as linguist 207
  marriage of 102, 103, 104
  to New Guinea 114–15
  second journey 105, 106, 107, 108, 109, 110
  son of 236
  third journey 112
Flierl (the Second), John 110, 112, **113**, 114, 116, 120, 122, 123, 126, 128, **129**, 150, 160, 184
  and Aboriginal customs 110–11, 121, 123, 125, 217

dismissal 130, 131, 132, 142
  on Diyari language 205
  as missionary and stock station manager 115, 128
Flierl, Luise (née Auricht) 102, 103, 104
Flinders Ranges 22, 31, 48, 76, 79, 81
  red ochre collecting 178
flooding 19, 52, 83, 98, 106–7, 134, 147
  of Coopers Creek 121, 136, 139, 150, 165, 187, 258,
  dependence of mission enterprise 140
  ferry service 121
  Reuther's death 194
food
  Aboriginal
    during mourning 37
    knowledge of 10
    gathering rights 22, 24
    handouts from stations 112
    increase rites for 29
    lack of 177
  Diyari 19, **41**, 56, 60, 64, 88–9
  of ex-Killalpaninna Aborigines 238, 250
  German, as pacification 14, 60
    dependence on stock 70
    diet 61, 152
    grown at mission stations 152
    supplied to Aborigines 43
    supplies 81–2
  mission Aborigines
    diet 179–80
    as part payment 180
  native
    after floodings 107, 112, 134, 165
    at Bucaltaninna 84
    at Killalpaninna 90, 107, 112, 134, 165
    scarce 43, 84, 88, 94, 114
  of semi-traditional Aborigines 238
Frederick the Great 4
Fritzsche, Gotthard Daniel 11, 12, 14, 15, 16, 82

Gason, Samuel
  on Diyari language and customs 203–4, 215, 217
  at Lake Hope 28, 35, 43, 50, 52, 55, 215
Gawler, Governor 13
genocide
  Aboriginal 1, 2, 3, 17, 71, 88
  culture 17, 88
German
  anti-German feeling (First World War) 232, 234, 235, 255, 256
  community, Barossa Valley 45, 58
  families to Murray River 245, 248
  fiancées 57
  language (*see also* language) 13
  missionaries in New Guinea 114

names for Aranda people 143
names for Killalpaninna Aborigines 186, 239
wedding 170
German Settlement
  at Barossa 11
  at Hahndorf 8, 10
  at Glen Osmond 7, 10
  at Klemzig 7
  at Tanunda (Langmeil) 11
Giles, Ernest 73–4
Gillen, Frank
  with Spencer 220–1, 223, 226, 227
goats
  at Killalpaninna 94, 134
  at Kopperamanna 134
  products at mission station 151, 152
  shepherding of 135
Goessling, Johann F. 45, 46, 47, 48, 50, 52, 53, 56, 57, 58, 59, 68
Gospel (*see also* New Testament) 3, 12, 17, 46, 55
  need to translate 209
  preaching of 15
Gosse, William 73, 74
Goyder, G. W. 57, 74
Great Artesian Basin 61, 101
  wells 101, 132
Great Stony Desert 110
Gregory, Professor 218–19, 222
Gumvale 163, 194, 229
Gustav 138

Hack, Bedford 61
Hahn, Dirk Meinert 7, 8
Hahndorf 8, 10, 12, 72
Hamburg 6, 11, 12
Hamilton, George 55, 56
Harms, Egmont 142
Harms, Ludwig 15, 16, 69, 77–8, 79
  language policy 203
Harms, Theodore 16, 49, 52, 56, 57, 58, 59, 72, 73, 74, 75, 77
health
  of Johannes Bogner's wife 165
  of Carl Meyer 84
  of missionaries 64
  of Johann Georg Reuther 118, 141, 162–3
  of Luise Wendland 58
heaven 63, 205
Heidenreich (Pastor) 50, 80
  president of UELCA 142
  purchase and sale of Hermannsburg 142
Heistermann, Wilhelmina (Dorothea) 57, **58**
hell 27, 62, 63, 205, 238
Hellmuth 50

Herbert River 108, 110
Hercus, Dr Luise 263
Hermannsburg at Lake Killalpaninna 52
Hermannsburg Mission Institute, Germany 15, 45, 49, 56, 58, 62, 68, 69, 71, 73, 74, 75, 77, 80
    connections severed by UELCA 142
    missionaries 19
    Mission Board 77
    mission fields 81
Hermannsburg ('New Hermannsburg'), Central Australia
    Aboriginal children 123
    Aboriginal wages 188–9
    Aborigines reverting to own culture 143
    accusations at 198
    Bogner at 142
    cattle drives 140
    income donated to 140
    missionaries
        ill 142–3
        rivalry with Spencer and Gillen 220
    purchased by Immanuel Synod 142–3
    ration depot 106
    scurvy deaths at 152
    sold by UELCA 142
    Strehlow at 118
    visit from Kaibel 141
Hermannsburger Missionsblatt 52
Herrgott Springs (Marree) 101, 111, 118, 131, 136, 140, 150, 154, 155, 172, 195, 234
    to Birdsville mailcoach 137
    bore 132
    railhead 138, 229
Hester, Jack 84
Hillier, Henry ('Harry')
    as artist 143, 229
    collection of artefacts 222, 229
    at Hermannsburg 143, 144
    at Killalpaninna 143, 208, 209
    Reuther–Hillier Map 143, 229
    translator into Aranda 144, 147
Homann, Elizabeth 62, 67
Homann, Ernst 45, **47**, 50, **51**, 53, 55, 56, 58, 60, 61, 62, 63, 64, 65, 66, 67, 68, 69, 71
    on Diyari culture 216
    Diyari dictionary 205
    on language learning 203–4, 205
    translations into Diyari 205, 206
Homann, Luise 59, 61, 65, 67, 241
Hookina 67, 76, 79
Hope, Lake 16, 22, 27, 28, 50, 51, 52, 55, 56, 73, 106, 187, 215
    Station 48, 49, 53
    survey beyond 98
Horn Scientific Expedition 220
Horrocks, John 46
Howitt, Alfred 16, 17, 30, 31, 35, 215, 119, 224
    on the Diyari 19, 20, 204, 215
    collaboration with Siebert 223–4, 225
    correspondence with Reuther 224
    as ethnographer–anthropologist 158, 215, 223, 224
    opposed to Reuther 225, 226, 227
Howitt's Depot 51
Hughes, Billy 234
Hunt, William 147, 208, 209

illness (*see also* disease)
    of Aborigines 65, 92, 111, 119, 128, 144, 191, 172, 180, 239
    of ex-Killalpaninna Aborigines 243
    of Germans 65, 68, 75, 76, 107, 154, 192
    of Hermannsburg (Central Australia) missionaries 142
    influenza epidemic 112, 184, 239
    medical treatment at Killalpaninna 122
    of Maria Pingilinna 122
    as relief, for mission Aborigines 126
    typhoid 153, 239
    venereal disease 184, 191, 239, 250, 262
infanticide 42, 67, 216
initiation 22, 26, 29–31, 40, 237
    of baptism 186
    ceremony 260
    mission Aborigines undergoing 94
    of Spencer and Gillen 220
    rites, Wangkangurru 98
Innaminka 31, 35, 51, 238, 242
Irrgang, Elizabeth 84, **85**
Irrgang, Johannes Gustav ('Jack') 84, **85**, 150, 231, 259, **261**
    cattle drives 140, 166
    on church organ 126
    as dentist 154
    as manager at Etadunna **133**, 166, 196, 211
    in Murray River area 249

Jacob, Elizabeth 84, 140, 147, 148, 155, 102, 249
    at Tanunda **248**, 249
Jacob, Johann Ernst 45, **47**, 155, 160, 189, 259
    accusations against Flierl the Second 132
    biography 81
    death of 164, 192
    as Diyari speaker 81
    as English speaker 81
    at Etadunna **133**, 138, 139
    house of 139
    as manager of shepherds 85, 86, **93**
    marriage of 84, **85**
    as sheep station manager 90, 128
    taking 'confessions' 168
    as teamster 60, 61, 65, 71, 73, 75, 79, 81–2, 84, 88, 264

wages of 136
Jaensch, Johannes Gottlieb 199–200, 233, 235
Jammilli 54
Jerkinna Cave 31, 33
Johannes (evangelist) 239, 254
Joseph ('old Joseph' Ngantjalina) **181**, 183, 187, 212, 239
  child of 184
  death of 252
  proselytised for Reidel 174, 184
  as Reuther's informant 218
Justice of the Peace 55, 70, 118, 178

Kaibel, Ludwig
  death of 236
  interviewed by commissioners 191
  president, mission committee 141, 177, 189, 198, 199, 200–1, 211
  and Reidel 170, 195, 196, 198
  and Reuther rumours 160, 162
  salary of 188
  visit to Hermannsburg 141
  visit to Killalpaninna 141, 190
Kandrimoku, Lake 27
Kardimarkara 29, 35
Kavel, August Ludwig (Pastor) 6, 7, 10, 11, 12, 13, 15, 16
Kempe, H. H. 80
Kennedy, Susie (née Maltilinna/Merrick) 239, 240, **251**, 252, 262, 263
Kidman, Sidney 136
Killalpaninna, Lake 17, 19, 22, 27, 35, 52, 53, 57, 59, 66, 69, 70, 71, 72, 73, 104, 140, **156**, 215, 223
  flooding of 106, 134, 147, 165, 264
  move back to 84, 88, 90
Killalpaninna Mission Station 2, 3, 54, 55, 59, 60, 61, **63**, 65, 67, 68, 69, 71, 72, 74, 79, 80, 102, 104, 105, 115, **127**, 155, 170, 188, 191, 199
  Aborigines
    1890s 119
    largest concentration of at 112
  Bogner at 142, 164, 166, 167, 168
  as cattle station 165, 231
  closure of as mission station 231
  as a community 111
  conditions of sale 232
  medical treatment at 154
  missionaries
    contribution of 264
    as translators and ethnographers 202, 203
  origin of name 35
  as refuge (*see also* refuge) 3, 108, 119
  revival, attempted 251
  Royal Commission investigation into 165, 199, 213
  ruins of 249, 254, **257**, 258, 259, 261, 264
  sale to Bogner and Jaensch 199–200
  visit from
    Herrgott police 131
    Kaibel 141
    mission committee 101
    scientists and ethnographers 118, 158
  water, lack of, at 134
King, John 50, 119, 215
Kintalakadi, Emil 218–19, 222
Klaatsch, Hermann 223
Klemzig 6, 7, 11, 12
Koch, Wilhelm 46, 59, 60, 62, 63, 64, 67, 153, 204
  death of 65
  and Diyari dictionary 205, 206
Koko Yimidir 114
Kopperamanna, Lake 17, 19, 22, 48, 49, 51, 52, 53, 59, 66, 73, 136, 151
  survey beyond 98
Kopperamanna Station
  Aborigines at 136, **141**, 154, 156, 177–8, 192
  after sale of mission leases 238, 240
  birth of Helene Vogelsang at 150
  bore 101, 111, 133, 136, 151, 154, 166, 244
  ferry service 121
  first house of Vogelsangs at 136, 137
  grazing of mission cattle 137, 188
  homestead 137, 138, 140, 151, 155, 166, 235, 245, 262
  ruins 258, **259**
  plains 35, 134, 252
  possibility of revival 252
  ration depot 52, 54, 55, 56, 59, 60, 80, **137**, **153**, 155, 242, 256
Kramer, C. W. 50, 52, 54
Kruse, Tom 257
Kujimukana muramura 36
kunkie (sorcerer, native doctor, magician) 35, 36, 38, 62, 63, 65, 122, 181
  as Rain-maker 35
Kurdaitcha (sorcerer, Queensland area) 238
Kuringii (ancestral Emu) myth 31, 32
kutchie (spirits) 29, 38, 63, 99, 187, 216
  as biblical Devil 215, 258
Kutikutithirinha (Rain Ancestor) 262

labour
  Aboriginal 43, 83, 105, 188, 196, 208, 214, 234, 242
  demand for 189
  employees, conditions for 260
  men 43, 82, 90, 91, 98, 105
  in Murray River area 245–6, 248
  stockmen 137, 140, 166, 240
  trained 111, 135–6, 188, 240, 260
  women 82, 92

workers' uniforms 135
German 133–4, 135
land (*see also* country)
Aboriginal 1, 2, 10, 24
land lease 133
application for 55, 70, 73
ceded from Aboriginal control 43–4
in centre of Australia 15
dispossession of 202
divisions in north of South Australia 190
grant to Reuthers 163
invasion of, at Lake Hope 16
Lake Eyre Basin 19
Cooper Basin 264
Diyari conception of 26
near Port Augusta 46
'land fever' 10
for mission station 133
as previous resource 57
for sheep station 72, 75
'waste land' 57, 74
Langmeil (*see also* Tanunda) 11, 15
church 15, 45, 84, 192
language
Aboriginal 22, 70, 90, 202, 205
Aranda 147
Diyari 22, 27, 60, 61, 63, 65, 67, 71, 75, 80, 158, 202–3, 263
Christian songs in 112
description of 206
documenting, contribution 264
language of mission station 197, 212–13
learnt by Flierl the First 87, 94, 99, 206; Luise Flierl 104; Flierl the Second 110; Jack Irrgang 85; Reidel 174, 211, 228; Strehlow 209; Vogelsang sons 166, 251
New Testament into 118
Reuther's dictionary 118, 211
spoken by Gason 55
services 139
translations into 92, 100, 112, 206, 207, 228
vocabulary 52
English 80, 205–6, 208, 213
at Bucaltaninna 90, 207
not taught by Flierl the Second 131
not taught in Reidel's time 197, 213
German 80, 110, 197, 213
translations by Theodore Vogelsang 255
Hillier, hymns into Aranda 144
languages taught in mission school 143, 209
translations into Wangkangurru and Jandruwonta 118
used by German community, Murray River 248
Yandruwantha 203
Leidig, Georg Freidrich (Pastor) 142, 170, 245
Leigh (Leigh's) Creek 47
Leipzig 3, 15
Leipzig Mission Society 15
Lights Pass 58, 59, 74, 116, 119
Love, John (Presbyterian minister)
visit to Killalpaninna 175, 176, 182, 204, 228
Low Bank 245
Lubra 82
Luther, Martin 3, 4, 17, 46, 80, 118, 142, 209
Lutheran Mission Society of Dresden 13, 14

McKinlay, John 243
McLean, Mick 262
McMahon, Thomas 130–1
Magdalene, Anna Maria **145**
marriage to Siebert 144
Mahuliliana, August 90
Maltilinna (Merrick), Anna 107, **109**, 239, 240, 252
marriage of 108
Maltilinna (Merrick), Florrie 239, 262
at Murray River 245
Maltilinna (Merrick), Frieda 232, 239, 240, 252, 262
Maltilinna (Merrick), Gottlieb 232, 239, 240, 252, 262
family of 258
Maltilinna (Merrick), Martin 239
at Murray River 245, 246
Maltilinna (Merrick), Rebecca 245, **247**
Maltilinna (Merrick), Timotheus 107, 193, 239, 245, **246**
death of 252–3
employed at cattle station 107
marriage of 108
at Murray River 245
relatives of **109**, 254, 257
son of (Tim) 245, 246
wages for 121
Manuwakaninna Station 48, 49, 50, 53, 55, 60
Maralinga 260, 261
Mardu 24, 25, 38, 39, 108, 205
Marduka 26, 29, 33
Marree (Herrgott Springs) 17, 234, 235, 238, 242, 244, 249, 250, 251, 254, 256, 257, 260, 262
marriage (*see also* Aboriginal weddings)
Diyari 22, 26, 39, 40, 41, 108, 110, 111
of Flierl the First 102
of Fritzsche 12
of Elizabeth Irrgang, first 84
of Jacob 84–5

by Lutheran pastors (Germany) 5
of mission Aborigines 95–7, 121, 243
proposal to Luise Wendland 58
of Reuther 116–17
of Vogelsang children 185
of Vogelsang (senior), first 58; second 84
Martin, the Rain-maker 183–4
massacres
  potential, of German missionaries 55
  Queensland 108, 114
  stories of 17
Meischal, J. 15, 16, 73
Meissel, G. 50
Meyer, Carl
  at Bucaltaninna 79, 80, 84, 87, 88, 90, 205–6
  dismissed 132, 160
  to Elim (Bloomfield) 115
  at Killalpaninna 92, 98, 150
Meyer, Pastor 13, 14
Milner, Mrs 55, 61, 65, 72, 73, 241
Mindari 33, 35, 41, 123, 125
Minkawonpala 29
Mirra Mitta 253, 257
Mirus, George 80
mission
  debts 75, 114, 165, 195–9, 233
  entertainment 154–8
  finance 91, 114, 141, 251
  income 70, 71, 81, 82–3, 114, 137, 138, 140, 166, 200, 244
  policy on venereal disease 184
  rallies and festivals 13, 16
  settlement, abandoned 240
  shop 125
  vegetable gardens 152, 155
  work in Australia 15, 16
moiety, Diyari
  of Anna and Timotheus Maltilinna 108
  matrilineal 24, 25, 36, 38
  totemic 26, 29, 33, 39
Mooloorinna Station (Dulkaninna Station) 245, 252
Moravian
  missionaries 17, 48, 50, 51, 52, 53, 55, 56, 57, 59, 60
  site of, mission 258
Morton, John 50, 55
Moses 254
Mount Lofty Ranges 8
Mulka Station 242, 244
  Bore 249
Mulligan River 20, 110
Mundowdna Station 67, 68, 69, 70, 71, 72, 80, 81, 238
Mungerannie Station 192, 238, 242, 243, 244, 250, 251, 253
mura (see also creation period, Dreaming) 22, 211

for Reuther 225, 226, 227
muramura (see also mythic being) 26, 27, 29, 30, 35, 36, 38
  as beginning of biblical Creation Story 216
  report by Flierl 99
  Reuther' interpretation of 217, 219, 224
  stories told in toas 229
murder
  Diyari revenge 41, 66
  at Lake Hope 17
  at Port Lincoln 13, 14
Murnpeowie Station 238, 252, 258
Murragurta 32
Murrapatirrinna Station 133, 144, 238
Murray, Ben 232, 239, 256, 259, 260, 262, 263
  baptised by Reidel **173**, 190
  brother of Ern 190, 246, **265**
  escape to Killalpaninna 190
  at Gallipoli 235–6
  as mission cameleer 190, 235
  in Murray River area 246, 248
  wages of 190
Murray River 245
  internment camp 256
Murtee, Johnny 262
myth 25, 28
  of Darana 27
  of Paltira 27
mythic being (see also muramura) 26
  ancestor 31, 38

Naylon, Jimmy 262
Neuendettelsau Mission Institute 75, 79, 80, 87, 106, 110, 111, 142, 144, 146, 172, 205, 236
  donation from 141
  missionaries to New Guinea 114
  mission journal 100
  Reichner and 102
  Reidel and 170, 174
  request for third missionary to 125
  Reuther and 119, 128, 162
New Guinea 236
  Evangelical Lutheran Mission of 114, 115, 128, 170, 172, 206
  Flierl the First to 114–15
  German missionaries in 114
  New Guinea Company 114
New Testament
  message for Luther 3
  reading, pre-breakfast 92
  translation into German by Luther 118, 217, 162
  translation into Diyari 90, 112, 118, 141, 142, 144, 158, 174, 180, 184, 186, 209, 210, 211, 212, 228, 241, 253, 259, 262
Neyi
  relationship, Henry Tipilanna to Flierl the First 100

role in pinja 39
used for Christ 212
use of as church elders 115
Neylon (also Neaylon or Naylon) family 155
Ngadada 39
  relationship, Henry Tipilanna to Flierl the First 100
  used for relationship with Christ 212
Ngarlangarlani, Lake (Lake Allallinna) 35, 167, 238
  site of Storm History 123, 182
Ninpilinna, Nathanael 108, 109
Nurnberg 119, 165

Ochre
  red 31, 178
  white 31, 32, 36, 37, 38, 97
    expeditions 32
    land grant for collection of 178
    myths and rites 33
    use of and trade in 32
Old Testament 52, 64, 262
  translation into Diyari 212–13, 229
Oodnadatta 238
opium 20, 72,
Oster, President 74

Palkilinna, Elias
  guide for Flierl the First 108, 109
  as shearer at Etaduinna 138
  wedding of 108
Paltira 28
  myth of 27
Papua (the Aborigines of Australia) 56, 59
Papua New Guinea 114
  people of 115
Parachilna 46, 178
  Creek 32
Perigundi, Lake 17, 25, 53, 55, 106, 243
  survey region of 98
Pestonjee Bomanjee 13
Pickally ('Mackey') 54, 55, 56, 61, 62, 63, 204
pinaru (*see also* Aboriginal elders) 22, 35, 38, 39, 88, 208
  challenged by Reidel 181, 182
  Jacob as 192
  'King John' 54
  missionary as 186
  mission committee as 186
  'old greybeards' 97, 111
  power of 94, 116, 125
  system still in operation 122, **179**, 243
  Vogelsang as 193
  Wangkangurru elders 98
Pingilinna, Johannes 90, 112, 257
  death of daughter (Maria) 122, **123**

to Elim (Bloomfield) Mission 115
  as shearer 138
  and wife **96**, 115
pintara 26, 28, 29
pinya 20, 38, 39, 66, 67, 89, 168, 180, 187, 212, 237
  baptised youths, engaging in 94
  killing 128
  leader 39, 180
  receptacle ('cup') for washing 38
  Reidel as victim of 196
pirauru (piranguru) 41
pitjantjatjara 260
pitjiri (pitchere) 20, 33, 88, 97, 110, 178
police 1, 238, 243
  arrest, pinja party 181
  discovery of diprotodont 220
  documenting Aboriginal customs 217
  in Germany 5
  massacres in Queensland 108, 114
  outpost, Kopperamanna 59, 60, 67, 155
    Lake Hope 16, 48, 50, 52, 54, 55, 215
  outstation 71
  ration depots 106
  protection 55, 56, 57
  report from Flierl the Second 128
  station, Mungerannie 192
polygyny 203
Pope 3, 170
Port Augusta 46, 48, 51, 61, 68, 71, 76, 81, 82, 87, 101, 254, 261
  hospital, Aboriginal ward 180
  trial of pinya party 128, 168
Port Lincoln 12, 13
Port Lincoln Mission 14
Port Misery (Port Adelaide) 6, 7, 11
Powell, Beryl 237, 240, 241, 243, 244, 245
Powell, Lance Kay 240, 241, 244, 245
  daughter of 240, 262
  purchase of Killalpaninna 237
Prince George 6, 7, 11, 84
Proeve, E. H. (Pastor) 251, 252, 256, 257, 258, 259, 260
Proeve, H. F. W. (Pastor) 258
Prussian 4, 5, 6, 11
  State Church 142

rabbits
  diet of 140
  plague of 139, 236
  skins of 166, 264
rain-making ceremonies 28, 35, 42
rations 52, 56, 57, 60, 61, 65, 71, 75, 81, 191, 238, 240, 244
  annual cost of 191
  at Bucaltaninna 204
  clothing from 64
  depot for 52, 106, 191, 242, 251, 261

at Killalpaninna 88, 94, 112, 119, 128, 164, 166, 180, 208, 232, 234, 237, 243
supply of 70, 80, **89**
of tobacco, Kopperamanna 138
wages paid plus 132
Reece, Johnny 262
Reformation (German) 3, 4
refuge
Killalpaninna as 2, 3, 66, 68, 88, 108, 119, 122, 128, 202, 208
Reichner, Gustav Julius
daughter of 116
death of 141
at Killalpaninna 102, 131
as president of mission committee 57, 70, 72, 73, 74, 79, 82, 98, 116, 126, 140, 143, 147, 149
at Tanunda 15
Reidel, Wolfgang
ant specimen named for 228
arrested 256
at Barossa Valley 170
clash
with mission committee 165, 170, 172, 176, 179, 195
with Bogner 176
with Kaibel 196, 198
and Diyari language 211–12, 228
first service in Diyari 174
interviewed by commissioner 191, 199, 213
at Killallpaninna 118, 170, 172, **173**, 174, 178, 179, 180, 181, 182, **183**, 184, 185, 186, 187, 188, 189, 190, 191, 193, 195, 196
marriage of 170
'new mission order' 174, 175, 176
offered parish, Queensland 197
pastor at Low Bank 249
pinya encounters 180, 181
punishment of mission Aborigines 182
requests visits to ex-Killalpaninna Aborigines 249, 251, 252, 255, 258, 259
resignation of 198–9
Reuther–Reidel house 240
salary of 174
translator, Old Testament 212, 213
trip north 172
wife of 170, 172, **175**, 176, 180, **239**
reincarnation
Diyari belief in 27
Reuther, Albert ('Bert')
birth of 150
visit to ex-Killalpaninna Aborigines 256
Reuther, Georg Edwin 150, 153, 258, 264
Reuther, Johann Georg 36, 118, 122, 123, 130, 134, 139, 142, 155, **161**, 190, **195**, 209, 222

accusations and suspicion of 119, 160, 162, 163
arrival at Killalpaninna 116
as biblical leader 118
biography of 119
as clerk and farmer 163, 194–5,
collector of artefacts 118, 219, 220, 229, 230, 141, 158
correspondence with Howitt 223
death of 194–5
dismissal of Flierl the Second 132
enforcing 'confessions' 121, 217
family of **149**
as general manager 132
health of 118, 119, 141, 159, 163, 194–5, 224, 226
interference at traditional ceremonies 118, 123, 125
journey to Hermannsburg 143, 150, 220
last baptismal service 159
left Killalpaninna 163, 194–5
as linguist and ethnographer 118, 146, 159, 194, 211, 217, 218, 219, **221**, 222, 223, 224, 225, 226, 227, 230
manuscripts 118, 219, 227, 228, 229, 255
marriage of 116–**17**, 119
on mission wives 149
placing 'spies' among mission Aborigines 121, 217
Reuther–Hillier Map 143, 229
Reuther–Reidel house **155**, 240
rivalry with Siebert 224
rivalry with Spencer and Gillen 220, 225-6
salary of 136
and school pupils 126, 128, 208
service at uprising 125
stock station manager 118, 134
and Yashchenko 222
Reuther, Pauline 147, 148, 162, **195**
duties at Killalpaninna 125, 126, 149, **221**
family of **149**
illness of 153
left Killalpaninna 163
marriage to Reuther 116–**17**, 119
as pianist 154
and Reuther's manuscript 229
revenge
of Reuther at uprising 125
of settlers at Port Lincoln 14
taken by Aborigines in Queensland 108
Riegert, Bernhard 115, 129
wife of 147, 148
ritual (*see also* ceremonies)
of Christmas 231, 241
death 38
Dreaming track 26
eating of the dead 36, 37, 38, 53, 63, 65, 67, 203, 216

European and traditional at Killalpaninna 180
increase 25, 29, 35
initiation 29
at Lake Perigundi 17
new mission 185
in pinya execution (*see also* pinya) 38
re-enactments 28, 30, 123
Rohrlach, 'Jack'
as manager at Kopperamanna 233
married to Bertha Vogelsang 233
as overseer 196
son of 255–6
Rosalee 100, 102, 207–8
Royal Commission into Conditions for Aboriginies (1912–16) 165, 191, 199, 200, 201, 213, 236, 243
Royal Shepherd 73
Ruediger, Theodore ('Jack')
cattle drive from Hermannsburg 140
child, death of 153
household 178, 185
joke on mission committee 158
left Killalpaninna 190, 197, 198
manager of cattle enterprise 196
squabble with Flierl the Second 130–1, 132
as teamster 130, 133, 139, 157, 164
wife of **91**, 147, 150, 222
Russell, Jimmy 256, 257, 263

sacred sites 26, 30, 219
fossil tree 219
Salt Creek 98, 102, 106, 107, 108, 109, 110
salvation
of the Aborigines 81, 116
no Diyari word for 27
Sandy, the Rain-maker 260
Scherer, Philip 229
Schilling, W. 252
Schmidt, Carl 73–4
Schmidt, Gerhard 256
Schmidt, Gottlieb 240, 245
sons of 255
Schmidt, Luise 239, 245, 248, 249
sons of 255
Schoknecht, Carl 68, 69, 70, 71, 72, 73
dictionary compiled by 205
as linguist 207
school 80, 205, 207
Aboriginal 62, 143, 151
literacy at 203
at Bucaltaninna 90, 205
building of, at Killalpaninna 91, 209, 143
in care of Vogelsang (senior) 84
children, work 176
closed 83, 164
continued after sale of mission leases 232

Diyari readers in 92
'German school' or 'colony room' 143
at Hahndorf 8
house 11, 66, 207
mission 62, 63, 64, 65, 67, 80, 98, 107, 204, 260
Moravian 52
in Murray River area 248
pupils at Killalpaninna 92, 101, 105, 110, 112
re-opening 166
room, as dining and church or Killalpaninna 92, 94, 95
teacher 79, 82, 90, 92, 110, 115
Schuermann, C. W. 12, 13, 15, 16
Schwarz, W. F. 80
Schwenningdorf 76
Second World War 254, 255, 257
Select Committee (SA) for Proposed Aborigines' Bill (1899) 154
sermon (*see also* service)
in Diyari 64, 94
first by Siebert in Diyari 144
open-air by Homann 51
sermon-letter by Reidel 258, 259
service (*see also* sermon)
at Aboriginal uprising 125
in Diyari
for Aboriginal weddings 97
at Bucaltaninna 204
at Killalpaninna 92
at Etadunna by Jacob 139
at Kopperamanna by Vogelsang (senior) 139
Lutheran, for ex-Killalpaninna Aborigines 246, 250, 251, 253, 254, 256, 259, 260
sheep 50, 61, 65, 66, 67, 70, 71, 72, 75, 76, 80, 82, 83, 84, 134, 189, 239
at Gumvale 163
under Jacob's care 85
of Kidman's drovers 136
killed by Aborigines 106
shearers
Aboriginal 105, 111, 155, 166
German 134, 155
shearing 133, 138, 150
station at Etadunna 138, 166
station at Killalpaninna 174
station, Lake Hope 16
suffering drought 87, 110, 140–1
threatened by rabbits 139
shepherds
Aboriginal 76, 85, 86, 90, 92, **93**, 105, 126, 196–7
English 71
at Etadunna 138, 166
ex-Aboriginal 250

Siebert, Otto 36, **145**, 147, 211, 227, 230, 257, 258
  as bush missionary 144, 218, 223
  collaboration with Howitt 223–4, 225
  collection of artefacts 229
  as ethnographer 144, 146, 158, 210, 218, 219, 224
  first sermon in Diyari 144
  illness of 146, 223
  informants of 219
  at Killalpaninna 144, 146, 208, 210, 217
  left Killalpaninna 146, 159
  marriage of 144
  wages of 136
Sillesia 5, 6, 11, 81, 82, 85
Simeon 112
Simpson Desert 108, 218, 262
sin
  no Diyari word for 27, 62, 64, 205, 216
sixth commandment (adultery)
  Aborigines and 35, 120, 121, 130, 159, 146, 165, 174
Skenner, P. T. 50
Skiold 11, 12
social evolutionists 2
  and Australian Aborigines 158, 203, 214, 219, 223
Sophia 50, 57
South Australia
  colony of 6, 11, 43
  emigration of Altlutherans to 6
  frontier 16
  government rations 60
  land grant to Reuthers 163
  north-east of 2
  population of 9
  South Australia Company 6, 13, 14
South, W. (protector of Aborigines) 239
South Australian Museum
  director (Stirling) 162, 220, 227
  exhibition of toas 264
  Reuther–Hillier Map 143
  Reuther's collection 118, 229
  Reuther's manuscript 229
  Theodore Vogelsang employed by 225, 258, 263
Spencer, Baldwin (Sir)
  accusations against Hermannsburg 198
  with Gillen 220–1, 226
  opposing theories to Reuther and Strehlow 224, 226, 227
spirit children 26, 28
Stirling, E. C. 162, 220, 227, 229
Stolz, J. J. 236
Strehlow, Carl
  Aranda language 220
  death of 143
  Diyari language learning 209
  at Hermannsburg 118, 119, 122, 128, 147, 166, 184, 202, 211
  journey to Hermannsburg 143, 150, 220
  at Killalpaninna 118, 142, 208, 209, 222, 230
  rivalry with Spencer and Gillen 220, 225
  translation of New Testament 142, 144, 158, 209, **210**, 211, 212, 217
Stuart, John McDouall 15, 73, 234
Stuckey, Samuel 48
subincision 30
Synod (Lutheran)
  Bethany Lutheran 12
  dissident, in Germany 11
  first in Australia 10
  General 73
    (South Australia) 254
  Immanuel (*see also* ELCA) 12
    South Australia (*see also* UELCA) 12, 15, 16, 45
  joint, mission committee 69, 70, 72, 73, 74, 75
  Lutheran, in America 142
  split into two 12, 15

Tankamarinna, Lake (Dulkaninna Station) 72
Tanunda (*see also* Langmeil) 15, 59, 65, 70, 72, 76, 80, 84, 87, 89, 102, 115, 130, 159, 160, 164, 166, 170, 192, 194, 203, 205, 232, 235, 236, 242, 249
Tassie and Company 81, 82
Teichelmann, C. G. 13
Terra Nullius 43
Tindale, Norman 255
Tipilanna, Henry ('Lame Henry') 90, 100, 111, 206, 207–8
  death of 112
toas 143, 229
totem
  cult, relationship Henry Tipilanna to Flierl (senior) 100
  matrilineal (marduka) 26
  patrilineal (pintara) 25
totemic, cult myth 24, 26
  ancestors 25
  clan 25, 26, 39
  soul 37
totemism, Spencer and Gillen 220
trachoma ('Sandy Blight') 53, 60, 62, 104, 110, 130, 262
trade
  in pitjiri 33
  in red ochre 32
trees
  cut for building 60
  Diyari, veneration of 28, 99
    muramura, to create 217

fossil tree 219, 229
typhoid (*see also* illness) 7, 104, 153, 239

Umberatana Station 47, 48
United Evangelical Lutheran Church of Australia (UELCA) or South Australia Synod 15, 16, 74, 75, 80,
  mission committee 72, 73, 79
  sale of Hermannsburg (Australia) 142
  severing connections with Hermannsburg (Germany) 142
  wages for Hermannsburg Aboriginal employees 188

Veit, Margarethe 57, **58**
Vogelsang, Anna 84, 102, 147, 148, 149
  contracted typhoid 153
  death of 258
  family 86, 90, 150
  at Kopperamanna 138, 151–2, **153**, **193**,
    after sale of 233, **234**
  left Kopperamanna 235
  at Low Bank 245, **248**, 249
  Silver Wedding Anniversary of 156
Vogelsang descendants 231, 239, 258, 261
  Bertha 233
  Dorothea 245
Vogelsang, Dorothea (née Heistermann) 66, 69, 72, 76, **78**
  death of 76
Vogelsang, Heinrich 76, **78**
Vogelsang, Helene 150, 151, **153**, 261
Vogelsang, Hermann (junior)
  conducting Diyari services 166–7
  death of 254–5, 256
  at Hermannsburg 254
  at Killalpaninna
    as choirmaster 154
    as schoolteacher 166, 231, 233, 235, 237
  at Kopperamanna 154
  visits to ex-Killalpaninna Aborigines 231, 246, **250**, 251, 252, 254
  wife of 182, 190, 251, 259
Vogelsang, Hermann H. (senior) 45, **47**, 48, 50, 54, **58**, 65, 66, 70, 71, 73, 75, **77**, 80, 90, 154, 259
  biography of 76, 77, 78, 79
  complaint against Reuther 162
  as cook at Etadunna 138
  death of 192–4
  described by Reidel 196
  ferrying across flooded Birdsville Track 121, 134, 136, 258
  grave of 258, 264, **265**
  at Killalpaninna 90, 91, 98, 128, 132
  at Kopperamanna 136, 137, 138, 139, 140, **141**, 151, **153**, 154, 166, 177–8, 185, **193**,
  medical and homeopathic treatment 150,
  154, 177, 146
  monument to 259
  near perished 83
  opposition to Flierl the Second 130, 131, 132
  second marriage 84, **85**, 156
  schoolteacher at Bucaltaninna 206
  taking 'confession' 168
  wages of 136
Vogelsang, Theodore 151, 168, 259
  artefacts (sacred) sent to 263
  as author 255, 263
  first contact, ex-Killalpaninna Aborigines 231, 249–50
  as general manager, Killalpaninna 166
  left Killalpaninna 241–2
  last trip north 258
  as overseer, Killalpaninna cattle station 231, 233, 235, 241
  preparing Reidel's house 172
  translating Reuther's manuscripts 227
  tutor to Reidel, Diyari language 174, 211
Von Leonhardi, Baron Moritz 194, 226, 227, 228
Von Meuller, Baron Ferdinand 106

wages
  Aboriginal 105, 121, 132, 136, 188, 189, 190, 240
    after sale of mission 233, 234
    demand for higher 187, 188
    at Hermannsburg 188, 189
    at Killalpaninna 196
    at other stations 188
  black and white (1884) 114
  Godfrey and 131
  of the Kolonisten 136
  lowered during 1901–02 drought 141
  of Reuther, Siebert, Wettengel and Kaibel 136
wagon
  German 8, 45–6, 47, 48, 54, 59, 60, 76
  horses 84
  Jacob's 67, 68
  mission 70, 79, 82, 87, 88, 101, **103**, 206
  spontaneous combustion of 82–3
Walder, H. 50, 51, 55
walkabout
  old men 24, 89
  mission Aborigines 92, 110, 120, 207
Wami Cata 262
Wangkangurru 22, **24**, 203, 207, 262
  boy 99
  at Bucaltaninna 90
  country of the 98
  informants for Reuther 218, 227
  language 211, 263, 264
  last at Lake Gregory 243

Timotheus Maltilinna as 108
Nathanael Ninpilinna as 108
translations into 118
Warburton Creek 112
Warburton, Peter Egerton 74, 140
Warburton River 140
water
　artesian 101, 235 (*see also* Great Artesian Basin)
　control of, Kopperamanna bore 136–7
　Diyari, source 20
　drinking 64, 65, 69, 72, 153
　at Etadunna 133
　at Lake Hope 16
　search for 107
　shortage 42, 46, 47, 51, 60, 67, 68, 70, 71, 72, 103–4, 151
　underground 22
　waterbag 83, 103, 109
waterholes 22, 29, 52, 53, 64, 66, 71, 83, 87, 103, 140
Watske, Frederick 60, 65, 66, 67, 70, 71, 73, 75
　wife of 69
weapons 1, 2, 16, 194
　boomerangs
　　burning of 115, 121
　　of Luise Vogelsang (Schmidt) 248
　Diyari 19, 20, **25**
　　boomerangs 107, 176, 180
　　used in pinya 38
　　women 21
　sword, German 79
　nuclear, at Maralinga 260
　and tools, ethnographic evidence 214, 228
Wendland, Luise 57, 58
Wendland, Willie 65
Wettengel, Nathaniel 125, 146
　at Hermannsburg 147
　at Killalpaninna 141
　marriage of 146
　as schoolteacher 146, 147, 151, **208**, 209
　wages of 136
Wettengel, Nicole 146, 147
Wilhelm III, Frederick 4, 11, 81
Wilyaru 30, 31, 34
Wimmera District 50, 73
Witchelina Station 259
Wittenberg 3, 4
women
　Aboriginal **41**, 82, 83
　　childbirth 150
　　ex-Killalpaninna 245
　　at Killalpaninna 92, 104, 105, 111, 125, 147, 149, 150, 176
　　offered for gambling debts 177
　　as prostitutes 178, 179
　　rumours, Bogner 235
　　and white labourers 135
　Diyari 19, 21, 22, 32, 33, 41–2, 63, 88
　　initiation rites for 29
　　in marriage 39–40
　　offered to missionaries 41, 52–3
　　role in pinya 38, 39
　　secondary wives (pirauru) 41
　　widows 37
　German
　　fiancées 57, 60, 61, 62, 68, 154
　　wives 97, 104, 105, 147, 152
wool
　from mission 71, 73, 81, 82, 83, 138, 140, 189, 190

Yashchenko, Alexander Leonidovich
　collection of artefacts 219, 222, 229, 230
　at Killalpaninna 128, 222

Zebra 7, 8
Zeullichav 6